Beyond Federal Dogmatics

Beyond Federal Dogmatics

The Influence of European Union Law on Belgian Constitutional Case Law Regarding Federalism

Stef Feyen

LEUVEN UNIVERSITY PRESS

ISBN 978 90 5867 938 3
D / 2013/ 1869 / 17
NUR: 828

Cover design: Friedemann BVBA
Typesetting: Friedemann BVBA

GPRC Guaranteed Peer Reviewed Content www.gprc.be

Every dogma, every philosophical or theological creed, was at its inception a statement in terms of the intellect of a certain inner experience.

FELIX ADLER, AN ETHICAL PHILOSOPHY OF LIFE 344 (1918)

We must avoid all dogma that blocks inquiry.

PHILIP SELZNICK, *Sociology and Natural Law,* 1961 NATURAL LAW FORUM 84, 94 (1961);
THE MORAL COMMONWEALTH: SOCIAL THEORY AND THE PROMISE OF COMMUNITY 21 (1992)

Law in action and the norms of law are not two independent spheres of existence, but different sides of one and the same reality. It is possible therefore to speak of two viewpoints, each mutually presupposing each other [...] [A] doctrinal study of law which ignores the social function of law must appear unsatisfactory when judged by the criterion of the interest that lies in the predictability of legal decisions [...] The judge is not motivated exclusively by the norms of law, but also by the social purposes and the theoretical insight into the social connections relevant to the furtherance of these purposes. For this reason, there [is] a demand for the doctrinal study of law to turn its attention to the realities of social life [...] [T]he real content of doctrinal propositions refers to the actions of the courts under certain conditions.

ALF ROSS, ON LAW AND JUSTICE 19-20, 40 (2004) (1959)

Table of contents

Foreword

Whereas many young researchers publish their doctoral dissertation as their first monograph, I am pleased to introduce this monograph, written by a junior researcher whose dissertation is yet to come.

In some respects, this book has characteristics which one could expect from a junior researcher: it tries to be innovative, explores issues from a (whole array of) different angle(s), and could be read as provocative. At the same time, the work radiates academic maturity in some other respects: the depth and width of the considerations taken into account are impressive, and even if some points might come across as provocative on a first reading, they seem well reflected and balanced on the whole. Finally – and I believe this to be the book's most important virtue – it not only identifies some of the most ardent methodological problems in constitutional and interpretative thinking, but also seeks to offer a (beginning of a) remedy. This remedy may not be worked out in complete detail – as the author moreover fully acknowledges – and one should not infer from my appreciation for the work that I agree entirely with its elaboration and with the amalgam of points it seeks to make; even so, I am convinced that the author – in an important area of constitutional thinking, *ie* the area of federalism – makes a significant contribution to how we can or should understand the jurisprudence of the Constitutional Court.

In that sense, he can be seen as riding a new wave of constitutional scholars with an interest in approaching Belgian problems pertaining to federalism from a new point of view. However, Feyen's work differs from the approaches of other scholars in at least two (related) ways. First, he seems to rely more on interdisciplinary insights, with an important focus on (legal) philosophy and theoretical/methodological issues. This creates a new perspective. Even if this angle might make Feyen's texts somewhat less accessible for legal scholars unacquainted with the philosophical jargon and the more reflexive and reflective way of thinking, it must be said that Feyen has done his utter best to make the texts readable, and vagueness seems to have been reduced to a minimum. Second, and maybe because of what preceded, the contentions Feyen makes and the theoretical framework of understanding of constitutional court jurisprudence in terms of a toolbox might allow for expansion beyond the limits of federalism case law. Admittedly, Feyen recognizes that the federalism focus might strengthen the theoretical point he tries to make, and he did not explicitly elaborate the theoretical point for other areas of jurisprudence. Nevertheless, it would surely be research-worthy to inquire whether his general point or approach – steeped in a rich philosophical anti-dogmatic tradition – can work in other areas of jurisprudence. Surely, Feyen's doctoral dissertation promises to have a lot more to say on this issue, at least in the area of freedom of expression.

Finally, I would like to emphasize that Feyen has wisely chosen the substantive angle through which he makes his (theoretical) point(s), *ie* the question about the influence of European law. This is a topic of research that continually requires further elaboration because of its ever-growing importance. Although in Belgian scholarship, some have spawned some kaleidoscopic considerations and thoughts about how European law influences Belgian constitutional case law, Feyen succeeds in offering a coherent view, axed upon his theoretical insights, which can be read autonomously. As such, the author adds another layer to the ongoing theoretical debate about constitutional pluralism and the problems associated with the multi-layered legal order(s), this time geared towards problems of federalism.

On the whole, this book is not a very easy read, but the richness of the insights offered in the volume and the clarity and ubiquity of the basic idea underlying the book – *ie* conceptualizing constitutional court jurisprudence in terms of the relationship between a toolbox used and rule of law values playing – make it a significant contribution to Belgian constitutional scholarship. They also make it a worthwhile read as a whole, or at the very least an important tool for reflexive criticism of those who engage in the practice of constitutional scholarship without a sufficient sense of pragmatism.

André Alen
Professor of Constitutional Law, KU Leuven
Judge in the Belgian Constitutional Court
Leuven, 21 January 2013

Reader information and acknowledgments

Reader information. This work was written for international and Belgian scholars alike. Opting for such a wide public obviously gives rise to some difficulties. On the one hand, to be accessible to the international scholars, and perhaps the Belgian ones who are not familiar with constitutional law, an introduction to Belgian federalism had to be written. For Belgian scholars of constitutional law, the chapters dealing with the basics (II and III) are arguably somewhat repetitive. On the other hand, this book aspires to be thorough, and make a point that is important in and for Belgian constitutional law as well. It engages Belgian constitutional scholars and it also offers jurisprudential and political considerations as support and nuance of my basic argument. This 'mixed' public has implored the construal of a text capable of accommodating 'mixed' needs. Here, I have first and foremost attempted to author a coherent text, which at the same time is not devoid of sufficient relevant nuances. Some debates engaged in might be thought to be more tangential to the general point, or of little relevance for non-Belgian constitutionalists. These debates I have consistently tried to either relegate to (some longer) footnotes, or published in grey font in the main corpus. Thus, I might hope that the text can be read as a self-sufficient and coherent whole, and that I have thus succeeded in reconciling the 'mixed' needs.

Acknowledgments. Many people contributed to the creation of this book in a myriad of ways. Understandably, naming everyone personally would take up too much space. Nonetheless, I am very grateful to my friends, my partner and my parents for offering me general support, without which this book would never have seen the light of day. I owe gratitude to my colleagues, not only for their moral support, but also for suggestions, debate and discussion in an intellectually stimulating cnvironment, in which an appetite for learning and enrichment is ever-present. My PhD supervisor, professor André Alen, who graciously accepted to write the foreword accompanying my work, further provided intellectual stimulation. I am moreover indebted to the co-supervisor of my PhD, emeritus professor René Foqué, who succeeded in always framing authors and thoughts in a broader philosophical perspective, and offering me interesting thoughts for reflections on theory (in its relationship to practice). Without a doubt, the Leuven University Press anonymous reviewer deserves special mention: (s)he pointed out, in the most constructive of ways, some important flaws in the first draft, which I hope I have been able to remedy. Moreover, it is through his/her extremely helpful and poignant suggestions that I can hope that this work can be read coherently. For editorial support, I like to thank Veerle de Laet of Leuven University Press. She has been pragmatically helpful and patient with me. Finally, I am indebted to FWO for allowing me the opportunity to pursue what I am passionate about, that is research: without the financial support of this institution, this book would never have been published. Of course, the usual disclaimers apply: all errors are mine alone, and I gratefully welcome comments at stef.feyen@law.kuleuven.be. Anyone whom I might have forgotten to mention can also contact me at this address. I pre-emptively extend my sincerest apologies to him, her, or them.

Some commonly used abbreviations

Law

Cons.	Belgian Constitution
SLIR	Special Law governing Institutional Reform of Aug. 8, 1980
LIRG	Law governing Institutional Reform in the German-speaking Community of Dec. 31, 1983
SLBI	Special Law governing Brussels Institutions of Jan. 12, 1989
SLCRF	Special Law governing Community and Region Financing of Jan. 16, 1989
SLCC	Special Law on the Constitutional Court of Jan. 6, 1989

The latter (special) laws are available in French and Dutch via www.juridat.be

The Constitution in English is equally available at www.dekamer.be/kvvcr/pdf_sections/publications/constitution/grondwetEN.pdf

Journals

CDPK	Chroniques de droit publique / Publiekrechtelijke Kronieken
JT	Journal des Tribunaux
RBDC	Revue belge de droit constitutionnel
RW	Rechtskundig Weekblad
TBP	Tijdschrift voor bestuurswetenschappen en publiekrecht

Tribunals and courts

CA	Court of Arbitration
Cass.	Court of Cassation
CC	Constitutional Court
COJ	European Court of Justice
CoS	Council of State

Other

BSG	Belgian State Gazette (the Belgian official journal [Belgisch Staatsblad / Moniteur belge])

Introduction

General purpose and method: beyond dogmatics

1. Dogma under pressure. In our "enlightened" times, the concept of dogma has acquired a rather negative connotation. Most people seem to believe that we should not accept dogma(ta) without constant, or at least potential critical reflection[1]. Even so, dogma continues to be relied upon in certain areas of life where we strive for a form of authoritative certitude, such as religion, or law. It seems as if our quest for stability here warrants the use of a modus of a thought that builds upon a set of premises that are accepted without constant critical re-examination, as authoritative. Dogma, in that very broad sense, can surely be understood as a notion underpinning the very foundations of law in different ways. Hence, jurisprudential thinkers have tried for a long time to explain how, why and to which extent dogma rules or plays in law: some have emphasized the entrenching or exclusionary function of the rules with which law works[2], others have tried to explain how dogma merely constitutes a framework within which or starting point from which legal reasoning can thrive critically and reflectively[3], and still many others have tried to explain how dogma figures in law in still different ways. Therefore it has been accepted by most scholars that dogma in one way or another, and "by implication" legal dogmatics[4], is a part and parcel of (the) law, or more precisely, thinking about (the) law. I want to make clear at the outset that – despite what the title might be read to suggest – I do not want to challenge this idea as such.

---

1 The *locus classicus* of this idea is IMMANUEL KANT, *Beantwortung der Frage: Was ist Aufklärung?* (1784) in 8 AKADEMIE AUSGABE 33, 35. This idea penetrates even the most fundamental level of reflection for some philosophers. Karl Popper, for instance, argued that even if 'we are prisoners caught in the framework of our theories; our expectations; our past experiences; our language [...] we are prisoners in a Pickwickian sense: if we try, we can break out' (*Normal Science and its Dangers, in* CRITICISM AND THE GROWTH OF KNOWLEDGE 56 (Imre Lakatos & Alan Musgrave eds. 1970)).

2 Some notable examples are JOSEPH RAZ or FREDERIC SCHAUER (*see for instance* references *infra* note 56).

3 *Eg* KARL LARENZ & CLAUS-WILHELM CANARIS, METHODENLEHRE DER RECHTSWISSENSCHAFT 51-55 (3d ed. 1995) (starting point, commenting on LUHMANN's conception); *compare* ROBERT ALEXY, A THEORY OF LEGAL ARGUMENTATION 250 *et seq.*, *esp.* 256 and 269-270 (R. Adler & N. MacCormick transl. 1989) (framework).

4 This term is virtually unknown to or unused by American scholars (Aulis Aarnio & Aleksander Peczenik, *Beyond the Reality. A Criticism of Alf Ross' Reconstruction of Legal Dogmatics* in MEANING, INTERPRETATION AND THE LAW 10, 25 (Aleksander Peczenik ed. 1986), according to Golding because American do not generally appertain a *scientific* view of law (MARTIN P. GOLDING, *My Philosophy of Law* in LEGAL REASONING, LEGAL THEORY AND RIGHTS 1 (2007); *also see* ALEKSANDER PECZENIK, SCIENTIA JURIS 2 (2005)).

2. Acceptance of dogma(tics) in law: theory and practice. The reasons why I do not challenge this idea as such are manifold. First of all, there has been a thorough debate, albeit without a unanimous outcome, on what legal dogmatics actually means or constitutes. Answering this question often coincides with tackling questions of a more general jurisprudential nature: accordingly, dogmatics will be seen as more *scientific* or *conceptual* in a system of conceptual jurisprudence, whereas it might be construed differently when one starts from different theoretical or methodological premises[5]. We will not delve into these issues in depth, considering that this book primarily serves a pragmatic purpose. Be that as it may, it will soon become clear to the reader that the book, which focuses on the question how European law influences Belgian constitutional case law on federalism, can, and indeed should, also be read as an attack on some of the remnants of a more *scientific*, *conceptual* or *systematic* view on thinking about law which has generally thrived within the thoughts of Belgian – and perhaps more widely: continental – constitutional law scholars. Indeed, even if some legal theorists have succeeded in starkly relativizing dogma (or the scope of dogmatics as a way of understanding and systematizing law), it is not always clear how this relativization has materialized within the practice of legal dogmatics itself, which can provisionally be described as the practice of commenting on, explaining and indeed systematizing – in our case: Belgian constitutional - law. This book tries to explore a theoretical framework that allows for considerations of how judges in fact decide constitutional cases, without however completely abandoning the dogmatic framework in which constitutional law in Belgium is generally understood.

3. Dogmatics in law: a central function. Abandoning that framework would indeed undercut many of the important functions that dogmatics can fulfill from a societal perspective. These will sound familiar to many legal scholars: law requires stability, it has a settling function, … Dogmatics, understood as legal doctrine studied and elaborated by *Rechtswissenschaft*, namely the whole of legal propositions which the courts distilled from (authoritative) sources or imposed upon litigants, and which scholars have used to systematize our

---

[5] For example, the attack of the *Freirechtsschule* (*eg* Von Jhering, Kantorovich, Heck or Ehrlich) on *conceptual jurisprudence (Begriffsjurisprudenz)* in Germany, or of French analogue (*the école libre*, with for instance Gény or Duguit) on the classic exegetic schools in France, with their concomitant attempts to rethink dogmatics are well known. For some historic contextualization, with reference to the problems discussed here, *see eg* Hasso Hofmann, *From Jhering to Radbruch: on the logic of traditional legal concepts to the social theories of law to the renewal of legal idealism* in A TREATISE OF LEGAL PHILOSOPHY AND GENERAL JURISPRUDENCE. 9 A HISTORY OF THE PHILOSOPHY OF LAW OF THE CIVIL LAW WORLD, 1600-1900, p. 301 (Damiano Canale, Paolo Grossi & Hasso Hofmann eds. 2009).

knowledge of the law, undoubtedly performs a stabilizing function. In fact, it could even be argued that without dogmatics, the law itself would become more or less unintelligible. Through definition and distinction, categorization and clarification of meanings and interrelationship(s) of concepts (conceptual analysis), dogmatics makes the law intelligible and coherent, and consequently explainable and predictable, thus allowing scholars to actually work with (the) law in practice. Accordingly: it should be clear that dogmatics, understood broadly as such, performs a central function in our understanding of law.

4. Beyond dogmatics? Why then, one should ask, does this book claim – or at least want – to go *beyond* dogmatics? Perhaps the title was somewhat of a misnomer: I might indeed be seeking to merely enrich dogmatics, rather than to go beyond that[6]. The problem here, as mentioned, is that there is no unitary conception of what dogmatics is: its meaning, use and function largely depend on context and legal practice[7]. It now seems to me that regarding the practice I am describing, that is Belgian constitutional practice, my analytical devises go beyond the framework currently established by Belgian scholars to explain Belgian constitutional law. It is for that reason that this book might be said indeed to reach beyond legal dogmatics[8].

---

6 *Compare eg* pertaining to fundamental rights protection, Roel de Lange, *De bijdrage van de rechter aan de ontwikkeling van de constitutie en de rechtsvormende taak van de rechter*, in Rechterlijk Activisme. Opstellen aangeboden aan prof. mr. J.A. Peters 147, 148 *et seq.* (Aernout Nieuwenhuis, Jan-Herman Reestman, Carla Zoethout eds. 2011) (trying to distinguish *conceptual* from *political* positivism, in order to redeem the possibility of dogmatics within a 'juristocratic' world). For some criticism of the use of dogmatic method vis-à-vis dogmatic objects, *see* Gerhard Struck, *Dogmatische Diskussion über Dogmatik*, 30 Juristen Zeitung 84 (1975) ('[d]ie Dogmatikdiskussion wird in einer typisch dogmatischen Manier geführt'). *Also see infra* Ch. 1.2.

7 'According to the traditional definition, the task of [the doctrinal study of law] is to produce knowledge about [valid] legal norms, as well as to systematize them. This definition is easy but problematic. It is more a point of departure than a well-founded conclusion or result from unambiguous premises' (Aulis Aarnio, Essays on the Doctrinal Study of Law 6 (2011)). At the same time, Aarnio adds that 'other fields of science [such as the sociology of law, law and economics, or comparative studies of law] have their own value, but in relation to [the doctrinal study of law] they are only sources of information. For instance, the sociology of law produces information that is valuable for understanding society, but, for [the doctrinal study of law], the best it can offer is to be a source of *practical arguments* that are used in legal reasoning to give support to the conclusion' (*ibid.* at p. 19 (*emphasis in original*)). According to Aarnio, the distinction reflects a different point of view (*ibid.* at p. 20 *et seq.*). *Also see* Struck, *supra* note 6, at p. 84 (referring to classic German thinkers, like Wieacker, Esser and Larenz on the issue).

8 *See*, in more detail, *infra* Ch. 1.2.

5. Method: exposition and demonstration. Now I have actually said a bit about the background of this book, but at the same time I have said nothing at all: there is no clear definition of dogma(tics) offered, I do not explain precisely how I want to go beyond dogma(tics) and what this would constitute, nor have I explained why going beyond dogma(tics) is useful in the context of constitutional/legal analysis (in Belgium). To the extent that my first chapter does not further elaborate, these issues will be addressed throughout the book, largely by means of a method of demonstration, enriched by some (light) legal philosophical analysis. I use this approach for several reasons: first, this book is primarily addressed to constitutional scholars, who might well be interested in theoretical analysis, but surely would rather want to focus on the constitutional issues, and on the constitutional framework offered here. Second, this is not a book worthy to be called a work in jurisprudence: the jurisprudential thoughts developed here are little more than ephemeral reflections unaccompanied by rigid conceptual, existential or comparative analysis. Yet, the book is undoubtedly driven by an interest in legal theory, and more particularly, in how legal theory forms our conceptions of how legal analysis should be performed: for that reason, it would be wholly unfair, and often indeed strange, to leave out *some* reflections which could start offering a justification for an approach which is different from more traditional lines of inquiry.

Explaining this difference through demonstration and exposition is all the more appropriate here, since the legal theoretical ideas I am using, and the form of analysis I am aiming for, is not really jurisprudentially innovative. Indeed, the toolbox concept that will be central to my analysis is not an invention of my own. I have appropriated it and sought to apply it in a distinct, and I believe novel way. At the same time however – and perhaps because it is novel – the concept is not elaborated in a full-fledged theory, nor will one find in this book a systematic approach to its application. In consequence, the book is merely a stepping-stone to further analysis, both in a theoretical and in a more practical sense. It offers a rudimentary framework to enrich the understanding of the classic approach to constitutional case law, but it surely does not work out that framework in staggering detail, nor does it want to claim truth for that framework as such.

6. Primary point of the book. Its primary point, then, – for which it would like to claim truth, or which it at least will try to defend – is methodological: a different approach to constitutional case law could enrich our understanding of this case law, and this approach should at least partially consist of a more pragmatic or instrumental analysis.

7. From purpose to object. If the point of the book is a methodological one, the legal materials to which the methodological considerations are made applicable, are situated in one area, that is federalism. This choice was conscious, in the sense that exploring the problem from the viewpoint of federalism – an area of law traditionally deemed to be closely related to politics – allows us to make our point more saliently. At the same time, I do not exclude that the form of analysis offered here could have a wider impact, on constitutional jurisprudence as a whole. Even so, our current research object remains federalism, and in what follows, I will further explain how this object is to be conceived of.

General object: federalism

8. Framing the object. In 1996, John Fitzmaurice considered a question that has become increasingly relevant since the 2007 and 2010 Belgian federal elections, the aftermath of which was constituted by a long and tiresome debate on a new institutional agreement. Even if this Institutional Agreement (coined *Butterfly Agreement*[9]) has now been reached[10], Fitzmaurice's question, that is: 'Whither Belgium?', has not really lost its relevance. For it is common knowledge amongst those familiar with Belgian politics that every stage of state reforms (partially) germinates the necessity for a subsequent one[11].

I refer to Fitzmaurice here, not so much because his question is the focal point of this book, but rather because his answer is illustrative of how we can start to understand federalism. He considered that '[o]utcomes will be determined by a complex dialectic between the internal dynamics of Belgian society and the balance between the two main communities and the external political, social

[9] In Dutch: *Vlinderakkoord*; in French: *l'accord papillon*. The name refers to the bow tie (*vlinderdas/noeud papillon*, *vlinder/papillon* being translated as *butterfly*) commonly worn by Belgium's current prime minister (and then chief negotiator), Elio Di Rupo.

[10] Een efficiëntere Federale Staat en een Grotere Autonomie voor de Deelstaten, Institutioneel akkoord voor de zesde Staatshervorming (Oct. 11, 2011) (hereinafter: Butterfly Agreement). It has even been partially implemented: *see* for an overview, http://www.law.kuleuven.be/icr/doc_6e_shv.

[11] *See* eg Patricia Popelier & Dave Sinardet, *Stabiliteit en instabiliteit in de Belgische federale staatsstructuur* in België: *quo vadis*? Waarheen na de zesde staatshervorming? 3, 3 (Patricia Popelier, Dave Sinardet, Jan Velaers & Bea Cantillon eds. 2012) ('[f]ederal states may be dynamic in nature: they are constantly searching for balance between the federated entities' autonomy and the coherence of the federal whole [...] But these reforms succeed each other much faster in Belgium than elsewhere').

and economic forces that play upon it'[12]. Correct as that consideration might be, the dialectic stands in need of some clarification, and this book will attempt to provide some clarification, albeit within specific constraints.

9. Legal analysis of federalism-related questions. These constraints are of particular importance when trying to explain a dialectic between different societal forces and various institutional structures, and the first constraint is rather obvious: I am not examining how Belgian federalism works in general, nor where it is heading towards. Rather, I am dealing with the particular question how Belgian fundamental rules concerning federalism are influenced by the process of ongoing Europeanization. Within this legal perspective, I need to further delimit the scope of my inquiry.

10. Analysis of constitutional court case law on federalism: the last word. First of all, I am not examining the European influence on Belgian legislation as such, or on case law as such. Rather, I primarily focus on the case law of the Constitutional Court in Belgium, which arguably 'has the final word'[13] in federalism matters. A constitutional court indeed generally decides upon modalities of the institutionalization of federalism, in that often measures institutionalizing federalism have been constitutionally enshrined, and constitutional law, in terms of judicial review of legislative measures, is first and foremost safeguarded by a constitutional court. This is at least the case in

[12] John Fitzmaurice, The Politics of Belgium: a Unique Federalism 267 (1996).

[13] Jan Velaers, De Grondwet en de Raad van State. Afdeling wetgeving 14 (1999). *Further compare* Popelier & Sinardet, *supra* note 11, at p. 11, 14-17 (on the importance of the CC as a mechanism of federal coherence); Marc Uyttendaele, Le Fédéralisme inachevé. Réflexions sur le système institutionnele belge, issu des réformes de 1988-1989 p. 530 *et seq.* (1991) (making a similar point, by construing the CA as one of the 'federal guarantees' and noticing (and criticizing) that the specificity of the CA, compared to other constitutional courts, lies 'in the rules that affix its composition and functioning, which are profoundly marked by the linguistic/communautarian dualism' (*ibid.* at p. 577)); Johan Vande Lanotte & Geert Goedertier, Handboek Belgisch Publiekrecht 92-93, 117-118 (6th ed. 2010) (acknowledging the growing importance of the judge in interpreting the Constitution); Jan Velaers, Van Arbitragehof tot Grondwettelijk Hof 6 (1990) ('[t]he establishment of the Court of Arbitration and the expansion of its competences were a 'conditio sine qua non' for the sought institutional reforms'), 24-25 and 55-57; *but also* Francis Delpérée & Anne Rasson-Roland, Receuil d'études sur la Cour d'arbitrage 1980-1990 p. 25-26 (1990) and Hervé Bribosia & Jean-Louis van Boxstael, Le partage des compétences dans la Belgique fédérale 28 (1994) (all arguing that the institution of the Court of Arbitration should be considered as a 'constituted authority'); André Alen & Patrick Peeters, *"Bundestreue" in het Belgisch Grondwettelijk Recht*, 1989-90 RW 1122, 1126-27 (discussing the debate about 'authentic' (sovereign) interpretation of the Constitution, at least at that time); Hendrik Vuye, *Het territorialiteitsbeginsel in de rechtspraak van het Grondwettelijk Hof en de Raad van State: eenduidig of meerduidig*, CDPK (10 year edition) 10, 35-36 (2007) (preaching plural views by 'highest courts' on constitutional matters as a virtue).

systems with a form of Kelsenian judicial review, and in Belgium, such a system is operative.

However, the aforementioned assertions require some qualifications. First, we should relativize the power of the 'final word'. It does not mean that all judgments of the Constitutional Court in federalism matters lead to a uniform application by all Belgian judges. Some remain contentiously reluctant to follow the case law of the Constitutional Court[14]. Moreover, a debate in Belgium continues about the proper effects of a Constitutional Court judgment, for instance in case of 'modulations'[15], which also threatens uniform application and thus relativizes the power of the final word.

Second, we should nuance the statement that foundational rules regarding federalism are constitutionally enshrined. In Belgium, indeed, the rules regarding the allocation of competences have often been 'deconstitutionalized' and regulated by *Special Laws*[16]. This is for instance the case for the competences of

---

[14] A famous example hereof is the different interpretation of article 4 of the Constitution by the CC and the CoS, regarding the effects of 'linguistic priority' (*see eg* André Alen & Rusen Ergec, *Het territorialiteitsbeginsel in de Belgische en Europese rechtspraak. Een poging tot synthese*, 1998 RW 417, 418-420; Velaers, De Grondwet en de Raad van State, *supra* note 13, at p. 44-52; André Alen & Koen Muylle, Handboek van het Belgisch Staatsrecht 314 *et seq.* (2011) or Vuye, *supra* note 13, at p. 12-33 (summarizing the dispute)).

[15] *See eg* Patricia Popelier, *De doorwerking van prejudiciële arresten van het Grondwettelijk Hof in de rechtspraak*, 2010 CDPK 392 (analyzing the effects of judgments vis-à-vis the judiciary in matters of preliminary references); Christian Behrendt, Le juge constitutionnel, un législateur-cadre positif: une analyse comparative en droit français, belge et allemand (diss. doct. Université de Paris I Panthéon-Sorbonne 2005) (analyzing the effects of judgments vis-à-vis the legislature); Claude Courtoy, *Rapport de la Cour d'arbitrage du Royaume de Belgique*, in 1 Les Relations entre les Cours constitutionnelles et les autres juridictions nationales, y comprmis l'interférence en cette matière, de l'action des juridictions européennes / The relations between the Constitutional Courts and the other national courts, including the interference in this area of the action of the European Courts (XIIth Congress of the Conference of European Constitutional Courts, Brussels, May 14-16, 2002) 283 (Michel Melchior, André Alen and Frank Meersschaut eds. 2005); *also see eg* Stefan Sottiaux, *Grondwetsconforme interpretatie garantie voor of aantasting van de scheiding der machten?* in 2 Leuvense Staatsrechtelijke Standpunten 193 (André Alen & Stefan Sottiaux eds. 2010) (criticizing the lack of coherence in use of modulations by the CC, and explaining how they can have different effects).

[16] Since the constitutional amendment process in Belgium is cumbersome (art. 195 Cons.), the 'Special Legislature' has been established so as to create an alternative form of entrenchment, which at least protects the two large sociological groups (*see* the quorum and majority requirement in art. 4 Cons.). There are other constitutional provisions requiring *qualified majorities (eg* art. 86-87 Cons.), but the Special Legislature has grown to be a specific form of normative power in Belgium, closely related to Belgium's federal structure. *See* Alen & Muylle, *supra* note 14, at p. 30 n40 (*but compare* CA No. 35/2003 (Mar. 25, 2003), B.19.4 (relativizing the autonomous meaning of 'special legislature')); *also see* Marie-Françoise Rigaux & Bernadette Renauld, La Cour Constitutionnelle 40-44 (2008); Patricia Popelier,

the Regions, which the Constitution does not regulate except in the most formal and abstract of ways[17]. Accordingly, the basic (contentious) rules governing the allocation of competences are not merely found in the constitutional text, but also in different (special) laws, such as the Special Law governing Institutional Reform (SLIR), the Law governing Institutional Reform in the German-speaking Community (LIRG), the Special Law governing Brussels Institutions (SLBI) and the Special Law governing Community and Region Financing (SLCRF). Other laws could be mentioned[18], but the aforementioned are the most important ones. Even if accordingly, some important rules governing Belgian federalism are not found in the Constitution, this does not undermine the coherence of our project, since we primarily focus on Constitutional Court case law. And the Constitutional can actually review legislation in light of what some authors have called a 'bloc de constitutionnalité', not only comprising the Constitution, but also other norms 'allocating competences'[19]. Even some executive norms can be counted amongst the latter[20]. This means, in Thomas Vandamme's words that in Belgium '[o]ne can change the constitution without changing the 'Constitution''[21]. Even so, and notwithstanding the fact that these competence allocating norms (also enshrined in (special) laws) are reference norms in the Constitutional Court's review, the Constitutional Court can also review the (Special) Laws in light of their own constitutionality[22].

11. Influence: a complex, but important concept. Next to the fact that I am limiting myself to an investigation of Constitutional Court case law on federalism, I will already devote a couple of words to the concept of "influence", which is a complex concept to work with. I will not *a priori* determine what influence means. Some preliminary considerations will be elaborated in a separate introductory chapter, but the issue is already touched upon to underscore the

Procederen voor het Grondwettelijk Hof 34-36 (summarizing the concomitant legal debate) or Vande Lanotte & Goedertier, *supra* note 13, at p. 121-129 (putting the debate in a broader perspective); *compare* Bribosia & Van Boxstael, *supra* note 13, at p. 19-20.

17 *Cf.* Alen & Muylle, *supra* note 14, at p. 294.

18 *See eg* Alen & Muylle, *supra* note 14, at p. 299-300 or Bribosia & Boxstael, *supra* note 13, at p. 24-37.

19 *Cf.* Bribosia & Van Boxstael, *supra* note 13, at p. 37-38.

20 *Eg* CA No. 39/97 (July 14, 1997); CC 57/2012 (May 3, 2012) B.10.3; *compare* CC 29/2010 (Mar. 18, 2010) B.5.3.

21 *Prochain arrêt: La Belgique! Explaining recent preliminary references of the Belgian Constitutional Court*, 4 Eu Cons 127, 131 (2008).

22 *Cf.* CA No. 8/90 (Feb. 7, 1990), B.2.3; *compare* Xavier Delgrange, *La Cour d'arbitrage enfonce un coin dans le bloc de constitutionnalité organisant la répartition des compétences législatives* (case note accompanying that case), 1990 Révue Régionale de Droit 166, 168; Rusen Ergec, *Des fissures dans le bloc de constitutionnalité*, 1990 JT 359-60.

importance of delimiting the denotation and sense[23] of the concept. Indeed, delimiting the meaning of the concept will accordingly delimit the purview of my inquiry. This delimitation will come about throughout this book, in connection with how I define and interpret the 'Belgian fundamental rules concerning federalism'. In this regard, it should be noticed that my primary focus, if anywhere, lies on the principle of exclusivity of competences, which is deemed to be of special significance within the dualist federal Belgian state structure.

This, I believe, will increase the coherence of my text. This does not mean, however, that European law cannot exert influence on other salient principles underlying the Belgian state structure (some of which might be – more or less directly – related to federalism). Some of the most important issues discussed in Belgian constitutional law, can be construed as having a direct relationship to European law. Two examples can suffice. First, the ongoing Belgian debate in 2011 about the concept of conducting current affairs[24] in light of European requirements to create a multiannual budget will not be dealt with. Political parties here disputed whether a resigning government could on its own create that budget[25], which obviously has ramifications in terms of exercising competences. Next to that, I leave aside the vivid controversy in Belgium over the implications of the *Melki* judgment[26] for article 26 SLCC[27] and more broadly the order of judicial review, the (indirect) relevance of which for federalism case law is quite evident too.

---

23 I add the Fregian distinction in order to allow for the possibility of integration, in which case the *denotation* of a European legal order (understood as its reference) would have to be reconstructed in terms of its *sense*; *cf. infra* Ch. 1.

24 The scope of competence of a resigning government, the content of which is determined by a constitutional general principle of law, *cf.* Patricia Popelier, *Lopende zaken: over een regering zonder vertrouwen en een parlement zonder motor,* 2008 CDPK 94, 96; Jan Velaers & Yves Peeters, *De 'lopende zaken' en de ontslagnemende regering*, 2008 TBP 3.

25 *Also see* Velaers, De Grondwet en de Raad van State, *supra* note 13, at p. 79-80 (arguing how article 10 of the Belgian Constitution has become partially moot because of European obligations).

26 Joined Cases C-188/10 and C-189/10 (GC; June 22, 2010) *Melki & Abdeli*, paras 52-57.

27 *See* (order) Case C-457/09 (Mar. 1, 2011) *Chartry*, para 24 (where the Court decided that the issue did not come within the scope of EU law); *also see eg* Jan Velaers, *Het arrest-Melki-Abdeli van het Hof van Justitie van de Europese Unie: een voorwaardelijk "fiat" voor de voorrang van de toetsing aan de Grondwet op de toetsing aan het internationaal en het Europees recht,* 2011 RW 770, 785 *et seq.*; Willem Verrijdt, *Should the EU Effectiveness Principle Be Applied To Judge National Constitutional Review Procedures, in* Liège, Strasbourg, Bruxelles: parcours des droits de l'homme. Liber Amicorum Michel Melchior 543 (Paul Martens ed. 2010). Much more has been written on the issue; for a short English summary of the problems in context, *see* Patrick Peeters, *The Belgian Constitutional Review Procedure under European Scrutiny*, 18 Eur. Publ. L. 411-422 (2012).

Even so, the principle of exclusivity of competence remains a mere focus indeed, since the principle is closely intertwined with other aspects of Belgian state structure, which require elaboration too.

12. Piecemeal approach, not geared towards exhaustivity, but towards the purpose and coherence. Even with these nuances, any claim to exhaustivity of analysis is precluded. Indeed, it could be argued that this monograph is an example of piecemeal – even subjective – inquiry, and I could only try to refute this argument by emphasizing that coherence was the first objective I had in mind when writing it. If I had to try to define the scope of my inquiry at the outset, I would say that my first focus lies on the *structural* aspects of Belgian federalism, and not so much on the substantive allocation of powers. I will further discuss this issue in my first chapter. Moreover, the book is obviously in form and function geared towards the point it seeks to make, which is – again summarily – that constitutional law can reach beyond the often deployed classic dogmatic approach and can be construed more in terms of not only abstract principles (rule of law values), but also instrumental-political rationales (tools).

13. Structure of the work. The objective of the book structures the content of this monograph as follows. After having delved into the concept of influence and offered some introductory remarks on the issue, together with some further jurisprudential considerations in light of the purpose of the work (Chapter 1), I offer some general considerations, in the form of an introduction to Belgian federalism, with a particular focus on the role of the Constitutional Court within the Belgian federal structure (Chapter 2). Afterwards, I aim at fitting these considerations in the established case law of the Belgian Constitutional Court regarding the allocation of powers (Chapter 3). In a subsequent chapter, a number of cases are discussed in which it could be argued that European law influences the established case law, at least within the scope I tried to delimit beforehand (Chapter 4). Finally, before concluding, I attempt to address some underlying explanations for this influence, and assess the future relevance of this influence in a more general way (Chapter 5).

1.

Influence and the toolbox concept: Some preliminary considerations pertaining to method

14. From influence to the toolbox concept. We mentioned that the object of our investigation would be how European Union law *influences* Belgian constitutional case law on federalism. "Influence", however, is a difficult concept to grasp here, because it may mean a myriad of things depending on the perspective, because the object and subject of influence do not always allow for a clear definition, and because of issues related to understanding how law in general should be conceived of. The latter reason will lead us to consider the toolbox concept we deploy here in order to enrich our understanding of Belgian constitutional case law relating to federalism.

1.1 Methodological problems pertaining to the object of the inquiry

15. Influence: ambiguities and perspectives. Influence is a concept that resists an easy or straightforward definition. One only needs to read a dictionary to perceive how the concept is fraught with ambiguity. For instance, influence can mean both 'an emanation of spiritual or moral force' and 'the act of power of producing an effect *without apparent exertion of force* or direct exercise of command'[28]. Even disregarding the ambiguity in these meanings, one can ask how influence can actually play in a legal sphere. A first possible perspective is a social theoretical one, which is geared towards *law*.

16. Influence in social theory. Although some system theorists, like Niklas Luhmann[29] or Günther Teubner[30] have argued that the "legal system" is operationally closed ("autopoietic") in the sense that it thrives within its own self-referential language games, Jürgen Habermas has offered some pressing arguments so as to conceive of legal discourse as 'open'[31]. The notion of influence is operationalized here in a legal context, but it does not seem very

[28] MERRIAM WEBSTER DICTIONARY. *Compare eg* to the OXFORD DICTIONARY definition ('the capacity to have an effect on the character, development, or behaviour of someone or something, or the effect itself').

[29] A SOCIOLOGICAL THEORY OF LAW 274 (Elizabeth King-Utz and Martin Albrow trans. 1985) (1972) (describing legal science as a discipline which 'sees law as a constellation of meaning in itself') and LAW AS A SOCIAL SYSTEM (Klaus A. Ziegert transl. Fatima Kastner *et al.* eds. 2004) (1993).

[30] LAW AS AN AUTOPOIETIC SYSTEM (Ruth Adler transl. 1993) (1989).

[31] BETWEEN FACTS AND NORMS. CONTRIBUTIONS TO A DISCOURSE THEORY OF DEMOCRACY 48-55. 207-209 and 330 *et seq.* (William Rehg transl. 1996) (1992).

helpful in our context. True, the social-theoretical debate can have an indirect effect on our construal of the notion of influence, but the questions authors like Luhmann or Habermas are answering, are primarily whether law is influenced by other *non-legal* spheres. Our question, here, however, *prima facie* seems to be narrower, as we are discussing influence by another *legal* order. Perhaps a more jurisprudential approach can be more fruitful in this regard.

17. Influence in "legal theory". We could start investigating legal theory or the philosophy of law, so as to learn what influence of one legal order on the other order means. *In abstracto*, to our knowledge this problem has not been elaborately discussed. But as applied to some more contentious issues, some (applied) legal theory can be read to have dealt with the issue[32]. However, this legal theory does not necessarily offer a clear definition of the concept either.

In relation to the problem of how to integrate the different (national) legal orders with the European legal order, the debate has recently been shaped by a discourse of constitutional pluralism[33]. In this spirit of pluralism (although

---

[32] On the importance of this legal theory for some dogmatic questions, *see eg* Stef Feyen, *The Economic and Monetary Union: caught between Brussels and Luxembourg* in FEDERALISM IN THE EUROPEAN UNION 392 (Elke Cloots, Geert De Baere & Stefan Sottiaux eds. 2012).

[33] *See, eg,* the famous introduction by Neil Walker (*The Idea of Constitutional Pluralism,* 65 MODERN LAW REVIEW 317 (2002) and *Multilevel Constitutionalism: Looking beyond the German debate* in THE MANY CONSTITUTIONS OF EUROPE 143 (Karlo Tuori & Suvi Sankari 2010)) (accordingly, I do not distinguish *a priori* between constitutional pluralism and multilevel constitutionalism, as developed by PERNICE in Germany); *also see* NEIL MACCORMICK, QUESTIONING SOVEREIGNTY: LAW, STATE AND NATION IN THE EUROPEAN COMMONWEALTH 117-18 (1999); Miguel Poiares Maduro, *Contrapunctual law: Europe's Constitutional Pluralism in Action* in SOVEREIGNTY IN TRANSITION 523-24 (2003); the 2008/6 I-CON issue (especially the contributions by Walker, von Bogdandy and Rosenfeld); the contributions in CONSTITUTIONAL PLURALISM IN THE EUROPEAN UNION AND BEYOND (Matej Avbelj & Jan Komarek eds. 2012); *compare* Alec Stone Sweet, *A cosmopolitcan legal order: Constitutional Pluralism and rights adjudication in Europe,* 1 GLOBAL CONSTITUTIONALISM 53 (2012) (in light of the ECHR); *also compare (more embedded in jurisprudence)* MICHEL VAN DE KERCHOVE & FRANÇOIS OST, LE SYSTÈME JURIDIQUE ENTRE ORDRE ET DÉSORDRE 190-199 (1988) (arguing that the legal system not only consists of rules and norms, but also of institutions, values, branches, ..., which create disorder in law, and which leads the authors to conceive of a legal system as a network, of which federalism is a prime example (*cf.* FRANÇOIS OST & MICHEL VAN DE KERCHOVE, DE LA PYRAMIDE AU RÉSEAU. POUR UNE THÉORIE DIALECTIQUE DU DROIT 192-93 (2002)) and R. Barendts, *De voorrang van het unierecht in persepctief van constitutioneel pluralisme,* 2009 SOCIAAL ECONOMISCHE WETGEVING 21, also published in English in 2009 EUCONS 438 (explaining how the *Costa v. ENEL*-principle (primacy) should be applied in concreto on the basis of theoretical considerations). *Further see* (for influence on dogmatics) Jaakko Husa, *The Method is Dead, Long Live the Methods! European polynomial and pluralist methodology,* 5 LEGISPRUDENCE 249 (2011). *Compare* MARCELO NEVES, TRANSCONSTITUTIONALISM (Kevin Mundy trans., 2013 forthcoming).

its ambit nor importance are unequivocally adhered to[34]), *influence* is a basic premise (or, depending on the semantics, one could even argue that influence is impossible as *integration* is the basic rule[35], or at least the aspiration). Even if this theoretical framework better succeeds than the old theories of monism and dualism to capture the relationship between legal orders intertwining, it does not help us to delimit the concept of influence as we would like to use it here, for several reasons. First, as we will explain further on, our theoretical framework to some extent differs from, or at least adds to[36], the discourse of constitutional pluralism. Second, even within this theoretical framework, the specific scope of influence, and its aspirations, are not clearly, or at least not generally, defined. And third, perhaps most importantly, our inquiry starts from a Belgian *practice*, and hypothesizes a theoretical framework applicable to that practice. As such the concept of influence has to remain underdetermined at this point, since we first need to examine what it is that might be subject of influence, and indeed its object.

18. Influence: object and subject. Indeed, in order to determine whether there is, and how there can be influence of European Union law on Belgian federalism, we will have know what we mean by (constitutional case *law* regarding) *federalism* and by (EU) *law*. This again, is a highly contentious issue, at least from a theoretical perspective. Of course, for practical issues, what the *law* is (or at least where to find its emanation for dogmatic purposes), does not seem to be so hard a question: many scholars agree that, in Belgium, one should start with different *legal sources*, so as to find provisions, principles or rules that are applicable to the case at hand. Be that as it may, to some extent, the theoretical debate on the meaning of law[37] can exert an influence on the

[34] Sometimes, for instance, a distinction is made between constitutional pluralism, multi-level constitutionalism, jurisdictional pluralism and also transconstitutionalism. For some critical reflections on the pluralist ideas as such, *see eg* Julio Baquero Cruz, *The Legacy of the Maastricht Urteil and the Pluralist Movement*, 14 ELJ 389, 412 *et seq.* (2008).

[35] As such, it could be said that "influence" as a concept disregards the primarily *dialectical* relationship between different legal orders. Insofar as dialectics (understood as *mutual* influence) are necessary to explain the relationship between the legal orders, the concept of influence itself becomes unworkable. On the other hand, a dialectical relationship existing between two legal orders does not preclude analyzing influence as a *one-directional* concept: in the latter case, however, one has to be aware of the danger associated with abstracting the dialectical characteristics of interaction.

[36] This is not to say that a discourse of constitutional pluralism cannot have an effect of reaching beyond classical dogmatics (see *eg* Giulio Itzcovich, *Legal order, Legal pluralism, Fundamental Principles. Europe and its law in three concepts*, 18 ELJ 358 (2012)).

[37] *See* Bribosia & Van Boxstael, *supra* note 13, at p. 13-90, *esp.* p. 31 (applying basic Kelsenian logic to distinguish a constitutional order from a constituted order and exploring the repercussions on the qualification of competences; *cf.* Hans Kelsen, Pure Theory of Law 221 *et seq.*

interpretation and solution of concrete legal problems in Belgium and the same holds for the theoretical debate about federalism[38]. Hence, theoretical issues regarding the meaning of law, but also regarding the meaning of federalism not only at times drive, but also sometimes conflate the debate in practice. We fully recognize the importance of these issues, but will not address them from a systematizing or abstract perspective.

19. Direct influence on federalist structure. Instead, we try to delimit the debate by specifying the question, thus delimiting the scope of our inquiry from a more specific (albeit probably more dogmatic) angle: we will thus limit ourselves to exploring the *direct* influence of EU law on *constitutional case* law regarding *federalism* from a *structural* perspective.

20. Substance vs. structure. Undoubtedly, European law has exerted direct influence on *substantive policy* areas in Belgium[39]. In light of this, one could argue – from an internal federalist perspective[40] – that EU law indeed influences

(Max Knight transl. 2002) (2d ed. 1967)) or UYTTENDAELE, *supra* note 13, at p. 598 *et seq.*, *esp.* 611 (trying to fit cooperation agreements into a Kelsenian pyramid). *See, more generally, eg* SCOTT J. SHAPIRO, LEGALITY 22 *et seq.* (2011) (explaining how 'many of the question that lawyers truly care about simply *cannot* be answered in a philosophical vacuum (*ibid.* at p. 31))

38 *See eg,* André Alen, Patrick Peeters & Jan Velaers, *Autonomie: een staatsrechtelijke benadering*, in VLAANDEREN OP EEN KRUISPUNT. SOCIOLOGISCHE, ECONOMISCHE EN STAATSRECHTELIJKE PERSPECTIEVEN (André Alen *et al.* eds. Report by the Leuven Club) 178-99 (1990); *also see* DAVID HALJAN, THE JUSTICIABILITY OF SECESSION? A THEORETICAL FOUNDATION FOR CONSTITUTIONAL ASSOCIATION AND DISSOCIATION (doct. diss. K.U.Leuven 2007) (to be published in 2013 titled CONSTITUTIONALISING SECESSION) (trying to bring secession, on the basis of a theory of associative constitutionalism, into the realm of the juridical, with a focus on international and Canadian law); *contra* 1 PATRICK PEETERS, PROBLEMEN VAN BEVOEGDHEIDSVERDELING EN BEVOEGDHEIDSUITLEGGING NA DE TWEEDE BELGISCHE STAATSHERVORMING. ANALYSE VAN DE AUTONOMIE VAN DE GEMEENSCHAPPEN EN DE GEWESTEN IN HET BELGISCH STAATSVERBAND – DE ARTICULATIE VAN DE BEVOEGDHEIDSVERDELING 149-150 (diss. doct. University of Antwerp, 1988; *but see ibid.* at p. 196 or 198 *et seq.* (invoking Kelsen in the concrete elaboration of Belgian autonomy, and criticizing the competence attribution of the Court of Arbitration), and *esp.* p. 170 ('the considerations of the Pure theory of law on the federal state are intrinsically linked to specific methodological basic points'); *compare* André Alen, *Enkele kanttekeningen bij het Belgisch federalisme, onder meer in het licht van bepaalde bondsstaatstheorieën* in BELGIUM: QUO VADIS 9, 19-43 (Acts of the conference of March 17, 24, and 31, 1999) (who refers back to Peeters' dissertation). For a general normative overview of federal theory, *see* THEORIES OF FEDERALISM. A READER (Dimitrios Karmis & Wayne Norman eds. 2005).

39 *See eg* Koen Lenaerts, *Federalism and the rule of law at the European Court of Justice*, 33 FORDHAM INTERNATIONAL LAW JOURNAL 1343 (2010) (discussing the influence of EU law on Member States' educational, direct taxation, health care and family law competences, which in Belgium, again, are allocated differently); *see also* François Tulkens, *La nature supraconstitutionnelle du droit européen et son impact sur la repartition de competences en matière de protection de l'environnement*, 39 REVUE DE DROIT DE L'ULB 201, 208 *et seq.* (2009).

40 From a "European" federalist approach, it is most obvious that EU law can influence the

the *internal* allocation of powers, for example in that some policy areas, competence on which having been allocated to the federated entities, are pervaded by European law requirements[41]. That is a form of direct influence on the *substance* of the law, and falls outside the scope of analysis, since our inquiry deals primarily with structure. Although Riccardo Vuillermoz's doctoral dissertation can be seen as offering important structural arguments, he primarily addresses the question of substantive influence[42]. In this book, we do not plan to add much to his analysis in this regard.

21. Direct vs. indirect. There are also forms of structural inquiry that fall outside the scope of our analysis, namely what we could call *indirect* influences. Several forms of this sort of influence can be conceived of.

For instance, one could argue that there is European structural influence as follows: notwithstanding the *principled* application in Belgium of the *in foro interno, in foro externo* principle[43], the federal government's competence is strengthened in that some "international safeguards" have been construed as exceptions to this principle and in that the federal government remains the first and foremost responsible on the international scene[44], which in turn diminishes the sub-entities' power insofar as they are obliged to (at least) cooperate and coordinate with the federal government[45]. This influence is structural (in that

allocation of competences between the member states (*including* sub-entities) and Europe, as becomes obviously clear in Lenaerts' article (*supra* note 39).

41 Lenaerts, *supra* note 39, at p. 1347 offers the example of Case C-65/03 (July 1, 2004) *Commission v. Belgium* (regarding access conditions for higher education, normally determined by the Communities in Belgium (*cf. ibid.* at §§ 6-8, referring to the Community legislation).

42 La Belgique, l'Espagne et l'Italie face à l'intégration communautaire. Quelle adaptation des rapports entre l'État et ses collectivités régionales, 40-48, 64-72, 79-89, 114-23, 138-45, 157-74, 205-20, 324-29, 334-43, 351-54; *also see* p. 283-86 and 300-04, but *esp. see* (focusing less on the institutional part, but rather on the *policy* implications) p. 382-86 (agriculture and fisheries), 396-99 (transportation), 403-08 (territorial planning), 412-17 (environment), 423-26 (employment and social policies), 428-30 (education), 432-39 (culture and health), 440 *et seq.* (transversal competences), 579-99 and 611-21 (discussing the duty to execute Community law in light of CA No. 6/97 (Feb. 19, 1997), also in light of coordination) (2003).

43 Art. 167, § 3 Cons.

44 *See* Alen & Muylle, *supra* note 14, at p. 738 *et seq.*, *esp.* 755-758 and 762-764.

45 Patricia Popelier, *Social federalism and the allocations of powers in a comparative law perspective – the case for shared powers* in Social Federalism: the Creation of a Layered Welfare State 97, 133 (Bea Cantillon, Patricia Popelier & Ninke Mussche eds. 2011) (mentioning (n192) this was the reason why German *Länder* sought a greater participation at the EU level); Popelier & Sinardet, *supra* note 11, at p. 20-21; Jan Beyers & Peter Bursens, Europa is geen buitenland 47-72 (2006) (*factually* describing how Belgian federalist institutionalization has become more cooperative under European pressures, especially for this issue; *also see ibid.* at p. 149 *et seq.* (regarding treaty revisions) and p. 173 *et seq.* (regarding implementation of

it occurs independently of the substance of the regulated policy area), but it is rather indirect, as it is not as such dealt with by the Constitutional Court in its elaboration of case law on Belgian federalism. Similar (arguably more institutional/political) indirect (and therefore not discussed) forms of influence can be discerned in (political science) discussions about 'institutional misfit'[46], or in broader legal-institutional debates regarding the powers of federated entities in light of the European Union (for instance their participatory powers), without direct connection to the case law of the Constitutional Court[47].

22. A tentative explanation of influence. These examples serve to show what I primarily tend to exclude from "influence" in this book: I will not deal with influence by the *substantive (policy)* aspects of European law, even if this

European law); a shortened English version of this book's point is presented in Jan Beyers & Peter Bursens, *The European Rescue of the Federal State: How Europeanization Shapes the Belgian State*, 29 West European Politics 1057, 1062-1073 (2006); *see also* Patricia Popelier & Wouter Vandenbruwaene, *The subsidiarty mechanism as a Tool for Inter-Level Dialogue in Belgium: On 'Regional Blindness' and Co-operative flaws*, 7 Eu Cons 204 (2011).

46 *See eg* Tanja A. Börzel, *Europeanization: How the European Union Interacts with its Member States* in The Member States and the European Union 14, 52 (Simon Bulmer and Christian Lequesne eds. 2005). *See*, for Belgium, Godelieve Craenen, *De bevoegdheidsverdeling inzake landbouw en zeevisserij, buitenlandse handel en ontwikkelingssamenwerking* in De Vijfde Staatshervorming van 2001 p. 123 at p. 139-40 (André Alen ed. 2002) (referring to the problem of the representation of the Regions in agricultural policies in the European Union); *compare Parl. Doc.* Senate 2000-01, No. 2-709/2, p. 1 (where an Amendment complains about Belgian loss of power within Europe, since a cooperation agreement stipulates abstention in case of disagreement between Regions).

47 For some (dispersed) analysis from a legal perspective, *see eg* Frank Ingelaere, *De Europeesrechtelijke raakvlakken van de nieuwe wetgeving inzake de internationale bevoegdheid van de Belgische Gemeenschappen en Gewesten,* Sociaal Economisch Tijdschrift 67, at 69-72 (1994); Jean-Victor Louis and André Alen, *La Constitution et la participation à la Communauté européenne*, 1994 Belgisch Tijdschrift voor Internationaal Recht 3; Karel Rimanque & Jan Wouters, De betekenis van de Grondwet voor de Europese rechtsorde. Beschouwingen in Belgisch Staatsrechtelijk en Europeesrechtelijk perspectief *esp.* 8-46 (1998); Michel Struys, *La Mise en oeuvre des obligations découlant du droit européen (La Belgique fédérale dans l'Europe fédérale)* in La Belgique Fédérale 483, 486 *et seq.* (Francis Delpérée 1994) or the texts (esp. Velaers' and Ingelaere's) compilated from the 5th Flemish Constitutional Law Conference (Internationale betrekkingen en federalisme (Godfried Geudens and Frank Judo eds. 2006)); *see also* 1 Nicole Plets, Het systeem van de Belgische fiscale bevoegdheidsverdeling: juridische evenwichtsoefning tussen autonomie voor de deelstaten en het behoud van de interne economische unie en monetaire eenheid in een federaal staatsverband 120 (diss. doct. Antwerp University 2004) (explaining the phenomenon in a wider legal context of allocation of competences); Roger Blanpain, *Arbeidsmarktbeleid in een federale staat. De bevordering van de uitwisseling van vraag en aanbod tussen werkgevers en werkzoekende werknemers op de arbeidsmarkt* in Sociaal Beleid en Federalisme (Staatsrechtconferentie 1998 – Vlaamse juristenvereniging) 155, 160 *et seq.* (Steven Vansteenkiste & Marc Taeymans eds. 1998) (describing for instance how a Court of Justice judgment forced the Flemish government to adapt its policies in employment mediation).

substantive European law influence on national law might cause a shift in the balance of power between the federal government and the federated entities. If *politically*, this shift of influence should not be underestimated[48], *legally*, and seen from our *internal* Constitutional Court perspective, it – *prima facie* – is not our primary concern here[49].

23. A Belgian perspective. But taking this internal perspective does not always make things easier. Detaching *substantive (policy)* from *structural-institutional* issues *within* Constitutional Court jurisprudence is not evident at all. To give but one example, the Constitutional Court, in explaining the principle of territoriality, has held that the 'review on the basis of the Constitution first occurs in light of the provisions allocating *material* competences which contain elements on the basis of which the validity of these criteria can be determined; insight into the *object, the nature and possibly the goal of the conferred material competence* is required so as to adequately adjudge the localization of the object of an adopted regulation within the territorial region of competence, determined by the Constitution'[50].

Perhaps one could argue that this is a generalization that can be intelligibly made without actually inquiring into the material competences. However, it will be the point of this book to actually starkly relativize the possibility of such abstract generalizations, which will be called reifications. One could again try to distinguish this issue and make it fall within the scope of our inquiry by arguing that this issue pertains to the *internal substantive (material)* issues of allocation of competences (and could therefore be included), whereas other issues, such as the influence of European law on the internal allocation of competences from a European case law perspective[51] is excluded.

---

[48] *See eg* Beyers & Bursens, *supra* note 45, at p. 47-72 (describing how Belgian federalist institutionalization has become more cooperative under European pressures).

[49] *Compare* Börzel, *supra* note 46, at p. 19 (distinguishing influence on the levels of *polity* (institutional organizational structures), *politics* (decision-making structures) and *policies* (outcomes), but emphasizing their mutual entanglement from a *factual* perspective). This does not mean that in the end, the political influence cannot have legal repercussions: the entire debate about increased cooperation (*eg infra* Ch. 4.3.3) could be framed in this way (*see eg* Popelier & Sinardet, *supra* note 11, at p. 20-21).

[50] *Eg*, CA No. 10 (Jan. 30, 1986) III.8.B.1; CA No. 17 (Mar. 26, 1986) III.3.B.7 (*emphasis added*); *see infra* Ch. 3.2.3.

[51] An example of such a perspective, with a particular focus on Belgian federalism, can be found in Edoardo Traversa's doctoral disseration (Intégration européenne et fédéralisme fiscal: deux processus incompatibles? (diss. doct. UCL and Bologna University 2007), published in 2010 as L'Autonomie fiscale des Régions et des collectivités locales face au droit communautaire. Analyse et réflexion à la lumière des experiences belge et italienne, and of which a useful summary is available in 70 Annales de Droit de Louvain 187 (2007)).

24. Limits of delimitation. However, it becomes clear that adding distinction upon distinction does not necessarily clarify a whole lot, and in the end might come across as merely arbitrary. Part of the point of this book will be that certain dogmatic distinctions can indeed be conceived of as concealing, rather than explanatory. Even so, we needed to clarify this at the outset, so as to at least make clear what we would not be doing in this book. Accordingly, even if the "boundaries" I have set myself here at the outset are necessary in order to create an entry point into the discourse, they will prove to be difficult to adhere to throughout the analysis conducted in this book[52].

A concrete example may serve to explain my point: when the Constitutional Court adjudicates upon a matter where the reference norm is article 6, §1, II, 2nd clause, 3° SLIR reserving the competence for international waste transports to the federal government in Belgium[53], should we conceive of that ruling as being influenced by European law? Surely it is in some way, since the Special Legislature, in creating this exception to the general competence for Regions in terms of waste policy, construed it *explicitly* on the grounds of a European requirement, that is article 24 of the Regulation on waste transfer, pursuant to which only one authority may be competent to apply the regulation[54]. On the other hand, in this case, it could be argued that it is not the *Constitutional Court* that is adapting allocation of competences under the influence of European law. That argument, then again, must to some extent fail since the Court itself decides to what extent it relies on *travaux préparatoires*[55]. Conclusion: the methodological problems remain...

Another example seems to be Herwig Verschueren, *The Impact of EU Law on the Devolution of Social Powers in the Member States* in FEDERALISM IN THE EU, *supra* note 32, at p. 265 *et seq.*

[52] *Also see* LUDWIG WITTGENSTEIN, PHILOSOPHICAL INVESTIGATIONS 69e, §201 (G.E.M. Anscombe transl., 3d ed. 2001) (1953) ('any course of action can be made out to accord with the rule') and WILLIAM G. LYCAN, PHILOSOPHY OF LANGUAGE 76 (2nd ed. 2008) (on the form of analysis of linguistic entities, in light of Wittgenstein's philosophy).

[53] Reserving the competence for (international) transports of waste to the federal government: *eg* CA No. 32/91 (Nov. 14, 1991) 5.B.1.6 (indirectly, via fiscal competences); *also see* CA No. 12/89 (May 31, 1989), IV.A.4 (argued by the parties), *compare* B.2 and B.4.

[54] *Cf.* CoS Advice, *Parliamentary Documents* [hereinafter: *Parl. Doc.*] Chamber 1991-92 Special Session [hereinafter SS], No. 600/2, at p. 19 (*but see* p. 20); Explanatory Memo, *Parl. Doc.* Senate 1992-93, No. 558/1, at p. 15, 19; Explanatory Memo, *Parl. Doc.* Chamber, 1991-92 SS, No. 600/1, at p. 4; *also see* Report, *Parl. Doc.* Chamber 1992-93, No. 1063/7, at p. 32-33 (on the differing definition of 'waste' under Belgian law by the CC and under European law by the Court of Justice, where the Prime Minister explicitly acknowledged that the 'Belgian allocation of competences must take the jurisprudence of the Court of Justice into account'; *ibid.* at p. 33; *cf.* CA No. 19/97 (Apr. 15, 1997) B.2.1-B.5). *Compare infra* No. 148.

[55] *Eg* CA No. No. 2/97 (Jan. 16, 1997) B.3.1.

25. Starting in practice as a concession, or perhaps necessity. As a matter of course, however, and perhaps necessarily in order to keep my discourse legally intelligible, I will have to rely on analytical differentiations that in fact can or should be understood as "reifications" of certain concepts[56].

Further on, I will revisit the problem of reification – which can by and large be understood as a fictionalization through objectification[57] –, but let me provide one simple example of possible reification at the outset. It has been pointed out that *in fact* the principle of exclusive territoriality, which is so seminal in (legal) Belgian federalism, is a fiction 'from a political perspective'[58]. Accordingly, the law will not as such take some *real* aspects of a certain relationships or state of affairs into account and objectify a relationship or state of affairs into a concept construed as self-containing and allowing for or at least striving for coherent explanation and elaboration. Law seems to do this often, if not all the time. This does not mean that such fictions – or this one – is useless: construing law on the basis of reifications (some "more fictional" than other, and some fictional in a different way) may, *pace* Bentham[59], be justified in terms of values we want the law to serve, such as equality, generality or legal certainty[60] (although also more pragmatic, institutional values could be referred to[61]). In fact, it could be argued that the *concept* of law itself, is to be construed as a justifiable fiction,

---

56 *See eg* Douglas Litowitz, *Reification in Law and Legal Theory*, 9 S. Cal. Interdisc. L.J. 401 (1999-2000); *compare* Frederick Schauer, Playing By the Rules. A Philosophical Examination of Rule-based Decision-making in law and life 18-22, 25-27 (1991).

57 *See infra* Nos. 33 and 163.

58 *Eg* Jean-Luc Dehaene, *Voorwoord* in Jan Beyers & Peter Bursens, Europa is geen buitenland. Over de relatie tussen het federale België en de Europese Unie 18 (2006); *compare* Uyttendaele, *supra* note 13, at p. 522 and 526 (who only pleads for nuancing the dogma of exclusive competences, which nonetheless remains (legally) valid).

59 Jeremy Bentham, *Legal Fictions*, Appendix A in C.K. Ogden, Bentham's Theory of Fictions 149 (1932).

60 *Cf. eg* Joseph Raz, *The Rule of Law and its Virtue*, 93 The Law Quarterly Review 195 (1977), *reprinted in* The Authority of Law 220 (1979); Lon L. Fuller, The morality of Law (2nd ed. 1969) (1964); Larry Cata Backer, *Reifying Law – Government, Law and the Rule of Law in Governance Systems*, 26 Penn St. Int'l L. Rev. 521 (2007-08).

61 *Eg* Geerten Boogaard, *De geheime politieke rol van de rechter. Over Institutionele realpolitik*, in Rechterlijk Activisme. Opstellen aangeboden aan prof. mr. J.A. Peters 17, 25 *et seq.* (Aernout Nieuwenhuis, Jan-Herman Reestman & Carla Zoethout eds. 2011) (discussing forms of institutional politics by the Marshall Court, and arguing that prudential arguments in judicial decisions create difficulties in terms of coherence/generalizability, and possibly also in terms of judicial duty: according to him, *Realpolitik*, even if it cannot be avoided, should be covered up); *also see* J.H. Nieuwenhuis, *Een discursieve grootheid. Discursieve beschouwingen over J.B.M. Vranken, Algemeen Deel, Zwolle 1995*, 1995 Nederlands Juristenblad 1387, 1391 ('such 'hypostazation' might be revealed by science to be a naive fiction; for practice this fiction has proved to be indispensable. *Lex semper loquitur*').

or perhaps more correctly as a self-fulfilling prophecy. However, elaborating on this matter requires broaching complex jurisprudential issues[62], and we will not tackle these issues as such in this book. Rather, we deploy the concept of reification in order to challenge some of the features of a system established in and by reified discourse, and not the system as such.

Accordingly, it is first and foremost *within the bounds* of these fictions (and sometimes perhaps excursing into the penumbra or periphery) that I will operate, or at least where my operation starts. I refrain from arguing – theoretically and specifically – how remaining within these bounds is to be justified, or even from answering how these bounds are to be set in detail. In that sense, I follow a practice of scholarship…

26. Still beyond dogmatics then? Even conceding this, I have opted for the admittedly slightly provocative title *'Beyond Federal Dogmatics'*. And the question then becomes: if the ambit of operation of the inquiry here is *'within the bounds* of this fiction (and sometimes perhaps excursing into the penumbra or periphery)', one could rightfully ask where and how dogmatics is left behind. I should re-emphasize here that it is not, or not necessarily. Indeed, it is not my plea here to leave any and all dogmatics behind. That – I believe – would be sheer impossible, as it is a form of legal thinking in which all lawyers are socialized. Nonetheless, I would want to argue that the explanatory potential of classic dogmatic thinking is shrinking, and that new modes of legal thought are warranted which have a greater explanatory potential.

Advocating a new mode of thought here by juxtaposing instrumentalism and rule of law values (which is, moreover, from a jurisprudential perspective not all that new), and by relying on the concept of reification in law, I do not pretend to have found a miracle solution for talking adequately about constitutional law, or not even about federalism in constitutional law. I would merely, and then still tentatively, suggest that trying to push and sometimes cross the boundaries of classically understood dogmatics can lead to fruitful lines of inquiry and increase constitutional scholarship's explanatory potential, even taking into account the specific function of constitutional scholarship and constitutional law.

---

[62] *Compare* (theoretically) RONALD DWORKIN, JUSTICE IN ROBES (2006) (emphasizing the interpretive nature of legal reasoning, and emphasizing the role of institutional (political; on this, *see* RONALD DWORKIN, JUSTICE FOR HEDGEHOGS (2011)) morality therein) *with* NEIL MACCORMICK, RHETORIC AND THE RULE OF LAW (2005) (trying to redeem the "legal positivist" reliance on the legal syllogism as a "core" of judicial reasoning).

1.2 The toolbox concept

27. Content driven by method. In order to push those boundaries, I will rely on the concept of legal principles/rules as tools, and the constitutional judge as a craftsman employing and deploying these tools, in order to find a solution which is both politically viable and does not encroach upon fundamental rule of law values. Accordingly, this is not merely an analysis of how European law influences Belgian federalism. Of course that is the content of the work, but the content is largely driven by a method of jurisprudence which tries to be innovative: hence the title. Let me try to further explain that.

28. Toolbox: historical roots and aspiration. Throughout the book, I will be relying heavily on the concept of a toolbox: the name is chosen to emphasize the often instrumental and indeed primarily pragmatic character of the Court's reasoning, harking back to an old jurisprudential tradition, namely that of (American) legal realism, the ideas of which were fostered and ripened throughout the traditions of legal pragmatism (*eg* Posner[63]), critical legal studies (*eg* Kennedy[64] or Tushnet[65]) and the 'political' approach to jurisprudence (*eg* Shapiro, Stone or Hirshl[66]). Although it harks back to the ideas of these great jurisprudential thinkers, it does not merely copy them. The book neither tries to expound a full-fledged jurisprudential theory of its own, nor does it want to delve into all the problematic details which jurisprudence *per se* gives rise to. However, it does explicitly rely on the thoughts of these thinkers to make a clear point, that is that a 'dogmatic' approach to federalism, certainly in a multi-level context, does not have the same explanatory, and perhaps even predictive[67], value as a more 'enriched' understanding of case law can have.

---

[63] *Eg* Richard A. Posner, How Judges Think (2008).

[64] *Eg* Duncan Kennedy, Critique of Adjudication (fin de siècle) (1997).

[65] *Eg* Mark Tushnet, The New Constitutional Order (2003); *see ibid.* at p. 120 (approvingly): '[f]or the realists, conclusions did not flow from principles: in a mature legal system whose doctrinal space was thickly populated, a judge given a principle articulated in some prior case could faithfully deploy that principle along with others equally available in the doctrinal universe to reach whatever result the judge thought socially desirable'.

[66] *Eg* Alec Stone, The Birth of Judicial Politics in France (1992); Alec Stone Sweet, Governing With Judges (2000); Martin Shapiro & Alec Stone Sweet, On law, politics & Judicialization (2001); Ran Hirschl, Towards Juristocracy (2004).

[67] Some of the (early) realists famously defended the thesis that a *factual* analysis of Court behavior would engender predictability (*see eg* Oliver Wendell Holmes Jr., *The Path of the law,* 10 Harv. L. Rev. 457, 461 (1897) ('[t]he prophecies or what the courts will do in fact, and nothing more pretentious, are what I mean by the law'); Karl N. Llewellyn, The Bramble Bush 5 (2d ed. 1951) ('[w]hat these officials do about disputes is, to my mind, the law itself') (*also see* at p. 57-60); Walter Weeler Cook, *Scientific Method and the Law,* 13 A.B.A. Journal 303, 308 (1927) ('[t]his past behavior of the judges can be described in terms of certain

29. The boundaries of explaining the toolbox model conceptually or analytically. It might now seem that the purpose of enriching a dogmatic understanding might presuppose a very constrained definition or description of what dogmatics is, or purports to do. One could approach this issue conceptually, starting for example from a classic conceptualization of dogmatics, like the hermeneutical one offered in the *Methodenlehre der Rechtswissenschaft* by Larenz. There 'dogmatics' (*Rechtswissenschaft*) features as a quasi-science purporting to explain the normative core of law through interpretation. One obvious problem with approaching this issue from a conceptual analytical angle is that a lot of scholars would be missing part of the conversation. To offer but the most obvious example: even if Larenz might be a classic example of what dogmatics has come to be understood, he does not represent the same 'classic' against which American legal realists were taking up their swords[68]. Indeed, Larenz clearly shows the limits of *Begriffsjurisprudenz*[69] and the subsumption model, and 'conceptual jurisprudence' with its subsumption model was indeed one of the strands of thoughts the realists were revolting against[70]. So then one can ask: how can one deploy 'realist' arguments against an author's conceptual elaboration that subscribes – so it seems – to some of the claims of the realists, or

generalizations which we call rules and principles of law')). I qualify the predictive value, however, because of several reasons, which I will not explain in detail. Suffice it to mention the most important reason, however, namely that this realist approach could deprive legal reasoning of its very nature, which I am not proposing, as this could eventually undercut some important rule of law values (Brian Z. Tamanaha, Law as a Means to an End 215 *et seq.* (2006); *compare* Stef Feyen, *Afwijkende meningsuitingen in het Belgische Grondwettelijk Hof* in 3 Leuvense Staatsrechtelijke Standpunten. De Europese Dimensie in het Belgische Publiekrecht 227, 272-273 (André Alen & Jan Theunis eds. 2012)). I do believe prediction might become possible in some cases, using generalization, which in turn keeps the inherent limits of the rule of law in mind.

68 They were primarily arguing against a formalist, Langdellian understanding of law (*see* Christopher C. Langdell, *Preface* to Selection of Cases on the Law of Contracts, reprinted in Stephen B. Presser & Jamil S. Zainaldin, Law and Jurisprudence in American Legal History 746-748 (5th ed. 2000), which was reviewed by Oliver W. Holmes, *Book Review*, 14 Am. L. Rev. 233, 234 (1880)), which came akin to *Begriffsjurisprudenz* (*but compare* Christopher C. Langdell, *Classifications of Rights and Wrongs*, 13 Harv. L. Rev. 537 and 659 (1900) (recognizing the power of induction)), at least in the sense that law was treated as 'an [autonomous] intellectual discipline independent of theology, moral philosophy, economics, or political science, one that involved the application of scientific methods to common law material' (Thomas C. Grey, *Modern American Legal Thought*, 106 Yale L.J. 493, 493 (1996)). *See further* M.H. Hoeflich, *Law and Geometry: Legal Science from Leibniz to Langdell*, 30 Am. J. Legal Hist. 95 (1986); *but compare* Brian Z. Tamanaha, Beyond the Formalist-Realist Divide 51 *et seq.* (2010).

69 Larenz & Canaris, *supra* note 3, at p. 45 *et seq.* (*also see* p. 25-35 – on the hermeneutical nature).

70 *See eg* Felix Cohen, 'Transcendental Nonsense and the Functional Approach', 35 *Columbia L. Rev.* 809, 809 (1935), referring to Rudolph Von Jhering, Im Juristischen Begriffshimmel 245 (11th ed. 1912).

more precisely that does not deny that some of the criticism the realists geared against "formalist" legal thinking, was sound in fact? Can the realist critique – steeped in the common law tradition and in common law jurisprudence – even be brought to bear on questions or issues of continental law and jurisprudence? Questions like these clearly bring to the fore the limits of analyzing 'strands of thought' from a conceptual analytic perspective. Furthermore, one should not forget that 'strands of thoughts' are often used to polarize excessively, as is clearly evinced by Brian Tamanaha's recent work[71]. Legal theorists indeed suffer from a felt need to categorize other thinkers, and of course, to distinguish oneself, this is a strategy that is rather easy to use. Notwithstanding the rhetorical implications of the title, this book will not be trying to paint a black and white picture: it will not generally sketch an approach of the past which it completely renounces, or even the vices of which it seeks to remedy. The book primarily tries to *show*, building upon existing analysis and trying to understand the limits of that existing analysis, how new ways of thinking might spawn or at least enrich our understanding of what the law is, at least in the area of federalism before the Constitutional Court.

With these caveats in mind, I will nonetheless have to situate the intellectual background against which I will conduct this analysis, and as mentioned, I will try to instill some instrumentalism into the reasoning of scholars about the Belgian Constitutional Court, and emphasize how this approach is relatively new in thinking about Belgian jurisprudence.

30. Realism: core thoughts. American legal realism (ALR) is a movement of thought endlessly reflected and commented upon. Furthermore, getting clear insight into the core thoughts of ALR is not an easy task. Not only have commentators greatly dissented over the meaning of American legal realism[72]

---

[71] *Supra* note 68 (who seeks to debunk both myths about "legal formalists" and "legal realists"); *but compare* (critically) Frederic Schauer, *Legal Realism Untamed*, VIRGINIA PUBLIC LAW AND LEGAL THEORY RESEARCH PAPER NO. 2012-38, 20 September 2012, available at http://papers.ssrn.com/sol3/papers.cfm?abstract_id=2064837, at p. 8 n20 ('even multiple counter-examples on one or the other side do not undercut the plausibility of a probabilistiscally accurate distinction. It is sometimes warm in January [...]').

[72] *See eg* Brian Leiter, *Rethinking Legal Realism: Toward a Naturalized Jurisprudence*, 76 TEX. L. REV. 267, 270-277 (1997), reprinted in BRIAN LEITER, NATURALIZING JURISPRUDENCE 15, 21-30 (2007) (distinguishing the "received view" of legal realism and their core claim, which according to Leiter is that 'judges respond primarily to the stimulus of facts' (*ibid.* at p. 21)); *also see* TAMANAHA, *supra* note 68, at p. 67 *et seq*. For a recent overview of the controvery (*also compare* with the subsequent note), *see* Schauer, *Legal Realism Untamed*, *supra* note 71, at p. 2 n3 (who contends that the conventional understanding of realism consists in the 'questioning of legal doctrine's determinacy, causal effects on decisions, and consequent accuracy in explaining and predicting legal outcomes').

– as the invocation of this tradition by several subsequent (though not always compatible) jurisprudential strands (pragmatism, critical legal studies, …[73]) evinces – but, as Tamanaha suggests, they have also distorted realist arguments in order to simplify things, and created a misleading narrative[74]. It is not wholly unlikely that the confusion was partly spawned by some schizophrenia within the realist movement at the time[75]. Keeping these preliminary caveats in mind – which should preclude any characterization of realism as simple instrumentalist thinking, or radical rule-skepticism – we could emphasize that there seem to be a few common points the realists sought to make.

Generally, their perspective was (more) on the law in action[76], and the real functioning of the law[77], and it is from this perspective that they became vastly critical of what they construed to be "classical legal thought"[78]. They argued against the classic search for pure, static – yes even geometric – principles[79] behind the chaos of everyday adjudication; in that regard, realists were often coined rule skeptics. They followed in the footsteps of Oliver Wendell Holmes who famously claimed that 'general propositions do not decide concrete cases'[80]. It should be emphasized right away that realists never really dispelled of rules altogether; however, they were highly critical of the predictive power of what Karl Llewellyn called 'paper rules'[81], and of the traditional elaboration of legal

[73] 'Contemporary American legal theory has also been powerfully affected by the Realist movement. The empirical orientation and the skepticism concerning the grip on social affairs of 'paper rules' characteristic of the Law and Society movement; the impatience with doctrinal reasoning and insistence upon judges' law-making power that infuses most Law and Economics scholarships; the aspirations to expose 'gaps, conflicts, and ambiguities' in the legal order and the fascination with the ideological functions of legal doctrine manifested in most Critical Legal Studies writings – all are traceable to the contentions of the realists' (American Legal Realism xiv (William W. Fisher III, Morton J. Horwitz & Thomas A. Reed eds. 1993)). These contentions, however, are not always accepted (*see eg*, as regards the connection between ALR and CLS, Wouter de Been, Legal Realism Regained (2008)).

[74] Tamanaha, *supra* note 68, at p. 5 (he argues that realists – too – have broadly conceived of judging in terms of a 'balanced realism').

[75] *Also see* American Legal Realism, *supra* note 73, at p. 49 *et seq*.

[76] A term already coined by Roscoe Pound, a proponent of a more sociological jurisprudence (*cf. Law in Books and Law in Action*, 44 Am. L. Rev. 12 (1910)).

[77] Cook, *supra* note 67, at p. 308 (1927); *see generally*, Tamanaha, *supra* note 68, at p. 65 et seq.

[78] Also often coined as "formalism" or "mechanical jurisprudence".

[79] But their arguments even held vis-à-vis more sophisticated "formalist" accounts of decision-making (Brian Leiter, *Legal Formalism and Legal Realism: What is the Issue?*, 16 Legal Theory 111 (2010)).

[80] *Lochner v. New York*, 198 U.S. 45, 76 (1905) (Holmes, *dissenting*).

[81] *See* Karl N. Llewellyn, *A realistic Jurisprudence – The Next Step*, 30 Colum. L. Rev. 431, 447 *et seq.* (1930) (only the 'real rules' – 'Factual terms. No more' (*ibid.* at p. 448) – predict adequately, whereas paper rules remain authoritative oughts, addressed *to* officials, which

concepts. Although they did not generally argue against paper rules as such, or against the employment of legal concepts[82], they underlined the importance of the 'knowledge that to classify is to disturb'[83] and the dangers of reification[84]. Surely, legal realists converged on some different other points of departure of analysis[85], but for our purposes, the focus on the practice of law, combined with a fairly deep distrust in the determinacy of (paper) legal rules[86], easily leads a scholar to the conclusion that the law is (partially) malleable[87], and can – and

---

'tacitly contains an element of pseudo-description' (*ibid.* at p. 449-450)). However, some more "extreme" realists – such as Jerome Frank (LAW AND THE MODERN MIND (1930) (who tries to debunk rule-guided behavior as a 'basic myth' of the law, even if from time to time, he leaves room for 'a limited degree of legal certainty' (*ibid.* at p. 12)) – did believe rules were completely causally inert, in that they had (almost) no influence on judicial decision making (of which Llewellyn was highly critical; *also see* Karl N. Llewellyn, *Some Realism about Realism – Responding to Dean Pound*, 44 HARV. L. REV. 1222, 1230 (1931); *see generally* KARL N. LLEWELLYN, THE THEORY OF RULES 63-76 (Frederick Schauer ed. 2011) (1938) and John M. Breen, *Statutory interpretation and the Lessons of Llewellyn*, 33 LOY. A. L. REV. 263 (2000)).

82 Llewellyn stated: '[l]ike rules, concepts are not to be eliminated; it cannot be done. Behavior is too heterogeneous to be dealt with except after some artificial ordering' (Llewellyn, *A realistic jurisprudence, supra* note 81, at p. 453). *Compare* KARL N. LLEWELLYN, CASES AND MATERIALS ON THE LAW OF SALES xi (1930) ('[t]his book is much occupied [...] with the difference between doctrine as a causal factor in inducing a decision and doctrine as a mere *ex post facto* justification of a decision already taken [...]. Doctrine is therefore emphasized, as doctrine must be; but it is emphasized as the first step in a wider process of seeing what law means of bringing it to bear on facts [...]').

83 Llewellyn, *A realistic jurisprudence, supra* note 81, at p. 453; he called it a 'process which can be excused only insofar as it is necessary to the accomplishing of a purpose', which necessarily had to imply 'scepticism as to the adequacy of the *received* categories' (*emphasis in original*).

84 '[C]ategories and concepts, once formulated and once they have entered into thought processes, tend to take on an appearance of solidity, reality and inherent value which has no foundation in experience' (Llewellyn, *A realistic jurisprudence, supra* note 81, at p. 453).

85 *See* Llewellyn, *Some realism about realism, supra* note 81, at p. 1236-1238 (where 9 common points of departure are mentioned, ie, (1) conception of law in flux, (2) conception of law as a means to an end, (3) the conception of society in flux, (4) the temporary divorce of Is and Ought for purposes of study, (5) distrust of the descriptive qualities of concepts and rules, (6) distrust in the operative quality of prescriptive rule-formulations, (7) the belief that cases should be studied more narrowly grouped, (8) insistence on evaluation of the law in terms of its effects and (9) on '*sustained and programmatic attack* on the problems of law along any of these lines' (*emphasis in original*)).

86 *Eg* 'there is less possibility of accurate prediction of what courts will do than the traditional rule would lead us to suppose' (Llewellyn, *Some realism about realism, supra* note 81, at p. 1241).

87 For confirmations hereof in realist literature, *see eg* FRANK, *supra* note 81; LLEWELLYN, *supra* note 67; Karl Llewellyn, *Remarks on the Theory of Appellate Decision and the Rules and Canons about how Statutes are to be construed*, 3 VAND. L. REV. 395 (1950); Max Radin, *The Theory of Judicial Decisions: Or How Judges Think*, 11 A.B.A.J. 359 (1925); *also see* Hanoch Dagan, *The Realist Conception of Law*, 56 U. TOR. L.J. 607 (2007); *compare* (on the malleability of facts) JEROME FRANK, COURTS ON TRIAL (1949) and some passages in his LAW AND THE MODERN MIND (*supra* note 81); *compare* Schauer, *supra* note 71, at p. 25 *et seq.* (emphasizing the

according to some realists – must be so construed as to best perform in practice the goal of the regulation at hand.

31. The toolbox: a novel method? Now one can wonder whether these core thoughts have not been sufficiently incorporated or at least taken into account in modern accounts about constitutional law, or at least in the conceptualization of the relationship between European law and municipal constitutional law.

As regards the latter conceptualization, a new era seems to have dawned. Whereas earlier, the question of hierarchy and supremacy – issues closely connected to a classic dogmatic understanding of law as either valid/invalid, construed within a logically coherent system – was central to academic inquiry, the focus now has shifted to a new discourse in which dialogue and heterogeneity are focal points, for which several names (often connected to slightly different conceptualization) such as constitutional pluralism, multi-level constitutionalism, or jurisdictional pluralism have been coined[88]. Although this shift could surely be construed as an improvement from the viewpoint of recognizing the relative nature of (the validity and/or application of) rules, our perspectives differs from these discourses in at least two respects. First, in our conceptualization, there is a more radical emphasis on instrumental and fact-responsive attitudes of courts. Surely, the courts will or at least should take other courts into account, preferably even enter into a dialogue with them, but the dialogical perspective seems a bit one-sided, since other considerations will play for the courts themselves when deciding whether and how to give form and content to a certain dialogue. We believe that these considerations are of importance to take into account. Second, our perspective – as we mentioned – is more internal, and does not start from the relationship between national and European law, but adopts the Belgian perspective.[89]

Modern Belgian accounts of constitutional law, on the other hand, also recognize the limited power of pure deductive reasoning, and acknowledge – albeit sometimes reluctantly – the importance of pragmatic arguments in the elaboration of the law by the courts. However, the pragmatism is mostly embedded *within* the classic doctrinal structure. For instance, as will be discussed further on, it is generally recognized that the Constitutional Court will allow for some exceptions to general rules (for instance the "rule" on territorial exclusivity); some even construe – sticking to the same example –

regularity of the 'real rules', as descriptive and prescriptive indicators of what a court would do); *also compare infra* note 109 (on H.L.A. Hart).

[88] *Supra* note 33 for some references.

[89] *Supra* No. 23.

territorial exclusivity as a principle, capable of being weighed. In the weighing process, pragmatic considerations (and indeed consequences) can also be taken into account. That is of course an (implicit) acknowledgment of the malleability of the norms at stake, but as we will try to further show, this does not go far enough in order to come close to descriptive, explanatory (or even normative) accuracy. Some authors even duly recognize, given that normative standards can be construed as principles, capable of being weighed, that principles often collide or at least pull in different ways. However, the underlying discursive rationality of the balancing exercise is generally thought to be internal, meaning that once one has determined the weight of one principle – a determination process that would occur taking relevant factual circumstances, and indeed also often consequences into account – and one has determined the weight of the other (relevant) principles, there is only very limited leeway for judges to intervene in the process of deciding a case[90]. "If pragmatism plays *then*, it surely must be an exception" – seems to be the underlying view. We contest the implications of this view, and emphasize that malleability goes quite a bit further, not only as regards the selection and elaboration of relevant principles, but also through concept (de)generation, and by many other means. These means, we describe as the Court's toolbox, which is at its disposal for the solution of legal questions. Most generally, the Court will be driven in its solution of cases by a want to reach politically feasible solutions. The equilibrium-rationale thus becomes overarching[91] and a driving force behind case law, which makes it hard to predict on the basis of purely legal analysis, all the more so in the sense that specific fact situations might ask for particularistic solutions[92].

Instead of recognizing this driving force within the extant doctrinal structures – which implies a set of limitations – this book pleads for a development of a framework in which the recognition is lifted to a new level: in that sense, I argue that the Court disposes of a true toolbox, with which it will "work"[93], in

---

90 For instance, Robert Alexy's theory, expounded in his *Theorie der Grundrechte* (*cf. supra* note 3), is often commented upon. He does recognize forms of (epistemic and structural) *discretion*, but these are arguably not central within his theory, but rather tangential to it.

91 *Also see* LLEWELLYN, *supra* note 81, at p. 87-102 (in terms of the goals of the legal order); *compare* MARK TUSHNET, RED, WHITE AND BLUE 193-194 (1988) (focus on policy analysis and policy considerations of judges).

92 *Compare* Joseph Hutcheson, *The Judgment Intuitive*, 14 CORNELL L.Q. 274 (1929) or Herman Oliphant, *A return to stare decisis*, 14 A.B.A.J. 71 (1928) (both on 'types of situations') with the more particularistic thoughts of for instance Frank (*Say it with Music*, 61 HARV. L. REV. 921 (1948); *Are Judges Human?*, 80 U. PA. L. REV. 17 and 233 (1931) or sometimes Llewellyn (for references, *see* Schauer, *supra* note 71, at p. 9 n23)).

93 I am loosely inspired here by Duncan Kennedy's use of the marxist concept of work (*Freedom and Constraint in Adjudication: A Critical Phenomenology*, 36 JOURNAL OF LEGAL EDUCATION

function of the interests involved at the time. These interests are not limited to legal interests – as commonly understood – but also include pragmatic considerations bordering on a form of (legal) politics[94]. Although the latter point – the (sometimes pervasive) instrumentality of constitutional court reasoning – will be recognized when talking to other academics, albeit in different degrees of persuasion and intensity, it has not been fully internalized in the structure of the study of constitutional law. The toolbox conception might take a first step in finding an adequate framework that allows for instrumental reasoning to be taken into account in a more serious way.

32. Legal dogmatics? A rather easy reproach to my exposition here would be the following: this might all be quite interesting, but it has little to do with 'legal science' (understood as *doctrine*, or *dogmatics*), as it asks different sorts of questions: it is thus 'law from a political perspective', or even 'legal sociology' of 'philosophy'[95]. The distinction between these approaches, however, requires a more profound understanding of what law is[96], and what we want to do with law, and hence, of what 'dogmatics' is[97]. Not wanting to explore the fine methodological distinctions here, not in the least because they are entangled with complex philosophical questions[98], I would just like to emphasize that I

518, 522 *et seq.* (1986), *reprinted in* CRITICAL LEGAL STUDIES 45, 48 *et seq.* (James Boyle ed. 1992)).

94 *Cf.* Llewellyn, *Some realism about realism, supra* note 81, at p. 1252.

95 Although some legal philosophers resists attempts to "naturalize" jurisprudence (*eg* JULES COLEMAN, THE PRACTICE OF PRINCIPLE 213 (2001) or Jules Coleman, *Methodology* in THE OXFORD HANDBOOK OF JURISPRUDENCE AND PHILOSOPHY OF LAW 350 (Jules Coleman & Scott Shapiro eds. 2002)).

96 *Compare* LON L. FULLER, THE LAW IN QUEST OF ITSELF (1940).

97 *Compare* for instance HANS KELSEN, HAUPTPROBLEME DER STAATSRECHTSLEHRE 7-11 (2d ed. 1923) *with* GEORG JELLINEK, ALLGEMEINE STAATSLEHRE 307 *et seq.* (1900) (on the normative power of the factual for legal research, in light of their system of law as a whole).

98 Such as the dichotomy between context of justification (which legal dogmatics is thought to focus on) and context of discovery (which is more subject to legal psychology, or legal sociology), which was introduced by positivist philosophers such as (critical rationalist) Karl Popper (THE LOGIC OF SCIENTIFIC DISCOVERY 7-9 (1934), and (logical positivist) Hans Reichenbach (EXPERIENCE AND PREDICTION 6-7 (1938)) in order to render philosophy autonomous in the view of empirical sciences, and often deployed in a legal context in order to maintain a "positivist" (Kelsenian normative) perspective. In that last regard, often the work of Richard Wasserstrom is cited (THE JUDICIAL DECISION 21 *et seq.* (1961) (who pleads for a neat dichotomy, and does not doubt the 'correctness of the descriptive generalizations' (*ibid.* at p. 20) of the realists, but doubts their methodological place in adjudicational theory and dogmatics)), as well as sometimes the work of Neil MacCormick (LEGAL REASONING AND LEGAL THEORY 15 *et seq.* (1978) (who argues that one should first try to work within the process of justification)) (*cf.* PECZENIK, *supra* note 4, at p. 3-6). Even so, there have been many critiques, both philosophical (*eg* PAUL FEYERABEND, AGAINST METHOD Ch. 14 (1975); THOMAS KUHN, THE STRUCTURE OF SCIENTIFIC REVOLUTIONS 3-5 (1962); WILLIAM V.O.

do not want to *a priori* categorize this approach as 'dogmatics', 'new dogmatics', 'sociology', or pure 'political speculation'... It might be all, or it might be none of the above. That is not the point. The point is that we enrich our understanding of a classic approach of dogmatics by taking into account factors which are generally not, or not more than tangentially or interstitially, considered as 'valid reasons'[99] in law. And, again, that brings me to the following question, which, approached from a legal reasoning perspective could be asked as follows: what makes a reason a *legal* reason? But that question itself presupposes a concept of law[100], and the elaboration of a theory of legal argument: as I said, I do not purport to offer a full-fledged theory (of the nature of law, or of legal argumentation) as such, but I do want to interrogate some issues related to legal argument(ation), and tentatively set up a framework which deals with some of the following questions: when scholars expound legal decisions, how should they understand the categories, frameworks, doctrines and concepts the Court works with, and perhaps even more importantly, should scholars look beyond the often strictly construed borders of these concepts and categories, for explanatory or predictive purposes? Our clear answer to the latter question would be yes. Answering the former question is more difficult, but we will try to show that some scholars fall in the trap of reification of concepts, categories, doctrines or frameworks.

QUINE, *Epistemology Naturalized* in ONTOLOGICAL RELATIVITY AND OTHER ESSAYS (1969)) and legal (*eg* BRUCE ANDERSON, "DISCOVERY" IN LEGAL DECISION-MAKING (1996) (who actually tries to rationalize the judicial discovery process); LEITER, *supra* note 72), sometimes explicit (for some examples, *see* the references in ANDERSON, *supra* this note at p. 20-29) but often implicit, vis-à-vis a strict dichotomy and this book can be understood as one of those critiques. Indeed, although it is reasonable to make a distinction, hardening this out into a dichotomy seems to cover up more than it can clarify. The related (Paul Hoyningen-Huene, *Context of Discovery and Context of Justification*, 18 STUD. HIST. PHIL. SCI. 501, 511 *et seq.* (1987); *compare* PECZENIK, *supra* note 4, at p. 5 *et seq.*) distinction between fact and norm has since time immemorial bothered lawyers in their dealings with it, and also philosophers have broken their heads over the distinction (*see eg* HILARY PUTNAM, THE COLLAPSE OF THE FACT/VALUE DICHOTOMY AND OTHER ESSAYS 7-66 (2002)). That is one reason why we do not enter into that debate as such, but circumvent it by the use of autonomous argument.

[99] Whether or not the "political", "institutional" or other considerations are valid reasons of law (which the realists did not presuppose (*cf.* LEITER, *supra* note 72, at p. 45), but for which an argument could be made (*see eg* DWORKIN, TAKING RIGHTS SERIOUSLY 31-39, 68-71 (1977); JUSTICE IN ROBES, *supra* note 62, at p. 41-43) for instance through the backdoor of the proportionality principle), is a separate, but potentially related question; *see* Frederick Schauer, *The Limited Domain of the Law*, 90 VA. L. REV. 1909 (2004).

[100] For an elaboration of this point (explaining how legal realists formulated a theory of adjudication which presupposed a classic (positivist) concept of law, and legal reasons), *see* LEITER, *supra* note 72, at p. 71-73, *and also see* at p. 121 *et seq.* *Compare* in this regard, KENNEDY, *supra* note 64, at p. 108 *et seq.*

33. Reification. Reification means, according to Lukács' classic description, that 'a relation between people takes on the character of a thing and thus acquires a 'phantom objectivity', an autonomy that seems so strictly rational and all-embracing as to conceal every trace of its fundamental nature: the relation between people'[101]. In law[102], this causes some mystical "objectification" of the legal order, which can turn out to be problematic to the extent that connection with the real world is lost: Wittgenstein and J.L. Austin in that sense showed that 'linguistic entities [- the instruments of law -] are not abstract objects that can be studied like specimens under a microscope'[103]. In that sense, also legal realists fought the idea of reification in law; as Llewellyn put it: 'categories and concepts, once formulated and once they have entered into thought processes, tend to take on an appearance of solidity, reality and inherent value which has no foundation in experience'[104]. Hence, realists conceived of this as a potential problem: '[c]ategories and classifications are tools to order our thinking, they should never be regarded as absolute realities'[105]. By and large, although not unconditionally, I think they were right[106]. However, matters are not as simple as that.

34. Rule of law values as backbench in a new conceptual framework. Although most legal realists recognized the constraining power of rules, they believed this power to be less pervasive than generally implied by judges and academia. Llewellyn called it 'leeway, a space admittedly bounded, within which a judge may act freely'[107]. We will try to make a similar point in this book: classic (dogmatic) treatments of Belgian constitutional law seem to have

[101] György Lukács, *Reification and the Consciousness of the Proletariat* in History and Class Consciousness 83 (Rodney Livingstone trans. 1971) (1968).

[102] A useful and simple introduction to some (more general) reification-problems with reference to theories of meaning can be found in Lycan, *supra* note 52, at p. 66 *et seq*. For more philosophical elaboration and an "application" in light of federalism, *see infra* No. 163. It might strike some as ironic that Lukács reification-argument was actually an argument *against* a form of instrumentalization. However, he was disconcerted with the instrumentalization of people (for it would lead to alienation), and not with the methodological question of how CC jurisprudence should be represented. Be that as it may, he had a specific conceptualization of law, too, which we mention further on (*infra* note 1023). This book cannot be read as an endorsement of his views of law.

[103] Lycan, *supra* note 52, at p. 76.

[104] Llewellyn, *A realistic jurisprudence, supra* note 81, at p. 453.

[105] Sanne Taekema, The concept of ideals in legal theory 90-91 (diss. doct., Katholieke Universiteit Brabant, 2000) (commenting on Dewey's innovations in pragmatic thought).

[106] *Compare* Oliver Wendell Holmes Jr., *Law in Science and Science in Law*, 12 Harv. L. Rev. 443, 460 (1899) ('[w]e must think things not words, or at least we must constantly translate our words into the facts for which they stand, if we are to keep to the real and the true').

[107] Quoted by Michael Ansaldi, *The German Llewellyn*, 58 Brooklyn L. Rev. 705, 755 (1992).

underestimated – or at least underarticulated – the pragmatic considerations that can play in the decision making process, and hence in the elaboration of and systematization of where the law as regards federalism in Belgium currently stands.

Even if that is the case, we do not want to go beyond the realists and keep emphasizing and acknowledging the importance of (rule-like) constraining impediments to complete judicial freedom and discretion[108]. Not wanting to focus too much on one kind of constraint, we employ the term 'rule of law'-values, and will further on elucidate what we mean by these values. We will also tentatively try to construct a conceptual framework that seeks to integrate 'rule of law'-values with the toolbox conceptualization of the "norms" used by the Constitutional Court. It will be shown that the relationship between tools and 'rule of law'-values is often problematic, and moreover very complex. We should mention at the outset that we are not entirely convinced that it is the best conceptual framework that can be offered, and as such do not claim truth for it. However, we are convinced that the framework can more fully explain constitutional law than current approaches do, without foiling the possibility of epistemological basis for legal valuation[109].

35. Generalizability of the framework? Now I want to leave open the question whether the conceptual model presented here is generalizable beyond the confines of federalism cases. It might be[110], but that is a different research question.

[108] On the importance thereof, *see* Tamanaha, *supra* note 67. For a short summary of the argument, with reference to Karl Llewellyn, Brian Z. Tamanaha, *On the Instrumental View of Law in American Legal Culture*, in On Philosophy in American Law 27 (Francis J. Mootz III ed. 2009) (where it is argued that the instrumental vision of law in the U.S. has been too ubiquitous, emphasizing the dangers thereof for the rule of law, which in turn has come to be understood more and more in instrumental terms too, resulting in a loss of a 'built-in core of integrity' (*ibid.* at p. 33)). Even if one does not accept the validity of such a justificatorfy account, for example on a Quinean basis (*see* Quine, *supra* note 98, at p. 82-83), one can still stress the importance of rule of law values with reference to the fact that a *causal* (descriptive) explanation always requires to take the normative force of reasons *qua* reasons seriously (*cf.* Leiter, *supra* note 72, at p. 65).

[109] *Compare* (*with reference to supra* note 98) Harvey Siegel, *Justification, Discovery and the Naturalizing of epistemology*, 47 Phil. Sci. 297, 309-313 (1980) ('psychological [and more broadly: empirical] information can never by itself give us good reasons for accepting some particular knowledge-claim to be true' (*ibid.* at 315)). As such we believe to debunk H.L.A. Hart's basis for criticism of the realist project (The Concept of Law 137-138 (Penelope A. Bulloch & Joseph Raz eds., 2d ed., 1994), if this was still necessary (*cf. eg* Leiter, *supra* note 72, at p. 59-80).

[110] As such, the toolbox concept might be said to reflect all instrumental forms of reasoning, whereas the rule of law values reflect 'authority reasons' (*cf.* Aleksander Peczenik, On Law and Reason 257 *et seq.* (2008); *also see* Patrick S. Atiyah & Robert S. Summers, Form and Substance in Anglo-American Law *esp.* 5 *et seq.* (1991)). However, such a generalization

On the one hand, there are some evident reasons why in federalism cases, this approach seems especially appropriate[111]. It is no secret that questions regarding federalism are closely intertwined with political considerations. Making some of these considerations more explicit, does seem to render the commentaries on the case law of the constitutional court more insightful and explicative[112]. On the other hand, the same reasons seem to make the approach less appropriate in federalism cases *for the Court itself*, especially because instrumentalism can put on different masks, and the question about the *ends* remains unsolved, or is at least relegated to the background here[113]. Indeed, as regards *federalism*, it is hard to state the underlying values except for speaking in metaphors of balance of power[114].

36. Added value of the framework? Then the question of course becomes how the conceptual framework would add value to the (perhaps admittedly flawed) existing conceptualization of case law. It might have more explanatory potential[115], but can it really ensure (more) predictability of decision-making? It might indeed 'enrich' dogmatic thinking about the law, but dogmatic thinking as it currently stands has the advantage of actually being relied upon by courts

---

risks running into deep theoretical problems. See for instance the interaction between Ronald Dworkin & Kent Greenawalt as regards the forms of reasoning Dworkin subscribed to in *Taking Rights Seriously* (*see* Kent Greenawalt, *Policy, Rights and Judicial Discretion*, 11 GA. L. REV. 991 (1977) and *also see* DWORKIN, *supra* note 90, at p. 294-330), or compare the Alexy-Habermas-debate on the axiological / deontological nature of adjudication and rights (for further reflection, *see* STEF FEYEN, PROPORTIONALITY: A MATTER OF PRINCIPLE, available at http://papers.ssrn.com/sol3/papers.cfm?abstract_id=1986135, at p. 75-93 and 99, n400). Moreover, it should work in a more refined model of legal reasoning (*see eg* GIOVANNI SARTOR, LEGAL REASONING. A COGNITIVE APPROACH TO THE LAW (2005)).

111 *Also see infra* Nos. 37 and 163.

112 The realists seemed to have offered a perspective for the practising lawyer first, instead of for the courts (*see eg* FRANK, *supra* note, at p. 47 note ('is primarily concerned with 'law' as it affects the work of the practising lawyer and the needs of the clients who retain him'); *also see* Holmes, *supra* note 67, at p. 457 ('appear before judges, or [...] advise people in such a way as to keep them out of court') – *see more generally* LEITER, *supra* note 72, at p. 70-71).

113 *Cf.* TAMANAHA, *supra* note 67.

114 *Also see infra* note 126.

115 If – as we can reasonably expect since prediction tracks justification – the leeway is comparable to that in the U.S., it will not be hard to be *more* explanatory than ordinary legal reasoning (called the legal model here): '[i]f various aspects of the legal model can support either side of any given dispute that comes before the Court, and the quality of these positions cannot be reliably and validly measured a priori, then the legal model hardly satisfies as an explanation of Supreme Court decisions. By being able to "explain" everything, in the end it explains nothing' (JEFFREY A. SEGAL & HAROLD J. SPAETH, THE SUPREME COURT AND THE ATTITUDINAL MODEL REVISITED 86 (2002)).

themselves when they 'speak' the law[116]; and often enough constitutional scholars will admit if not write that the facts of *and* surrounding the case are of utter importance, which can be partially "recuperated" through doctrine itself, for instance through proportionality review, or reliance on principles rather than rules.

That might all be true, but we believe that our model still has two advantages. First, it allows for a combined empirical-normative analysis, which could even result in more predictability. Not only relying on the normatively stated reasons of a case, but also systematically investigating case law in the broader factual context would indeed raise understanding, and with the deployment of the correct empirical method, could make cases more predictable[117]. This book might lack a rigid empirical(-scientific) method when one enters the terrain beyond classic legal reasons, and therefore a reader should not make bets on the outcome of the next case involving federalism and European law based on this book. Even if – accordingly – this book does not set out a detailed set of criteria along the lines of which predictions for future cases can conclusively be made, it does try to show the increased explanatory potential. Second, even if a dogmatic approach to law has succeeded in "recuperating" or "redeeming" some of the points made by "realist" criticisms, other points fail to be internalized, for instance because they are wholly incompatible with the basic ideas of judging impartially and under law. In other words: the domain of what is considered *legal* may have expanded, but some reasons are *per se* excluded as being legal (*eg* "I'm hungry"[118]), and our model does allow for such reasons to be taken into

---

[116] PECZENIK, *supra* note 4, at p. 6-8.

[117] Although for the model to be *scientifically predictable*, a model should be construed which is much less rudimentary than mine, taking every relevant factor pertaining to judging into account (which might indeed be an impossible task). Even leaving aside the question of free will, judgment and an inquiry into consciousness here (*eg* DANIEL C. DENNETT, CONSCIOUSNESS EXPLAINED (1991) (arguing that an explanation might be scientifically feasible)), it could seriously be questioned whether this will ever be possible. Be that as it may, being *more* explanatory than the legal model (*supra* note 115), our model – by taking factors into account which are *relevant* to the decision – will generally allow for a *more* reasoned prediction to be made.

[118] ALR is often caricatured as contending that a decision is based on what a judge had for breakfast. This is a caricature indeed, although it should be noted that even the fact *when* a judge had breakfast has been 'proven' to play an important part in the decision-making process (*see* Shai Danziger, Jonathan Levav & Liora Avnaim-Pesso, 'Extraneous Factors in Judicial Decisions', 108 *PNAS* 6889-92 (2011) (where researchers found that the chance of parole in front of Israeli judges highly increased when appearing before them after a snack or a meal)). That the latter is a form of irrationality – or rather: an exhaustion of rationality (*cf.* DANIEL KAHNEMAN, ONS FEILBARE DENKEN 49-50 (2011)) – does not detract from the conclusion that *in fact*, such quirky factors might (and indeed do often) play in decision-making.

account[119] (although it should by no means be read as a justification of such reasons). This does not mean that the model is immediately useful for a judge as a replacement of classic dogmatic thinking[120], but it might nonetheless enrich it.

37. Judicial activism? Perhaps some will view all this indirectly as an attack on the Constitutional Court, which – so it might be said – imposes its own values on the legal order, but this is certainly not the point I seek to make here, nor is it a point I would subscribe to for that oversimplified reason[121]. Judges constantly impose values on fact situations, partially constrained by laws and procedures, but at the same time deducing and imposing values out of legal meaning. This is almost always the case, even in simple civil cases, and especially in human rights cases.

In federalism cases, the Court occupies a particularly important position because it can *institutionally* serve as a 'neutral' arbiter[122], the authority of which is by and large accepted. That, however, does not give it legitimate power to speak the law into the Constitution without proper reasoning. Even if it might be the case that the Court indeed cannot make its toolbox conceptualization of

---

[119] It should be noted that here an inconsistency on our part might be thought to arise, since the distinction between *rule of law* values and the *toolbox* indeed presupposes an idea about what law is. According to LEITER, an entire concept is even presupposed in such a context (*supra* note 72, at p. 71-73). Although we agree that some conceptualization or vague idea of what is legal and what is not is needed to work out the model, no rigid definition or analytical configuration in terms of necessary and sufficient conditions has to be expounded in order to (1) make an argument work for practice (as Leiter moreover recognizes (*ibid.* at p. 70 *et seq.*)) or (2) to make the argument meaningful, as concepts can be thought of as in flux; *compare* KENNEDY, *supra* note 64, at p. 25.

[120] In fact, some have argued that judges should believe in 'slightly inaccurate or oversimplified accounts of decision-making' (Scott Altman, *Beyond Candor*, 89 MICH. L. REV. 296, 299 (1990)). Moreover, it is obvious that a judge has a job to do that differs from the commentator, and should take different principles into account when expounding "the law" (*see eg* PECZENIK, *supra* note 4, at p. 2).

[121] As Leiter amply shows, it does not follow from the recognition of a 'naturalized' jurisprudence (or in our case: view of the case law of the CC) that this is a proposal to change the outlook of adjudicative practices themselves (LEITER, *supra* note 72, at p. 114-117; *but compare* at p. 106 n15). More precisely, the fact that the legitimacy of (in the sociological sense of acceptance) of constitutional argument might be at stake when such an argument veers from the use of common "modalities" (*eg* PHILLIP BOBBIT, CONSTITUTIONAL INTERPRETATION 28; *also see* p. 12-13 (1991)), this does not imply *per se* that the illegitimacy of a more theoretical reflection upon such argument is established as soon as this reflection diverges to some extent from extant practice (LEITER, *supra* note 72, at p. 139). *Compare infra* No. 66, *especially* note 298.

[122] *Compare eg* James B. Kelly & Michael Murphy, *Shaping the Constitutional Dialogue on Federalism: Canada's Supreme Court as Meta-Political Actor*, 35 PUBLIUS 217 (2005) (arguing in terms of shared responsibility, where the CC is thought to complement the role of the constitutional and political actors).

the law explicit on all accounts[123], because this would undermine its authority and would bring strive and conflict into its walls[124], it surely could patch up some of its lines of reasoning or strengthen its 'principled' approach[125] taking into account the consequences more explicitly, even from a different conceptual perspective. It remains most important, however, that legal scholars can adopt a stance which is not so much focused on explaining and predicting the law through rigid doctrinal systematization, but are conceptually capable to take into account the other factors which have contributed to the discussion, trying to square them into a theoretical model which is not only better suited as a systematization, but at the same time upholds the important values which the current dogmatic system serves.

[123] For some reasons (or motives) should clearly not be accepted as legal reasons, even if – in terms of the psychology of decision-making – they may have played in decision making process. If this book seeks to throw into doubt the necessarily normative nature of legal scholarship (/dogmatics), it surely does not plead for a open and clear politization of the Court system, for instance by judges who openly ground their decisions on either descriptive generalizations or non-legally construed reasons (if not, there would be no *"grounding"; compare supra* note 98).

[124] Or because judges are just unaware of the underlying reasons for their decisions (*cf. supra* note 120).

[125] *Compare supra* No. 31.

2.

Belgian federalism: A cursory overview

38. *Compromis à la belge.* On the whole, Belgium's federal structure must be understood as a 'complex set of compromises that was the product of a series of protracted political negotiations'[126]. These negotiations dealt primarily with Flemish aspirations for (cultural) autonomy, Flemish fear of 'Frenchification' of the Brussels periphery, Walloon aspirations for economic autonomy, and minority protections, both for the Francophones in Belgium as a whole, and for the Flemish inhabitants of the 'Frenchified' Brussels periphery[127].

The negotiations proceeded in stages: up till now five grand packages of institutional reforms have been adopted. The first package in 1970 created balances in light of the establishment of Belgium's two kinds of federated entities, notably the (Cultural) Communities and Regions. The second state reform in 1980 expanded the competences of the Communities and established those of the (two large) Regions in a special law (SLIR). The third package in 1988

---

[126] Robert Mnookin & Alain Verbeke, *Persistent nonviolent conflict with no reconciliation: the Flemish and Walloons in Belgium*, 72 LAW AND CONTEMPORARY PROBLEMS 151, 167 (2009). *See* Hugues Dumont, *Etat, Nation et Constitution. De la théorie du droit public aux conditions de viabilité de l'Etat belge* in BELGITUDE ET CRISE DE L'ETAT BELGE 73, 108 (Hugues Dumont et al. eds. 1989) ('Belgian federalism is perceived as a mode of pacification and not as a political project'); Alen, *supra* note 38, at p. 19 (noticing that there was neither a true 'legal' project: 'if there is one thing missing from all consecutive institutional reforms, it was legal theoretical analysis'); Jan Velaers, *België is een federale Staat, samengesteld uit de gemeenschappen en de gewesten (art. 1 G.G.W.): een commentaar in het licht van federale theorieën* in BELGIUM: QUO VADIS, *supra* note 38, at p. 41 *et seq*. *Also see* LUC HUYSE, OVER POLITIEK (2003) (explaining how these negotiations have more or less worked in the Belgian consociational model (Lijphart) of democracy to mitigate two foundational discords in Belgian politics, *ie* the religious one and the economic one, but not (quite to the contrary) the third, linguistic one; *cf.* André Alen, *'De tien geboden van de Staatshervorming'* in ZEVEN KNELPUNTEN NA ZEVEN JAAR STAATSHERVORMING 5, 5-7 (André Alen & Louis-Paul Suetens eds. 1988). *Also see* WILFRIED DEWACHTER, DE DUALISTISCHE IDENTITEIT VAN DE BELGISCHE MAATSCHAPPIJ 17 (nuancing this consociationalism by emphasizing the importance of political parties in these negotiations). *But see* Paul Vermeulen, *Advies*, 1975 TBP 417, 420 *et seq*. (arguing, from a Foucauldian perspective, that consociationalism does not work in Belgium, because of Francohpone dominance). *Compare* Frank Delmartino & Kris Deschouwer, *Grondslagen van het Federalisme* in FEDERALISME. STAATKUNDIG, POLITIEK EN ECONOMISCH 9, 24-29 (Interuniversitair Studiecentrum voor Federalisme ed. 1994) (arguing that consociationalism is a specific form of federalist thinking) *with* André Alen, *Het Belgisch Federalisme* in *ibid.* at p. 178-181 (describing how consociationalism in Belgium has led to political elitism, which both creates and is rooted in a whole set of other societal evolutions that can be deemed problematic).

[127] ALEN & MUYLLE, *supra* note 14, at p. 287-289; *also see* Mnookin & Verbeke, *supra* note 126, at p. 167-172 (also mentioning the growing lack of solidarity and the issue of internal transfers). For a relevant nuance, with an emphasis on the problem that Brussels has always constituted, *see* Wouter Pas, *Federalisme met gemeenschappen én gewesten: een tussenstand van moeilijkheden, mogelijkheden en voorstellen*, 2011 TBP 486, 488 ('[e]ssential is that the creation of Communities was necessary because of the specific situation of the bilingual language area. In fact, it is only here that Belgian federalism needed a correction or a modification of its fundamentally territorial character').

fully transferred the competence on education to the Communities, and further expanded the competences of the Regions. The fourth state reform package in 1993 above all institutionally updated the renewed allocation of competences and the fifth package in 2001 expanded the competences of the Regions and refinanced the federated entities to some extent[128]. The sixth package of state reforms has been politically ratified and partially awaits legal implementation: it promises institutional reform, further transfers of competences and financial reform and should for the largest part be implemented by the 2014 elections[129].

39. Fundamentals of federalism. The protracted series of negotiations have resulted in an idiosyncratic form of federalism. One could wonder now, whether federalism is not always in some way idiosyncratic[130]. Somehow it will always be: political scientists have tried to pin down what constitutes the essence of federalism for a long time. Authoritative in this regard, is Kenneth Wheare's elaboration of the 'federal principle'[131], and it could be said that Belgium indeed adheres to that principle. Even so, legal and political discussions have been conducted about the question whether Belgium really is a federal country, notwithstanding its confirmation in article 1 of the Constitution. Those debates might be interesting, but they have been conducted elsewhere, and for our purposes (starting in Belgian practice), we can suffice with what Belgian authors conceive to be the fundamental tenets of federalism. Notwithstanding some disagreement, most Belgian authors recognize at least two 'laws' of federalism, namely autonomy for the federated entities and participation of these entities in the federal enterprise[132].

---

[128] This description of course is flawed: for a more elaborate discussion of the different stages of reforms, *see* the standard reference works mentioned in Alen & Muylle, *supra* note 14, at p. 293-294 n19-21 and n25-27.

[129] For an overview, *see* www.law.kuleuven.be/icr/doc_6e_shv; *also see* Jan Velaers, *De zesde staatshervorming, eerste fase: BHV, de randgemeenten, Brussel en de democratie,* 76 RW 1002 (2012-2013). Next to referring to the Butterfly agreement, some references are made to the reports preceding the conclusion of the Agreement, especially the unaccepted Dewever and Vande Lanotte Reports (Bart De Wever, Verslag aan Koning Albert II (2010) and Johan Vande Lanotte, De Zesde staatshervorming: onderhandelingsnota (2011)), but also the Di Rupo report which served as a basis for the Butterfly Agreement (Elio Di Rupo: Een efficiëntere federale staat en een grotere autonomie voor de deelstaten (2011)).

[130] *Cf.* Charlie Jeffery, *Belgium, as seen from elsewhere* in Social Federalism, *supra* note 45, at p. 267. This of course harks back to the problems we elaborated in Chapter 1.

[131] Kenneth C. Wheare, Federal Government 10, 14 (4th ed. 1963) (1946); *but see* S. Rufus Davis, The Federal Principle. A Journey through Time in Quest of Meaning 10-11 (1978) (arguing that 'the federal principle has come to mean what it does because the United States has come to be what it is')

[132] Often relying on Burdeau, *eg* Delmartino & Deschouwer, *supra* note 126, at p. 13-14; *also see infra* note 215.

Some authors have added other 'laws', such as cooperation[133], equality of the federated entities[134], superposition of two 'state' levels[135] or the existence of a court to rule on conflicts of competence[136]. However, important to note here is that the federal practice is more important than the Constitution by itself[137] or than some ideal-typical concept, at least when we want to assess constitutional court case law regarding federalism. As the Vice-Prime Minister recalled in 1988, '[t]he most important thing to know is not whether the new system is federal, confederal or prefederal, but to know exactly who does what'[138]. Be that as it may, in order to understand the basic tenets of the Belgian state structure, it will not suffice to merely look at the allocation of competences from a legal perspective. Some theoretical framework, and indeed context needs to be offered.

40. Understanding the federal structure: more than allocation of competences. Keeping that in mind, it seems that the best way to describe Belgium in terms of its federal structure, is by emphasis on Belgium's doubly stratified federalism[139] (**1.1**), couched in a confederal decision-making process on the national level[140] (**1.2**), on which a Constitutional Court has to rule (**1.3**).

---

[133] *See eg* ANDRÉ ALEN, BELGIUM: BIPOLAR AND CENTRIFUGAL FEDERALISM 17-21 (1990).

[134] *See eg* Francis Delpérée, *La voie fédérale* in BELGITUDE, *supra* note 126, at p. 56-57; *compare* UYTTENDAELE, *supra* note 13, at p. 369 *et seq.*

[135] *See eg* UYTTENDAELE, *supra* note 13, at p. 45-46; *also see* Rusen Ergec, *Institutionele analyse van het Federalisme* in FEDERALISME. STAATKUNDIG ..., *supra* note 126, at p. 45.

[136] Ergec, *supra* note 135, at p. 47.

[137] Alen, *supra* note 38, at p. 10-11.

[138] Report on behalf of the Commission (Cerexhe & Erdman), *Parl. Doc.* Senate 1988 SS, No. 405/2, at p. 51.

[139] On doubly stratified federalism in connection with the sixth state reform, *see* Wouter Pas, *De Dubbele gelaagdheid van het Belgische federalisme: quo vadis* in QUO VADIS, *supra* note 11, at p. 111-156 and his earlier contribution, mentioned *supra* note 127.

[140] Karel Rimanque, *Réflexions concernant la question oratoire: Y a-t-il un Etat belge?* In BELGITUDE, *supra* note 126, at p. 65-67.

2.1 A doubly stratified federal structure

41. Four language areas. Belgium is divided into four non-overlapping language areas: three monolingual territories (Dutch, French and German) and one bilingual area (the Brussels Metropolitan area)[141]. These areas have not as such been imbued with legal personality, but are legally important in determining the competences of the federated entities in Belgium, that is, of the Communities and Regions[142].

Not only are these language areas important in determining the territorial scope of application of the respective competences of the Regions and the Communities, but also in the sense that the Constitutional Court derives from article 4 of the Constitution (enshrining the language areas) a 'constitutional guarantee of linguistic priority' [143].

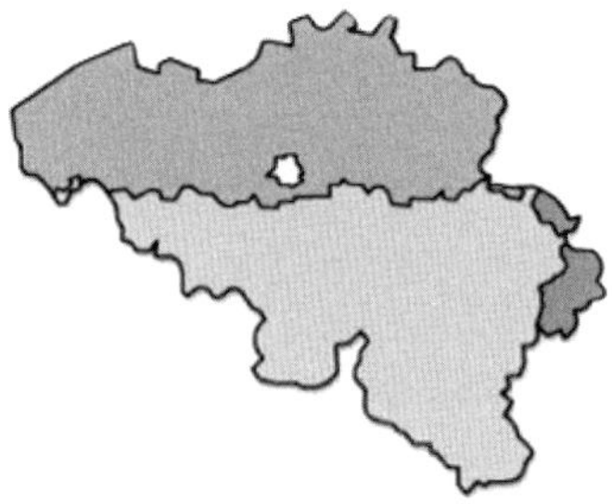

Figure 1:
Language areas (4) in Belgium

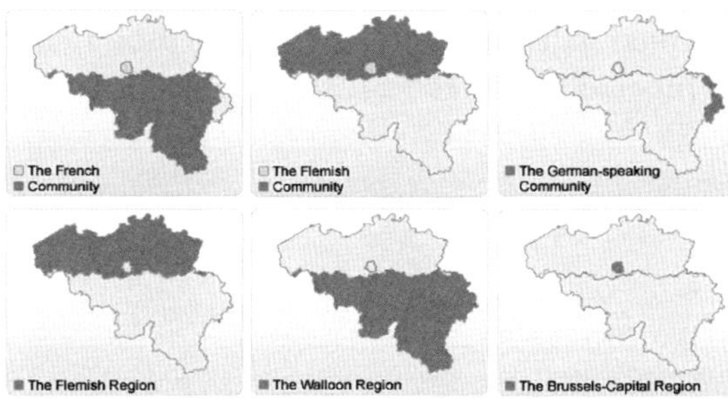

Figure 2:
Communities (3) and Regions (3) (source: www.belgium.be)

42. Communities and their competences. Belgium is composed of three Communities: the Flemish, the French and the German(-speaking) Communities[144]. They are generally competent in educational, cultural, person-related

[141] Article 4 Cons. *See Figure 1.*

[142] *Cf.* HENRI STORME, RELATIE TUSSEN DE TERRITORIALE BEVOEGDHEIDSVERDELING EN HET CONFLICTENRECHT IN EEN FEDERALE STAAT. BELGIË EN DE VERENIGDE STATEN 211-13 (diss. doct. Ghent University 2009), published in 2010 by Larcier (page references to the latter version).

[143] CA No. 17 (Mar. 26, 1986) 3.B.6 (arguably as obiter dictum); *see* CA No. 26/98 (Mar. 10, 1998) B.4.1 ((connected to) dictum); *cf.* references mentioned *supra* note 14.

[144] Art. 3 Cons. *See Figure 2.* It should be noted that symbolicism (in linguistics) is important in the Belgian Constitution, for in the French official version, *'la Communauté française'* is mentioned first, and in the German official version, *'die Deutschsprachige Gemeinschaft'* comes first; *see* CHRISTIAN BEHRENDT & FRÉDÉRIC BOUHON, INTRODUCTION À LA THÉORIE GÉNÉRALE

and linguistic matters in their own monolingual territories, and the Flemish and French Communities are competent vis-à-vis monolingual institutions in the Brussels area[145]. Pursuant to the Constitution[146], the SLIR further specifies the competences conferred[147] to the Communities[148], which they exercise by decree.

43. Oversimplification. This description disregards or at least oversimplifies an important peculiarity in Belgium, *ie* Brussels. With regard to the competences vis-à-vis the monolingual institutions, it should be noted that aforementioned was a severe simplification. The Constitution, in cultural matters, makes Communities competent vis-à-vis institutions that 'due to their activities, must be deemed to be exclusive part of one or the other communities'[149] and in 'person-related' matters, the same holds for institutions that 'due to their organization, must be deemed to be exclusive part of one or the other communities'[150]. Even if, according to the *travaux préparatoires,* 'every Community decides for itself which criteria a Brussels institution should fulfill to be acknowledged as an institution which is an exclusive part of that Community'[151], generally, that will

---

DE L'ETAT 125 n401 (2009). A similar linguistic quarrel has arisen as regards the name of the smallest Region: sometimes it has been coined Brussels Region (*eg* art. 3 Cons.), whereas elsewhere, the notion of Brussels Metropolitan Region has been used (*eg* art. 136, 138, 163 and 166 Cons.); *compare* VELAERS, DE GRONDWET EN DE RAAD VAN STATE, *supra* note 13, at p. 41 (referring to a 1989 CoS advice which implies that the difference is not merely terminological, but might convey a 'different institutional meaning').

145 Art. 127-130 Cons.

146 Art. 127, §1, 2nd clause (vis-à-vis cultural competences) and art. 128, §1, 2nd clause (vis-à-vis 'person-related' competences).

147 The 'residual competences' remain – for now (*see* art. 35 *juncto* art. 38-39 Cons.; Patrick Peeters, *Vlottende residuaire gewest- en gemeenschapsbevoegdheden in de federale Belgische staat: een zinvolle en haalbare kaart,* 1990 TBP 79) – at the federal level. They are, however, not *directly* reviewed in light of article 35 (*eg* CC 31/2011 (Mar. 2, 2011) B.3.2-B.3.3; *see* CC 9/2001 (Jan. 27, 2011) B.3.1-B.3.2; CC 57/2012 (May 3, 2012) B.2.1-B.2.3). *See infra* Nos. 72-73.

148 *See* art. 4 (cultural matters) and 5 ('person-related' matters) of the SLIR. *Also see* art. 6*bis* (scientific research), art. 6*ter* (development cooperation), art. 8 (infrastructure), art. 9 *juncto* 87-89 (services, institutions and corporate participations), art. 10 (implied competences), art. 11 (criminal competences), art. 14 (pre-emptive purchasing right), art. 16 *juncto* 81 (on international cooperation) and art. 79 (expropriations (*eminent domain*)). Some limits are also construed there (*eg* art. 16*bis-ter*: forbidding the denaturation of the extant guarantees for linguistic communities; *see also infra* No. 104), and sometimes cooperation is facilitated or enforced (art. 92*bis-ter*, and diffused stipulations in the articles 4-6).

149 Art. 127, §2 Cons.

150 Art. 128, §2 Cons. *See further* on 'person-related matters', *infra* note 473.

151 Report (Lindemans & De Stexhe), *Parl. Doc.* Senate 1977 SS, No. 100/27, at p. 7. *See further*, as regards its determination, STORME, *supra* note 142, at p. 230-34: VELAERS, DE GRONDWET EN DE RAAD VAN STATE, *supra* note 13, at p. 410-12, 416-19.

be linguistically determined[152]. Accordingly, the Communities are competent in Brussels for institutions, but not vis-à-vis persons. In fact, it has been generally accepted that there is no 'sub-nationality' in Belgium[153]. Even so, quite some discussion has arisen about the legal consequences thereof. The debate about whether social security legislation can be federalized, in light of the fact that the Communities cannot reach persons as such, is a good illustration of the issue. Whereas Xavier Delgrange argued that forcing people to make choices to adhere to this or that institution violates the prohibition on sub-nationality[154], Jan Velaers contended that from the perspective of the principle of equality, no problem had arisen in this regard[155]. Accordingly, notwithstanding consensus on the principle, its implications are not always clear[156]. Due to its excessive complexity, I will not discuss in detail how Community competences are exercised in Brussels. Suffice it to say that – in general – regarding bicultural competences, the federal government remains competent pursuant to its residual competence, whereas regarding 'bi-person-related' competences a separate federated entity called the Joint Community Commission has been made competent[157]. When the Communities themselves are competent (vis-à-vis mono-linguistic institutions), they exercise their powers through subordinate organs in Brussels[158]. Even if from time to time reference is made to Brussels or the German-speaking community, the primary focus here is on the largest

[152] *Ibid.* at p. 8, 10-11; *also see* French Community Decree (July 1, 1982) on establishing criteria [...], *BSG* Aug. 27, 1982; Alen & Muylle, *supra* note 14, at p. 381.

[153] *See eg* Report (Lindemans & de Stexhe), *supra* note 14, at p. 7 (where the Minister for institutional reforms 'resolutely denounces' the idea), 10; Alen & Muylle, *supra* note 14, at p. 379-380; Peeters, *supra* note 38, at p. 188 *et seq.*

[154] Xavier Delgrange, *Bruxelles et l'hypothèse de la défédéralisation de la sécurité sociale* in Autonomie, solidarité et cooperation. Quelques enjeux du fédéralisme belge au 21e siècle. Autonomie, solidariteit en samenwerking. Enkele belangen van het Belgisch federalisme in de 21ste eeuw at p. 235 and 265, and *see esp.* 260-63 (Philippe Cattoir *et al.* eds. 2002).

[155] Jan Velaers, *Brussel en de hypothese van de defederalisering van de sociale zekerheid* in *ibid.* at p. 301-02

[156] *See* François Rigaux, *Les règles de droit délimitant leur propre domain d'application*, 1983 Annales de Droit de Louvain 285, 316 ('there does not exist, in designating the persons who are the destinataries of the norm of the Community, any personal criterion'); *also see* Storme, *supra* note 142, at p. 227 *et seq.* (commenting on the link between the institutions and the personal choice of citizens, resulting in a 'landscape of uncontrolled competition between regulations').

[157] *Cf.* art. 128 and 135 Cons.

[158] Art. 136 Cons.; *also see* art. 166 Cons.

federated entities. More specifics on Brussels are found in the SLBI[159] and on the German-speaking Community, the LIRG[160] should be consulted.

Next to that, it should be noted that the story elaborated here might have simplified matters in other respects as well. First, there are some constitutional exceptions to the Communities' competences, materially as well as territorially. For instance, the federal government remains materially competent for retirement pension regulation in educational matters[161]. Territorially, exceptions are made as regards the linguistic competence for some municipalities having a special linguistic status[162]. Moreover, there are differences between the distinct Communities: thus, the German Community is not competent for regulating languages in social relations[163]. Going into the details here would go beyond the purpose of this section, which primarily serves as an introduction.

44. Community decrees. Communities can adopt decrees, as legislative instruments. A decree has force of law, meaning that there is – in principle – no subordination of a decree to a (federal) law or to other decrees[164].

Some nuances are called for here, too, however, pertaining to the idea of non-subordination.

First, insofar as[165], for instance, the competences of the German Community are regulated by (normal federal) law, the decrees it adopts are subject to "review" under these (normal federal) laws. Bribosia and Van Boxstael explain this by referring to an incorporation of some laws into the 'bloc de constitutionnalité'[166].

Moreover, in Brussels, the Joint Community Commission can issue *ordinances*[167], which are subject to limited judicial review by the ordinary judge[168], which is

---

[159] Regarding Community competences, see *esp.* art. 63 *et seq.*

[160] *Esp.* art. 4.

[161] Art. 127, §1, 2°, c) Cons.

[162] Art. 129, §3, first dash Cons.

[163] *Compare* art. 129, §1, 3° *with* art. 130, §1, 5° Cons.

[164] Art. 127, §2; art. 128, §2; art. 129, §2 and art. 130, §2 Cons.

[165] *Compare* art. 125 Cons.

[166] Bribosia & Van Boxstael, *supra* note 13, at p. 37-38; *also see* CA No. 92/2003 (June 24, 2003), B.3.3 (where the Court explicitly recognizes that rules allocating competences need not even have force of law); *compare* Explanatory Memo (accompanying bill on institutional reform in the German-speaking Community), *Parl. Doc.* Chamber 1982-83, No. 622/1, at p. 1 (trying to ensure 'maximal concordance' with the other Communities); Report (Schijns) on the Revision of the Constitution, *Parl. Doc.* Chamber 1979 SS, No. 10-16/4, at p. 3 ('similar autonomy').

[167] *See* Alen & Muylle, *supra* note 14, at p. 387.

[168] Art. 9 SLBI *juncto* art. 69 SLBI.

not the case for decrees, at least not in light of rules allocating competences in the strict sense, since here the Constitutional Court, in virtue of articles 141 and 142 of the Constitution, is exclusively competent[169].

Then again, because many conferrals of competence (indirectly) refer to existing (federal) legislation[170], the question arose whether this existing legislation should be considered as 'mummified' for the purposes of allocation of competences[171]. The Constitutional Court has rejected that view[172]. As such, as the Council of State explained (without endorsing the process), by adjusting legislation that is important in light of the allocation of competences, the federal legislature can indirectly limit or define the scope of the competences of the federated entities[173]. Conversely, it has been acknowledged that federal legislation dating prior to the institutional reforms may have been implicitly modified through that institutional reform[174]. Be that as it may, the Court, by relying on the

[169] For more information on the legal instruments in English, *see* the short introduction in Stef Feyen, *The Regional Interpretative Decree: in search for a Right Answer*, available at http://ssrn.com/abstract=1742367, at p. 3-6.

[170] *See eg* CA No. 27 (Oct. 22, 1986), 4.B.1 (arguing that art. 13, §2 SLIR is a rule governing allocation of competences); Uyttendaele, *supra* note 13, at p. 421, 445-46, 465; Steven Vansteenkiste, *Coherenties en incoherenties in de persoonsgebonden aangelegenheden* in Sociaal Beleid en Federalisme, *supra* note 47, at p. 85, 100, 108-110.

[171] Bribosia & Van Boxstael, *supra* note 13, at p. 78-79; Jean-Marie Van Bol, *Les matières communautaires et régionales,* 1981 JT 633, 641-42.

[172] CA No. 28 (Nov. 28, 1986) IV.4.B.2.c-d; CA No. 42 (Nov. 10, 1987), III.4.B.2.b.2 (it follows from the economy of article 13, §3 SLIR that 'the special legislature has wanted to render the financial, budgettary, and administrative control techniques that are valid at the national level [...] applicable in the same way for the Institutions of the Regions and Communities' and, therefore, the Decree cannot stipulate that the federal legislation the SLIR refers to, is merely applicable as it stands at the time of entry into force of the decree).

[173] CoS Advice (joint chambers), *Parl. Doc.* Senate 2000-01, No. 2-709/1, at p. 45-46.

[174] CA No. 65 (June 15, 1988) 1.B.2, 2.B.3 (regarding the 1962 federal law on expropriation); *also see* CA No. 2/2003 (Jan. 14, 2003) B.3.2-4 (applying article 42 of the Judicial Code (per analogy)); *compare* 1B Alen & Muylle, Compendium van het Belgisch Staatsrecht 261-62 (2004); Velaers, De Grondwet en de Raad van State, *supra* note 13, at p. 426 (all arguing that art. 30 Cons. (linguistic freedom) has been implicitly reviewed by the adoption of art. 129, §1 and 130, §1, 1st clause, 5° Cons., which seems to find support in CA No. 16 (Mar. 25, 1986) III.B.2). The same has been argued for art. 39 (*eg* 3 André Alen, Handboek van het Belgisch Staatsrecht 251 (2d ed. 1997)); possibly *contra* CA No. 17 (Mar. 26, 1986) III.3.B.5 (article 129 has not implicitly changed the meaning of articles 8 and 162 Cons.). *Also see* art. 94, §§1-2 (federal law remains applicable as long as the federated entities have not exercised their competences) and 83, §§2-3 SLIR (even when not having exercised their competences, the executive power is transferred to the federated entities' executive branches). *But see eg* CA No. 108/2000 (Oct. 31, 2000), B.1.4.1 (relativizing the reference practice for 'organic laws' regarding hospitals – the federal competence is not limited to that law, nor does it comprise the entire law – precisely on the ground that otherwise the federal legislature could make abuse of the hospital law to influence competence allocations).

travaux préparatoires and intentions of the Special Legislature, does ossify certain concepts or terms arranging the allocation of competences[175], notwithstanding the fact that these concepts have been construed using prior ordinary legislation. The issue will be revisited, but it is mentioned here, because this 'logic' might thwart the equal legal force of decrees indeed. As such, this already provides a taste of the leeway the Constitutional Court has accorded itself in the interpretation of decrees in light of the allocation of competences.

45. Regions and their competences. Next to the Communities, there are three Regions, which partially territorially overlap with the Communities, but are different legal entities[176], that is the Flemish Region, the Walloon Region, and the Brussels Metropolitan Region[177]. After the Constitution gave a blank check[178] to the Special Legislature, the SLIR in staggering detail[179] confers competences to the Flemish and Walloon Regions. Their decrees have respective force of law in the Dutch and French language areas[180].

46. Oversimplification: Brussels and asymmetry. Next to that, it should be mentioned that also in a Regional sense, Brussels is somewhat of a special case, which we will not deal with *in extenso*[181]. Moreover, Brussels is not the only

---

175 For a clear example, *see* CC 75/2012 (June 14, 2012) B.11.

176 There is no full fusion of the Flemish Community and the Flemish Region (ALEN & MUYLLE, *supra* note 14, at p. 353-354), even if the attributes of the Flemish Region's legal personality are exercised by the Flemish Community (art. 3, 2nd clause SLIR). *Also see further* notes 200-201.

177 Art. 2 Cons.; *see Figure 2*.

178 Art. 39 Cons. *Also see* art. 134 Cons. *Cf.* ALEN & MUYLLE, *supra* note 14, at p. 294.

179 Art. 6 SLIR reads somewhat like chaos. Even if headings have been inserted on Regional competences (regional planning, environmental and water policy, soil planning and nature conservation policy, housing policy, agricultural policies and sea fishery, economy, energy, subordinate governance, employment policy and public tenders and transportation), these do not have explicit legal value and merely serve as 'indicators' of the treated matter (Explanatory Report, *Parl. Doc.* Senate 1979-80, No. 434/1, at p. 9; *cf.* UYTTENDAELE, *supra* note 13, at p. 420-24, 427-435, 441-452 (describing three different levels of autonomy of politics)) – whatever that might mean, at least in light of the interpretive difficulties arising in interpreting and qualifying different rules and principles allocating competences and the exercise of (alleged) competences.

180 Art. 19, §3 *juncto* art. 2 SLIR and art. 5 Cons. *Also see* art. 7, 2nd clause *juncto* art. 2, §1 SLBI.

181 In particular because the Region adapts ordinances instead of decrees. Like bipersonal ordinances (*supra* No. 44), these (regional) ordinances have legislative force (art. 7, 1st clause SLBI;) and come within the jurisdiction of the CC (VELAERS, VAN ARBITRAGEHOF TOT..., *supra* note 13, 110-12), but are subject to limited judicial review (art. 9 SLBI). Unlike bipersonal ordinances, they are additionally subject to limited administrative review (art. 45 SLBI). There is one important difference (*compare* Feyen, *supra* note 169, at p. 57 n319) in material powers between Brussels and the other Regions: it notably, like the Germanophonic Community, lacks constitutive autonomy (ie the rights accorded in art. 118, §2 and 123, §2 Cons.; *cf.* art. 4 SLBI; ALEN & MUYLLE, *supra* note 14, at p. 384-385). However, the Butterfly

'asymmetric' phenomenon in Belgian federalism[182], but we refrain from further elaborating on this issue here.

47. Fiscal competences. What we do want to stress is that not all federated powers are conferred in the SLIR[183]: indeed, one yet undiscussed competence of vast importance has been conferred by the Constitution itself, namely the fiscal competence. Indeed, article 170, § 2 of the Constitution regulates the taxing powers of the federated entities: it stipulates that a community or a regional tax can only be levied to the extent that the federal laws have not set forth 'the exceptions, the necessity of which is proved'[184]. As we will discuss below, in that light, the fiscal powers are often conceived of as concurrent powers. In order to ensure that the federated entities enjoy sufficient revenue, the SLFCR sets out a complex mechanism of financing, consisting of different forms of revenue[185]. We will not examine this law in detail here.

Agreement promises to abolish this difference (*supra* note 10, at p. 11-12 (*also see* p. 9)): *also see* Senate Proposals and the CoS advices, *Parl. Doc.* Senate 2011-12, No. 5-1754/1-2 and 5-1755/1-2.

[182] *See eg* art. 138 Cons. (according legislative competence to the French Community Commission (*CoCoF*)) or art. 139 Cons. (German Community may exercise competences of the Walloon Region) or art. 137 Cons. *juncto* art. 1, §1 SLIR (the Flemish Community exercises (with some modalities – *eg* art. 50 and 76 SLIR) the competences of the Flemish Region). These asymmetries however, are sometimes said to have a political effect on the exercise of powers (*eg* Raphaël Born, Hugues Dumont & Géraldine Van der Stichele, *La Communauté française dans le fédéralisme coopératif belge*, in AUTONOMIE, SOLIDARITÉ..., *supra* note 154, p. 435).

[183] Accordingly, the *Constitution* determines that it is not only the federal government which is supposed to ensure sex equality (art. 11*bis* Cons.), guarantee the right to a private and family life (art. 22 (2) Cons.), safeguard the rights of the child (art. 22*bis* (4) Cons.), protect certain economic, social and cultural rights (art. 23 (2) Cons.), preserve certain educational freedoms (art. 24 Cons.), or secure informational freedom (art. 32 Cons.). On the "quality" of this determination (and its competence-allocating character), *see* Margo Merckaert, *Status Quaestionis van de bevoegdheid inzake grondrechten*, 2013 TBP 162, 164 *et seq.*

[184] A specific federal law (generally) stipulates that the federated entities cannot levy taxes (nor surcharges or reductions) on matters that are already object of a federal tax (Art. 1 law (Jan. 23, 1989) regarding fiscal competence, BSG Jan. 24, 1989).

[185] The Regions are financed through *regional taxes* (*eg* inheritance tax, traffic taxes, ... - which might be modulated (*cf.* art. 4, 5, 8 and 11 SLFCR) and a so-called 'composed' tax (art. 6, §2 SLFCR), which is revenue generated by (federal) personal taxes conferred to the Region on the basis of population (art. 7, §2 SLFCR), vis-à-vis which the Regions might adopt limited and coordinated (*cf.* art. 9-9*bis* SLFCR) surcharges or reductions. Moreover, Regions can use loans to finance themselves (art. 49 SLFCR), as can the Communities moreover (*cf.* art. 1, §1, 3° SLFCR). The latter collect revenue from a so-called 'divided tax' (art. 6, §1 *juncto* art. 1, §1, 2° SLFCR), which in essence is a federal tax (Personal tax and VAT), the revenue of which is divided amongst the Communities, and from a special endowment (art. 1, §1, 2*bis* SLFCR). Finally, Regions and Communities may levy 'retributions', which are (*but see* VELAERS, DE GRONDWET EN DE RAAD VAN STATE, *supra* note 13, at p. 608-617) specific (non-fiscal) levies which compensate for services granted to a specific retribution-payer, with

2.2 Bipolar and centrifugal federalism institutionalized

48. Need to go beyond the allocation of competences in the strict sense. This general description of the allocation of competences might have given the impression that there is no real rationale or drive behind institutional reform in Belgium. Surely there is: the stages of institutional reform – each in their own way – were answers to salient and often ardent political question arising at the time[186]. We mentioned that Communities emerged from the Flemish quest for cultural autonomy and Regions emerged from the Walloon aspirations for economic revival. These explanations, however, were only partial (and of course, simplified). Even if the result of the Belgian process of federalization is the doubly stratified federal structure that I described above, it is impossible to understand Belgian federalism as a whole – and henceforth, the federalism jurisprudence of the Constitutional Court – without taking into account the (legal) effects that the *bipolar* and *centrifugal*[187] nature of Belgian federalism have produced.

---

a specific competence-allocating meaning (whereas fiscal competences do not need to be linked to the material competences, levies in the sense of art. 173 Cons. do: *Cf.* CA No. 55/96 (Oct. 15, 1996) B.4.2.4 or *eg* CC No. 89/2010 (July 29, 2010); *see* Bruno Peeters, *De begrippen belasting, last en retributies in de artikelen 110 en 113 van de Grondwet,* 1988 RW 241). Although this short overview by no means lists all nuances and exceptions, it should be mentioned that the German-speaking Community is financed differently (primarily through endowments: *see* ALEN & MUYLLE, *supra* note 14, at p. 576 *et seq.*), and that transfers amongst entities generally occur (art. 48 SLFCR).

[186] *Eg* Alen, *supra* note 38, at p. 7, 13; I PLETS, *supra* note 47, at p. 76. That there was a rationale does not however mean that there was an underlying, coherent political project: *cf. supra* note 126 (*compare* the distinction in light of note 98).

[187] A great English introduction (even if it is somewhat outdated now) is the booklet by ALEN, *supra* note 153 (who introduced the concepts into Belgian constitutional law). Alen develops his points more thoroughly, both from a political and from a historical perspective and adapts them to the consequences of the Fourth State Reform in Alen, *Het Belgisch Federalisme, supra* note 126, at p. 135 *et seq.* For an analysis from a specific *legal* point of view, *see* the basic works in constitutional law (both English, Dutch and French), mentioned in Feyen, *supra* note 169, at p. 2 n2; *adde* M. PACQUES, DROIT PUBLIC ÉLÉMENTAIRE EN QUINZE LEÇONS (2005); RUSEN ERGEC, INTRODUCTION AU DROIT PUBLIC (2nd ed. 2003); JAN VELAERS, STAATSRECHT: ELEMENTEN VAN HET PUBLIEK RECHT (2007). Even if this list is not exhaustive at all, I should mention that less recent basic treatises (*eg* by Mast or Velu), or downright older treatises (*eg* by Orban or Wigny) are not mentioned here, nor are the constitutional comments by themselves (*eg* by Rimanque or Velaers). Some (all too) short English (political science / sociological) introductions to Belgian federalism (some are more accurate / up to date than others), are, for instance, ALEN, *supra* note 153 (offering a short legal introduction to Belgium, which is by now somewhat outdated); MICHAEL BURGESS, COMPARATIVE FEDERALISM: THEORY AND PRACTICE 115 *et seq.* (2006) (offering a socio-political analysis of how duality is coped with in Belgian State structure); Frank Delmartino, *Belgium after the Fourth State Reform: Completed*

49. Bipolarity: federal bicameralism and dualist protective measures. The *bipolar* nature of the Belgian federation reflects itself not only in the lack of a true federal bicameralism, which is discussed first, but also, and perhaps more importantly, in a whole array of *dualist* protective measures, which will be discussed subsequently, and which will be judged in light of the constitutional structure of the Belgian federation, as one composed out of three Communities and three Regions.

50. (Lack of) "real" federal bicameralism. Generally, from a comparative constitutional perspective, a Second federal Chamber (Senate) has often functioned as a springboard for participation by the federated entities in the federal decision-making process. Accordingly, so goes to normal rationale, it is

---

Federalism or confederalism in the making? in THE REGIONS – FACTORS OF INTEGRATION OR DISINTEGRATION IN EUROPE 117 (Gisela Färber & Murry Forsyth eds. 1996) (debating (*esp. ibid.* at p. 131 *et seq.*) whether the Belgian structure should be coined federalist or confederalist); JAN ERK, EXPLAINING FEDERALISM: STATE, SOCIETY, AND CONGRUENCE IN AUSTRIA, BELGIUM, CANADA, GERMANY AND SWITZERLAND 31 *et seq.* (2008) (offering a historico-sociological narrative on the grounds of Belgian federalism); THOMAS O. HUEGLIN & ALAN FENNA, COMPARATIVE FEDERALISM: A SYSTEMATIC INQUIRY 140 *et seq.* (2006) (offering an example of what not to read: the data provided are too limited to offer insight, and contain factual mistakes); Wilfried Swenden, *Why is Belgian Federalism not more asymmetrical* in FEDERALISM BEYOND FEDERATIONS: ASYMMETRY AND PROCESSES OF RE-SYMMETRIZATION 13 *et seq.* (Ferran Requejo and Klaus-Jürgen Nagel eds. 2011) (arguing that the duality of Belgian's social substratum lies at the basis of its institutional structure, notwithstanding the formalization of a doubly stratified federalism); RONALD WATTS, COMPARING FEDERAL SYSTEMS 26 *et seq.*. (3rd ed. 2008) (a great political science introduction which succeeds in pointing out some of the underlying difficulties in the Belgian construction) and Peter Wagstaff, *Belgium: a new federalism* in REGIONALISM IN THE EUROPEAN UNION 74 (Peter Wagstaff ed. 1999) (offering a short history of institutional reform, with an emphasis on social factors influencing it); *also see* KRIS DESCHOUWER, THE POLITICS OF BELGIUM: GOVERNING A DIVIDED SOCIETY (2009) (offering a political science introduction to Belgian society, with a focus on the post-2007 political crisis); Luc Hooghe, *Belgium: From Regionalism to Federalism* in THE TERRITORIAL MANAGEMENT OF ETHNIC CONFLICT 73 (J. Coakley ed., 2nd ed. 2003) (summarily describing the sociological and political background of the Belgian State Reforms); Luc Hooghe, *Belgium: Hollowing the Centre* in FEDERALISM AND TERRITORIAL CLEAVAGES 55 (Ugo Amoretti and Nancy Berneo eds. 2004) (emphasizing the territorialization of Belgian politics and the concomitant 'hollowing' of the federal government's powers as a condition for peace in Belgian society) and ELS WITTE & H. VAN VELTHOVEN, LANGUAGE AND POLITICS: THE BELGIAN CASE IN A HISTORICAL PERSPECTIVE (1999) (focusing on the evolution of language laws since the end of the 19th century, and describing their influence in the process of progressive Belgian federalization). The most detailed systematized inquiries into matters of allocation of competences, have occurred in a series by Die Keure, called DE BEVOEGDHEIDSVERDELING IN HET FEDERALE BELGIË (Geert Van Haegedoren and Bruno Seutin eds.). From 1999 up till 2012, 16 different booklets have been published exploring different 'matters' of allocation of competences, ranging from 'use of languages' (No. 12 by Velaers in 2001) over environmental policies and water policies (No. 1 by Lavrysen in 1999) to functional decentralization (No. 14 by Baeten and Vandendriessche in 2007) and agricultural policy (No. 16 by Judo in 2011).

ensured that the interests of the federated entities are taken into account at the federal level, at least pertaining to matters in which these federated entities are deemed to have a stake. In Belgium, things are slightly different. As the Belgian Senate has not (yet) been construed as an Assembly of federated States[188], in accordance with the federalist principle of participation, other guarantees have been construed so as to allow (the population of) the (large) federated entities (that is, by and large the 'communities'[189]) to 'participate' in the federal decision-making process.

51. Dualist protective measures. This 'participation' – or perhaps it is better to speak of interest protection – is ensured by the institutionalization of a whole array of what could be coined 'dualist protective measures'. More precisely, the bipolarity of the Belgian federation is reflected in a wide array of protective measures accorded to the Francophone community at the federal (institutional) level[190],

---

[188] *See eg* Patrick Peeters, *Enkele algemene problemen van bevoegdheidsverdeling en bevoegdheidsuitlegging na de tweede Belgische staatshervorming* in ZEVEN KNELPUNTEN, *supra* note 126, at p. 58 *et seq.*; *cf. supra* note 126 (on federalism theories). For the reasons described below, it is uncertain whether a conceptualization of a Senate as a Second (State) Chamber would work in Belgium; *see* references, *supra* note 33. Even so, the Butterfly Agreement stipulates that the Senate will become a more direct reflection of the federated entities. At the same time, however, it reduces its competences, and thus not making it into a 'Second Chamber', accordingly weakening an already comparatively 'weak' institution (*cf.* Ronald L. Watts, *Participation of federated entities in federal policy-making* in FEDERALISM: TURNING DIVERSITY INTO HARMONY, SHARING BEST PRACTICES (Third International Conference on Federalism, Brussels, Mar. 3-5, 2005) 464, 470-474, *esp.* Table II (2005))). *Compare eg* VANDE LANOTTE, *supra* note 73, at p. 8-9, 55; DE WEVER, *supra* note 72, at p. 5; DI RUPO, *supra* note 129, at p. 19-20 to the 2006 political agreement, as mentioned in Patrick Peeters, *De Senaat opnieuw ter discussie. Zin en onzin van een statenkamer in (con)federaal België*, in DE GRONDWET IN GROOTHOEKPERSPECTIEF. LIBER AMICORUM DISCIPULORUMQUE KAREL RIMANQUE 213, 236 (Bruno Peeters & Jan Velaers eds. 2007).

[189] This term (without the capitalization) is used merely from a sociological (factual) perspective, as it has *no* legal value as such. As was discussed (*supra* notes 154-155), subnationality in Belgium has been radically denounced from a legal point of view. Moreover, as will be discussed, this finds (one of) its legal translation(s) in the principle of exclusive territoriality (*cf.* CA No. 33/2001 (Mar. 13, 2001) B.4.4; *adde* CoS Advice (June 28, 2011), *Parl. Doc.* Flemish Parl. 2011-2012, No. 1568/1, § 7).

[190] Mostly, these protective measures have been worked out '*neutrally*', in the sense that the constitutional or legal provisions do not – at face value – reveal for which community they have been inserted. Factually, however, it is almost always the case that the protection can be brought back to Francophones at the federal level and Flemish at the Brussels level. This, on the other hand, does not mean that their protective scope is limited to their factual rationale, even if some legislation refers explicitly to facts in order to establish a status quo (*see eg* art. 16*bis-ter* SLIR, which are nonetheless rendered 'neutrally' applicable with reference to facts (*eg* Jürgen Vanpraet, *De bescherming van de "bestaande garanties" in de faciliteitengemeenten en Brussel*, 2011 CDPK 503, 505-506, 509-510; *cf.* JÜRGEN VANPRAET, DE LATENTE STAATSHERVORMING 217 *et seq.* (2011)). On the neutrality issue, further *see* Stef Feyen, *De Raad van State en de Zesde Staatshervorming*, 2013 TBP (forthcoming), *esp.* Nos. 25-30). *Compare* VANDE LANOTTE

with concomitant measures for the Flemish inhabitants of Brussels[191].

52. Special laws. The most important protective measure on the federal level is probably the 'rigidification' of legal measures by Special Laws[192]. This rigidification (and thus protection) applies to almost all matters regarding the allocation and determination of *competences* in the strict sense[193], but also for matters with a more indirect or tangential impact on competence allocation in Belgium, such as the determination of the competences of the Constitutional Court[194], or the regulation of language use in the municipalities with special linguistic facilities[195]. In all these matters, no decision can be taken without consent of the two large (*bipolar*) Belgian communities, as the qualified majority required by article 4 of the Constitution, requires a majority of votes cast in each *linguistic group*[196] of the Federal Chambers. Moreover, the Constitutional Court determined that the 'special majority requirement necessarily is part of the system of allocation of competences'[197].

& GOEDERTIER, *supra* note 13, at p. 1458 n194 (who conceive of these protective measures as 'rules governing the allocation of competences' in the sense of the jurisdiction of the CC).

191 This does not imply symmetry. For instance, during the 2001 State reform, the protection for Flemish inhabitants in Brussels was somewhat dimished, so as to prevent institutional gridlock. Some authors lamented the increasing lack of symmetry (Frank Judo, *De Brusselse instellingen en de bescherming van de minderheden*, in DE VIJFDE STAATSHERVORMING VAN 2001, *supra* note 46, at p. 272-73), but the CC by and large approved of this (CA No. 35/2003 (Mar. 25, 2003) B.19.8: 'even if the organization of Brussels Institution, vis-à-vis the protection of the smallest group, shows a certain parallelism with the organization of federal institutions, articles 10 and 11 of the Constitution do not imply that the legislature should necessarily organize the Brussels institution in the same manner as the one prescribed by article 4 (3) of the Constitution for the federal institutions'). Accordingly, the symmetry is not complete, in fact nor in law. For instance, in the Brussels Parliament, protection is afforded by a fixed division of seats (art. 10 SLBI), an alarm bell procedure (art. 54 SLBI), a requirement of an overridable majority per linguistic group for important matters (art. 28 SBLI), equal representation (art. 34, §1, SLBI), consensus decision-making (art. 36, §1 SLBI), and other measures (*see eg* art. 35 SBLI, art. 36, §1 SLBI, *in light of* CA No. 35/2003 (Mar. 25, 2003) B.13.6, B.16.6, B.16.8; *compare also* art. 72, 4th clause SLBI, art. 75 SLBI and art. 60, 4th clause and 76, 2nd clause SBLI).

192 Art. 4 Cons. (*cf. supra* note 16).

193 Excepting the German Community (*but see* art. 130 Cons.), and some technical measures.

194 Art. 142 Cons.

195 Art. 129, §2 Cons.

196 Art. 4 Cons. The Chambers are divided in linguistic groups (art. 43 Cons.), which largely coincide with the two large Communities (*also see* art. 1 Law (July 3, 1971) dividing the legislative chambers into linguistic groups [...], BSG July 6, 1971 *juncto* art. 87*bis* (4) Electoral Code); some debate has emerged about the German representative, and the 'senators of right', but we will not further delve into that issue here.

197 CA No. 18/90 (May 23, 1990) B.16.2. If these measures undeniably have an impact on competence allocation, and the latter, for instance, now first and foremost protects the rights of Francophones in the Flemish Brussels periphery, the special majority requirement at first

53. Alarm bell procedure. The linguistic groups are also important for the so-called alarm bell procedure[198], which brings issues on the table of the Cabinet, which in general is required to decide by consensus[199]. Using this procedure, a legislative bill can be temporarily evacuated from the legislature, when a three-fourths majority of a linguistic group presents an alarm bell motion. This procedure has been used twice (1985 and 2010) and both times, the Legislature was dissolved before the procedure fully ended. The procedure confirms the bipolar nature of Belgian federalism. [200]

54. Equal representation. Next to the linguistic groups and the alarm bell procedure, the technique of equal representation has often been used, especially in the country's most important institutions. For instance, linguistic parity is strived for in the federal Cabinet[201], in the High Council for the Judiciary[202], in the Constitutional Court[203], in the other important courts and in the central administrative services (at least starting from the 'directors' level)[204].

55. A true danger: veto powers. There is a palpable danger that the aforementioned instruments for the protection of minorities (or more precisely: *a* minority)

– paradoxically – was a Flemish demand (Jan Clement, Taalvrijheid, bestuurstaal en minderheidsrechten. Het Belgisch model. Een constitutionele zoektocht naar de oorsprong van het territorialiteitsbeginsel en de minderheidsrechten in de bestuurstaalwetgeving 827 (2003)).

198 Art. 54 Cons. Some exceptions are made. A similar procedure has been inserted for the Brussels decision-making process (art. 31 SLBI), which is the case for some of the other guarantees as well (*eg* parity), but which I will not further discuss. *See supra* note 191.

199 The composition of the federal Cabinet is constitutionally enshrined: possibly excepting the Prime Minister, the Francophones and Dutch-speakers are equally represented there (art. 99 (2) Cons.). The consensus is a constitutional custom, which implies that when disagreement emerges in the Cabinet, either a Member can acquiesce in the majority's decision, or (s)he can resign. Alternatively, the whole federal Cabinet may resign (*eg* Alen & Muylle, *supra* note 14, at p. 339-340; Vande Lanotte & Goedertier, *supra* note 13, at p. 798; Uyttendaele, *supra* note 13, at p. 312-13).

200 Even if the dissuasive function of this procedure has been highly contested (*eg* Uyttendaele, *supra* note 13, at p. 304-07; Hendrik Vuye, *De alarmbel. Op zoek naar de juridische en de politieke draagwijdte van artikel 54 Grondwet: verzoeningsprocedure of grendel?*, 2008 CDPK 69, 86-87), it should be emphasized that the mere existence of the procedures confirms the *bipolar* nature of the Belgian federation (*ibid.* at p. 80). Moreover, although the German Community, for instance, is protected by other measures (*also see* Vande Lanotte & Goedertier, *supra* note 13, at p. 746-47), for instance the 'conflict of interest'-procedure, the latter only has dilatory effects (art. 142, §§2-3 Cons. *juncto* art. 32 Ordinary Law on Institutional Reform, *BSG* Aug. 15, 1980; *also see* CA No. 201/2004 (Dec. 15, 2004) B.4-B.5.2 (stressing the difference between conflict of interest and adjudication)).

201 *Cf.* Supra note 199.

202 Which plays a central role in the selection of most judges – art. 151, §2 Cons.

203 Art. 31 (*and* see art. 55) SLCC; *cf. eg* Uyttendaele, *supra* note 13, at p. 533-36

204 *Eg* Clement, *supra* note 197, at p. 825-26; Rimanque, *supra* note 140, at p. 67.

become *veto powers* landing any progressive forces into a stalemate[205]. It has often been pointed out that the lack of meaningful federal parties in Belgium in that sense also constitutes a problem[206]. Moreover, some have emphasized that this phenomenon takes on an extra dimension, in the sense that the 'parties' in dispute will be forced into a 'joint-decision' trap, that is, a situation where governments race to the bottom to find a lowest common denominator just to be able to make a decision[207].

56. A false danger: anomaly. It has further been pointed out that the protective measures are somewhat anomalous in the competence-structure of the federal state[208]. Uyttendaele for instance argues that, since this dualism is a residue of the unitary state, that these cannot be 'analyzed as actual rules regarding the functioning of a federal State'[209]. He seems to want to argue that they have little to do with Belgian *federalism.* I disagree. Notwithstanding some paradoxes and historical anomalies, federalization in Belgium cannot be historically, normatively, empirically or sensibly legally uncoupled from the protection accorded to the French at the federal level (and to the Dutch at the Brussels level). Of course I do not imply that federalism in Belgium cannot be conceived of differently than in its current form[210], but rather, I intend to convey that every further state reform has to take the 'large dualism' underlying the Belgium situation into account[211]. Even if it should be acknowledged that an assertion like

[205] *Eg* Alen, *supra* note 153, at p. 7-8 (with references); Wilfried Martens, De memoires: luctor et emergo 771 (2006); Popelier, *supra* note 45, at p. 129-30; Popelier, *supra* note 11, at p. 30-31; Robert Senelle, Kronieken van een Vlaamse Staatswording 74-76 (1999); *also see* Rimanque, *supra* note 140, at p. 67.

[206] *Eg* Alen, *supra* note 38, at p. 16; *see* Watts, *supra* note 187, at p. 75 *et seq.*; Nancy Bermeo, *Position paper* in Federalism: turning diversity, *supra* note 188, at p. 336 (with further political science references).

[207] *See* Fritz W. Scharpf, *The Joint-Decision Trap. Lessons from German Federalism and European Integration*, 66 Public Administration 239 (1988); *also see* Fritz W. Scharpf, *The Joint-Decision Trap Revisited*, 44 Journal of Common Market Studies 845 (2006) (adding a dimension of "non-political" decision making). *Compare* Johanne Poirier, *Layered Social Federalism: From the Myth of Exclusive competences to the categorical imperative of cooperation …* in Social Federalism, *supra* note 45, at p. 286-87 (arguing that when competences would become more *shared*, the danger of this trap would be exacerbated in Belgium).

[208] *Eg* Uyttendaele, *supra* note 13, at p. 297-301, 372, 402; Plets, *supra* note 47, at p. 87-90.

[209] Uyttendaele, *supra* note 13, at p. 317-18.

[210] *Eg* Stefan Sottiaux, De Verenigde Staten van België 60 *et seq.* (2011); Johan Vande Lanotte, De Belgische Unie bestaat uit vier deelstaten (2011). *See generally* on this point Pas, *supra* note 127.

[211] Vande Lanotte & Goedertier, *supra* note 13, at p. 960; *cf.* Francis Delpérée, *Où va la Belgique*, 1982 JT 216 ('[e]very day, Belgium becomes a bit more of a dualist State').

this one, borders on taking a political stance[212], first, it is acknowledged that the protective measures are to a large extent conceived of as necessary in the current situation[213], and second, the *dualist* protective measures (which can constitute an overall balance) have legal repercussions which cannot be underestimated[214].

57. Centrifugality. This institutionalization of protective measures at the federal level cannot be seen apart from the *centrifugal origins* (of perhaps: nature) of Belgian federalism. It is probably the case that – *by and large* – the Flemish have sought more autonomy than the French-speaking part of Belgium (disregarding any considerations on Brussels, for a moment). In this sense, a 'fear' has emerged, which lies at the basis[215] of many of the aforementioned protective measures[216] and which ensures that debates about the proper institutionalization of federalism are generally of a very delicate nature[217].

---

[212] *Eg* TERZAKE (May 16, 2011), *Interview with Caroline Gennez*, available at http://www.deredactie.be/permalink/1.1025161; TERZAKE (May 26, 2011), *Interviews with Rudy Demotte and Kris Peeters*, available at http://www.deredactie.be/permalink/1.1032732 and http://www.deredactie.be/permalink/1.1032730 (on the respective "Francophone" and "Flemish" views on Regions and Communities in Belgium).

[213] *Eg* Hugues Dumont, Christian Franck & François Ost, *Belgitude et crise de l'Etat belge: de la boutade à la recherche d'une nouvelle citoyenneté* in BELGITUDE, *supra* note 126, at p. 263, 291; Wilfried Dewachter, *L'identité dualist de la société belge*, in *ibid.* at p. 133; Swenden, *supra* note 187, at p. 13 *et seq.*

[214] *See eg infra* note 218; *also see* Patrick van Ypersele, *Quelques réflexions "catastrophistes" sur les risques que comportent les divergences de contrôle en matière d'union économique et d'unité monétaire entre la Cour d'arbitrage et la Cour de Justice des Communautés Européennes*, in L'UNION ÉCONOMIQUE ET L'UNITÉ MONÉTAIRE EN BELGIQUE (Acts of the Study day of May 15, 1992) 121, 124 (Xavier Delgrange ed. 1993) (noticing that the centrifugal force underlying Belgian federalism is a relevant point of difference between the EMU as inserted in the SLIR and the EMU as consecrated in European law).

[215] It is at least one of the factors that play. It should on the other hand be emphasized that in *any* federation, an adherence to the federal leval should be either presupposed or protected, since cohesion is often presupposed to outweigh autonomy in a federation (ALEN, *supra* note 153, at p. 22 (relying on Mast); ALBERT V. DICEY, INTRODUCTION TO THE STUDY OF THE LAW OF THE CONSTITUTION 75 (8th ed. 1915) ('[t]hey must desire union, and must not desire unity') ; Dumont, Franck & Ost, *supra* note 213, at p. 288 (quoting 2 GEORGES BURDEAU, TRAITÉ DE SCIENCE POLITIQUE 118 (3d ed. 1980) (describing that a federal state needs 'un *esprit national* seul capable d'assurer la cohésion de l'ensemble' (*emphasis by Dumont, Frank & Ost*))).

[216] *Compare* (in Brussels, where the argument about the logic of fear can also be defended, although matters are more complex there) art. 5*bis-ter* SBLI (which mirror (*cf.* CA 35/2004 (Mar. 10, 2004) B.3.1) art. 16*bis-ter* SLIR).

[217] It has often been argued that the Flemish political class wants to further construe Belgium on a dualist basis, so as not to be 'outvoted' by two other (Wallonia / Brussels) federated entities which are primarily Francophone, whereas Francophones generally prefer building Belgium on the basis of the Regions, in which case Brussels should be conceived of as a full-fledged Region (Resolutions Fl. Parl., *Parl. Doc.* 1998-99, Nos. 1339-1343 (currently referred to as *The Flemish Resolutions of 1999*, where the Flemish wish is expressed to construe the Belgian federation on a dualist basis); *also see* the 'Octopus memorandum', attached to the

58. The drive: ad hoc pacification. It appears then that two aspects are distinctively ingrained in Belgian federalism. On the one hand, pacification in Belgium takes on a very important dimension. This is not only recognized institutionally, as described above, but is also reflected in the Constitutional Court's case law[218]. On the other hand, the different phases of institutional reform are by and large *ad hoc* pacifying answers to salient problems of the time, the result of which is that Belgium lacks a true *political (federal) project* of its own[219]. This assertion does not undermine the legal ingenuity of the different stages of institutional reform, but rather reflects a concrete reality, which Karel De Gucht aphorized as follows: 'Belgium is a permanent diplomatic conference'[220].

Flemish Government's government plan (*Parl. Doc.* Flemish Parl. 2009, No. 31/1, 107 *et seq.*). *Compare also* Providing trust, taking responsibility, *Parl. Doc.* Flemish Parl. SS 2004, No. 31/1, at p. 97-99 *with* Declaration of the Regional Politics of the Walloon Government (July 20, 2004), *Parl. Doc.* Walloon Parl. SS 2004, No. 10/1, at p. 37).

[218] This is the case in different ways: both directly (*eg* CA 18/90 (May 23, 1990) B.9.1-B.9.2 (on the 'Pacification Law'); CA 26/90 (July 14, 1990) 6.B.7-6.B.8, 7.B.2 (on European elections); CA No. 35/2003 (Mar. 25, 2003) B.13.4-B.13.5, B.14.2 (on the 2001 Special Law on State Reform); CA 35/2004 (Mar. 10, 2004) B.4.1-B.4.2 (on art. 5*bis-ter* SBLI) (granting the (special) legislature a large margin of appreciation), or indirectly (*eg* as principled exclusivity of competences is understood as conflict-avoiding competence structure, built to pacify; *cf.* Report (Cerexhe & Erdman), *Parl. Doc.* Senate, 1988 SS, No. 405/2, at p. 28).

[219] *Eg* Alen, *supra* note 38, at p. 13-14; FRANK INGELAERE *et al.*, DE BEVOEGDHEIDSVERDELING IN HET FEDERALE BELGIË. LAMBERTMONT: DE STAATSHERVORMING VAN 2001 at p. 283-84 (2002); *also see* Feyen, *supra* note 169, at p. 54 *et seq.* (explaining how it is even hard to *reconstruct* a theory of federalism for Belgium). Remarkable in this regard, is the accusation of Martens – a former Belgian PM, during the 1980 and 1988 reforms –, that there is an increasing 'lack of vision and coherence' pertaining to a federal project (MARTENS, *supra* note 205, at p. 783); Popelier & Sinardet, *supra* note 11, at p. 31.

[220] Isabel Albers, '*Bestuurbaarheid van België is fundamenteel probleem*' (Karel de Gucht interview) DE STANDAARD Feb. 2, 2009. Even if this aphorism is often used by Flemish nationalists in their separatist discourse, I try to employ it more 'neutrally', to characterize – what I above referred to as – the confederalist mode of decision-making at the federal level. That is why I take no interest in the second part of the quote ('and this ever becomes worse'). *See* Wouter Pas, *Confederale elementen in de Belgische federatie*, 2009 TBP 67. This does not mean that no criticism has been elaborated in this regard, however, for instance by constitutional scholars, *eg* Karel Rimanque, *De nieuwe kleren van de Keizer. Over schijn en werkelijkheid in de Staatshervorming*, 1984-85 RW 641, 647.

2.3 The Constitutional Court situated in the Belgian federal system

59. From Court of Arbitration to Constitutional Court. The Court of Arbitration, when established in the early 1980s, was conceived of primarily as a sort of moderator in this metaphorical conference.

The Court of Arbitration's existence was enshrined in the Constitution in 1980[221]. From its first ruling in 1985 up till 1989, it was primarily governed by a (regular, thus not special) law[222]. The law in several senses reflected the limited scope of the Court's review: for instance, only 'institutional petitioners' could directly bring a case before the Court at that time (individuals had no standing). Before, in the period from the First State Reform (1970) up till the Court's first judgment, conflicts of competence were to be (theoretically) referred to a (never established) 'section competence conflicts' within the Council of State or to the Legislative Chambers, depending on the case.[223] However, since the need for an actual arbitrator became all the more pressing in 1980, when more competences were conferred to the federate entities, the Court's establishment was deemed necessary. It is within this context that we have to situate the Court's former name: the Court of Arbitration[224].

Accordingly, initially, the Court was competent to decide conflicts of competence (as it still does). Throughout the years, however, its jurisdiction has gradually expanded. In 1988, it became competent to review laws in terms of their conformity to the principle of equality (and article 24 of the Constitution)[225];

---

221 *BSG* July 20, 1980.

222 *Ie* Law (June 28, 1983) regarding the establishment, competence and functioning of the Court of Arbitration (BSG July 8, 1983, with an *errandum* on July 28, 1983).

223 *See* Law (July 3, 1971), *BSG* July 6, 1971 and art. 28 Regular Law (Aug. 9, 1980) on Institutional Reform, *BSG* Aug. 15, 1980.

224 'Only [the Court] renders coexistence of Communities and Regions within the State possible' (Francis Delpérée & François Tulkens, *La création de la Cour d'arbitrage*, in La Cour d'arbitrage. Actualité et perspectives 15, 41 (Francis Delpérée ed. 1988). *Adde* Report (Suykerbuik & Van Cauwenberghe, *Parl. Doc.* Chamber 1979 SS, No. 10-9/4°, at p. 3 and *Integral Report* Senate (July 28, 1980), No. 87, at p. 2642). On the name, *see* the discussion in *Parl. Doc.* Chamber, 1979 SS, No. 10-9/1°, 2°, 4°, where Prime Minister Martens confirmed that it was not the intention to establish a full-fledged constitutional court (*Integral Report* Senate (July 29, 1980), No. 88, at p. 2652), which was deemed 'essential' (*Integral Report* Senate (July 29, 1980), No. 87, at p. 2641); *see* Velaers, Van Arbitragehof..., *supra* note 13, at p. 92-94.

225 *Cf.* SLCC, which at the time was the Special Law (Jan. 6, 1989) on the Court of Arbitration, BSG Jan. 7, 1989. Importantly, from hence on, natural and legal persons could directly petition for annulment (*cf.* art. 2 SLCC).

in 2003, the Court's jurisprudential expansion of its competences into a (quasi-) full-fledged constitutional court was expressly confirmed[226] and finally, in 2007, its name was adjusted in this sense: as of now the Constitution provides that for the whole of Belgium, one Constitutional Court exists[227].

60. The equality test: broad but not all-encompassing. Some important qualifications must be added, however. Surely, the Court has seriously expanded its jurisdiction, but it still does not guarantee enforcement of the entire Constitution. It works often *via* the articles 10 and 11 of the Constitution, and as such has accorded itself quite a bit of leeway to decide upon the extent of its proper jurisdiction.

In the *Biorim* case[228] the Court was inspired by the ECtHR in elaborating its *equality test*. As the refrain went then: 'the constitutional rules of equality of Belgians before the law and of non-discrimination do not exclude that a distinction in treatment is instituted according to certain categories of persons, insofar as there is an objective and reasonable justification for the criterion of distinction. The existence of such a justification must be assessed with reference to the goal and the consequences of the norm [...]; the principle of equality is violated when it is established that the deployed means are reasonably

[226] Because the Court – when it for instance wanted to review a measure in terms of freedom of expression (art. 19 and 25 Cons.; *also* art. 10 ECHR) – had to find a way to establish a distinction between two categories of persons (equality review), which sometimes led to artificial reasoning (*cf.* Explanatory Memo, *Parl. Doc.* Senate 2000-01, No. 2-897/1, at p. 2), the Special Legislature decided to (formally) expand the Constitutional Court (and avoid any detours) by allowing a direct review in terms of the rights of Title II, and art. 170, 172 and 191 Cons. A direct review of norms in light of European provisions, however, was not accepted at that time (even if there had been some on-and-off debate about inserting a provision in to the Constitution (art. 32*bis*) referring to the ECHR earlier – *see* Jan Theunis & Arne Vandaele, *De (geplande) wijzigingen inzake de bevoegdheid en de werking van het Arbitragehof* in De Vijfde Staatshervorming van 2001, *supra* note 46, at p. 279 at p. 288-89, 301-304 (André Alen ed. 2002); *also see* Pieter Vanden Heede & Geert Goedertier, *De doorwerking van het internationaal recht in de rechtspraak van het Arbitragehof*, in Doorwerking van internationaal recht in de Belgische Rechtsorde 239, 244-47 (Jan Wouters & Dries Van Eeckhoutte eds. 2006)). However, regarding European law – although art. 3, §2 SLCC in 1989 already established the term to bring annulment proceedings against laws consenting to treaties was shortened (60 days instead of three months) – the 2003 modification brought one further limitation to the Constitutional Court's review powers in preliminary proceedings: thence on, laws consenting to constitutive treaties regarding the European Union or the ECHR and its Protocols, could no longer be reviewed in these proceedings (art. 26, §1*bis* SLCC).

[227] Art. 142 Cons., as altered by the Constitutional Revision of May 7, 2007, BSG May 8, 2007 (with an *errandum* on Oct. 31, 2007). Judgments predating No. 73/2007 (May 10, 2007), accordingly will be cited by referring to CA (Court of Arbitration). Judgments since then, will use CC (Constitutional Court); *cf.* Report (Collas), *Parl. Doc.* Senate 2007-08, No. 4-514/3.

[228] CA No. 23/89 (Oct. 13, 1989) B.1.3.

disproportionate to the purported goal'. This definition has been refined over the years: for instance 'of Belgians' is exsected now, it is one *principle* of equality and non-discrimination, and next to the goal and consequences, one has to take into account the general principles of the Belgian legal order ('the nature of the principles valid at hand'), but the idea by and large remains the same. Well, at least, if 'idea' is conceived of as *expansion* of jurisdiction. Accordingly, whereas in *Biorim*[229] the Court still only allowed a protection of 'the enjoyment of all rights accorded [...]'[230], it expanded this quite quickly to rights and liberties in international treaties *read together* with the articles 10 and 11 of the Constitution.[231] At that time, treaties had to be 'self-executing', but nowadays, this is not a requirement anymore[232]. Moreover, 'rights and liberties' were interpreted very widely, so as to encompass EU Directives as well[233] and when treaty provisions protect rights analogous to those enshrined in Title II of the Constitution, the detour via articles 10 and 11 of the Constitution is not necessary anymore since 2004[234]. In the meantime, the Court also made itself competent to review articles 10 and 11 of the Constitution together with (certain) general principles of law[235]. This short summary of course lacks depth and width to be really informative, but merely purports to show, first, how the Court expanded its own jurisdiction in equality jurisdiction (by expanding the conditions of its application), sometimes going very far[236], second, how the Court has not eschewed looking to supranational law – which sets the stage for further investigations in Chapter 4 – and third, that the Court has indeed quite some leeway when interpreting the confines of its own jurisdiction – an issue I will further elaborate.

---

229 *Ibid.* B.1.2.

230 Where a (silent) *in the Constitution* should be added.

231 CA No. 18/90 (May 23, 1990) B.11.3.

232 Since CA No. 41/2002 (Feb. 20, 2002) (*compare* No. 51/94 (June 29, 1994) B.5.6).

233 *Eg* No. 7/95 (Feb. 2, 1995) B.5.1 *et seq.*; *but see* No. 94/2003 (July 2, 2003) B.36.3 and B.38; *but compare* CC No. 144/2012 (Nov. 22, 2012) B.9.3 (confining the breadth of its review powers, in comparison with the CoS in light of European requirements) and B.13 (European law widening the Court's jurisdiction in this regard) – *cf.* Hervé Bribosia, *Applicabilité direct et primauté des traités internationaux et du droit communautaire. Réflexions générales sur le point de vue de l'ordre juridique belge*, 1996 Belgisch Tijdschrift voor internationaal recht 32, 72.

234 No. 136/2004 (July 22, 2004) B.5.3.

235 No. 72/92 (Nov. 18, 1992).

236 *Eg* CC No. 29/2010 (Mar. 18, 2010) B.5.3 ('the Court can review whether the legislature has abided by its international obligations as they stem from the [...] Directive').

This leeway is obviously also present in the substance of equality review. True, the equality test has often been thought of to consist of several prongs[237]. First, in its comparability prong, the Court establishes whether a pertinent comparison between different categories is possible[238]. In the goal prong, sometimes also referred to as the non-arbitrariness prong, the Court assesses whether the distinction created in the legislation strives for a sufficiently justified goal[239]. Furthermore, the Court ensures that the distinction relies on objective factors, and it reviews whether the criterion or criteria of distinction are pertinent or adequate to reach the set goals (suitability prong / adequacy prong)[240]. Finally, during proportionality review, the Court weighs the different legal interest in play, taking both the goal and the consequences of the legislation into account. Formerly, the Court generally did not apply a 'least-restrictive means'-test, as the *Biorim* case shows. However, nowadays, it does so in some cases, certainly when fundamental rights are at stake[241]. Nonetheless, it still recognizes, from time to time, the need for judicial restraint, and is not entirely unambiguous on the matter[242]. Accordingly, the there is leeway in the intensity of the text. Moreover, it could be argued, in particular because the prongs have not always been deployed as such, that they indeed are post-hoc rationalizations trying to attenuate (or even to reify) the 'empty' character of equality review.

Next to ambiguity over the intensity of the test, and the best representation of how it is conducted, there has also been quite some debate over the breadth of the test. In that sense, it could be doubted whether the Court is indeed a full-fledged Constitutional Court. Without wanting to elaborate too far on this issue, it should be noted that the Court apparently cannot review *all* Constitutional provisions. Whereas it declared itself competent to review norms in light of article 144 in conjunction with articles 10 and 11 of the Constitution so as to establish whether a right was political or civil in nature[243], in light of article 63 *juncto* articles 10 and 11 of the Constitution so as to exert control over

[237] *Eg* Jan Theunis, *Het Gelijkheidsbeginsel. Juridisch interpretatiekader, met bijzondere aandacht voor 'corrigerende ongelijkheden' en doorwerking in private rechtsverhoudingen* in Publiekrecht. De doorwerking van publiekrecht in het privaatrecht 129, 135-146 (1997).

[238] *Eg* CC No. 60/2007 (Apr. 18, 2007) B.2.3; CA 144/2003 (Nov. 5, 2003) B.5.3; CA No. 76/92 (Nov. 18, 1992) B.3; *compare eg* CA No. 69/2000 (June 14, 2000) B.3.2 (seemingly mixing different prongs).

[239] *Eg* CA No. 138/2002 (Oct. 2, 2002) (where the forbidden goal was to interfere in pending cases).

[240] *Eg* CA No. 140/2001 (Nov. 6, 2001) B.6-B.7; No. 55/2011 (Apr. 6, 2011) B.7.2.

[241] *See* already No. 74/92 (Nov. 18, 1992) B.3.5-B.3.6, B.3.8.

[242] *See eg* CC No. 81/2011 (May 18, 2011) B.4.5.

[243] CA No. 14/97 (Mar. 18, 1997).

the construal of an electoral district[244], in light of articles 116 and 136 juncto articles 10 and 11 of the Constitution[245], in light of articles 41 and 162 juncto articles 10 and 11 of the Constitution to ensure that provincial interests remain with the provinces[246], or in light of article 151 juncto articles 10 and 11 of the Constitution to scrutinize the public prosecutor's discretionary powers[247], the Court is neither competent to either *directly* review in light of articles of the Constitutions not mentioned in the its competence attribution (article 142 of the Constitution), nor can it employ the articles 10 and 11 of the Constitution to review *all* articles of the Constitution. For instance, it is generally not believed to be competent to check how a legislative norm came about[248]. Even if apparently, the relationship with articles 10 and 11 of the Constitution was not invoked[249], the Court found itself incompetent to review norms in light of the constitutional revision procedure[250]. This, on the other hand, does not mean that the Court cannot review some of these provisions at all: some of them can be construed *as* rules governing the allocation of competences, for which it is competent[251]. Next to that, the Court sometimes relies on the (deeply unpredictable) comparability test[252] to exclude some reviews[253]. Whereas, when fundamental rights at in play, the Court does not generally pay a whole lot of attention to the comparability[254], it does tend to pay increasing attention to comparability in other cases[255]. Maybe some stable doctrine of comparability will emerge in the coming years, but what becomes clear from the aforementioned picture, is that the Court has a lot of leeway and faces limited jurisdictional and doctrinal constraint.

244 CA No. 30/2003 (Feb. 26, 2003).

245 CA No. 35/2003 (Mar. 25, 2003).

246 CA No. 173/2004 (Nov. 3, 2004).

247 CA No. 182/2004 (Nov. 16, 2004).

248 No. 35/2003 (Mar. 25, 2003) B.2.2 ('in principle'); *but compare* No. 177/2005 (Dec. 7, 2005) B.17.4 and No. 144/2012 (Nov. 22, 2012) B.13. *Also see* David Keyaerts, *De Europeanisering van het Belgische Staatsrecht* in 3 Leuvense Staatsrechtelijke Standpunten 3, *supra* note 67, p. 47, at p. 69 *et seq.*

249 CC No. 54/2009 (Mar. 19, 2009) A.2.1.

250 *Ibid.* B.8 (on art. 195 Cons.).

251 *See eg* CC No. 8/2011 (Jan. 27, 2011) B.9.2 (on art. 160 Cons. being such a rule; it would seem hard to call upon this article in the framework of art. 10-11 Cons.)

252 *Cf. infra* notes 694-695.

253 *Eg* CC No. 63/2010 (May 27, 2010) B.3-B.4.

254 *Eg* CC No. 142/2009 (Sep. 17, 2009) B.3 (the comparable category becomes the *abstract* idea of persons for whom the guarantee is indeed upheld) or even more clearly, *see* No. 186/2011 (Dec. 8, 2011) B.4 *juncto* B.15.

255 For other examples, *see* Vande Lanotte & Goedertier, *supra* note 13, at p. 357-61.

61. Competence and rights jurisdiction. In general, the Court's review has been divided into two categories. In its *competence* jurisdiction, the Court checks whether legislative measures[256] violate 'the rules established by or in virtue of the Constitution to determine to distinct competences of the State, the Communities and the Regions'[257] (briefly: rules allocating competences). In its *rights* jurisdiction, the Court ensures that legislative measures do not violate 'title II "The Belgians and their Rights" and the articles 170, 172 and 191 of the Constitution'[258]. The majority of the Court's docket is made up out of rights jurisdiction cases[259]. We already discussed the large contours of this jurisdiction above, in the context of the articles 10 and 11 of the Constitution. Our focus in the next chapters lies primarily on competence jurisdiction. However, one of the reasons why we could not pass over rights jurisdiction in silence is because of a certain sense of entanglement of both jurisdictional categories.

First, the categorization is not perfectly reflected in the legal texts. Accordingly, article 142 of the Constitution mentions three categories of review. Notwithstanding these categories, which can by and large be explained historically, article 1 of the Special Law on the Constitutional – the relevant article pertaining to annulment proceedings – does distinguish between the two. Article 26 of that Special Law – the relevant article for preliminary references to the Court – however, again distinguishes between three: next to the categories of article 1, *ie* competence jurisdiction and rights jurisdiction, it adds the possibility for the Court to adjudicate upon conflicts between legislative measures which

[256] These are not only laws, decrees and ordinances (*cf.* SLCC), but also special majority laws (*cf. supra* note 22) or decrees (*eg* CA No. 7/96 (Jan. 18, 1996)), "laws" adopted during the wars (CA No. 115/99 (Nov. 10, 1999)), decrees by the *CoCoF* (*cf. supra* note 182), and – in *substance* – laws assenting to international treaties (CA No. 12/94 (Feb. 3, 1994)) and cooperation agreements amongst federated entities (CA No. 17/94 (Mar. 3, 1994)) or laws validating legislative delegations (*eg* No. 6/99 (Jan. 20, 1999)). Arguably, also ordinances by the Joint Community Commission can be reviewed (Storme, *supra* note 142, at p. 313-14, with references). *Also see* CA No. 168/2006 (Nov. 8, 2006), B.1 (Decrees by National Congress) and CC No. 126/2008 (Sep. 1, 2008) B.6 (laws referring to executive decisions). *Compare* CA No. 10/92 (Feb. 13, 1992) B.3 (even if the Court can sanction lacunaes in legislation, it does not have jurisdiction to rule upon 'implicit refusals' to legislate). Although it is principally incompetent to review the relationship between the legislative and the executive branch (*eg* CC No. 71/2011 (May 12, 2011), B.9; *also see* No. 10/2009 (Jan. 15, 2009) B.2.3), it has developed a more or less sophisticated jurisprudence on so-called legislative delegations, *see* Alen & Muylle, *supra* note 14, at p. 388 *et seq.*; *also see* Vande Lanotte & Goedertier, *supra* note 13, p. 1193-97 (regarding taxes); *compare* Stef Feyen, *Het Hof van Cassatie en het Grondwettelijk Hof op weg naar een nieuw conflict*, 2012 RW 1358.

[257] Art. 1, 1° (annulment) and art. 26, §1, 1° (preliminary references) SLCC.

[258] Art. 1, 2° (annulment) and art. 26, §1, 3° (preliminary references) SLCC.

[259] Up till April 2011, approximately 12,5 percent of the final judgments directly involved division of competences (395 out of the 3130: 12,6%).

do not imply an excess of competences[260]. The *travaux préparatoires* on this article are however somewhat sketchy[261], which is not surprising, in light of an important Court of Cassation Judgment[262] rendered on the issue of norm conflicts without excess of competence.[263] Up till now, the Court has not yet relied on this 'third' jurisdictional ground to adjudicate any cases[264]. Indirectly, it has been deemed relevant in the context of the principle of territorial exclusivity, but we will not revisit the issue explicitly.

62. Rights and competence jurisdiction: overlap and interference. Furthermore, the fields of jurisdiction intertwine in the case law in different sense. Admittedly, the Court itself relies on the jurisdictional *summa divisio*: for instance, established case law dictates that – in principle[265] – the Court first reviews measures in terms of their conformity to rules allocating competences[266]. Be that as it may, a myriad of entanglements and connections exists between rights and competence jurisdiction.

This particular issue of entanglement seems to have lost scholarly interest, however[267]. Most would accept that some form of entanglement exists, but it is also clear that entanglement does not mean acceptance of a *fully holistic* forms of reasoning[268]. It might be the case that scholars are not interested, in that

260 Art. 26, §1, 2° SLCC.

261 As are the professorial opinions, added in the Report Herman-Michielsens and Lallemand (quoted *infra* note 437).

262 (June 11, 1979) *Vandenplas,* 1978-79 Arresten van het Hof van Cassatie 1992 (with a conclusion by A-G Lenaerts).

263 *See* the Senate answer in the preliminary proceeding in 1981-82 RW 103; *cf. Parl. Doc.* Senate 1980-81, No. 631/1. *Also see* Cass. (Mar. 30, 1981) *Van Hoet* 1981-82 RW 104 *juncto* Cass. (Feb. 8, 1982) *Van Hoet (final)* 1982-83 RW 919 (both with case note by Paul Van Orshoven). More elaborately on this issue, *see* Bribosia & Van Boxstael, *supra* note 13, at p. 68-70; Storme, *supra* note 142, at p. 303-22; Marc Uyttendaele, Précis de droit constitutionnel belge. Regards sur un système institutionnel paradoxal 983-85 (3[d] ed. 2005); Velaers, Het Arbitragehof, *supra* note 54, at p. 25-60 (all with further references).

264 *But compare* No. 26 (Oct. 21, 1986) 1.B.1; *compare* Report (Lallemand-Baert), *Parl. Doc.* Senate 1988-89, No. 483/2, at p. 51-52 (on why it was not removed from the SLCC in 1988).

265 Sometimes exceptions are made, often without any explanation (*eg* CC 71/2011 (May 12, 2011)).

266 *Eg* CC 50/2011 (Apr. 6, 2011) B.6.2.4-B.7.

267 However, from 1985 up till 1989, when the Court could only review legislative measures in terms of the rules allocating competences, many scholars noted that the Court also relied on other provisions of the Constitution, and accordingly expanded its review powers (*eg* Peeters, *supra* note 38, at p. 204-13).

268 For an example, *see* CC No. 23/2009 (Feb. 18, 2009) B.6-B.7.2 (a violation of the art. 10, 11, 27, 128 and 130 *juncto* art. 5, §1 SLIR and the principle of linguistic equal representation as it follows from article 99 (2) Cons. were invoked, but the Court did not follow the holistic logic here; *compare infra* note 708).

some interconnections are rather obvious, and from a relational perspective unproblematic[269]: one can think then about articles which function as standards for review, both in terms of rights jurisdiction, as in terms of competence jurisdiction. For example, next to ensuring a principle of fiscal equality and legality in the exercise of any taxing power, article 170 of the Constitution also clearly[270] imposes a rule governing competence allocation[271]. However, less obvious, and more interesting are the connections that are made in the argumentative structure of the Court's jurisprudence. We have already mentioned one, viz. that *pacification* (understood as a corollary of Belgian federalism) can serve as a legitimate justification in the multi-tiered equality test the Court has elaborated to review compatibility with articles 10 and 11 of the Constitution[272]. This is an issue that plays an important role in what follows. A multitude of other (less obvious) examples could be discussed, some more relevant to our purpose than others[273]. Interesting for us is for instance the

---

[269] This of course presupposes an 'article' to be the relevant unit of analysis for comparison in light of entanglement. Even if this presupposition can easily be undermined, it nonetheless remains the case that the 'interconnection', by a legal audience, can be thought of as 'obvious'.

[270] To be precise: 'clearly' should be viewed in light of the Constitutional Court's jurisprudence or in light of the purpose of the provision at hand. Indeed, it is important to underscore that – *generally* (*compare* art. 30*bis* SLCC (on forms of cooperation) and the aforementioned art. 16*bis-ter* SLIR or art. 5*bis-ter* SBLI (which according to some authors are rules allocation the division of competences (*eg* Vande Lanotte & Goedertier, *supra* note 13, at p. 1457-58; *also see* Alen & Muylle, *supra* note 14, at p. 64-65), for which some support can be found in case law (*eg* CC No. 124/2010 (Oct. 28, 2010) *esp.* B.12 – even if the case as a whole does not follow the logic of the normal competence jurisdiction)) it is the Court itself that determines what is to be understood under 'rules established by or in virtue of the Constitution for determining the distinct competences of the State, the Communities and the Regions'.

[271] It stipulates that (§2) 'a tax for the community or the region can only be levied by (decree or ordinance). The law stipulates vis-à-vis these taxes the exceptions of which the necessity is apparent'. Accordingly, here the primacy of the fiscal law over the fiscal decree is established (*also see infra* note 537).

[272] *See esp. supra* note 218.

[273] Amongst the less relevant ones, these might come to mind as examples:

- Whereas the Court – in principle – cannot review *executive* measures under its equality jurisdiction, it has done so in light of its competence jurisdiction (possibly relying on art. 159 Cons.). Accordingly, the Court reviewed a rule governing the allocation of competences of an executive nature in light of the principle of equality, or more precisely, as regards the legality of the measure determining the general principles of the administrative and pecuniary statute of civil servants (CA No 31/95 (Apr. 4, 1995) B.3.3-B.3.5 *et seq.*; No. 45/95 (June 6, 1995) B.4.2-B.4.6; *also see* No. 39/97 (July 14, 1997) B.4.4.1-B.5);
- Sometimes, it depends on the interpretation of a law, whether a provision infringes upon the principle of equality, or upon the rules governing the allocation of competences (*eg* CC No. 3/2010 (Jan. 20, 2010) B.17 *et seq.*);
- In Judgment 41/2010 (Apr. 29, 2010) B.3-B.4, the Court reformulated a preliminary reference in equality jurisdiction (on the compatibility of art. 92, § 2 SLIR with art. 10-

following connection: whereas freedom of trade, is generally recognized by the *d'Allarde* Decree, which can be invoked before the Court read together with the articles 10 and 11 of the Constitution, the Court has also accepted reliance on (a connection between 10 and 11 Constitution and) article 6, §1, VI (3) of the SLIR (the EMU-provision)[274].

The most important entanglement can be described as follows: the Court will not find different regulations comparable or unequal by themselves insofar as they are established by autonomous legislatures in the federal system[275]. Sometimes, the Court reached this point in another way[276], arguing that the Court cannot review constitutional provisions themselves: it has to respect the choices made in the Constitution. But stating that is stating the obvious, and the relevant question of course becomes twofold: first, what measure of discretion (or autonomy) has to be accorded to the federated entities? Next to that, to which extent does the Court have to take considerations of institutional competence into account, or in other words, to which extent does it have to respect the compromises made in institutional matters? Generally, it will respect the political compromise as far as possible, both from the viewpoint of discretion[277], as from the viewpoint of judicial deference[278]. However, the issue does open up room for debate and

11 Cons.) to a question regarding hte allocation of competences (then again, however, reviewing under the EMU-provision).

274 *Eg* No. 6/96 (Jan. 18, 1996) (where no connection was made with 10-11 Cons.: *cf. infra* on EMU); No. 2/2009 (Jan. 15, 2009) *esp.* B.22.1 (implicitly, in language) or No. 9/2011 (Jan. 27, 2011) B.26.1 *et seq.* (where such a connection was made); *compare* 29/2010 (Mar. 18, 2010) B.6.3 (the *d'Allarde* Decree cannot stand on its own as a reference norm)). For how these points are, or at least could be deemed relevant, *see infra* No. 111.

275 This is established jurisprudence (*eg* 37/92 (May 7, 1992) B.3), even if it has been formulated differently from time to time (*compare eg* CC 111/2007 (July 26, 2007) B.12-B.13 *with* CC No. 3/2010 (Jan. 20, 2010) B.26).

276 There might however be legal consequences ensuing from this distinct approach: since, for instance, the Constitution did not determine anything explicitly about regional competences (art. 39 Cons.), the review of the Fifth State Reform (*cf.* Nos. 35/2003 and 35/2004) had to rely on an explicit justification (not as such enshrined in the constitutional text), instead of on a verdict of non-comparability. It is even unclear in light of recent case-law whether the doctrinal structure (*ie* the verdict of non-comparability when Constitutional choices are involved) can be upheld (*eg* No. 63/2010 (May 27, 2010) B.3-B.4 (preliminary ruling on articles 68-69 SLIR).

277 *Eg* No. 35/2003 (Mar. 25, 2003) B.21.2-B.21.3 (on the distinct treatment of Brussels vis-à-vis its municaplity competences).

278 *But see* No. 30/2003 (Feb. 26, 2003) and No. 73/2003 (May 26, 2003) (both on Brussels-Hal-Vilvorde, an issue that is now solved (*see further* Velaers, *supra* note 10); *compare* ECtHR Case No. 9267/81 (Mar. 2, 1987) *Mathieu-Mohin Clerfayt*, para 57) and No. 35/2003 (Mar. 25, 2003) (where some provisions regarding Brussels were nonetheless invalidated)). *Also see* Karel Rimanque, *De paradoxale werking van het gelijkheidsbeginsel*, 1992-93 RW 1, 14.

interpretation, and such a debate might have important consequences, not only in general[279], but also with regard to European law. For as we will see further on, the interaction between these fields of jurisdiction can cause tensions, in particular when noticing that European law provisions, insofar as they can exert an influence on constitutional jurisprudence, often enter into the argumentative structure of the Court via its *rights* jurisdiction[280].

[279] For another example in the same regard, *see* Feyen, *supra* note 190, Nos. 31 *et seq.*
[280] For further reflection and implications, *see infra* No. 116 *et seq.*

3.

The Belgian Constitutional Court and federalism

3.1 Different ways of examining (case-)law

63. General examination. Constitutional Court Judge André Alen explains:

> [d]uring the first years, the Court of Arbitration has laid the foundations for the allocation of competences [case law], which has resulted in a wide conception of the competences of Communities and Regions, without however, when necessary, losing track of the unity of policy, and in the upholding of an exclusive territorial division of competences. These foundations were clearly affirmed in the subsequent phases and can as such be deemed to be "established jurisprudence"[281]

This general characterization of the first five years of Constitutional Court jurisprudence refers to three *tools* the Court has used during its first years, *ie* exclusivity, a broad interpretation of federated competences and the economic and monetary union which requires unity of policy from time to time. Alen further explains that in the 1989-2003 period, the Court, pursuant to some adaptations of the SLIR, relaxed its interpretation of implied competences and expanded the notion of the economic and monetary union, at the same time allowing for a limited 'deviation' from the rule of territoriality. Moreover, he notices how there has been a change of interpretation of the reserved competences, and how more competences were construed as "parallel". Since 2003, the most important evolutions were – again according to Alen – in the jurisprudence on telecommunication and radiodiffusion matters, where the Court decided that, although these competences resort under different legislatures, the principle of proportionality forces the legislatures to work together, at least when infrastructure is in question. Finally, he believes that the Court's recognition of the principle of federal loyalty might have some further effects on the future.[282]

This description seems to be an adequate general categorization of what had been happening in the Constitutional Court, at least up till the beginning of 2005. Afterwards, no real revolutions seem to have occurred. Perhaps the

---

[281] André Alen, *Twintig jaar grondwettigheidstoezicht op wetgevende normen. Krachtlijnen van de rechtspraak van het Arbitragehof van 1985 tot en met 2004*, in 20 JAAR ARBITRAGEHOF 5, 6 (André Alen ed. 2005).

[282] *Ibid.*, at p. 7-16. He was right about this, as evinced by the new institutional agreement of October 2011 (*supra* note 10), where it is decided that the Court may review legislation in terms of 'the principle of federal loyalty' (*ibid.* at p. 11).

growing tendency to refer to the European Court of Justice for preliminary rulings should be underscored. It can also be noted that in for instance in Case 202/2009[283], the Court allowed an alone-standing argument based on the principle of proportionality and federal loyalty, which seems to underscore Alen's point, even if the Court *generally* still does not read any other arguments into the principle of federal loyalty than proportionality requirements[284]. It could also be argued – although it might be too early to call this assertion grounded – that the Court is confronted with an ever more assertive Flemish Government in terms of a wide interpretation of its own competences[285], which could result in a new interpretation of implied competences. The latter might be somewhat a-historic though[286]. Even so, because of a limited distance, it is harder to describe a general evolution of the case law after 2005.

At the same time, explaining case law from such a generalist perspective elides the required depth. More importantly even, it presumes, rather than explains, certain concepts and ways of thinking, such as the concept of "implied competence" or that of "economic and monetary union". These concepts require some sense of analytic examination in order to procure understanding.

64. Reframing of dogmatic analysis. However, characterizing the Court's jurisprudence more *analytically* poses serious dangers, at least when one construes analytic examination in the traditional (dogmatic) style. Even if some forms of modern dogmatics allow for a more *case by case* approach – an approach which comes closer to understanding competence case law than mere abstract concept analysis does[287] – an overemphasis on the particularities would elude any theory's aspirations of generality. We try to redeem (part of) that generality (methodologically) by reframing the arguments commonly figuring in dogmatic analysis as tools. Without this adaptation, generally, the analytical scheme easily pushes someone into the groping arms of dogmatics, which does not seem appropriate as an explanatory or predictive device, as we explained

---

283 (Dec. 23, 2009) B.12.1-B.17; *compare* CC No. 31/2010 (Mar. 30, 2010).

284 *Ibid.* B.17. *But compare infra* Ch. 3.3.3.

285 *Eg* the disputes about the Flemish Care insurance, the Flemish Habitational Code, the decree on land and buildings policy, … which are all discussed further on, but also, the establishment of administrative jurisdictions, or other interferences into the federal competence regarding the judicial order (*also see infra* note 598, *esp.* the reference to Vanpraet's contribution).

286 For the other arguments, I rely by and large on the 2004-2011 yearbooks of the Constitutional Court. The principle of mutual recognition deserved a special mention there too (*see* 2010 yearbook, at p. 29 *et seq.*), but we will discuss that principle further on (*infra* Nos. 86 and 110).

287 *Cf.* '[I]t is actually difficult to trace the boundaries between national and regional competences. Only experience, and case-by-case solutions may be clarifying' (Grégoire Brouhns, *Débats* (presided over by Jean-Paul Abraham) in L'UNION ÉCONOMIQUE, *supra* note 214, at p. 63).

above. Accordingly, we will try to explain how the Court can use different "doctrines", "principles", or what one could generally call arguments in its elaboration of the law in order to construe results which are commensurate with the overarching politico-legal necessities.

65. Other arguments. This, of course, does not mean that the tools we are describing here are the only arguments which are available to the Court, or which are important. Quite on the contrary: the Court does take other arguments into account, such as those relating to 'hierarchy of norms', purely factual elements, and not in the least, what I have called 'rule of law'-values (coherence, precedent, or a ('clear') text – as explained below). One specific 'rule of law'-value I will not further elaborate in the context of European law, but which seems quite important is the (clear) text of the "procedure" before the Court[288].

Accordingly, admissibility requirements can be construed as 'rule of law'-values. For instance, although the Court is not overly formalistic in this regard, non-institutional petitioners must have a sufficient (personal, legitimate, direct, actual) interest in having a norm annulled that prejudices them[289]. Now one could ask whether (the text imposing) this admissibility requirement truly constrains the Court. Is it not the case that this 'rule of law'-value admits of different interpretations?[290] More generally, is it not the case that other admissibility requirements similarly give the Court quite a bit of interpretative leeway: for instance, is it not the case that the Court – vis-à-vis the requirement that arguments and facts are formulated in the petition[291] – can exercise important discretion in the interpretation of exactly how well an argument must be formulated?[292] Or more drastically even, can't the Court just set aside admissibility requirements by raising *ex officio* arguments?[293] These questions can all be answered in the affirmative, which shows, first, that (the text imposing) admissibility requirements (as rule of law values) are not conclusively self-explanatory and, second, that they admit of being used as *tools* as well. Notwithstanding these important caveats, the text imposing (and principles underlying) admissibility

[288] Certainly for annulment proceedings, this could be construed as an instance of "clear text" constraint (*compare infra* notes 504-505).

[289] Art. 2, 2° and 5 SLCC; *see eg* Riet Leysen, *Het belang als ontvankelijkheidsvereiste in het beroep tot vernietiging voor het Arbitragehof* in 1 PRÉSENCE DU DROIT PUBLIC ET DES DROITS DE L'HOMME. MÉLANGES OFFERTS À JACQUES VELU 403 (1992).

[290] *Cf.* Rik Ryckeboer, *De belangvereiste bij beroepen tot vernietiging bij het Arbitragehof inzonderheid wat betreft het collectief belang van verenigingen zonder winstoogmerk* in 20 JAAR ARBITRAGEHOF, *supra* note 281, at p. 76.

[291] Art. 5-6 SLCC.

[292] Also in light of the rationale, *eg* CC No. 93/2008 (June 26, 2008) B.3.

[293] *See* art. 90 (2) SLCC; *eg* No. 140/2008 (Oct. 30, 2008) or No. 129/2011 (July 14, 2011).

requirements do have some constraining effect. For instance, the Court will deem itself to be "more or less" bound by the principle of judicial passivity (and the prohibition on *ultra petita* rulings[294]), which can sometimes turn into a very *imposing* rule of law value. "More or less" implies that escape routes are available – the most obvious one of which of course are *ex officio* arguments – but from the viewpoint of the self-understanding of the Court and its will to abide by the imposed 'rule of law'-values, it will not (or should not) – as a rule – easily (or without argument) set aside these constraints. "Set aside" might be a potentially deceptive use of language here, as the Court – for instance – has a textual basis[295] which does not prohibit different interpretations, nor forbids using it in light of a rather pragmatic (instrumentalizing) rationale. Accordingly, one could argue that even in instrumentalizing these (available) provisions, the Court indeed faithfully *follows* the 'rule of law'. But is the Court still really *bound* in that case? That question requires independent (jurisprudential) argument, which we refrain from offering here. Even so, what the aforementioned does show is, first that the distinction between 'rule of law'-values and pragmatic (*toolbox*) reasoning does not necessarily translate into a strict dichotomy, and thus allows for a dynamic construal of the case law of the Court. Next to that, and that was our point, it shows that someone who attempts to gain a full understanding of the interplay between freedom and constraint in Constitutional Court adjudication cannot suffice with rendering intelligible that interplay in light of topical 'federalism-related' arguments, but requires a broader understanding of that interplay in light of 'procedural' and other 'general' legal arguments (*eg* the hierarchy of norms, general legal principles, *et cet.*) as well. Our focus here, nonetheless, lies on 'federalism-related' arguments.

66. Hierarchy? It does not seem wise to impose a (dogmatic) hierarchy amongst the tools within the toolbox. That is not only the case because these are mostly principles, by nature prone to being weighed[296]. More fundamentally, the imposition of a rigid hierarchy within the toolbox would undermine the very idea that the arguments are tools. That the arguments function as tools does not impede that the Court adheres to a more or less basic (or perhaps even solid) argumentative structure throughout its reasoning in competence jurisdiction[297].

[294] *Eg* No. 8/2009 (Jan. 15, 2009) B.5.2.

[295] *Cf. supra* note 293.

[296] *Eg* RONALD DWORKIN, *supra* note 99, at p. 22-23.

[297] Per argument, this goes roughly as follows: elaboration of the contested measure (and its goal), statement of the relevant competence-allocating provision, exploring the latter's rationale, qualifying the measure either under or outside that competence heading, and often also checking whether there are repercussions in terms of different competences, in the latter case, mostly using the principle of proportionality or implied competences, sometimes even relying

The tool-like nature can be reflected within this structure, for instance by the variegating emphasis laid on different aspects or elements during the process of elaboration of constitutional argument. This emphasis can be explicit, or rather implied within the structure of the case as a whole. Ascertaining such an implied emphasis can sometimes be hard, as we need not accept *a priori* that what the Court says fully coincides with what it is doing[298]. On the other hand, when the Court does indeed diverge from the basic argumentative structure, this could be perceived as a clue that the Court is indeed reasoning in a tool-like nature. Hence, appearances of argumentative structural integrity (which could form the basis for a dogmatic hierarchization) notwithstanding, the idea of (dogmatic) hierarchy amongst tools cannot easily be squared with the instrumental nature of the Court's reasoning.

Be that as it may, we might distinguish between some *foundational* principles, and principles which are more *incidental* to competence jurisdiction. It could be argued that the principle of exclusivity and the principle of conferral are foundational within the Belgian scheme of competences. Next to that, some would proffer that (con)text, federal loyalty, EMU, proportionality and implied powers are more or less incidental principles in the toolbox. The distinction between foundational and incidental principles has no direct relationship, however, with a sense of hierarchy, understood as precedence in case of conflict of norms, or in another dogmatic sense. It rather has to do with frequency of occurence, chronology or logical priority in the (traditional) conceptual and argumentative structure, as is explained by different Belgian scholars in terms of rules and exceptions, principles and deviations, et cetera... Traditionally, for instance, it is thought that, when a Community adopts a decree that violates the principle of proportionality it will (chrono)logically, albeit not necessarily explicitly, be established first that the "power" first remained within the contours of the conferral and exclusivity so understood, but that the "exercise" of the power breached the allocation of competences. More generally, Belgium's traditional scholarship by and large accepts that exclusivity is a bedrock of the allocation of competences: generally it will describe (textual) arguments abnegating this exclusivity (such as article 170 of the Constitution, which institutes a "concurring competence") as exceptional in frequency of occurence. Succinctly: conventional Belgian scholarship seems to accept that the entire idea of Belgian federalism is duly premised on the basic principles that (1) the federated entities

on or distinguishing different cases.

298 I am loosely inspired here by Duncan Kennedy's exposition of the marxist concept of work (*supra* note 93), but it has been a central point of realist jurisprudence to emphasize the distinction between what a judge is saying and what he is (actually) doing.

have conferred competences and (2) that the general allocation of competences has tried to establish a system in which exclusivity reigns. Without these two premises, the elaboration of the so-called 'incidental principles' does not even seem to make sense.

However, as we will show further on, this distinction (between foundational and incidental) should strongly be relativized, especially with reference to the case law of the Constitutional Court. Although it might have its merits in general theories of federalism, one could consider abandoning it in the explanation of the case law of the Constitutional Court. Even so, be it without the full power of my conviction, and at best for general educational or organizational purposes, I have structured the rest of this chapter on the basis of the distinction, which – I hope – will have become somewhat spurious after reading the chapter.

3.2 "Foundational" principles

3.2.1 Conferral

67. Logic and the Constitutional Court's trinity. Principally, federated competences in Belgium are conferred competences[299]. Logic only seems to dictate that what has not been conferred, remains behind. The Court goes beyond logic in that it infers from this general principle, or when interpreting it, several interpretative principles or basic arguments pertaining to the different competences: amongst these figure the extensive interpretation of conferred competences and the strict interpretation of competence reservations. That at least is the view of traditional Belgian scholarship on Constitutional Court case law. As we will try to show, however, the guidance offered by these principles or basic arguments is very limited, sometimes because a strange disjunction has occurred between a/the rationale and the concrete implementation of the arguments in cases (thus reifying the argument, possibly concealing more than revealing, let alone explaining), at other times because the principles or basic arguments are not sufficiently determined, in particular with reference to their interaction with other arguments.

68. Extensive interpretation of conferral and homogenous competences. First, generally, without prejudice to possible 'exceptions', conferred competences must be interpreted extensively. Scholars mostly derive this principle from arguments made by the Court, such as the following one:

> [t]he constitution and the special legislature, unless they have determined otherwise, must be deemed to have attributed *full competence* to the communities and regions to adopt rules proper to their conferred competences, and this without prejudice to the possibility – if needed – of reliance on [implied competences][300].

---

[299] Art. 38-39 Cons. The conferral presupposes an Act of the Special Legislature or of the Constituant Assembly, *see eg* CoS Advice, *Parl. Doc.* Chamber 1986-87, No. 797/17, at p. 8 ('a law adopted by a normal majority cannot confer new competences to Community organs') and CoS Advice, *Parl. Doc.* Chamber 1985-86, No. 101/4, at p. 2.

[300] Established jurisprudence since CA No. 25 (June 26, 1986) III.B.1 (*see already* CA No. 8 (Jan. 22, 1986) III.(11).B.1; *also see* CA No. 7/85 (Dec. 20, 1985) III.6.B.1 (on the narrow interpretation of the commercial publicity competence)). For a recent confirmation, *see* (albeit without mentioning the implied competences) CC No. 50/2011 (Apr. 6, 2011) B.10.1. In more recent judgments (*but see already* CA No. 24/94 (Mar. 10, 1994) B.3 (on cultural patrimony) and CA No. 2/97 (Jan. 16, 1997) B.3.1 (without specification)), the Court often adds: 'unless stipulated otherwise, the special legislature has attributed the entire policy pertaining to the competences conferred to Communities and Regions' (*eg* CC No. 29/2011

Accordingly, the Court states that – as a rule – it will interpret conferred competences widely. Although this has often been accepted as a general principle – probably because the Court repeats it so every so often – the legal-dogmatic importance of it should be duly put in perspective. True, this principle constitutes a clear affirmation of the autonomy of the federated entities in Belgium, but it is not entirely clear what – in general – could be said to follow from such a principle. Its explanatory – and especially predictive power – is very limited indeed.

Some argue that the principle can indeed explain the case law, when it is not just conceived of as a corollary of the principle of conferral as such, but rather as the result of a *homogenous* conferral of competences[301]. Increasing homogeneity, so it has been argued, has indeed been the 'big picture'-rationale behind different phases of institutional reform. But at the same time, a quasi-numberless amount of times it has been argued that the Special Legislature has not reached that goal, owing to the fact that competences are still scattered over the patchwork that is the SLIR. The latter argument seems hard to deny (even if it could be argued that it is not the *scattering* by itself which is problematic, but rather its content[302]). The former argument is more complex to assess, as it depends on what we understand by 'rationale'. If it is to be interpreted in terms of an 'intention', it brings several psychological and philosophical connotations and concomitant difficulties to mind. Interpreting 'rationale' differently, will imply making or at least presupposing contentious hermeneutical and legal-philosophical judgments as well, again opening up an area for debate. Even if we try to sidestep these difficulties and approach the issue more phenomenologically, a first reading through the different *travaux préparatoires* of the 1988 State Reform[303] cannot help but to give the impression that two groups of children are playing a yes-no game over whether or not this reform will help to make the 'competence blocks' more internally coherent. Despite these apparent difficulties, those relying on a general argument about homogeneity (being able to explain case law) generally fail to address these issues. Therefore, it seems that the idea of homogeneity lacks a *general* explanatory potential, and adds little to the dogmatically quite empty statement that competences should be interpreted extensively.

(Feb. 24, 2011) B.4.3; CC No. 139/2012 (Nov. 14, 2012) B.4.2). A connection could be made in this regard to the wish to confer homogenous packages of competences (see *infra* this paragraph; *also see eg* CA No. 2/97 (Jan. 16, 1997) B.3.1). For some further references (up till 1997), see Velaers, De Grondwet en de Raad van State, *supra* note 13, at p. 269 n110.

301 *Eg* Bribosia & Van Boxstael, *supra* note 13, at p. 182 *et seq.*

302 *Cf. eg* Uyttendaele, *supra* note 13, at p. 422-23.

303 Chamber Bill 516 and Senate Bill 405.

Now one might wonder what it means when the Court indeed invokes the idea of homogenous competences, which it has admittedly done on several occasions: for instance, Regions have a 'homogenous packet of competences' in the area of registration taxes[304] or in the area of taxes on automatized leisure machines[305]. It could be the case that the 'homogenous packet of competence' is a mere synonym for 'full competence' or 'entire competence', and some authors seem to think it is[306]. Dogmatically or semantically, they might be right, although being right here does not seem to mean a whole lot, since the principle is empty, for what does 'fullness' or 'entirety' indeed imply? A more plausible explanation – however – would account for a difference in the use of language, and it will come as no surprise that symbolically one could at least argue that 'homogenous packet of competences' is stronger than (mere) 'entire policy'. The former 'magical' words in that regard could perhaps indeed have a meaning, not so much at the 'word-analytic' level, but rather from a symbolic angle. This seems to concur with the existing case law. It seems to us that the deployment of the stronger language (of homogeneity, instead of mere 'full competence') mostly serves to either defuse any interpretation imposed by *travaux préparatoires*, which is possibly ambiguous or contrary to the holding[307], or to be very strict vis-à-vis 'excesses' of competences, which could be interpreted as rather marginal[308]. Accordingly, the Court seems to use it as a rhetorical device (and thus a *tool*) to underscore an argument that requires reinforcement in the face of (strong) counter-arguments. Admittedly, the contention remains speculative, since only two cases have been adduced in evidence. Even so, an analysis such as the preceding one – going beyond classic dogmatic concepts and categories, and not eschewing the possibility of judicial politics – seems to have more explanatory power (although one could doubt whether it can really guide future cases).

69. Reservations. Next to that, according to traditional Belgian scholarship, it follows from the principle of conferral that an entity may not impinge upon

---

304 CA No. 45/2004 (Mar. 17, 2004) B.5.1.

305 CC No. 124/2008 (Sep. 1, 2008) B.8.3.

306 *Eg* Vande Lanotte & Goedertier, *supra* note 13, at p. 1005n3.

307 *Eg* CA No. 45/2004 (Mar. 17, 2004), B.4.1-B.5.2 (where the Court set aside an interpretation suggested in the *travaux* (distinguishing gifts from shares without counter-obligation) in favor of what it considered to be a more systematic interpretation of the legislation regarding registration taxes on gifts); *also see* CA No. 2/97 (Jan. 16, 1997) B.3.1 (on barge services).

308 *Eg* No. 124/2008); *but compare* CC No. 95/2010 (July 29, 2010) B.23.2 (suspension) and CC 124/2010 (Oct. 28, 2010) B.20.2 (annulment) (which nonetheless is a judgment (on the Flemish inspection of Francophone schools in the Brussels periphery, albeit on Flemish territory), in which the Court seems to speak from both sides of its mouth, probably because of the very sensitive *communautarian* problem it is called upon to solve here). On the latter *infra* note 190 and *infra* Nos. 86 and 104.

competences that are either expressly conferred upon other entities, or which remain with the federal state as residual powers[309].

Matters expressly reserved to other entities can take on two different configurations: they can be reserved by the Constitution[310], or by the Special Laws. Competences explicitly formulated as exceptions in the SLIR are manifold: examples include the exclusion of 'broadcasting federal government messages' from the broadcasting competence[311], the exclusion of sickness and invalidity insurance from the health policy competence[312], the exclusion of establishing product norms from the environmental competence[313], or the exclusion of employment law and social security from the economic competence[314]. Matters can also be exempted from a competence but at the same time conferred to a different federated entity, as is the case for monuments and landscapes[315]. Such a patchwork has given rise to names like 'partitioned exclusive competences'[316]. Even if this notion (distinguishing the competences from concurrent or parallel competences) might create insight from an educational perspective, it does not seem to offer a lot of guidance in concrete cases, not only because a lot will depend on the content of the particular competence allocation, but also because questions can arise as regards the adequacy of the distinct concepts deployed to capture the form of competence allocation. The 'qualification' of different *kinds* of competences is indeed often a matter of dispute. Even if there is consensus about a certain qualification at some point, it can turn out to be of a dynamic nature. Plets, for instance, argues that in the economic sphere, some

---

309 *Eg* CC No. 49/2011 (Apr. 6, 2011) B.8.1.

310 *Eg* article 127, §1, 2° Cons. makes the Communities competent in education (*'fully competent'*, moreover – cf. CA No. 8 (Jan. 22, 1986) III.(11).B.1), but it nonetheless reserves 'determining the beginning and the end of the duty to learn' (a), 'the minimal conditions for granting diplomas' (b) and the 'pension regulation' (c) to the federal government).

311 Art. 4, 6° SLIR.

312 Art. 5, §1, I, 1°, c) SLIR.

313 Art. 6, §1, II, (2) SLIR.

314 Art. 6, §1, VI, (6) 12° SLIR.

315 *See* art. 4, 4° and art. 6, §1, I, 7° SLIR.

316 *Eg* Alen & Muylle, *supra* note 14, at p. 398; Louis-Paul Suetens & Riet Leysen, *Staat, Gewesten en Gemeenschappen. De technieken van bevoegdheidsverdeling. De rol van het Arbitragehof*, in Staat, Gemeenschappen en Gewesten 45, 50-51 (Roger Blanpain *et al.* eds. 1989); Popelier, *supra* note 45, at p. 104-05; Vande Lanotte & Goedertier, *supra* note 13, at p. 967-68; Uyttendaele, *supra* note 13, at p. 105 and 407. The Court has nonetheless accepted this name in the case of federal tariff policies in energy matters (CC No. 89/2012 (July 12, 2012) B.4.2, applying it to the (unforeseen) tariffs charged by distribution/transmission system operators to electricity producers, *because* these tariffs influence the price paid by the customer (B.4.3)).

'parallel' competences have become 'limited concurring' competences[317]. The latter assertion of course provides some sort of insight (in the sense that it may point out that the Court pays more attention to a Belgian economic union as a whole), but it does not constitute a solid benchmark for future cases, primarily due to a lack of conceptual representational power.

70. Constitutional reservations and article 19 SLIR. As regards interpretation of competence reservations, two principles are generally thought to apply.

When competences are reserved by the Constitution, article 19 SLIR is of importance, which stipulates: 'Article 10 [*implied powers*[318]] remaining in full force, the decree regulates the matters meant in articles 4-10 [*these are the nominatim conferrals*] without prejudice to competences that have been reserved to the law by the Constitution after [1980]'[319]. This article has given rise to many interpretative disputes.

Belgian constitutional scholarship for example struggled for a long time (and actually still struggles, although it has now become clear that the redaction of article 19 SLIR is seriously flawed[320]) with the question – in light of a formal hierarchy of powers *and* in light of the competence attribution *ratio temporis* – whether (and which) reservations have *constitutional* legal power or the legal power of a *special law* (and its consequences)[321]. Whereas the Constitutional Court decided that – in principle – the foundation for reserved competences should be found in article 19 SLIR[322], and that accordingly, the use of the word 'law' in the constitutional provisions pre-dating institutional reform does not have legal consequences in terms of federalism[323], a lot of discussion remains about specific provisions and about the extent to which these provisions reserve competences

---

317 PLETS, *supra* note 47, at p. 108.

318 *See infra* Ch. 3.3.4.

319 Art. 19, §1 (1) SLIR. This 'translation' is more a paraphrase than a strict translation: the original versions are confusing since two exceptions have been made ('behoudens' and 'onverminderd' / 'sauf' and 'sans préjudice de'), but they seemingly have a different object. The first exception (*implied powers*) applies to the whole, whereas the second exception (*reserved powers*) applies to the matters in articles 4-10.

320 *See* Wouter Pas & Brecht Steen, *Met het nodige voorbehoud. Het grondwettelijke voorbehoud aan de formele en aan de federale wetgever (Deel II),* 2005 TIJDSCHRIFT VOOR WETGEVING 34, 34-35.

321 For a concrete example of a dispute: *compare* ALEN & MUYLLE, *supra* note 14, at p. 411-412 *with* Wouter Pas, *De door de Grondwet aan de "wet" voorbehouden aangelegenheden. Vroeger en nu* in DE VIJFDE STAATSHERVORMING VAN 2001, *supra* note 46, at p. 57-60 or Johan Vande Lanotte, *Slottoespraak van de Vice-Eerste Minister, Minister van Begroting, Sociale Economie en Maatschappelijke Integratie op het Colloquium "De Vijfde Staatshervorming van 2001* (Leuven, Nov. 16, 2001)", in DE VIJFDE STAATSHERVORMING VAN 2001, *supra* note 46, at p. 309-15.

322 CA No. 44 (Dec. 23, 1987).

323 *Cf.* CA 35/2003 (Mar. 25, 2003) B.12.6.

to the Constitution[324]. Hence, the Court solves these interpretative issues case by case[325].

Notwithstanding the disputes about this article, its rationale might at first sight seem more or less clear, and thus capable of providing guidance to future cases: the Court should take into account the fact that institutional reform has proceeded in steps, and should (temporally) align its interpretation with this rationale. This was at least how the rationale was clarified by those who amended article 19, §1 SLIR in 2001[326]. However, the (latter) rationale existed long before already[327], and the Court of Arbitration did not always (merely) infer from article 19 SLIR the need to take into account the fact that institutional reform proceeded in steps. Instead, for instance, article 19 SLIR was believed to reserve competences to the federal legislature, especially in the criminal field[328]. When read together with the Court's inference that article 10 SLIR could – at that time – not be applicable to reserved matters, unless there was an explicit conferral[329], one remains confused as to the concrete guidance or explanation offered by this "principle". What remains intact of this principle, is that when a competence, in the Constitution, has been reserved to a 'law', this does not necessarily mean that the Constitutional legislature intended it to be arranged by federal law[330]. The question then of course become – given earlier interpretation by the Court of Arbitration – how much guidance such an argument actually provides.

---

[324] *See eg* Pas, *supra* note 321, at p. 39-45 or Pas & Steen, *supra* note 320, at p. 38-43.

[325] *Eg* CA No. 168/2004 (Oct. 28, 2004) B.4.2 (on jurisdictions of courts).

[326] Specifically in the context of article 162 Cons.: *see* Explanatory Memo, *Parl. Doc.* Senate 2000-01, No. 2-709/1, at p. 4-6; Report (Moens & Monfil), *Parl. Doc.* Senate 2000-01, No. 2-709/7, at p. 8-9, 17-18; *also see* p. 74-85, 154-59, 239-43 and Report (Coveliers & Poncelet), *Parl. Doc.* Chamber 2000-01, No. 1280/3, at p. 8-9, 61-62, 95.

[327] *Compare eg* CA No. 65 (June 15, 1988) IV.1.B.2 and IV.2.B.3 (arguing that institutional reform can implicitly change laws adopted beforehand, in this case, the 1962 law on eminent domain).

[328] *Eg* CA No. 44 (Dec. 23, 1987) III.B.4 *et seq.*; CA No. 11/89 (May 11, 1989) III.B.2 *et seq.*; CA No. 18/89 (June 29, 1989) B.5 *et seq.* or CA No. 15/90 (Apr. 5, 1990) B.16 *et seq.* (waste cases); *also see* CA No. 20/89 (July 5, 1989) B.2 (on abortion information); CA No. 41/90 (Dec. 21, 1990) B.2 (on the competence of the CoS)) or CA No. 13/92 (Feb. 27, 1992) 5.B.2-5.B.3 (ground water).

[329] *Eg* CA 14/89 (May 31, 1989) IV.2.B.2 (on expropriation). Sometimes this case law is still relevant in more recent judgments (*eg* CA No. 29/2011 (Feb. 24, 2011) B.4.4 (on a claims right for citizens on behalf of their municipality in environmental matters)).

[330] Its primary use was indeed to have the matter regulated by the legislative, instead of the executive (as a reaction against the '*ruling by executive decree*' ('besluitenregering') of William I of the Netherlands, ruler over Belgium during 1815-1830). *See, generally,* 1 André Alen, Rechter en Bestuur in het Belgische Publiekrecht: de grondslagen van de rechterlijke wettigheidskontrole (diss. doct. Leuven University 1983) (published by Kluwer in 1984).

71. Reservations in (Special) Laws and strict interpretation. Conversely, when a (special) law reserves a competence, it has often been proclaimed that this should be interpreted strictly[331]. This interpretative assertion, too, should be taken with a pinch of salt. And here is why. Whereas the exceptions, for instance, should be meaningful – as the Court explained in Judgment No. 7 regarding commercial advertising[332] –, there is no impediment for them to be 'merely theoretical' in some other cases[333], and in still other cases, they may

[331] *See* ALEN & MUYLLE, *supra* note 14, at p. 393 (n453 claims it is established jurisprudence); DELPÉRÉE & RASSON-ROLAND, *supra* note 13, at p. 102; VANDE LANOTTE & GOEDERTIER, *supra* note 13, at p. 973; *compare* BRIBOSIA & VAN BOXSTAEL, *supra* note 13, at p. 186-87 (framing the 'strict interpretation'-rule as a neutral corollary to the large interpretation of the conferrals, but immediately mentioning the transversal 'exceptions': afterwards they construe the principle of proportionality as the 'supreme regulatory mechanism in dividing competences' (*ibid.* at p. 189)); *compare* UYTTENDAELE, *supra* note 13, at p. 496-97 (stressing the (general) transversal nature of exceptions). *Seemingly contra*: Yves Lejeune, *Sur les méthodes d'interprétation des règles répartitrices de compétence* (case note accompanying CoS (Apr. 4, 1986)), 1987 JT 267, 268 (allocation of competences is neutral). Suetens and Leysen can be construed as taking a middle position here (*supra* note 316, at p. 56). The Court itself first mentioned this (in the context of commercial publicity) in No. 7/85 (Dec. 20, 1985), III.6.B.1. There it was mentioned as an application of a general rule ('every exception should be interpreted narrowly') in an argument going the other way. This has not always the case in subsequent cases – in fact, this very line has never, to my knowledge, reoccurred literally in any Constitutional Court judgment.

[332] (Dec. 20, 1985) III.6.B.1-III.6.B.2 (commercial advertising was a federal exception up till 1988).

[333] Proposal Geysen *et al.*, *Parl. Doc.* Chamber 1991-92, No. 600/1, at p. 5. Although this was merely a proposal, that was not adopted as such (rescinded on May 21, 1995), the remark pertains to the federal government's power to establish minimum norms vis-à-vis drinking water (a competence that, before 1993, was allocated to it by way of art. 6, §1, II, 2° SLIR). As such, the remark is relevant, for the period up till the 1993 modification of the SLIR (at least from 1989 on, when the federal competence reservation was made; *cf.* art. 4, § 6 Special Law (Aug. 8, 1980) modifying the SLIR, *BSG* Aug. 13, 1988). *Cf.* LUC LAVRYSEN, DE BEVOEGDHEIDSVERDELING IN HET FEDERALE BELGIË. LEEFMILIEU EN WATERBELEID 14 (1999). *Compare* CoS Advice Chamber 1990-91, No. 1767/1, at p. 11 (where it was confirmed that the two large Communities' autonomous taxing powers, pursuant to article 170, § 2 Cons. (explicitly referencing them), is by and large academic, since 'strangely, it has no single useful consequence')). *Also see* Report (Schiltz & Denker), *Parl. Doc.* Senate 1992-93, No. 558/5, at p. 90-91; ALEN & MUYLLE, *supra* note 14, at p. 587 (calling them '*quasi* impossible'); *contra* Paul van Orshoven, *De fiscale aspecten van de vierde Staatshervorming* in HET FEDERALE BELGIË NA DE VIERDE STAATSHERVORMING 108-09 (André Alen & Louis-Paul Suetens eds.) (relying on the autonomy exception to the principle of equality to justify taxes on Brussels institutions). Velaers, however, rightly notes, insofar as the non-subnationality principle must constitutionally stand, that a cooperation agreement between the two large communities will be a necessity, which is probably why the 'analogy' with the former case (regarding water policy) does not work (VELAERS, DE GRONDWET EN DE RAAD VAN STATE, *supra* note 13, at p. 596). However, it remains the case that some competence allocations seemingly *are* merely theoretical, at least vis-à-vis the two large Communities (Report (Arts), *Parl. Doc.* Senate 1991-92, No. 100-15/4, at p. 11).

actually be transversal[334] or wide[335]. This does not mean that there is straight-up contradiction here, for the distinction has an explanation: in one set of cases, the Special Legislature itself – expressing its will in the *travaux préparatoires* – defined the federal competence as being by and large theoretical, which was surely not the case in the commercial advertising case we referred to[336]. Furthermore, the passage in which 'meaningful' was mentioned in Judgment No. 7 pertains to the limits of implied powers. Moreover, arguments can be found in both in theories of interpretation and the *travaux préparatoires* of the SLIR and the Constitution (even if they are sometimes ambiguous[337]) to argue that the social security exception – which was at stake in the last cases referred to – works transversally[338].

Even so, the complexity of these explanations impedes removing the 'pendular impression' of competence interpretation[339]. True, some principles do come back time and again, and on that basis, scholars can hardly be said to be wrong in enlisting these as basic dogmatic arguments deployed by the Court. However, here we merely try to look beyond the classic dogmatic principles, because debate about the particular scope of application (in reference to other 'tools')

[334] A prominent example hereof is the social security exception, which was inserted as an exception to the Regional competence in economic policy, but has been construed to also prevent Communities from regulating this area (*see eg* CA No. 88/93 (Dec. 22, 1998), B.5.4; No. 53/99; *compare* CA No. 33/2001 (Mar. 13, 2001) B.3.9.3). *See eg* Bribosia & Van Boxstael, *supra* note 13, at p. 187. Nonetheless, it could be argued, that *all* exceptions to conferred competences in the SLIR are transversal (*compare* CA No. 25 (June 26, 1986), III.2.B.1-3 (Communities are competent for rules governing fire protection *and* for conditions of establishment, notwithstanding the fact that the latter are excepted from regional competences in economic policy) *with* CA No. 36 (June 10, 1987) III.4.B.2 (where the exception on establishment conditions is rendered transversal); *see* on this overruling, Jan Velaers, *Het Arbitragehof: 'Een grondwettelijk hof met een beperkte bevoegdheid'. Een overzicht van dertig maanden werking*, in Zeven Knelpunten, *supra* note 126, at p. 161-62 (trying to dogmatically cope with the change); *but compare* (conceptually) Vanpraet, *supra* note 190, at p. 155 *et seq.*

[335] In a case regarding obligatory reports on environmental effects, the Court for example *considered* that the federal energy competence (postulated as 'exception' sub art. 6, §1, VII (2) SLIR) is 'wide' (CA No. 57/95 (July 12, 1995) B.7). It might be telling that it again *held* in that case that the obligation to submit such reports did not violate the regional competence (*ibid.* B.8).

[336] This refers back to Case No. 7, mentioned *supra* note 332. Nothing specific was mentioned in the Explanatory Report accompanying Senate Bill 434 (*Parl. Doc.* Senate 1979-80, No. 424/1).

[337] *See* Martens' answer to Hugo Schiltz' question, *Integral Report* Chamber 1979-80 (July 3, 1980) at p. 2330.

[338] *See eg* Velaers, *supra* note 155, at p. 272-75.

[339] Uyttendaele, *supra* note 13, at p. 551, as confirmed in Uyttendaele, *supra* note 263, at p. 975.

and the specific meaning of these principles remains largely unsolved until the Constitutional Court rules on a concrete and specific case[340].

72. Residual powers and article 35 of the Constitution. Next to the 'wide' conferral and 'strict' exceptions, we are faced with undetermined[341] residual powers which – perhaps peculiarly – remain with the federal government.

The latter peculiarity is rooted in the centrifugal nature of the Belgian federation. Article 35 of the Constitution has sought to reverse this logic, but as long as this article is not implemented, the residual competences indeed remain with the federal government[342]. Alen rightly noted in 1989 that the implementation of article 35 might actually take a while[343]. In 2003, he still believed that Belgium probably still has to wait some time for its 'Copernican revolution'[344]. That is probably right: next to immense political hurdles, important unresolved legal issues probably will obstruct a speedy implementation of the article[345].

73. Residual powers: meaning in constitutional reality. If the rationale of residual competences is to cover the entire societal field with possible competences that have not been named, this does not seem to have been their functioning in constitutional reality.

---

340 *Cf.* Brouhns, *supra* note 287, at p. 63.

341 One could argue that neither the conferred powers are *determined* in the sense that the Court itself mostly decides what rules allocating different competences *are* (arguably, the analytical distinction made here between determining which they *are* and interpreting what they *mean* is somewhat flawed, but the Court itself does from time to time make the distinction). A nice example is CA No. 24 (June 24, 1986) 5.B.1 (*compare* 5.B.4-5.B.5) or CA No. 27 (Oct. 22, 1986) 4.B.1 (arguing that article 13, §3 SLIR should be understood as a rule allocating competences, in which case 'allocation' is understood broadly, as either conferral, or modulation or restriction).

342 *See* on this issue, the recent contributions by Sébastien Van Drooghenbroeck and Jan Velaers in SCHARNIER- OF SLEUTELELEMENTEN IN HET GRONDWETTELIJK RECHT / ÉLÉMENTS CHARNIÈRES OU ÉLEMENTS CLÉS EN DROIT CONSTITUTIONNEL (Alexander De Becker & Emmanuel Vandenbossche eds. 2011) 87 and 155 or the article by Willem Verrijdt, *De Omkering van de residuaire bevoegdheden: sleutel of slot,* 2011 (Special Number State Reform) TBP 503.

343 André Alen, *De bevoegdheidsverdeling tussen de Staat, de Gemeenschappen en de Gewesten – enkele algemene bedenkingen na de derde Staatshervorming,* 1989 TBP 139, 149; *also see* Van Drooghenbroeck, *supra* note 342, at p. 90-92.

344 ALEN & MUYLLE, *supra* note 14, at p. 41; *also see eg* Report (Antoine & Uyttendaele), *Parl. Doc.* Chamber 1988 SS, No. 516/6, at p. 23; *also see* Jean-Luc Dehaene's comments in DE HERVORMINGEN VAN DE INSTELLINGEN. TWEEDE FASE 165 (André Alen & Louis-Paul Suetens eds. 1989) and HET FEDERALE BELGIË NA DE VIERDE STAATSHERVORMING 271 (André Alen & Louis-Paul Suetens 1993) (arguing that art. 35 will only be "implementable" when a system of concurrent competences is established in Belgium).

345 *See eg* André Alen & Francis Delpérée, *De residuaire bevoegdheden,* 1991-92 RW 345; Peeters, *supra* note 147; Geert Van Haegendoren, *De residuaire bevoegdheid: troef of joker?* 1990 TBP 88.

On the one hand, it should be noted that the concept of residual competences – taken on its own – does not imply any rule of interpretation[346]. Authors who accordingly speak of 'second degree'[347] or 'factual'[348] residual competences are entering a discourse of reification, as they completely detach the rationale of an abstract notion from its meaning – even if they recognize it[349]– and impose upon it a 'new' meaning in concrete circumstances, sometimes inferring consequences from this meaning[350].

On the other hand, vis-à-vis these competences, the Court has had the chance to develop its own constitutional policy: by qualifying certain norms as falling under a *residual* competence, the Court can in fact rupture a potential connection and thus forgo subsumption under a conferred or reserved competence. Various sources have served as inspiration for the Court to decide that a norm should remain *residual*: for instance, it has relied on a reading of an international treaty in which competences had been divided[351] or also on a reading of the Constitution[352]. Even so, there are no conclusive ways to determine what is in nature un(der)determined. Hence, whether a competence will be residual or not stands to be a matter of grave uncertainty. Admittedly, one could argue that, to the extent that the Court is bound by precedent the new competence area, enunciated as being residual, might put pressure on future qualifying operations of norms. The telecommunication versus radiodiffusion competence saga that took place in the early 2000s might be deemed to constitute a suitable example of the latter: whereas the competence over radios has been conferred to the Communities[353], the Court held, more or less implicitly in 1998[354], and explicitly in in 2000[355], that 'telecommunication' falls outside its scope[356]. In that

---

346 *Eg* PEETERS, *supra* note 38, at p. 237; Alen, *supra* note 38, at p. 33-36; Suetens & Leysen, *supra* note 316, at p.54-57; VANDE LANOTTE, *supra* note 13, at p. 973; Velaers, *supra* note 342, at p. 165-67; *compare* (from the perspective of deontic logic) CARLOS E. ALCHOURRON & EUGENIO BULYGIN, NORMATIVE SYSTEMS 31-34 (1971).

347 BRIBOSIA & VAN BOXSTAEL, *supra* note 13, at p. 133-135; UYTTENDAELE, *supra* note 13, at p. 405-411.

348 VANDE LANOTTE & GOEDERTIER, *supra* note 13, at p. 969.

349 UYTTENDAELE, *supra* note 13, at p. 133; VANDE LANOTTE & GOEDERTIER, *supra* note 13, at p. 973.

350 *Eg* BRIBOSIA & VAN BOXSTAEL, *supra* note 13, at p. 135-147.

351 *Eg* CA No. 109/2000 (Oct. 31, 2000) B.5.3.1.

352 Accordingly, 'reserved' matters and 'residual competences' are not necessarily neatly divided: *eg* No. 17/86 (Mar. 26, 1986) III.3.B.5 (where the Court, on the basis of articles 8 and 162 of the Constitution, decided that the 'eligibility requirement' competence had remained national).

353 Art.4, 6° SLIR.

354 CA No. 76/98 (June 24, 1998) B.10-B.11.

355 CA No. 109/2000 (Oct. 31, 2000) B.5.3.1-B.5.4.

356 *See already* CA 76/98 (June 24, 1998) B.10-B.11; *see infra* Nos. 100, 137 and 139.

sense, one could ask where exactly the difference with conferred and reserved competences is situated, as tensions – sometimes indeed-grave uncertainty – in the qualification process also occur(s) vis-à-vis these. We believe that the specificity of residual competences lies in the more explicit initial *policy*-making power. Once the Court has enunciated one, it will be hard to later assert that – lacking any textual constitutional reform – it is no residual power anymore[357]. But even here guidance is only limited, as the Court does not loose its power completely: similarly to reserved and conferred competences, it can – in a next operation, where a rule *prima facie* seems to resort under a previously enunciated residual competence – still distinguish (implicitly or explicitly).

3.2.2 Material exclusivity

74. Material exclusivity as underlying precept. Material exclusivity, generally understood as the absence of concurrent powers, is a second underlying precept of the Belgian system. Even if many authors signal deviations and nuances in the principle of exclusivity, there is unanimous consent that this principle lay at the foundation of Belgian institutional reforms. This consent seems reasonable, if one deems the *travaux préparatoires* to be (quasi-) authoritative evidence[358]. Velaers explains that even if a minority position held competences to be possibly concurrent (in the event of norm conflicts without excess of competences) and even if the *travaux préparatoires* adjoined to the first law on the Constitutional Court were somewhat sketchy on this point, the *travaux préparatoires* adjoined to the constitutional amendments were not. Even if the first law remained sketchy, no sensible person could deny that exclusivity was the underlying *Leitmotiv* and foundation.

The *foundations* should be understood (chrono)logically here in the first place. Reading through the *travaux préparatoires* of the first (1970) and second (1980) state reform, there is almost no way of denying that exclusivity lay at its basis. However, some authors have emphasized that in the three subsequent stages of institutional reforms (1988-1993-2001), there has been a growing emphasis on

[357] *Cf.* STORME, *supra* note 142, at p. 439 n1622; *compare infra* Ch. 4.4.2.

[358] Some have tried to infer from art. 129 Cons. (which confers the regulation of language use, explicitly 'excluding the federal legislature') that exclusivity has been *constitutionally* recognized, or that exclusivity (on the basis of the interpretative principle *inclusio/expressio unius est exclusio alterius*) does not hold in other areas. It was convincingly argued however, that this insertion into art. 129 first and foremost tried to solve a possible conflict with art. 30 (Walter J. Ganshof van der Meersch, *Réflexions sur la révision de la Constitution,* 1972 JT 480, 483; Luc Veys, *De "exclusiviteit" van de federatief opgedeelde normatieve bevoegdheden: rechtsvergelijkende inzichten,* 1990 TBP 135, 142); *also see* JAN VELAERS, HET ARBITRAGEHOF 37 *et seq. (*1985).

the non-tenability of rigid exclusivity[359], which has been countered with different measures, such as inserting (or more precisely: acknowledging) overarching principles such as EMU, allowing for some concurrent competences, and institutionalizing (sometimes compulsory) cooperation mechanisms[360]. Legally, this results in a different methodological inquiry: instead of neatly trying to delimit different spheres of competences, the question becomes about delimiting 'the amount of policy influence'[361]. Be that as it may, from a foundational angle, the principle of exclusivity remains intact within the Belgian system.

At that foundation, the principle was intended both to ensure the autonomy of the federated entities and to avoid conflicts of competences. Viewed from these purposes and particularly in light of the constitutional case law, it could be argued that the principle could not as such, or at least did not in fact unequivocally reach its goals.

75. Necessary autonomy? As regards the autonomy, it has already been mentioned that there are exceptions abound to be found in the distribution of the allegedly 'homogeneous' packages of competences. Sometimes, using the term 'exceptions' might even sound a bit disingenuous. In educational matters, for example, it used to be commonplace to say or jest[362] that the entire education competence had been devolved, except for education[363]. The same has been said about the Region's economic policies. Yet all of course depends on the perspective or the baseline given that 'autonomy' has no predetermined meaning in federalism matters. Whether a Region or a Community can be conceived of as autonomous requires an elaboration of the notion of autonomy and a determination of the criteria according to which autonomy

---

[359] *See eg* (all with references, amply confirming) Alen, *supra* note 38, at p. 33-35; Alen & Muylle, *supra* note 14, at p. 397; Bribosia & Van Boxstael, *supra* note 13, at p. 62-66 and 92 *et seq.*; Peeters, *supra* note 38, at p. 271-75, 303-10; Plets, *supra* note 47, at p. 107; Uyttendaele, *supra* note 13, at p. 471-72; Vande Lanotte & Goedertier, *supra* note 13, at p. 963 and Velaers, De Grondwet en Raad van State, *supra* note 13, at p. 274-75. What could be noted however is that the 1977 Egmont Pact – which was never adopted by Parliament – did rely on concurrent competences quite extensively (*see* Chamber Bill 461 (1977-78)).

[360] *See* Patrick Peeters, *Over de bevoegdheidsverdeling en de bevoegdheidsrechtelijke kwalificatie van normen*, 1984-85 RW, 706, 716-18; Velaers, De Grondwet en Raad van State, *supra* note 13, at p. 274; Veys, supra note 358, at p. 135-37. According to Alen, the principle of exclusivity could only remain operative because of an evolution to cooperative federalism (Alen, *supra* note 38, at p. 35).

[361] André Alen & Patrick Peeters, *Samenwerkingsverbanden tussen de Staat, de Gemeenschappen en de Gewesten* in Staat, gemeenschappen en gewesten 71, 76 (Roger Blanpain *et al.* eds. 1989).

[362] Between 1970 and 1988, when the exceptions were formulated very extensively, reserving the entire 'School Pact' to the federal government.

[363] *Cf.* Velaers, De Grondwet en de Raad van State, *supra* note 13, at p. 399-400.

can be 'measured'. That elaboration, determination and measurement are tasks for which political scientists or philosophers are better suited than legal scholars and hence, my contention here should not be misunderstood. I do not allege that the federated entities in Belgium are not autonomous: they surely are (to some extent, and – as regards the Regions – to a much larger extent than initially foreseen). What I do want to contend is that *exclusivity* itself does not necessarily ensure autonomy. Even up till 1988, the Court argued that 'education' was an exclusive competence for the Communities. No one, however, would have sensibly argued back then that the Communities could develop an autonomous educational policy. Hence, whether a legislature is autonomous or not first and foremost depends on the *content* and *circumscription* of the competences[364].

On the other hand, there is a point in contending that exclusivity ensures autonomy, but then it is meant *exclusivity* as compared to *concurrent* powers, in which case a rule of conflict often solves the conflict in favor of the federation. Even the existence of such concurrent powers, however, does not necessarily imply a breach of autonomy: amongst other factors[365], the decision-making capacities of the federal level should be assessed. For instance, in case of a so-called competence with derogatory effect (also known as alternative concurrent competence[366]) the federal level indeed needs to be able to make a decision, without which the autonomy of the federated entities remains assured. This capacity, in turn, seems to partly rely on the decision-making structure[367].

Accordingly, even if exclusivity works as an interpretive tool in arguments over the delineation of packages of competences, it cannot ensure autonomy in the abstract sense intended by the *travaux préparatoires*. This does not mean that it has not assured autonomy in some areas (it surely has), or that is has not helped to establish autonomy in others (that could also be argued)[368]. It just

[364] On the other hand, it cannot be denied that the *content* and *circumscription* of competences is partly determined by whether they are of an exclusive nature or not. When they are exclusive, the competences (*under the conditions in the next paragraph*) safeguard autonomy in general.

[365] *See* Popelier, *supra* note 11.

[366] Which, according to some, is (therefore) not even a 'real' concurrent competence (*eg* Veys, *supra* note 358, at p. 140).

[367] *Eg* veto powers (*also see supra* Nos. 54-55).

[368] *See eg,* on how autonomy is a driving factor in the construction of the principles the Constitutional Court deploys, Delpérée & Rasson-Roland, *supra* note 13, at p. 98-103, 106-107 (1990); *also see* Alen, Peeters & Velaers, *supra* note 38, at p. 178-199 (noticing that 'mutual exclusivity [...] is probably the most emphasized component of autonomy' (*ibid.* at p. 193), but taking a broader perspective on the issue, including theoretical considerations); *compare* André Alen, *Le principe de subsidiarité et le federalisme belge* in Le Principe de Subsidiarité 461, 467 (Francis Delpérée ed. 2002) or Popelier, *supra* note 45, at p. 113-14 (noticing that concurrent powers often coincide with centralistic tendencies).

means that there is no necessary abstract connection between exclusivity and autonomy.

76. Necessary conflict avoidance? On the other hand, exclusivity was intended to *in principle* avoid conflicts, since – in the abstract – concurrent powers would need a 'conflict solution'[369]. There has been quite some debate about how true this is in the abstract and this debate has often been analytically quite strong (as often debates inspired by the Germans are)[370]. Although interesting, and sometimes even illuminating, it should be noted that within the debate, spatial and hierarchical images are constantly relied upon or at least presupposed. As we will explain further on, such *more geometrico* analysis of competence allocation is seriously flawed, and often lacks explanatory insight, at least when applied to the case law of the Constitutional Court. That point is actually self-evident: exclusivity might perhaps be geared towards avoiding conflicts, but once a case has reached the Constitutional Court, presumably (or at least potentially) a conflict does exist.

Accordingly in light of the abstract and principled rationales underlying the exclusivity precept, not a whole lot can be said about solving concrete cases that come before the Constitutional Court. Of course these principles matter, but describing the allocation of competences in Belgium only with reference to them, fails to grasp the complexities that a Constitutional Court has to grapple with, primarily because they do not attach these principles to the *object* that should be qualified under the *competences*. Admittedly, some authors have duly emphasized that this qualification process (often characterized as a process of (or preceding) subsumption[371]), is of utter importance[372]. However, it is clear that within this process of subsumption, *arguendo* accepting that this is the best logical representation of the process, the premises of the logical operation require vast

---

369 Often characterized as a *rule of conflict*: however – from the perspective of (deontic) logic – if a rule of conflict is already there, than there is no conflict anymore, since it is solved by the rule. *Also see* Bribosia & Van Boxstael, *supra* note 13, at p. 57-70.

370 The debate was seemingly initiated by an article by Pluymen and Perin (1983 JT 17), which caused some explicit reactions in scholarship (*see eg* Peeters, *supra* note 360, at c. 719 *et seq.*; Veys, *supra* note 358, at p. 137 *et seq.*), but could be argued to continue in the work of many authors, at least presuppositionnally (for instance, in how they differently 'categorize' competence allocations), and sometimes more explicitly (Henri Storme, for instance, in his doctoral dissertation (*supra* note 142) tries to more or less undermine the assumption that exclusivity – in the abstract – avoids norm conflicts).

371 Peeters, *supra* note 360, at c. 725.

372 *See eg* Peeters, *supra* note 38; Bribosia & Van Boxstael, *supra* note 13, at p. 173 *et seq.*; Vanpraet, *supra* note 190, at p. 9-29 and 77 *et seq.*; Velaers, Grondwet en Raad van State, *supra* note 13, at p. 276-78.

elaboration. Legal scholars and courts sometimes pretend otherwise, accordingly reifying the terms constituting the premises of the subsumption process[373].

77. Elaboration, qualification and subsumption: separate categories? Generally, authors analytically distinguish between the *elaboration* of the competences in the abstract, and the qualification of concrete legal regulations under these abstract categories. Befitting regular legal jargon, they argue that even if a concrete provision of a law often has connecting factors with several competences, the Court nonetheless *subsumes* every concrete legal provision under one competence concept. In spite of recognition that *elaboration* and the *subsumption* are 'closely intertwined'[374], they insist on analytically separating them. Such separation can be somewhat misleading, since it does not sufficiently emphasize the entanglement of the questions[375]. Some authors sketch the essence of the operation as trying to 'detect the most meaningful connecting factor'[376]. Admittedly, the support they find in the Court's argumentation is vast[377], and of course, this formulation of how 'qualification' or 'subsumption' works, is in some sense valid indeed[378]. It nonetheless does not take enough 'intervening' factors (indeed other available tools) into account, and sets itself prone to the danger of a fallacy of misplaced concreteness (reification). Moreover, arguments in judgments can sometimes also be read differently: for instance, in the

[373] For a legal theoretical (Heideggerian/Esserian) basis for this assertion, *see eg* Robert Alexy, *Juristische Interpretation* in RECHT, VERNUNFT, DISKURS: STUDIEN ZUR RECHTSPHILOSOPHIE at p. 75-76 (1995) (discussing the concept of *Vorverständnis* in light of the hermeneutical circle: 'Man kann daher sagen, daß dem Zirkel des Vorverständnisses das *Postulat der Reflexion* korrespondiert' (*emphasis in original*)), and (more analytically) Robert Alexy, *On Balancing and Subsumption: a structural comparison*, 16 RATIO JURIS 433, at 433 (2003) ('[t]here are two basic operations in application of law: subsumption and balancing'). Other theoretical precepts can explain my assertion too, *compare eg* MACCORMICK, *supra* note 62, at p. 52 or MARCUS GALDIA, LEGAL LINGUISTICS 81 (2009) (who surmises that all legal doctrine in the sense of dogmatics 'tends towards the reification of legal language'). I refrain from exploring this issue further here, at least from a purely legal theoretical perspective.

[374] *Eg* Velaers, *supra* note 334, at p. 153 (who nonetheless severs the issues analytically further: *ibid.* p. 153-69 versus p. 169-77); *also see, more generally,* STONE SWEET, GOVERNING WITH JUDGES, *supra* note 66, at p. 93.

[375] We recognize that detaching (or better: merely distinguishing) these questions can have a value in law generally, and even in federalism law, but we starkly want to relativize its explanatory (and certainly predictive) potential.

[376] *Eg* VELAERS, DE GRONDWET EN DE RAAD VAN STATE, at p. 276; *cf.* Velaers, *supra* note 334, at p. 173.

[377] *Eg* already in CA No. 11 (Feb. 25, 1986) III.2B.3.a ('dominant aspect' ('*overheersende aspect*'/'*aspect dominant*')); reformulated as 'center of gravity' ('*zwaartepunt*' / '*élément prépondérant*'), *eg* CA No. 73/2000 (June 21, 2000) B.4.1; CA No. 184/2002 (Dec. 11, 2002) B.7; CA No. 109/2006 (June 28, 2006) B.9.2; CC No. 2/2009 (Jan. 14, 2009) B.11.2; CC 87/2009 (May 28, 2009) B.10; CC 45/2012 (Mar. 15, 2012) B.12.

[378] *Cf. supra* note 375.

aforementioned case No. 11 it is held that 'the distinction made by the special law between the concepts 'credit politics' and 'economic expansion' requires that every *concrete* measure must be subsumed under a specific competence'[379]. Would it be too much of a stretch in interpretation to see this as a mere confirmation of exclusivity as a *solution* here (rather than as a starting point of reasoning, or as an independent argument), since the SLIR makes two different entities competent for these 'concepts'?[380] This reading – which does not accept the strict dichotomy between elaboration and subsumption – seems to be reinforced by a multitude of other judgments, in which the Court deploys different competence concepts (belonging to a *single* legislature) in order to justify a specific measure: in a recent judgment, for instance, it invoked *both* the subordinate governance competence and the housing jurisdiction of the Regions in order justify a limitation on the review capacities of audits[381]. Accordingly, representing constitutional review of concrete legislative norms in light of the exclusivity principle as first qualifying these norms and henceforth subsuming them under abstractly elaborated competence concepts seems to be problematic indeed.

78. Exclusivity as a solution. Even if one accepts that the Constitutional Court does make the analytical distinction itself from time to time, it seems to understand *exclusivity*, in its familiar formula, as meaning that (territorially) 'the subject of each regulation of a [...] legislature must be able to be localized within the territory for which he is competent, so that *every concrete relation and situation can only be regulated by one legislature*'[382] and (materially) '*every legal situation* in principle *can only be regulated by one legislature*'[383]. True, this assertion is not wholly unconnected to the *principle* of exclusivity in the abstract.

---

379 *Emphasis added.*

380 *But compare* No. 11 (Feb. 25, 1986) III.3.B.1.

381 CC No 9/2011 (Jan. 27, 2011) B.7 (invoking both art. 6, §1, VIII SLIR and art. 6, §1, IV SLIR).

382 Established jurisprudence since CA Nos. 9 and 10 (Jan. 30, 1986) (respectively) III.5.B.1 and III.8.B. These were cases pertaining to the decree Lagasse-Lepaffe and the so-called September Decree, regulating language in social relations, which were adopted by the (respective French and Flemish) Communities. For the Regions, the same principle plays (*see eg* CA 56/96 (Oct. 15, 1996) B.21), even if it was only literally taken over in CC 33/2011 (Mar. 2, 2011) B.5, where is was not art. 127, 128, 129 or 130 Cons. that had established a system of exclusive territorial competences, but rather art. 5 and 39 Cons., read together with art. 2 and 19, §3 SLIR (and in this case, art. 2, §1 and 7 SLBI). *Also see* (for yet another, shorter formulation) No. 125/2001 (Nov. 20, 2001) B.7.1.

383 Established jurisprudence*: eg* CA 76/2000 (June 21, 2000) B.4.1, as still confirmed in CC 25/2010 (Mar. 17, 2010) B.4.3. *Compare* CA No. 11 (Feb. 25, 1986) III.3.B.1 (where the Court does not speak of a concrete situation, but about the competences *in abstracto*). Notice a(n important) change of language: whereas in 1986, the Court does not employ 'in principle', it does so in its more recent formulation of this consideration. For territorial competences, this change has not taken place.

However, these contentions first and foremost seek to solve cases *in concreto*. This concrete exclusivity accordingly does not so much *prevent* conflict (in case law)[384]; it rather *solves* it[385].

"Solving" needs an immediate qualification here, for it is often the case that in a concrete dispute a judge must still *apply* the jurisprudence of the Constitutional Court in light of the governing provisions of law[386]. The Constitutional Court indeed will not adjudicate upon the applicability of the norm regarding the concrete dispute in preliminary reference proceedings[387], except when it is

---

384 Given the *de facto* (and partial legal) precedential value of CA judgments, prevention can also occur. Furthermore, much depends on the characterization of *conflict*: some would argue that no such conflict exists – *in abstracto* – in the case of (so-called) parallel competences, which – again – depends on the concrete measures in particular cases (*see eg* CC 17/2009 (Feb. 2, 2009) B.106.2) (on the penalization of horizontal discriminations, in which case the federated entities may themselves penalize specific acts on the basis of their own competences).

385 'A grey norm becomes black or white, to the extent that it is rather black or rather white' (Velaers, *supra* note 334, at p. 200 (who nonetheless used this phrase in a slightly more limited context, *ie* that of competence *qualification*)). Bribosia and Van Boxstael try to capture this idea by elaborating the dual structure (hypothesis – dispositive) of legal norms (*supra* note 13, at p. 93 *et seq.* and 173-179 (the latter section is not wholly convincing because of the (admittedly articulated and relativized, but) strained distinction between material and instrumental competences).

386 *See eg* CC No. 179/2009 (Nov. 12, 2009), B.10-B.12 (merely providing further guidelines for the interpretation of an authorization to the executive, pertaining to the tension in competence allocation between regulation of well-being at work (federal) and preventive healthcare (Community)); CC 165/2009 (Oct. 20, 2009) B.4-B.6 (similarly providing guidelines for such an authorization, pertaining to the tension between Community competences and the federal competence to regulate the exercise of medicine'; *also see* B.8-B.9 and B.10-B.11); *also see eg* CC No. 117/2010 (Oct. 21, 2010) dictum (formulating an interpretative reservation, which might make the decree at hand harder to apply); *compare* CC No. 144/2009 (Sep. 17, 2009) B.13 and B.17 (offering a general interpretative framework in which the judge *a quo* can decide whether the executive crossed the line between the federal competence in energy policy (transportation and production) and the regional competences regarding roads, waterways and their accessories, dikes and sea walls) or CC 47/2009 (Mar. 11, 2009) B.4.3 (on the relationship between contract law (rent) and the Flemish Code on Habitation in relationship to civil remedies to be applied by the judge *a quo*). *Also compare supra* note 15.

387 *Eg* CA No. 12 (Mar. 25, 1986) 3.B.1. This argument notwithstanding, there has been quite some discussion about the extent to which the Constitutional Court can interpret the law under review itself, for instance through interpretative reservations, reformulations of the preliminary reference, qualification, *et cet.* (*compare supra* note 15). For an example of the latter, *see* CC No. 52/2009 (Mar. 19, 2009) B.3.1-B.5.2 (contemplating whether a provision regarding Green Electricity Certificates should be categorized as an administrative sanction or as a tax/retribution, and deciding that it is a sanction); *also see* CC No. 71/2011 (May 12, 2011) B.4-B.6. For a further example of 'interaction' in this domain, *see* CC 187/2008 (Dec. 18, 2008), *compare* B.3.2 *with* B.6 *and* B.16 *et seq.* (where the Court ruled that interpreting a 'criminal exclusion ground' (disqualifying any prosecution on criminal grounds) too widely would interfere with federal competences – quasi-limited to the circumstances of the case, and accepting the judge's interpretation, but also offering another one (and further ruling on the basis of the latter; *also see* CC No. 112/2008 (July 31, 2008) (similar)).

manifest that the reviewed law is not applicable to the case[388]. Accordingly, the solution the Constitutional Court offers is one to a legal question that properly falls within its jurisdiction.

79. Exclusivity as a solution and avoiding conflict in concreto. Most forms of reasoning that have been found 'in between', that is, between the grand starting principle of exclusivity (preventing norm conflicts) and the solution of a conflict by the Constitutional Court, have been characterized as 'exceptions to', 'deviations from' or 'nuances in' the principle of exclusivity. Probably these characterizations are correct – if one accepts the abstract nature of the analysis – but viewed from the concrete situations (norms) at hand, they miss the point. On the one hand, as we showed above, the principle of exclusivity in the abstract does not function as an independent legal argument, and as such does not control cases. On the other hand, the principle of exclusivity (practically) always applies, in so much as for every concrete situation, the Constitutional Court ensures that no conflicting regulations arise[389].

Here, I provisionally leave aside the important, but onerous question what a conflict of norms consists in. For instance, what about a Region imposing stricter requirements than the federal legislature? Without going into details, it seems that, to some degree, the competence allocating tools take such questions conceptually into account.[390] However – and notwithstanding the specifying and clarifying power of deontic logic[391] - important questions will remain, for instance because premises still need to be interpreted[392].

---

388 *See eg* CC No. 69/2011 (May 12, 2011) (on procedural provisions regarding appeal); *also see* CC No. 73/2011 (May 12, 2011) (non-applicability in light of No. 25/2007); *compare* CC No. 70 (May 12, 2011) (clearly preferring one interpretation of the law – B.5). *Also see infra*, on Care insurance (*cf. eg* Henri Storme, *Vlaamse Zorgverzekering: Grondwettelijk Hof beslecht maar lost niet op,* Juristenkrant (Feb. 11, 2009) 4-5; Storme, *supra* note 142, at p. 363-66 (on the unclear semantics of CA 72/96) and 405 (relying on the next reference pertaining to Care Insurance); Jan Velaers & Jürgen Vanpraet, *De materiële en territoriale bevoegdheidsverdeling inzake sociale zekerheid en sociale bijstand (II)*, 2009 TBP 195, 207). *Compare* Karel Rimanque, Jan Gijssels & Patrick Peeters, *Stilzwijgende toegekende bevoegdheden*, 1980 TBP 226, 242 (recognizing implied competences as 'a result of interpretative reasoning').

389 At least to the extent necessary in light of the jurisdiction and the contentious questions raised by the legislative norms (*compare supra* notes 386 *et seq.*).

390 *See eg* Velaers, *supra* note 334, at p. 175-77 (discussing how 'parallel competences' are grounded in the possibility of a 'differentiated regulation', meaning that the rules adopted by different legislatures must be able to coexist without contradiction, and making a link with implied powers (*cf.* CA No. 7 (Dec. 20, 1985), III.6.B.1) in this regard).

391 *See eg* Lars Lindahl, *Conflicts in systems of legal norms: a logical point of view* in Coherence and Conflict 39, 40-47 (Bob Brouwer *et al.* eds. 1992) (on the distinction between disaffirmation, compliance conflicts and unrealizability)).

392 *Cf.* Karel Rimanque, De Regel is niet steeds recht. Het labyrint van de rechtsnormen

80. A pragmatic Court. As will be shown in what follows, the toolbox concept abstractly explained above fits the case law in a more coherent way. Again, this is not meant as a form of criticism vis-à-vis the Constitutional Court *per se*, but rather as an explicit acknowledgment of its pragmatic vision[393].

The recognition of pragmatism here does not mean that the decision of the Court – according to the famous trope often attributed to Jerome Frank – depends on what he had for breakfast[394]. Rather, I acknowledge what Oliver Wendell Holmes argued, namely that '[t]he law embodies the story of a nation's development through many centuries, and it cannot be dealt with as if it contained only the axioms and corollaries of a book of mathematics'[395]. Broaching this subject in detail would surely lead me too far, and we refer to our first chapter's arguments on the issue to theoretically frame it. I hope to adequately show, however, how the classic (dogmatic) elaboration of arguments fails on a number of accounts, and how there is a need for a more (pragmatic) conceptualization of (material) exclusivity.

And let me finish by adding this: the pragmatism does not necessarily run counter to the rule of law values (also) embodied by the Court. A certain amount of pragmatic reasoning arguably – although the *travaux préparatoires*

NA DE STAATSHERVORMING 12-15 (1990). Some authors nonetheless use a conceptual framework which is too rigid to notice this (*eg* 1 SÉBASTIEN VAN KOEKENBEEK, PRINCIPES FONDAMENTAUX DU CONTENTIEUX CONSTITUTIONNEL BELGE 56-58; *also see* T. De Pelsmaeker, *De verhouding tussen federaal en gefedereerd recht in België en de Bondsrepubliek Duitsland: het verband tussen normencollisie en bevoegdheidsverdeling*, 2001 TBP 71, *esp.* 72 *et seq.* (on art. 31 Basic Law)*; compare* ALCHOURRÓN & BULYGIN, *supra* note 346, at p. 121 *et seq.* (trying to explain interpretation in a rigid logical framework)). *Also compare infra* notes 498-499.

393 'In the great run of cases which come before the courts, the *selection* of principles, and the determination of whether the facts are to be stated in terms of one or another minor premise, are the chief tasks to be performed' (FRANK, *supra* note 81, at p. 72 (*emphasis added*)). *See eg* Alen & Ergec, *supra* note 14, at p. 423-424 ('the Court is not called upon to adjudicate according to the classic patterns and syllogisms and does not do dogmatic work'); UYTTENDAELE, *supra* note 263, at p. 955-56; Velaers, *supra* note 133, at p. 200-01; *also see* Sébastien van Drooghenbroeck, *De la révolution copernicienne et des nouvelle forces motrices. Considérations diverses sur la répartition des compétences à l'aube de la sixième réforme de l'Etat* in BELGIË, QUO VADIS?, *supra* note 11, at p. 243 *et seq.* ('the creative part of the activity of the constitutional judge is inevitable in light of rules allocating competences, although perhaps recent, that in their flanks show uncertainty and the indeterminacy of the achieved political compromises' (*ibid.* at p. 244)); *compare, generally,* WALTER VAN GERVEN & STEVEN LIERMAN, ALGEMEEN DEEL. VEERTIG JAAR LATER. PRIVAAT- EN PUBLIEKRECHT IN EEN MEERGELAAGD KADER VAN REGELGEVING, RECHTSVORMING EN REGELTOEPASSING 238-248 (2010) (arguing that there is increasing 'pragmatism' (*ibid.* at p. 239-240) in the enlarged field of adjudication in Belgium).

394 But *compare, supra* No. 36.

395 OLIVER W. HOLMES, JR., THE COMMON LAW 1 (Digireads.com publishing 2005) (1881).

are not entirely clear on this[396] – was foreseen by the (special) legislature, which seems to have been reflected in the composition of the Court. The Court indeed comprises six politicians, next to six legal scholars[397]. And the linguistic parity rule (combined with the rules regarding voting and seat composition[398]) also indicate(s) that the legislature took into account the possibility of pragmatic reasoning. Accordingly, pragmatic solutions have always been on the mind of the special legislature instituting the Constitutional Court, whether it was a *Court* or not.

3.2.3 Territorial exclusivity

81. A contentious principle, 'solved' by the Constitutional Court. Let us now turn the coin of the principle of exclusivity and glimpse at its territorial side.

The principle of territorial exclusivity is one of the most contentious principles in Belgian Constitutional law.

Whereas Flemish scholars generally subscribe to a (strictly) territorial nature of Belgian federalism, Francophones are often said to dispute this territorial nature, and more specifically, the territorial nature of Community competences

396 *Compare eg* Report (Suykerbuyck & Van Cauwenberghe), *Parl. Doc.* Chamber 1979 SS, No. 10-9/4°, at p. 6 ('more than a mere legal institution') *with* Integral Report Chamber No. 93 (July 22, 1980), at p. 2666 (where Mr. Baert states that whereas the Court of Arbitration 'in a normal way adjudicates upon conflicts of competence', it differs from the CoS, which is a 'strictly judicial institution') *and* Integral Report Senate No. 88 (July 28, 1980) at p. 2647 (where Mr. Demeyer stated that the Court of Arbitration only adjudicates upon legal questions) *or* Integral Report Senate No. 87 (July 28, 1980) at p. 2640 (where Mr. Destexhe recognized that is in essence a 'jurisdictional organ').

397 *Cf.* Storme, *supra* note 142, at p. 314.

398 *See* art. 54-60*bis* SLCC. On the issue, and how it relates to problems of federalism, *see eg* Francis Delpérée, *La Cour d'arbitrage et le Fédéralisme belge*, in Federalisme et cours supremes / Federalism and Supreme Courts 167, 169 (Edmond Orban et al. 1991) (asking the rethorical question whether it is necessary to underline 'the parallel between the structural transformations of the Belgian state and those that define the establishment of the Court of Arbitration' and explaining how the Constitutional Court serves to preserve, perfect and orient the dualist Belgian federal enterprise). Also the nomination could be said to reflect this pragmatism (*eg* CoS Advice (Joint Chambers), *Parl. Doc.* Senate 1981-82, No. 246/1, at p. 51). This issue has been relevant before the Court, especially as regards the application of article 6 EHRM (*compare* No. 32 (Jan. 29, 1987) III.B.b.7.2 (article 6 is not applicable to the Constitutional Court, except the 'reasonable delay'-requirement) *with* Nos. 35-36/94 (May 10, 1994) (article 6, in light of case *Ruiz-Mateos* (ECtHR) is in fact applicable to the Constitutional Court's preliminary reference procedure) and No. 50/97 (Sept. 17, 1997) (to the Constitutional Court's annulment proceedings). *See, for more reflections*, Feyen, *supra* note 67, at p. 266 *et seq.* and *infra* No. 130.

and hence territorial exclusivity[399]. To the extent that in its arguments before the Constitutional Court, the French Community relied on the 'personal' interpretation of federalism, this is surely correct. [400] However, the juxtaposition should not be exaggerated. On the one hand, some reputable Francophone scholars now readily accept the principle of exclusive territoriality[401]. On the other hand, many (mostly non-legal) authors, both Flemish and Francophone, describe the Communities' competence in Brussels as being (partly) *personal*[402]. This, in light of the non-existence of sub-nationality in Belgium, is of course disputable, perhaps even 'a common misunderstanding'[403]: we should prefer to use the word *institutional* to describe the competences of the Communities in Brussels[404], at least from a *formal* point of view. In practice, institutions of course can reach people, and the Communities have worked through these institutions to reach the members of their language in Brussels[405]. Notwithstanding these nuances, it should be clear that the (alleged) French opposition to the (strict) idea of territoriality still exerts very strong symbolic (political) power[406].

---

399 *Eg* ALEN & MUYLLE, *supra* note 14, at p. 323-324; *also see* VELAERS, DE GRONDWET EN RAAD VAN STATE, *supra* note 13, at p. 408-09 (nonetheless pointing out that the Francophone Chambers of the CoS never accepted the 'personal' nature of communities, and using the word 'French Community' instead of 'Francophones')

400 *Also see eg* CA No. 70 (Dec. 14, 1988) III.B.5.g *juncto* A.2 (relying on article 27 ICCPR).

401 *Eg* (Alen &) Ergec, *supra* note 14; FRANCIS DELPÉRÉE, LE DROIT CONSTITUTIONNEL DE LA BELGIQUE 618 (2000); *contra* UYTTENDAELE, *supra* note 263, 986 *et seq.* (calling the Court's jurisprudence here 'eminently subjective' (*ibid.* at p. 991)).

402 *Eg* many of the introductions mentioned *supra* note 187; *also see* PLETS, *supra* note 47, at p. 57 n235 (however, relativizing at p. 78).

403 Work Session Proceedings (Brems, Van Drooghenbroeck, Bonbled) in FEDERALISM: TURNING DIVERSITY INTO..., *supra* note 188, at p. 65; even stronger: Alen, Peeters & Velaers, *supra* note 38, at p. 215

404 *Eg* Alen, Peeters & Velaers, *supra* note 38, at p. 215-16; VELAERS, VAN ARBITRAGEHOF TOT..., *supra* note 13, at p. 122; *cf.* Rigaux, *supra* note 156, at p. 315-16.

405 *Eg* Delgrange, *supra* note 154, at p. 255-56 (critical about using spending powers through institutions to reach persons, mentioning the case of free bus tickets); VELAERS, DE GRONDWET EN RAAD VAN STATE, *supra* note 13, at p. 419 (referring to Flemish care insurance)). *Also see* STORME, *supra* note 142, at p. 221-25.

406 Intervention in a Plenary Session on the Policy Declaration, *Integrated Report*, Chamber (May 11, 2005), CRIV 51/PLEN 135 at p. 6: 'You were prepared to offer French-speakers in the municipalities with a special linguistic status additional rights. You were prepared to factually facilitate the annexation by Brussels of the Flemish border municipalities. You were even prepared to give up the principle of territoriality, one of the foundations of the federal state, for which Flemish people – also Flemish liberals – have fought for decades. That was a scandalous attitude you brought to bear there. You would let the French Community become active within Flemish borders. That in May 2005, a Flemish Prime Minister would let the French Community become active within the borders is beyond imagination, despicable and beyond decent political words' (by Pieter De Crem, a relatively 'mainstream' Flemish Christian Democrat politician). *See* Intervention in a Plenary Session, *Integrated Report*, Chamber

Accordingly, the issue of territoriality has always been a burning issue in Belgian politics and constitutional law. It should not come as a surprise then that the SLCC left unclarity about the matter[407]. However, the Court of Arbitration brought some clarification soon enough. It held that the Belgian system of competences does not only rely on a material exclusivity of competences, but also on a territorial exclusivity, meaning that every *territorial* norm conflict must be accompanied by an excess of competence, which can be invalidated by the Court. The Court formulates it as follows:

> The[...] provisions of the Constitution have established an exclusive allocation of competences. Such a system presupposes that the subject of each regulation of a [...] legislature must be able to be localized within the territory for which he is competent, so that every concrete relation and situation can only be regulated by one legislature.

(Sep. 13, 2002), CRIV 50 / PLEN 266, at p. 8. *Also see eg* Interventions in the Foreign Relations Committee on the second Nabholz Report, *Integrated Report*, Chamber (Sep. 18, 2002), CRIV 50 / COM 828, at p. 4 (Els Van Weert), p. 8 and 28-29 (Paul Tant) and p. 20 (Ferdy Willems). *Compare* Question by Roel Deseyn to the secretary of public corporations on the application of the principle of territoriality by the Flemish Government, *Questions and Answers* (Oct. 10, 2006), QRVA 51/140, at p. 27504-27505 (to be assessed in light of the Constitutional Court's jurisprudence on limited extraterritorial effects of regional/community decrees). On why symbols in this regard may matter, see Dumont, Franck & Ost, *supra* note 213, at p. 286 *et seq.* ('[t]he Belgian State is sure to die off quickly, if it would appear that it could no longer benefit from the indispensable support of a carrying myth that finds its double emanation in Belgian citizenship and in a Belgian federal fidelity', *ibid.* at p. 290-91). On the other hand, even if some conceive of territoriality as intrinsically connected to the establishment of the Westphalian state itself (*cf.* art. 2 (4) UN Charter; *see* Hugues Dumont, *Au-delà du principe de territorialité: fédéralisme, intégration et subsidiarité*, 1999 APT 64; *see eg* ECtHR No. 23885/94 (Dec. 8, 1999) *ÖZDEP v. Turkey*, para. 41 (*a contrario*, on the principle of territorial integrity of the state)), it is conceivable for a personal view on federalism – and in fact some very authoritative authors have defended the idea (*eg* Will Kymlicka, *Two models of pluralism and tolerance* in TOLERATION. AN ELUSIVE VIRTUE 96 (David Held ed. 1996) (describing a 'liberal' and 'communautarian' model of religious minority protection, the latter on the basis of group rights, in which some theoretical justification of personal federalism can be found)) – to leave an imprint on the modern state (*compare* Wouter Pas, *Personal Federalism and Human Rights* in FEDERALISM: TURNING DIVERSITY INTO..., *supra* note 188, at p. 380 (idea of personal federalism can be useful in terms of minority protection, but not for structuring federalism as a whole)).

407 *Supra* No. 61. The Constitution itself, arguably, does not offer any conclusive arguments either (Velaers & Vanpraet, *supra* note 388, at p. 197), nor does the SLCC or its predecessor law (STORME, *supra* note 142, at p. 309 *et seq.*).

> Taking constitutional provisions into account, the [Parliaments] may determine the criterion or criteria, through the application of which the subject of their adopted regulation, according to their insight, is localized within their competence area. The chosen criteria, nonetheless, are subject to the Court's review [...].
>
> Review on the basis of the Constitution first occurs in light of the provisions allocating material competences which contain elements on the basis of which the validity of these criteria can be determined; insight into the object, the nature and possibly the goal of the conferred material competence is required so as to adequately adjudge the localization of the object of an adopted regulation within the territorial region of competence, determined by the Constitution[408].

82. Territoriality: hard to get a grip on. The idea of exclusive territoriality, as it is shaped by the Constitutional Court, is somewhat more impenetrable than the notion of material exclusivity. A number of reasons seem to account for this.

The language used here vis-à-vis the notion of exclusive territoriality seems somewhat more rigid than that of material exclusivity. To be concrete, it lacks the 'in principle' which is generally attached to the considerations regarding material exclusivity[409]. Even so, the Court does allow – according to the text – that several criteria may (potentially) be employed to determine the territorial scope of the regulation.

---

[408] CA No. 9 (Jan. 30, 1986) III.5.B.1; No. 10 (Jan. 30, 1986) III.8.B.1; No. 17 (Mar. 26, 1986) III.3.B.7; No. 29 (Nov. 18, 1986) III.3.B.1-III.3.B.2; *see* No. 51/2006 (Apr. 19, 2006) B.9.1-B.9.3 (almost the same wording, with the third paragraph paraphrased); *also see* CA No. 54/96 (Oct. 3, 1996) B.7.1; No. 72/96 (Dec. 11, 1996) B.7.1, *also see* B.7.4; No. 22/98 (Mar. 10, 1998) B.4.1; No. 30/2000 (Mar. 21, 2000) B.2.1; CA No. 56/2000 (May. 17, 2000) B.3; No. 92/2003 (June 24, 2003) B.13.3; CC No. 11/2009 (Jan. 21, 2009) B.12.3 (only the first paragraph – sometimes paraphrased); *compare* CC No. 33/2011 (Mar. 2, 2011) B.5 (paraphrasing and adopting to the Regions only the first paragraph). Even those thoroughly in favor of constitutional court adjudication of norm conflicts without excess of competence, acknowledge that the Court characterizes the matter as a conflict of competence (*eg* STORME, *supra* note 142, at p. 335-36, 361-62). *Also compare* CA 4/98 (Jan. 21, 1998) B.2 and B.5.2 (the Court must investigate material exclusivity *before* judging upon the issue of territoriality).

[409] *Also see* UYTTENDAELE, *supra* note 263, at p. 988.

In a case pertaining to juvenile protection, the Court held that '[t]o be compatible with the constitutional rules, the chosen localization criteria must render it possible to situate the place where organs for juvenile protection act, within the competence area of a single legislature. Given the goal of juvenile protection, this will *normally* be the family residence of the minor. If the minor does not have a family residence, the place will have to be determined where the minor is educated and raised. The referring judge should determine that place keeping the factual elements into account, and thereafter apply the decree of the territorially competent community'[410]. However, the Court in this case duly emphasizes the subsidiary nature of the second criterion of localization employed by the Decree here[411].

Next to the equivocal language, it should be noted that there are far less cases on the principle of territoriality than cases involving problems of material exclusivity. One important reason for this is that – perhaps under influence of the 'strict' jurisprudence – federated entities do not often establish the scope of their competence *ratione loci*. Thus, it normally is up to regular judge – in *applying* the decrees and ordinances – to establish the territorial scope of competences[412]. Accordingly, it would be interesting to take the jurisprudence of other courts reviewing regulations in light of the territoriality principle into account[413]. But in that hypothesis, it would not be the decrees or ordinances (or laws) that violate the Constitution, but the executive measures, which fall beyond the scope of our inquiry[414].

Finally, the explicit connection made between territorial competence and material competence, through 'the object, the nature and possibly the goal of the conferred material competence' makes the matter rather complex indeed, certainly in light of the lack of a general political federal project and in light of the obscure patchwork functioning as a template for material competence allocation. As a result, the principle itself – or more precisely *how* it can be used as a tool – is hard to get a grip on.

---

[410] CA No. 72/96 (Dec. 11, 1996), B.7.6.

[411] *Ibid.* B.8. In that light, the question has arisen whether they are indeed distinguishable (STORME, *supra* note 142, at p. 364). *Compare* CoS No. 179.511 (Feb. 12, 2008) 4.2.2.2, 4.2.2.4 and 4.2.3.1 (recognizing the 'principled' nature of the exclusive territoriality).

[412] *Cf.* CA No. 72/96 (Dec. 11, 1996) B.7.2, B.9.

[413] *Also see eg* VELAERS, DE GRONDWET EN DE RAAD VAN STATE, *supra* note 13, at p. 408-12 (recapitulating the CoS advices on this matter).

[414] *Cf.* CA No. 22/98 (Mar. 10, 1998) B.7.1; *but compare* No. 30/2000 (Mar. 21, 2000) B.4.2-B.4.3. *Also see* STORME, *supra* note 142, at p. 251-52 (arguing that the Constitutional Court should nonetheless set forward 'framework' criteria to deploy).

83. Carrefour: exacting scrutiny. That is illustrated by the (notable[415]) controversy over whether the Court in the so-called *Carrefour*[416] cases actually created an *exception* to this (seemingly – or at least semantically) rigid rule of territorial exclusivity.

These cases all pertained to French Community budget items, which allocated funds as 'cultural promotion subsidies', or so at least the French Community contended before the Court. The Court acknowledged in *Carrefour I*, that the

> territorial limitation due to the nature itself of promoting culture, does not imply that the community competence ceases to exist merely because of the fact that the taken initiatives could have consequences outside the area for which the involved community takes care as regards culture, pursuant to article 127 of the Constitution. The possible extraterritorial consequences of measures promoting culture, however, may not hamper the cultural policy of the other community. The territorial limitation does not flout anyone's right to his freely chosen cultural development, regardless of the linguistic area in which he finds himself[417].

At the same time, however, on the basis of the fact that the object of the *Carrefour I* allocation was the endowment of municipalities with a special linguistic status[418], the Court could not accept the budget item as geared towards cultural promotion. Its real object, the Court held, was the protection of minorities, and there was no constitutional foundation to exercise unilateral competences with extra-territorial effects in this area[419]. Accordingly, the budget item was invalidated[420]. In later budgets, the Francophones tried to rely on the cultural 'extra-territorial effects' argument of the Court, but the Court never allowed it, because apparently, the Court never believed that it was the intention of

---

[415] *Cf.* Frederik Gheeraert & Stany Vaes, *Het Arbitragehof: Quo Vadis* 2001-02 Jura Falconis 3, 8 (where former Court of Arbitration President Boel – the interviewee – had these judgments figure amongst the most important ones the Court ever rendered).

[416] The name of the saga originated from one of the associations intended for subsidies in the municipalities with special linguistic facilities. The association edited and published a homonymous magazine that many Flemish residents resented. *See* Storme, *supra* note 142, at p. 386-92.

[417] CA No. 54/96 (Oct. 3, 1996) B.7.2.

[418] *Ibid.* B.8.2

[419] *Ibid.* B.9.

[420] *Ibid.* dictum. Or at least the budget item itself was annulled, and there was an interpretative reservation for art. 1.

the Francophone Community to really promote culture rather than to protect minorities[421]. Instead, the Court refused to accept the justifications by the French Community, which relied on its earlier jurisprudence. Gencrally, the Court acknowledges that if no territorial scope of application has been determined, the legislature has to be deemed to have acted constitutionally[422]. This idea has implicitly been endorsed by the SLCC[423]. Even so, the Court now formulates this as a rebuttable presumption[424], which can be 'contradicted by reality'. This 'reality' should be assessed, not merely by what actually happened[425], but can also be apparent from the *travaux préparatoires*[426]. Whereas in *Carrefour* cases I and II[427], the Court still acknowledged that statements made in the *travaux préparatoires* could not supersede a text, and there only made a reservation (albeit an *explicit* one), the Court in 145/2001 actually *annulled* the provision, and took the lack of any contrary explanation as a sufficient ground (together with the *travaux préparatoires* of the previous judgment) to judge that the budget item in the 1998 budget was allocated unconstitutionally[428]. It accordingly performed a quite exacting scrutiny vis-à-vis the budget items.

---

421 CA No. 22/98 (Mar. 10, 1998) B.4.2 (a mere change of form cannot provide a legal basis for the past or the future for a subsidy the Court has invalidated) and B.5.1 (the program has not been abolished, it was mere transferred); No. 50/99 (Apr. 29, 1999) B.5 (making an explicit reservation about interpreting the budget allocation contrary to the aforementioned judgments); No. 56/2000 (May 17, 2000) B.4.3 (even if not the same words are used as in the previous cases, the Court should search for the real object of the contested provisions) and No. 145/2001 (Nov. 20, 2001) B.8 (noticing that there is no other explanation for the funds allocation than the explanations provided in the previous judgment, and therefore effectively invalidating the provision, insofar as it allocates funds contrary to the constitutionally determined allocation of competences). *Compare* No. 67/96 (Nov. 28, 1996) (suspension claim rejected). *Also see* Vuye, *supra* note 13, at p. 33-34 (arguing that the Court was looking for an efficacious solution to the problem).

422 *Eg* CA No. 22/98 (Mar. 10, 1998) B.7.1 and (more explicitly) No. 56/2000 (May 17, 2000) B.5. This is the application of a longstanding rule of Belgian law, according to which 'it is certain that the creators of [a law] have not wanted to confer power upon the government to take measure violating the Constitution' (Cass. (Apr. 20, 1950), *Waleffe,* 1950 Arresten van het Hof van Cassatie 517, 518 or 1950 Pasinomie (I) 560, 562).

423 Storme, *supra* note 142, at p. 309-10 (explaining why there is no alternative to art. 26, §1, 2° SLCC in annulment proceedings); *cf.* Rigaux, *supra* note 156, at p. 324-28.

424 CA No. 56/2000 (May 17, 2000) B.5-B.6; *also see* CA No. 30/2000 (Mar. 21, 2000) B.4.2-B.4.3 (applying it vis-à-vis part-time art education).

425 *Ie* the actions of the executive; *cf.* No. 30/2000 (Mar. 21, 2000) B.4.3.

426 CA No. 56/2000 (May 17, 2000) B.6; No. 22/98 (Mar. 10, 1998) B.7.2.

427 CA No. 22/98 (Mar. 10, 1998) B.7.3; No. 50/99 (Apr. 29, 1999) B.5.

428 No. 145/2001 (Nov. 20, 2001) B.7-B.8; *compare* B.9-B.10. *Also see* Storme, *supra* note 142, at p. 318-19.

84. Extra-territorial effect as an exception? Dogmatic dispute. The question then arose whether this 'extra-territorial effect' was really an exception to the general rule of territorial exclusivity[429].

On the one hand, there was exacting scrutiny of the objective (read through the intention or motivation) of a certain measure, but the question remained whether this should be perceived as an application of the principle of proportionality that was also enunciated in these cases, or rather as a flat denial of territorial effects altogether in case of minority protection. Some authors' contentions seem to point in the direction of a reading in the former sense[430], whereas other authors seem to lean towards the latter sense[431]. The Council of State does not seem to comprehend the Court's jurisprudence as pertaining to *proportionality* application, but rather as an operation of (re-)qualification[432].

[429] This issue can also be framed in a larger logico-theoretical debate on the meaning of rules and principles. *Compare, eg* DWORKIN, *supra* note 99, at p. 25 (arguing that a rule can be distinguished from a principle because of the principled enumerability of exceptions to rules; *but compare ibid.* at p. 73 *et seq.* (explaining how it is mostly a 'matter of exposition')) *with* Robert Alexy, *Zum Begriff der Rechtsprinzips,* 1979 RECHTSTHEORIE 59 (Supp.), *reprinted in* RECHT, VERNUNFT, DISKURS: STUDIEN ZUR RECHTSPHILOSOPHIE 177, 188-89, *esp.* n64 (1995) (arguing that new exceptions can always be construed (either reduced, or extended) through conjunctive *casu quo* disjunctive addition of a negated fact) and ALEXY, *supra* note 3, at p. 44 *et seq.* (conceiving of principles and rules as 'reasons of a very different nature' (*ibid.* at p. 45), where principles are construed as optimization requirements and rules as 'norms which are always either fulfilled or not [...] contain[ing] fixed points in the field of the factually and legally possible' (*ibid.* at p. 48), [which] display another 'prima facie character' (*ibid.* at p. 57); *compare infra* on defeasibility, note 735).

[430] For a reading that seems to point that way, *see* STORME, *supra* note 142, at p. 385 n1492 (referring to CoS No. 158.547 (May 9, 2006); No. 66.078 (Arp. 25, 1997); No. 154/635 (Feb. 7, 2006) and No. 66.657 (June 10, 1997) – even if Storme here refers (*ibid.* at p. 385-86) to the principle of federal loyalty; *but compare ibid.* at p. 388 (where he points out that the principle of proportionality is part of the principle of federal loyalty)) and (more explicitly) p. 388-89 (the Court 'veiled its balancing of interests as a requalification of the subject of the regulation in question' (*ibid.* at p. 388))).

[431] André Alen & Patrick Peeters, *The Competences of the Communities in the Belgian Federal State: The principle of Exclusivity Revisited,* 3 EPL 165, 172-73 (1997) (remarking that it was strange that the Court invalidated the provisions of the budget relying on article 127, § 2 Cons., which indeed determines the territorial competence of the Communities in *cultural* matters).

[432] *See eg* CoS No. 101.706 (Dec. 10, 2001) 3.2.4 (disallowing the establishment of a consultative council for the French in the periphery (inspired by 'solidarity amongst Francophones'), as this constituted a measure of minority protection); CoS No. 179.511 (Feb. 12, 2008) (where the CoS nullified the re-establishment, even if a different 'motivation' was offered by the French Community Council ('creating a space for dialogue' with the 'Brussels periphery'), as it stressed that measures promoting culture cannot be confused with measures protecting minorities (*ibid.* at 4.2.2.3), and held that because the dialogue did not first and foremost pertain to the periphery (the users of FCC services), but rather to Francophones (*ibid.* at 4.2.3.2), it should be requalified as a measure protecting minorities) (*but see* STORME, *supra* note 142, at p. 389-91 ('the detour through requalification of the subject of regulation to minority protection was

Accordingly, dogmatically, uncertainty remains.

On the other hand, the Court never spoke of an extraterritorial *competence*, but rather of a (mere) extraterritorial effect, which – then again – was inherent to the competence[433]. It is nonetheless hard to push these issues into distinct encompassing categories, which causes dogmatic confusion. For instance, some authors – admittedly in an aphorism in the given example – give the impression that no *conflict* of laws can emerge from cumulating subsidies[434]. But 'subsidies' cannot coherently constitute a dogmatic category to be subsumed under 'effects', since the *Carrefour* cases clearly show that subsidies indeed may give rise to conflict of norms. Others suggest that *international* extraterritorial regulation by Communities and Regions might be a germane level of analysis, as the principle of territoriality is asserted not to play there[435]; even if this assertion is carefully nuanced, it is not sure in light of what follows about Europe whether this category is tenable.

---

unnecessary and even unhappy')). *Compare* CA No. 42/2005 (Feb. 23, 2005) B.11 (where the Court held constitutional obligations regarding the conservation of munition imposed by the French Community to obtain a French Community recreational shooting licence, even if the location of the munition was in a different Community; *see* STORME, *supra* note 142, at p. 381-84).

[433] *Compare eg* DELPÉRÉE, *supra* note 401, at p. 613 (stressing that the *effects* are merely 'natural', seemingly implying that they can be part of each competence exercise) and Jean-Claude Scholsem, *Observations sous l'arrêt du 3 octobre de 1996 de la Cour d'Arbitrage*, case note accompanying CA No. 54/96, 1996 JOURNAL DE PROCÈS 31 (stating that, 'if the money is not burried in the garden (in which case, one can strictly talk about localization), any expense, which enters an open economic circuit, always has certain 'extra-territorial' effects', and thus implying that the extra-territorial effect is only a natural corrolary of expenses (or costs)) and STORME, *supra* note 142, at p. 339 (the principle of exclusivity of *regulators* does not imply an exclusivity of *norms*, since this primarily depends on the matter at hand), 366 (on the distinction between competent authority and applicable law) *with* Rigaux, *supra* note 156, at p. 319 n34 (leaving no room for extraterritorial effects indeed); Vuye, *supra* note 13, at p. 24-25 (on the one hand, arguing that the possibility of extraterritorial effect will depend on the nature of the measure at hand, but at the same time stressing that the extraterritoriality must come as an *accessorium* (rather than as an inherent trait) of the measure in play and on the other hand, stressing that the approach of the Court (requalification) differs from the abovementioned considerations) and Dries Van Eeckhoutte, *Het grondwettelijke territorialiteitsbeginsel en de internationale samenwerking: zijn walvissen rare vogels in de Belgische bevoegdheidsverdeling?* 2006 CDPK 841, 848-49 (arguing that the 'exacting' nature of the scrutiny of the Court is more or less undone or at least mitigated by the fact that the legislatures may themselves decide upon the criteria employed to create a territorial connection).

[434] *Eg* Jan Velaers, '*In foro interno et in foro externo*': *de internationale bevoegdheden van gemeenschappen en gewesten* in INTERNATIONALE BETREKKINGEN EN FEDERALISME 3 (Frank Judo & Guy Geudens eds.) (2006) ('1000 EUR federal development aid and 1000 EUR Flemish development aid are not in conflict… it is 2000 EUR').

[435] Van Eeckhoutte, *supra* note 433, at p. 852 *et seq*.

Be that as it may, the *Carrefour* jurisprudence is not entirely unparalleled, as the Court is said to have relied on it in later cases again. For instance in the cases pertaining to the radio broadcasting competence, the Court developed arguments which are very similar to the *Carrefour* jurisprudence, notably holding that it follows from the nature of the radio competence that extraterritorial effects might be involved[436]. Although these cases show a clear parallel with the *Carrefour* jurisprudence, it has been hard to coherently capture in a dogmatic way what the similarity consists in. Hence, these cases proffered no conclusive argument for either side in the dogmatic debates on the relationship regarding the place of the principle of proportionality within *Carrefour* jurisprudence or on the distinction between competence and effect.

85. A failure of dogmatics. The underlying issue could be dubbed both *conceptual* and *jurisprudential*.

Conceptually, a similar distinction as the one made vis-à-vis material competences should be underlined: whereas the *abstract* principle of territoriality should be conceived of as a behavioral standard which (primarily) directs federated entities to determine the scope of application of their regulations in a manner that does not unduly impinge upon the territorial competence of the other federated entities, the *concrete* territoriality requirement (which indeed is informed by the meaning of the former) sets forth a closed system of competences, in the sense that, in the end, when norm conflicts arise, the principle of territoriality will be taken into account when solving concrete norm conflicts. This somewhat goes against the common understanding of a 'closed system of competences', as it is often postulated at the *abstract* (mere competence) level[437]. This common

[436] CA 92/2003 (June 24, 2003) B.14.2 (where it was held that a French Community decree setting out a roster in which different radio frequencies are distributed 'in the French Community' does not infringe the territorial competence of the Flemish Region, as the criterion used is pertinent (B.13.4), and the Court does not see how the French decree would impede Flemish policy in this regards (*compare* A.11: stressing the unilateral character of the measure and the possibility of interference), nonetheless adding that 'it is up to the concerned governments to coordinate the matter in question' if they find this appropriate (B.14.2 *juncto* B.10)). Some other cases involved extraterritorial effects as well, but are not discussed in depth here. *Compare eg* CA No. 44/2005 (where the extraterritorial effect does not seem to be within the nature of the competence, even if a connection could be made; *cf.* Storme, *supra* note 142, at p. 382-83): CC No. 2/09 (Jan. 15, 2009) B.14 (if installations, which are not situated on Brussels territory, but nonetheless emit radiation (measurable on Brussels territory), are regulated by a Brussels ordinance, then there is no excess of competence, since otherwise the Brussels measures would be 'rendered inefficacious or ineffective').

[437] *Eg* the advice of the CoS in Report (Herman-Michielsens & Lallemand), *Parl. Doc.* Senate 1981-82, No. 246/2, at p. 356-59 (CoS); *compare ibid.* at p. 363-70 (where Mertens de Wilmars is pleading for a partly open system of competences, nonetheless still in the abstract mode of thought); *but see ibid.* at p. 380 (where Velu acknowledges that the 'antinomy is

understanding, in which one infers from the abstract closure the impossibility of concrete norm conflicts (in territorial application), rests on a conceptual confusion about the meaning of territoriality in the case law of the Constitutional Court. Instead of dogmatically conceiving of it as a principle operating at an abstract level, the principle can only make sense from a more practice-oriented, concrete perspective. On the one hand, this is caused by the connection between material and territorial competences, for which the Constitutional Court usually employs the standard of *pertinence*, in combination with the freedom for the entities to choose their own criteria of territorial application[438]. On the other hand, the jurisprudential issue set forth below has to be taken into account[439]. This does not mean that the abstract principle is bereft of importance, or that there is no close connection between the abstract principle and its concrete repercussions. However, we should duly recognize that norm conflicts have a great deal more to do with practice than with (abstract) theory or dogmatics[440], and that therefore, the dogmatic (abstract) category of the principle of territoriality encounters difficult problems.

A germane example of how *concrete* conflict solution takes shape are the cases regarding the 'seat of exploitation'-criterion where the Court did determine the (only) adequate criterion of application in light of material competences. The Court in these cases had the advantage that it could easily connect the territorial requirement to the material competence (social *relations*), thus allowing for the construal of a connecting factor that would *generally* avoid conflicts. An easy connection is not always available, however: sometimes the Court will be obliged to either employ a form of conciliatory interpretation (or more broadly, presume a situation of absence of concrete norm conflict[441]) or

---

usually expressed when the two norms that contradict each other, are applied to a certain case'; *also* see *ibid.* at p. 416; *but compare ibid.* at p. 387).

438 *Cf.* Peeters, *supra* note 38, at p. 214-21; *also see* Storme, *supra* note 142, at p. 249-50, 339 *et seq.*; *also see* p. 308, 436-37; *also see* Velu's opinion in *Parl. Doc.* Senate 1981-82, No. 246/2, at p. 398-99.

439 *Also see* Storme, *supra* note 142, at p. 248-49 (further pointing out that territorial scope cannot be set in stone through qualification, as – arguably – can be the case for the scope of material competence).

440 Chaïm Perelman, *Les antinomies en droit. Essai de synthèse* in Les Antinomies en droit 392, 393-96 (Chaïm Perelman ed. 1965) (but the system's coherence requires them to be solved, either from the perspective of legislative coherence, or from the perspective of judicial duty to adjudicate); *also see* Alf Ross, On Law and Justice 18 (2004) (1958).

441 *See eg* No. 42/2005 (Feb. 23, 2005) B.11 (on a decree imposed obligations on marksmen to keep their guns and ammunition separately stored: in order to be licensed, marksmen had to declare in a statement of honor that this obligation would be fulfilled; since this statement took place in the French Community and since it pertained to a French Community license issued by the French community, it was irrelevant whether the storage would occur in the

just decide which criterion is not only pertinent, but also necessary[442] (at least in light of the necessity to avoid concrete norm conflict[443]). If the Court takes the latter option, material competence allocation will often be implicated, as there is a need to reciprocally coordinate connecting factors[444]. And as such, the principle of territoriality is not so much about preventing conflicts (anymore), but rather about solving them, in a pragmatic way. In Storme's words, the judges 'are doomed to realize the exclusive system'[445]. From all this, we can probably infer that, even if the Court accords discretion in principle to federated entities to adopt their own connecting factors[446], it renders some of them (apparently)

French Community. Moreover, Flemish and German-speaking license-holders would be allowed to shoot in the French Community too. Accordingly, in this regulation the Court saw no norm conflicts (although interference in norms could easily arise)) or No. 2/2009 (Jan. 14, 2009) B.14 (calling for cooperation by the Regions on ionizing radiation regulation, but accepting that the Brussels norm can apply to institutions located outside of the Brussels Region (although here too, interference with other norms could easily arise)).

442 Jan Velaers, *Het Arbitragehof herstelt de rechtszekerheid. De arresten van 30 januari 1986 inzake het taalgebruik in de sociale betrekkingen*, 1986-87 RW 1953 (approving); *but see* Marc Uyttendaele, *Observations sous l'arrêt de la Cour d'arbitrage du 26 juin 1986,* 1986 JT 564, 566 (calling the freedom 'more apparent than real', as confirmed in more recent writings, *eg* Uyttendaele, *supra* note 263, at p. 986-88); *compare* Storme, *supra* note 142, at p. 362-67 (on how the Court does what it says it would not, *ie* formulate a rule of conflict in cases of youth assistance and as such, implicitly deploying art. 26, §1, 2° SLCC).

443 *See eg* Raymond Vander Elst, *Antinomies en droit international privé* in Les antinomies en Droit, *supra* note 440, at p. 175-76 (discussing different antinomies in terms of their intensity) or Paul Foriers, *Les antinomies en droit,* in *ibid.* esp. at p. 37-38 (summarizing how the problem of antinomies may interact with different tenets and rules of interpretation).

444 Storme, *supra* note 142, at p. 338.

445 Storme, *supra* note 142, at p. 252; *also see* at p. 218 ('the principle of territoriality cannot be more than the starting point requiring a further concretization, the outlook of which [...] may be very diverse'), p. 246 (distinguishing the territorial sphere of validity from the territorial scope of application). *But compare ibid.* 217-18 (on 'binding force') *with* p. 246 (on validity) and notice the conceptual confusion.

446 *Compare* Henri Storme, *Vlaamse Zorgverzekering. De lange weg naar een geschikte aanknopingsfactor,* 187 Nieuw Juridisch Weekblad 614, 621 (2008) ('[t]he Constitution determines what the territory of the Communities is, but does not determine in which way a legal relationship should be situated within that territory which leads to the application of the law of the corresponding Community. The criterion [of residence in the Care insurance case] indeed *fits* the requirements of an exclusive territorial allocation of competences, but it is neither *required* nor *justified* by it. The acceptability of the connecting factor can not only be measured by the exclusivity of territorial competences, but must be reviewed in light of other elements: the objectives of a rule, the impact of a rule-makers policy, its budgetary implications, the expectations and interests of individuals, the general constitutional framework, and the entrenchment in the European and international context' (*emphasis in original*)) *with* Henri Storme, *Juristenkrant, supra* note 388, at p. 5 (arguing that the Constitutional Court, on the basis of the EMU, had the opportunity to impose just one valid connecting factor). On the unclarity of the disjunction in light of European law requirements, *see eg* Storme, *supra* note 142, at p. 401-02 (commenting on No. 51/2006 regarding Flemish care insurance) and 406-

compulsory[447], generally for (pragmatic) reasons of coordination and conflict-avoidance.

At the same time, what should not be forgotten is that (some of) the review procedures before the Court *are* abstract indeed, in different senses: on the one hand, the annulment procedure is abstract in the sense that the Court adjudges the legislative measure on its face (and it will accordingly have to decide whether it is possible or probable that a concrete norm conflict will ensue). On the other hand, there might be *abstraction* in the sense that the Court sometimes deals with virtual norm conflicts: then, the Court will conduct a similar operation (assessing the possibility of concrete norm conflict), since apart from norm A under scrutiny, no other norm will be available on the basis of which it could be adjudged whether an explicit and concrete conflict arises[448]. According to some, the latter abstraction is the direct translation of exclusivity[449], which would imply that the Court indeed can assess the principle in the abstract. Even if I will not elaborate in detail here, I think such a conceptualization and explanation of how the Court deals with virtual norm conflicts is deficient, since it presupposes or at least insists too rigidly on an *a priori* determination of competence allocation[450].

In a second, *jurisprudential* – more precisely, norm- and competence-theoretical – sense, the question emerges what the reach of the principle of exclusive territoriality is. Does it pertain primarily to the territorial *scope* of application of a certain norm, or does it also influence the particular territorial *modalities* or *conditions* set forth in or by a norm?

An answer to that question presupposes that such a distinction can be made intelligibly. Some authors argue that both the (territorial) *scope* and the *modalities* are part and parcel of the protasis[451] of any norm and should therefore

13 (commenting on Case C-212/06 and No. 11/2009) and 436-37, *esp.* n1621 (the facultative nature does not take several competence allocating principles into account, nor international law).

447 Uyttendaele points out, in light of Cases Nos. 9 and 10 (seat of exploitation as connecting factor), that the liberty to choose connecting factors is 'more apparent than real' (Uyttendaele, *supra* note 442, at p. 566, as confirmed for instance in Uyttendaele, *supra* note 263, at p. 986-88). *Compare* Storme, *supra* note 142, at p. 362-67 (on how the Court does what it says it would not, *ie* formulate a rule of conflict in cases of youth assistance and as such, implicitly deploy art. 26, §1, 2° SLCC) and at p. 406 *et seq.* (criticizing the Court for imposing the place of residence criterion in the care insurance case; *cf.* previous note).

448 *Eg* No. 65 (Oct. 18, 1988) IV.1.B.1.

449 *Eg* Van Koekenbeek, *supra* note 392, at p. 59-62; *cf.* Bribosia & Van Boxstael, *supra* note 13, at p. 58.

450 Instead of construing the determination from a more relational perspective.

451 Construing a norm as a hypothetical proposition (*if X (factual constellation) obtains, then Y (legal consequence)*), the protasis (or antecedent) is X, whereas the apodosis (or consequent) is Y (*see*

not be distinguished. This view, for instance, could be attributed to Kelsen: '[t]he sphere of validity of a norm is an element of its content'[452]. François Rigaux, however, nuances: '[t]he distinction between a disposition that delimits the material domain of application of rules in internal law and a disposition that determines its spatial domain [...] seems to be striking'[453]. This nuance is justified: it is not because, in a Kelsenian theoretical framework, both territorial *scope* and territorial *modalities* are part of the protasis of a norm, that they cannot be distinguished. Accordingly, even in a Kelsenian comprehension of norms, a distinction can intelligibly be made[454]. Then again, sometimes, the modalities and the scope are closely intertwined[455], for instance resulting from the fact that the territorial scope of a measure may be inferred from some territorial (or, for that matter, material) modalities, be they implicit or explicit[456]. We will highlight below how this can give rise to specific problems in the relationship with European law[457], but for now it suffices to argue that this jurisprudential distinction has a bearing on the dogmatic conundrum elaborated above.

Perhaps indeed, the distinction between disallowed territorial infringement and allowed (limited) extraterritorial effects can in some regards be brought back or at least related to these conceptual and jurisprudential issues. However, the Court's own theoretical framework – distinguishing extra-territorial scope / exercise of competences from (inherent) extraterritorial effects – does not address (m)any

eg Rupert Schreiber, Die Geltung von Rechtsnormen 3-40 (1966); Gidon Gottlieb, The Logic of Choice: An investigation of the concepts of rule and rationality 36, 39, 43-47 (1968); *also see* MacCormick, *supra* note 98, at p. 43, 45 (opting for *'operative facts'* instead of protasis) or Schauer, *supra* note 56, at p. 23 (opting for *factual predicate* instead of *protasis* and *consequent* instead of *apodosis*)). How norms (or their sphere of validity) in general should be represented, moreover, has been object of quite some jurisprudential debate, which we will leave aside for now.

[452] Kelsen, *supra* note 37, at p. 13.

[453] Rigaux, *supra* note 156, at p. 296. Even so, sometimes the territorial scope can be delimited within a material provision of law, even implicitly, from the 'global objectives pursued' (*ibid.* at p. 302-04; *but see* p. 314 *et seq.*).

[454] *Eg* No. 50/2011 (Apr. 6, 2011) B.64 *et seq.* (where a requirement of a sufficient nexus was set forth in order to be able to acquire goods in certain municipalities).

[455] *Eg* CC No. 107/2009 (July 9, 2009) B.9.1-B.9.3 (where the territorial scope of application of a decree was inferred from the fact the school inspection occurred for all minors, *residing* in a particular zone).

[456] *Eg* CC No. 107/2009 (July 9, 2009) B.9.1. *Compare* CA No. 42/2005 (Feb. 23, 2005) B.9 (where the scope of application of the regulation was so construed that a *material* requirement was imposed extra-territorially). Even so, concrete cases will still require a concrete resolution (which will often have to resolve possible conflicts); *eg* Storme, *supra* note 142, at p. 426-28.

[457] *Compare* No. 101/2008 (July 10, 2008) B.27-B.37 and B.42.1-B46 (on a requirement of being prepared to learn a language in order to be eligible for social housing *in some Brussels or linguistic border peripheral municipalities*, the Court refused to refer the case to the COJ).

of the underlying theoretical issues involved, and as such procures confusion. This is not the place to address what is the best way to theoretically conceptualize the Court's *Carrefour* jurisprudence. I merely offer some (theoretical) factors which go beyond the classic dogmatic framework and which may serve as more adequate explanations of the debates surrounding the *Carrefour* conundrum. But if we want to be able to explain more fully (or even predict) how the Court will respond to future cases – if that is possible at all – it seems that practice (and a pragmatic attitude) is more informative altogether.

86. The Court's thinking in practice: avoiding destabilization. Although it is clear that in many cases, the principle of exclusive territoriality does not as such constitute a problem[458], it could be argued that, *most generally*, in the cases

[458] Of all the cases that have come before the Court, only a very limited number directly engage the problem of territorial exclusivity of federated entities' competences. In his doctoral dissertation, Storme identifies five principal areas in which the Constitutional Court has produced some jurisprudence pertaining to territorial exclusivity, *ie* language use in social matters, youth assistance, amateur sports, subsidizing cultural initiatives and care insurance (*supra* note 142, at p. 332-33). Next to the *Carrefour* cases (on subsidizing cultural initiatives) discussed above, - insofar as these do not overlap – the cases mentioned *supra* note 382, and their direct applications (*see* Nos. 12, 13, 15, 16, 18, 19, 20, 21, 22 and 23 (Mar. 25, 1986 (12 through 16), May 20, 1986 (18), June 12, 1986 (19) and June 25, 1986 (20 through 23)) respectively III.3.B.2.a *et seq.*, III.B.3.a *et seq.*, III.B.2 *et seq.*, III.B.1 *et seq.*, III.B.2.a *et seq.*, III.B.1.a *et seq.*, III.B.1.a *et seq.*, III.B.1.a *et seq.*, III.B.1.a *et seq.* and III.B.1.a *et seq.* (application of No. 10 on use of languages in social matters in preliminary proceedings); *compare* No. 72/95 (Nov. 9, 1995) B.9 *et seq.*, *esp.* B.13.2 (limitation of the material competence in social relations, excluding offers and pre-contractual relations); No. 26 (Oct. 21, 1986) III.4.B.1 (application of No. 9 on language use in social matters in a preliminary proceeding); *also see* No. 29 (Nov. 18, 1986) III.3.B.1 *et seq.* (analogous application of No. 9; *cf.* No. 30 (Dec. 16, 1986) III)), the following cases could be mentioned: CA No. 11/98 (Feb. 11, 1998) B.15-B.18 (without localization criteria, there can be – in principle – no violation; *compare* No. 53/99 (May 26, 1999) B.7.4 (cannot decide a same preliminary reference twice, although the problem had reoccured in argumentation (*see* A.11))); No. 74/99 (June 30, 1999) B.9 (applying art. 129, §2, 2nd dash Cons.); No. 124/99 (Nov. 25, 1999) B.8.3 *et seq.* (right to free gathering of news); No. 30/2000 (Mar. 21, 2000) B.2.1 (on art education in one of the municipalities with special linguistic status); No. 33/2001 (Mar. 13, 2001) B.4.1 *et seq.* (on Flemish care insurance); No. 92/2003 (June 24, 2003) B.12 *et seq.* (on extra-territorial radio broadcasting); No. 119/2004 (June 30, 2004) B.2.4 (on travel agencies in Brussels) No. 42/2005 (Feb. 23, 2005) B.9 (on recreational shooting); No. 44/2005 (Feb. 23, 2005) B.12.2 *et seq.* (on how to delimit the Communities territorial competences on education in Brussels); Nos. 56/96 (Oct. 15, 1996) B.7.2-B.7.3; 85/2008 (May 27, 2008) B.6.2 *et seq.* and No. 41/2010 (Apr. 29, 2010) B.5.1 (all three on regional cross-border taxi licences, but *compare* the first and the last judgments; *adde* No. 40/2012 (Mar. 8, 2012) B.7.2); No. 2/2009 (Jan. 15, 2009) B.13 *et seq.* (on non-ionizing radiation control in Brussels); No. 107/2009 (July 9, 2009) B.8 *et seq.* (on extramural education); and the several cases on the Flemish inspection of Francophone schools in the communities bordering the linstuigic border (and on how to combine the reading of art. 16*bis-ter* SLIR and art. 127 Cons.) Nos. 95/2010 (July 29, 2010) (suspension), 124/2010 (Oct. 28, 2010) (partial annulment) and their progeny in 2011 (Nos. 57/2011 (Apr. 28, 2011) (where there was however no real scrutiny of the principle of territoriality) and No. 60/2011 (May 5,

it does, the Court performs exacting scrutiny if a federated entities' measure is *anticipated* or *intended* to destabilize the fragile equilibrium between the federated entities. This requires further explanation and qualification.

First, without fear of serious destabilization, the Court shows more restraint: rigid analytic conceptualism (on territoriality) is certainly enslaved by pragmatism here[459].

Second, the distinction drawn here between 'intent' and 'anticipation'[460] on the one hand, and the meaning of 'exacting scrutiny' on the other hand require some elucidation. Whereas it seems clear that the Court in *Carrefour* was convinced that the intent of the French Community was to fund a specific form of minority protection[461], in some other cases, the distinction is less clear. For instance, as regards the school inspection cases[462], people can (reasonably)

2011)). *Also see* STORME, *supra* note 142, at p. 251-52, 318-19 (noting that many problems will have to be solved by the regular judiciary; *cf. supra* No. 78).

459 *See* Velaers & Vanpraet, *supra* note 388, at p. 202 (the principle of territoriality does not play 'insofar as the territorial competence of the other federated entity is not endangered'). *Also see* CA No. 2/97 (Jan. 16, 1997) B.17.1-B.17.2 (in exercising its international competences, a Region may (obviously) take extraterritorial considerations into account, *in casu* the trajectory of ships towards the ports for which it is competent); Van Eeckhoutte, *supra* note 433, at p. 855-56, 863 (arguing that the principle does not play in international relations). Van Eeckhoutte's position should be nuanced in light of CC No. 107/2009 (July 9, 2009) B.13.1, where the Court recharacterized the extra-territorial factor in its decision (the fact that it pertained to the recognition of diplomas of foreign schools) so as to render it compatible with the internal principle of exclusive territoriality.

460 I rely here on a dictionary definition of anticipation and intention (and therefore I do not want to broach issues of psychological nature, or even concomitant philosophical-hermeneutical questions). Anticipation in this regard is weaker than real intention: when one anticipates, one could be said to merely 'speak or write in *knowledge* or *expectation* of later matter', whereas when one intends, one actually 'has in mind as purpose or goal' (MERRIAM-WEBSTER DICTIONNARY). The distinction is often course not always neat and thus sometimes becomes blurred.

461 On how this can be derived, *see* CA No. 56/2000 (May 17, 2000) B.6.

462 Mentioned *supra* note 458; *also see supra* note 308. In these cases, a 2009 Flemish decree was reviewed which determined that general provisions regarding Flemish education were to be applied to Francophone schools too, for instance in municipalities having a special linguistic status, in the Brussels periphery (No. 124/2010), and elsewhere along the linguistic border (No. 60/2011). More concretely, these schools would have to (1) implement the Flemish development goals and final objectives (unless the Flemish Parliament ratified a deviation), (2) accept school inspection by Flemish inspectors, (3) apply an educational plan approved by the Flemish government and (4) contract with a Flemish Centre for Student Guidance. The Court, simplifiedly, accepted that some of these measures infringed upon the existing guarantees for the Francophones, protected by art. 16*bis* SLIR (with reference to a 1971 Special Law which would guarantee Francophone inspection of the Francophone schools) and argued that not allowing for a (timely) deviation under (1) would impinge upon the principle of federal loyalty *juncto* the idea of mutual recognition.

disagree about whether there was an intent or anticipation (or perhaps even only counterfactual normative knowledge[463]) by Flanders that the federation would or could be destabilized. We could even try to coalesce intent and anticipation under the heading of 'reasonable expectation'[464]. Next to that, these school inspection cases exemplify the difficulties surrounding the meaning of *exacting* scrutiny. On the one hand, it could surely be argued that the Court performed intensive scrutiny in these cases (their sheer length, compared to other cases, can be construed as evidence for that). On the other hand, the exact opposite could be argued as well, namely that the Court deferred to the political compromise of 1970-1971. Even so, the 1970-1971 compromise was construed strictly, so as to occasion a conceivable *balanced* outcome for both the Francophones and the Flemish.

Succinctly, the Court compromised internally. The latter adds an additional twist to the idea of exacting scrutiny, and perhaps more generally, to cases in which federalism plays, especially politically salient cases where the intensity of preferences of judges for this or that outcome (or line of reasoning) is greater. I do not address the issue separately, but the school inspection cases are certainly not the only cases in which the Court has sought an internal compromise, formulated to fit extant doctrinal structure. More generally, this seems to be exactly what the Court does in (hard) federalism cases. How to square this hypothetical, yet not wholly unlikely (empirical) finding (which is entirely commensurate with a toolbox conceptualization of the Court's jurisprudence) with rule of law values, is a tougher question though, which I will not address at this stage[465].

---

[463] In the sense that 'it ought to have known, but did not in fact'.

[464] *Compare infra* Ch. 3.3.2.2.

[465] What can be mentioned here is that sometimes the principle of territoriality might stand in the way of dogmatically coherent stabilization. In the school inspection cases, the Court apparently found an internal compromise to have French Community inspectors inspect francophone schools in the Flemish municipalities with special linguistic status. Here, the Court had to explicitly stipulate (keeping article 127 Cons. in mind) that 'article 5 of the June 21, 1971 Special Law could not imply that the territorial scope of application of decrees of the French Community regarding pedagogical inspection, educational plans, goals and pedagogical provisions, could be extended to cover the aforementioned schools and sections, nor that these decrees are applicable vis-à-vis them as such' (CC No. 124/2010 (Oct. 28, 2010) B.34.1; *cf.* No. 95/2010 (July 29, 2010) B.36; No. 60/2011 (May 5, 2011) B.20.4; *cf.* Laurent Maniscalco, *Les droits linguistiques en matière d'enseignement: de la contractualisation aux règles répartitrices de compétence*, case note accompanying CC Nos. 95/2010 and 124/2010, 2012 RBDC 192, 213-216 and 222-228). It is very unclear how such an assertion can be squared with the rule of law value of legality: on which legal basis (in the territorial sense) would Francophone inspection then be allowed? Accordingly, this demonstrates that the Court has to make choices in the toolbox, but too, that these choices must be (attempted to be) reconciled with each other in light of rule of law values, which is far from evident. *Also see infra,* next paragraph.

Finally, on the one hand, the territorial 'conflict-avoiding' credo does not mean that this is the *only* relevant explanatory variable. This is of course already clear from the *toolbox concept* we employed, but I wish to underline it once again. First, there are other 'doctrines', 'principles', 'rules', or (in our framework) 'tools' that can interact with the principle of territoriality. Recently, for instance, the Constitutional Court explicitly recognized the principle of *mutual recognition* as a basic principle in Belgian constitutional law[466]. More broadly, the Court has argued that the legislatures may in any case take into account facts and legislation from outside its own territory while legislating[467]. Second, there might be a relevant distinction between abstract and concrete review in play[468]. And third, 'conflict-avoiding' can be understood from two different perspectives: the Court not only seeks to avoid conflict between the different federated entities within the Belgian framework, but it also seeks to avoid conflict between itself and the legislature, by deferring to the legislature from time to time (at least insofar as there is no conflict of the first kind impending or imminent)[469]. The grounds for this judicial deference (or restraint), however, fall beyond the scope of this work.

Even if this balancing-searching engine behind Constitutional Court case-law regarding territorial exclusivity might be thought of as too general to have real predictive value, especially when one realizes there is no *a priori* structural relationship with qualifications and other *tools* (thus justifying that the Court's

[466] *Inherent* in the EMU; *see* CC No. 41/2010 (Apr. 29, 2010) B.5.3; *also see* CC No. 129/2011 (July 14, 2011) B.4.3-B.4.4 (in educational matters); *adde* CoS Advice, *Parl. Doc.* Senate 2003 SS, No. 3-89/1, at p. 11-12 (recognizing that other regional governments are bound by the issuance of a taxi licence) and implicitly CC 40/2012 (Mar. 8, 2012) B.7.1. *Compare* art. 1*ter* SLFCR (enshrining a cooperation principle against double taxes; *see* INGELAERE *et al.*, *supra* note 219, at p. 228); *also compare eg* Butterfly Agreement, *infra* note 10, at p. 39 (on the mutual recognition of driving schools). It is not certain that the principle of mutual recognition – if we analogize with European law – will bring more clarity to the fore (*see eg* Christine Janssens & Lieve Hoornaert, case note accompanying Court of Justice case *Liga Portuguesa*, 2010-11 RW 211, 213-14; *also see infra* note 629 and accompanying text).

[467] CA No. 51/98 (Mar. 20, 1998) B.4.2.

[468] *Compare eg* No. 72/96 (Dec. 11, 1996) B.7.6 (where in preliminary proceedings, the Court gave some more detailed directions to the judge *a quo*) *with* No. 11/98 (Feb. 11, 1998) B.17 (where the Court seemed more rigorous in the determination of its own competence). *Cf.* STORME, *supra* note 142, at p. 369-70, 384 (Storme here relies on art. 26 §1 2° SLCC to more or less justify a difference, which is not necessary, since it can follow from the nature of the proceedings themselves).

[469] *See eg* Boogaard, *supra* note 61; *also see eg* VELAERS, VAN ARBITRAGEHOF TOT..., *supra* 13, note 95-101.

case law can be predicated as *ad hoc*[470]), this by no means impairs the arguments against the lack of explanatory potential of dogmatics.

87. The issue of Brussels. Brussels, a quandary when it comes to territorial exclusivity, further complicates matters. Whereas the issue is not so much salient as to Regional matters (as for this purpose, a Brussels territory has been delineated)[471], as to Community matters, there is only a limited *institutional* competence[472], supplemented by competences of the Joint Community Commission in bi-person-related matters[473], and by the residual competences of the federal government in bi-cultural matters. Even if the details of this arrangement fall beyond the scope of our inquiry, four judgments on the principle of territoriality involved Brussels, which therefore are shortly discussed here.

In No. 124/99[474], the Court invalidated a provision of a Flemish decree which sought to guarantee a right to free news gathering, insofar as it was applied to mean that that every broadcasting service which belonged to or was recognized by the Flemish Community had a right to access events and to record there if the organizing institution exclusively belonged the Flemish Community (due to its organization)[475]. The Court here rigidly applied article 127 of the Constitution and imposed an interpretation in which the rights could only be guaranteed vis-à-vis institutions which – due to their *activities* – should be deemed to resort exclusively under the Flemish Community competence[476]. The Court accordingly here did not seem to follow the pragmatic justifications of the Flemish government[477] to employ the 'organizational' criterion.

---

470 *Cf.* Storme, *supra* note 142, at p. 251 (underlining the necessity of casuistic approach due to a lack of coherence in (material) allocation of competences; *but compare ibid.* at p. 387 n1498 (critical of Alen & Ergec's considerations on pragmatism)).

471 *See eg* CA No. 56/96 (Oct. 15, 1996) B.7.2-B.7.3 on renting cars with drivers and taxis and its progeny (*cf.* Storme, *supra* note 142, at p. 428-31).

472 *Cf. supra* No. 47.

473 Art. 135 Cons. *juncto* art. 7, 62-63 SLBI. 'Person-related matters' are very hard to define (*compare* Rimanque's replacement of 'person-related' by other vague concepts (*Parl. Doc.* Flemish Council 1984-85, No. 312/1, at p.8) *with* Delpérée's try, which to some extent seems to distort the idea (*supra* note 401, at p. 825). What is sure is that the 'communicative' aspect that was emphasized during the constitutional amendment process (*eg* CoS Advice, *Parl. Doc.* French Community Council 1984-85, No. 172/1, at p. 7 *et seq.*), was not withheld as a dispositive criterion by the Court (CA No. 66 (June 30, 1988) III.2.B and No. 67 (Nov. 9, 1988) III.4.B).

474 Nov. 25, 1999.

475 *Ibid.* B.8.4 and B.8.6.

476 B.8.7.

477 A.7.2.

In No. 33/2001[478], the Court decided that a Flemish decree imposing contributions to (partly) finance a system of care insurance could be applied to Brussels, insofar as the obligations of the scheme only applied to (care insurance) institutions[479]. Since the Flemish legislature had not imposed specific obligations on residents in Brussels (allowing them a free choice to either join or not join the scheme)[480], the constitutional provisions on territorial competences were not violated. The Care Insurance issue will be brought up again in a different light below[481].

In No. 119/2004[482], the Court decided that when the French Community Commission allows for travel agencies to provide services outside their seat of exploitation (a prohibition was federally instituted in the 1960), the fact that this allowance does not hold for travel agencies in Flanders or "Flemish" travel agencies in Brussels, 'is due to the limits that spring from the territorial and material competence of the French Community Commission'[483]. The Court here seems to implicitly accept that there might be such a thing like Francophone unicommunautarian travel agencies, which are sufficiently localized insofar as the connecting factor is the seat of the travel agency[484]. However, the markets where the travel agencies may sell their services must also be localized in the Brussels Metropolitan Region area[485].

Case No. 44/2005[486], finally, involved the question how to delimit the Communities' educational competences in Brussels, when language use comes in play,

---

478 Mar. 13, 2001.

479 B.4.4.

480 B.4.3.

481 Different, in the sense that 'even if the Regions would have been competent, the problem of European law, and of the connecting factors "residence" versus "working place" would have posed itself in exactly the same way' (Pas, *supra* note 127).

482 June 30, 2004.

483 B.2.4; *also see* B.4.2

484 *Cf.* Jean-François Neuray, *La réglementation du tourisme en région bruxelloise: une nécessaire mise au point*, 2006 Revue de la Jurisprudence de Liège, Mons et Bruxelles 232, 233-34 (critical on this point).

485 *See* Wouter Pas, *Federale loyauteit, de bevoegdheid inzake toerisme en unicommunautaire reisbureaus. Enkele bedenkingen bij het arrest 119/2004 van het Arbitragehof*, 2005 TBP 147, *esp*. 160-64); Storme, *supra* note 142, at p. 227-34, 353-54, 370-76, 379-86 (discussing how the constitutional language is problematic and forces the legislatures to resort to a lot of pragmatism; *see esp*. p. 374). On how Brussels can constitute vast problems in practice, however, *see* (next to the abovenmentioned references to Storme's dissertation), *eg* Laurence Gallez & Thomas Bombois, *Les Infrastructures et les centre sportifs locaux*, 2004 Revue de Droit Communal 5, 40-45 (on problems of localization pertaining to building and financing sports infrastructure in Brussels).

486 Feb. 23, 2005.

for which the Communities are not competent in Brussels in conformity with article 129 of the Constitution. In this case, the Court set up a dual construction, on the one hand arguing that the Communities themselves are competent to determine the criteria on the basis of which an institution should be thought of the exclusively appertain to one or the other community, and on the other hand conceiving of the legal provisions in play (articles regulating the use of language) as setting forth such criteria[487], which confirms the point we made before.

Evaluations of the Court's Brussels jurisprudence, at least in this respect, have generally not been so generous, mostly because of doctrinal incoherence[488], which confirms the point we made before.

88. Territoriality as a tool-like principle. To conclude, the principle of territoriality is what it is: a *principle* (deployed as a tool), which posits an abstract requirement of a nexus to the territory of the entity legislating. This principle in action before the Constitutional Court implies that, when a federated entity decides to delimit its own competences *ratione loci*, the limitation should be *sufficiently* linked to the territory of the entity (in light of the competence at hand). In order to assess that sufficiency, the Court (also) has to take the stability of the country as a whole into account. The Court employs different concepts out of its toolbox to accomplish this. The territoriality principle *pragmatically* works as one of these tools.

These are, according to a majority of constitutional scholars, the basic principles underlying Belgian federalism. Accordingly, primarily in light of these principles, the influence of European law will be discussed further on. We have tried to explain how these principles should not be conceived of *more geometrico*, but first and foremost as pragmatic tools. Although this explanation can account for some of the jurisprudence, the Court's (federalism) toolbox obviously consists of more than merely these tools, which we turn to in what follows.

---

[487] B.12.2.

[488] *See* Wouter Pas's contribution in 2006-07 Tijdschrift voor Onderwijsrecht en Onderwijsbeleid 234, 236 (on the constitutional distinction between organization and activities); *also see* Storme, *supra* note 142, at p. 375-76 (praising the result, lamenting the means); *compare* Eddy Clybouw, *Het Arbitragehof en de Bamahervorming. Enkele beschouwingen bij het arrest van 23 februari 2005*, 2004-05 Tijdschrift voor Onderwijsrecht en Onderwijsbeleid 506, 515 (praising the Court for its pragmatism); *compare too* CoS Advice, *Parl. Doc.* Flemish Parl. 1991-92, No. 502/1, at p. 211-18 (on the justificatory relevance of the distinction between universities and other schools pertaining to language use regulation), as (negatively) evaluated by Velaers, De Grondwet en de Raad van State, *supra* note 13, at p. 425 *with* CoS Advice, *Parl. Doc.* Flemish Parl. 2002-03, No. 1571/1, at p. 258-59. *Further compare* CoS No. 156.418 (Mar. 15, 2006) *Paleis Stoclet* (on the difficulty of localizing movables, for which the Communities are competent in Brussels and the breadth of the term 'institution' in art. 127, § 2 Cons.).

3.3 "Incidental" principles in the toolbox

3.3.1 Specific "(con)textual" constraints

89. Underlying principles and categories. Continuing our investigation of Belgian constitutional scholarship, it should be noted that most commentators recognize that next to exclusive powers, there are (exceptionally) some parallel powers (in which case the entities can exercise competences next to each other), and some concurrent powers (in which case, in Belgium, the federal government always seems to have something more to say than it does under 'regular' exclusive competences). Scholars seem to find it very hard to precisely define what this 'more' is. The reasoning is generally thought to occur in specific categories – such as parallel, or concurrent powers – or through well established principles, such as the principle of verticality, which is generally thought to mean that *unless otherwise stipulated*, in Belgium, the entity which is responsible for legislating a certain competence object, is also responsible to execute and administer the legislative policy decided upon.[489] However, these categories and principles generally cannot do the explanatory work commentators expect them to do.

90. Deficiency, as illustrated by the principle of verticality. Well-established as the principle of verticality might be in the abstract, we incur similar issues as the ones we treated above: in short, there is a deficiency in overly abstract categories, which in doctrinal accounts are generally presupposed to integrate into a coherent whole[490].

The case law – also the Constitutional Court's – on the issue of distinguishing legislation from execution (*legality*) is vast[491]. A good example of the difficulties associated with (what are thought to be) (the exceptions to) the principle of verticality is found in some earlier cases of the Court.[492] According to the competence allocation in force at that time, the Regions were competent to *execute* the measures regarding placement of unemployed persons *established* by the federal government. The Court nonetheless adds that a legislative organ need not necessarily impose this establishment: also the executive organ (or

[489] *See eg* CA No. 65 (June 15, 1988) IV.2.B.1. This stands in contradistinction to other forms of federalism, such as German executive federalism.

[490] Vanpraet, *supra* note 190, at p. 50 *et seq.*

[491] Rest assured, I will not quote it. I focus on cases with a clear link to federalism. *Compare too* Feyen, *supra* note 256, at p. 1370 *et seq.*

[492] CA No. 58 (June 8, 1988) III.B.4.5-III.B.4.6; CA No. 71 (Dec. 21, 1988) III.2.B.3 or CA No. 2/89 (Feb. 2, 1989) III.B.3 (on similar legislative validations).

its services) may partake in the establishment as a 'normative competence'[493]. What is important, nonetheless, is that the Regions remain competent to take individual measures. Accordingly, there is a complex intertwining of different functions and organs at play[494] that resists simple categorizations as those expounded by the commonplace definition of the principle of verticality. Even if it might be the case that there are principled (indeed 'rule of law'-related) reasons to distinguish between *legislating* and *executing*, such as the sophisticated one elaborated by Habermas[495], this does not justify a stringent, concomitant dogmatic distinction per se. All the more so, this is the case because of underlying theoretical issues: for instance - it has been (controversially) contended by Kelsen that '[a]pplication of law is at the same time creation of law [...]. It is not quite correct to distinguish between law-creating and law-applying acts [,b] ecause [...] every legal act is at the same time the application of a higher norm and the creation of a lower norm. [Accordingly,] the constitution is created in application of the basic norm'[496]. Apart from justifications for the difference, it is clear that quite some judicial ingenuity is required to be able to determine (as the case might be), whether a specific norm / act is of a legislative or an executive/administrative nature. Accordingly, the principle of verticality is far from (self-) explanatory, neither in a dogmatic sense, nor in a more theoretical-analytic sense.

More generally, although there is *some* explanatory value in categorizations like parallel powers, concurrent powers, or the principle of verticality (certainly from a point of view of *teaching* federalism), their explanatory potential (from the point of view of *understanding* the case law of the Court) is rather limited, or at least more limited than generally thought. Attempting to formulate predictable, conclusive or even straight-forward rules, for instance on the basis of the aforementioned categories, seems destined for failure, not only for the reasons elaborated above, but also for reasons explained below. Taking a more action-oriented perspective seems to be more informative here.

---

493 In No. 58, it expressly adds that this should not be confused with (what is now) art. 108 Cons., which is a central article in separation of powers doctrine; *compare eg* CA No. 5/91 (Mar. 26, 1991) III.B.2 (where the Court talks about a division of normative competences in the context of (old) art. 6, §1, VIII, 1° SLIR).

494 *Also see infra* note 544, with specific reference to Nos. 2/89 and 79/92 in light of the separation of powers doctrine and Peeters, *supra* note 188, at p. 71 (noting the intricate connection between federalism and separation of powers issues).

495 Habermas, *supra* note 31, at p. 175 ('[t]he *priority of laws* legitimated in democratic procedures has the cognitive meaning that the administration does not have its own access to the normative premises underlying its decisions' (*emphasis added*)).

496 Kelsen, *supra* note 37, at p. 234.

91. The Court in action generally: playing with text and context. What the Court seems to do, in general, is to have a look at the provisions in play[497], at the *travaux préparatoires* of the relevant provisions, at its own case law, and at the general legislative framework (broadly or more narrowly, often including purpose and consequences) in which a particular measure has been adopted. It depends on this '(con)text' as a whole[498], whether or not a measure will be allowed to pass or not. Of course, this 'action-oriented' approach does not by itself offer conclusive or predictable rules either, as it is too general for that.

Moreover, it does not seem that the variables ("legal sources", or sources of legal reasoning) at play here (within the meaning of "'(con)text' as a whole") interact in an *a priori, more geometrico* way. Spending time on each and every one of them separately (and analytically) will accordingly thwart my purpose, which is to construe a general framework within which the arguments of the Constitutional Court can be adequately (and more realistically) conceptualized. This again brings us back to the general notion of tools, which – we assume – can be *mutatis mutandis* applied to these different sources of legal reasoning, not only because leeway is afforded to the Court in *interpreting*[499] the texts *sensu stricto*[500], but more importantly because the interpretative activity of the Court in a broader sense[501] allows for it to play with the sources of legal reasoning. All

---

[497] I take 'in play' here to mean argued for by the parties (*but compare supra* note 293 (on *proprio motu* arguments; *also see* VELAERS, VAN ARBITRAGEHOF TOT ..., *supra* note 13, at p. 507-09); *eg* CC No. 97/2011 (May 31, 2011) B.7.3 (where an argument arising from European law (the 2nd and 3rd Electricity Directive) was raised *ex officio*)). This is a first and foremost pragmatic assertion: it does not discount some theoretical problems involved by the issue of *Vorverständnis* (*see supra* note 373). In fact, these additional problems underscore my general point, although I will not further reflect on them theoretically (*compare infra* note 500).

[498] In preliminary proceedings, especially the facts of the case may play a role (Marc Bossuyt, *De verhouding tussen de hoogste rechtscolleges*, speech delivered in Leuven (PDS) on Nov. 8, 2010).

[499] A recent *sensu stricto* (and arguably more semantically classic, but therefore not hermeunetically uncontested (*cf. eg* STANLEY FISH, IS THERE A TEXT IN THIS CLASS (1980))) definition of interpretation in this regard has been proferred by Barak (PURPOSIVE INTERPRETATION IN LAW 3 *et seq.* (2005), who basically argues that 'linguistics sets the boundaries of legal interpretation [:] the end of every interpretive process must remain within the bounds of language' (*ibid.* at p. 19), and as such does not pertain to either filling gaps, deciding conflicts between texts, correcting mistakes in a text, and other '"non-interpretive"-doctrines' (*see* his p. 61 *et seq.*).

[500] For a recent example as to how, *see* CC No. 97/2011 (May 31, 2011), where the Court decided that distribution tariffs should also be included within the meaning of 'tariffs' (of which the normal meaning is consumer prices and industrial prices for energy) for which the Belgian federal government is competent, as 'these tariffs influence the consumer price' (B.5.3).

[501] Thus incorporating for instance problems of proof, problems of classification, problems of interpretation (*sensu stricto*) and problems of relevancy (*cf.* MACCORMICK, *supra* note 62, at p. 39-43 (*also see passim*) (*compare* FERNANDO ATRIA, ON LAW AND LEGAL REASONING 47 (2002) ('insistence upon *indeterminacy of meaning* as the master explanation of legal disagreement is clearly insufficient')), but also on the conflicts between rules, which in an even more 'stark'

this does not mean that the Court will not try to treat like cases alike[502], or more generally, that it will not try to adhere to the rule of law in general, or its more concrete conceptualized requirements (what we have coined rule of law values). Neither does this mean that there are no easy cases; surely there are[503]. What we do repudiate is that the simplicity of a case can be the result of some unshakable dogmatic doctrine, according to which – presumably – conclusive results can be reached. The easiness of a case does not depend on such adages as a 'clear text' doctrine[504], which is not only susceptible to (theoretical) criticism on its own, but should also be relativized in light of some other judgments[505]. Instead, it is a function of interplay of complex underlying arguments and presuppositions, none of which can or should be reasonably disputed, the result of which is that a case is perceived of as easy[506]. At the same time, as we will try to show in what follows, the underlying arguments and presuppositions, and the conceptual apparatus legal dogmatics has developed to deal with these, very often can be

sense shows the 'often murky nature of the law, and the corresponding need for the exercise of judgment' (SHAPIRO, *supra* note 37, at p. 237). It could also be deemed to incorporate, as for instance treated in the context of the Belgian division of competences by VANPRAET, principles like that of *lex specialis* (*cf. supra* note 190, at p. 148-155, *and see* critically, Stef Feyen, review of *De Latente Staatshervorming*, 2012-13 RW 279, 282).

502 This is, for its part, a more or less established rule of law requirement. *See eg* FULLER, *supra* note 60 (most of his eight principles of legality (*see* p. 33 *et seq.*) are closely related to this requirement; *cf. eg* p. 157-58, p. 218-19); *also see* JOHN RAWLS, A THEORY OF JUSTICE 206-14, esp. 208-09 (2nd ed. 1999) (1971) (describing the requirement as 'justice as regularity', applied to the legal system to become 'the principle of legality'); *also see* JUDITH N. SCHKLAR, LEGALISM: LAW, MORALS AND POLITICAL TRIALS 113-18 (1964) (explaining how following rules impartially constitutes a virtue, which cannot be easily followed in social practice); *compare* ARISTOTLE, NICOMACHEAN ETHICS 88-89 (W.D. Ross transl. 1999) (exposing the requirement as a correction to legality) or Herbert L.A. Hart, *Positivism and the Separation of Law and Morals*, 71 HARV. L.R. 593, 624 (1958) (who describes the requirement not as justice of the law, but as 'justice in the administration of the law'); *but compare* David A. Strauss, *Must Like Cases be Treated Alike?* (Chicago Public Law and Legal Theory Working Paper No. 24), available at http://ssrn.com/abstract_id=312180 (who refuses to conceive of this precept as a requirement with independent *moral* force).

503 *Eg* Case No. 15/90 (Apr. 5, 1990) B.17, B.21 (whereas art. 11 SLIR explicitly determines that 'the provisions of Book I of the Penal Code are applicable' (to criminal sanctions of the federated entities), the Walloon Region had here decreed that these were indeed applicable 'excepting article 85'); *also see* CA No. 52 (Mar. 17, 1988) III.B.5 or CA 11/89 (May 11, 1989) III.B.10. Even if *in principle* it would have been possible to construe some kind of nuance, exception of deviation here, a *prima facie* reading of these provisions seems to indicate that this is an easy case (*cf.* SHAPIRO, *supra* note 37, at p. 31).

504 *Eg* No. 193/2004 (Nov. 24, 2004) B.10.

505 *See* eg Feyen, *supra* note 169, at p. 7-8, 15-16, *esp.* n77.

506 The theoretical literature about the distinction between hard and easy cases, especially in American scholarship is vast. However, here is not the time or place to further explore it in depth.

reasonably disputed. The main problem is not so much the scholars' ideas, but their fixation on them[507].

All this, hopefully, will become clearer when we further elaborate the *incidental* principles in the Court's toolbox below.

92. Parallel competences. Competence allocations have been called *parallel*, by and large, when a matter – a competence object – may be regulated by different legislatures separately (and applied cumulatively and independently)[508].

93. Dogmatic concepts caught between text and context and the meaning of parallel competences: the difficulty of bringing norms under competence headings. The parallelism of competences might find inspiration in the text[509], but in some cases, it is just enunciated by the Court[510]. Even so, the distinction between both is not always entirely clear, and wrought with some complexity, especially when read in combination with other constitutional doctrine.

The case of constitutional rights provides a germane example of the latter complexity. Whereas the protection of fundamental rights was deemed to be a federal *residual* competence during much of the 1990s[511], the Court decided

[507] *Cf.* Daniel A. Farber & Suzanna Sherry, Desparately Seeking Certainty. The Misguided Quest for Constitutional Foundations (2002) (who argue that 'no single grand theory can successfully guide judges or provide determinate – or even sensible – answers to all constitutional questions. Only an amalgam of theories will do' (*ibid.* at p. 5)).

[508] *See generally* Alen & Muylle, *supra* note 14, at p. 397 *et seq.*; Peeters, *supra* note 38, at p. 288; Plets, *supra* note 47, at p. 62; Popelier, *supra* note 45, at p. 102, 108-09; Suetens & Leysen, *supra* note 316, at p. 51-53; Uyttendaele, *supra* note 13, at p. 452 *et seq.;* Vande Lanotte & Goedertier, *supra* note 13, at p. 967 *et seq.*, 1008 *et seq.*

[509] *Eg* in the Constitution, which, vis-à-vis several constitutional rights, provides that both the federal states as the federated entities guarantee the protection of the right (*eg* art. 22*bis* (2) Cons.). *Compare* CA No. 124/2000 (Nov. 29, 2000) B.4.2 (more general conclusion). Moreover, the competence regarding scientific research has been deemed to be parallel (art. 6*bis*, §1 and §2, 1° SLIR; *cf.* CA No. 34/92 (May 7, 1992) B.1; CA No. 76/2000 (June 21, 2000) B.3.2; CC 57/2012 (May 3, 2012) B.10.2). *Also see* art. 31, § 6 SLIR (on political party financing). *Compare* art. 6, §1, VI (1) 2° and (5) 2° SLIR, which Alen deems to be parallel competences (Alen & Muylle, *supra* note 14, at p. 398-399). Even so, whereas both clauses expressly stipulate 'controlling credit institutions' (although in (5) this might be connected to savings), (5) expressly mentions that *only* the federal government is competent. I will not go into the *travaux préparatoires* or scholarship commenting on this relationship, but suffice it to re-emphasize that the *textual* grounds are not always self-explanatory in this regard.

[510] *Eg* CA No. 11 (Feb. 25, 1986) III.1.B.3 (public financing of industry); CA No. 15/99 (Feb. 10, 1999) B.2.2. (providing guarantees vis-à-vis import, export and investment risks).

[511] *See eg* CA No. 14/91 (May 28, 1991) B.3.2-B.3.3 (on the right of response as a necessary corollary of the free press); *also see* Patrick Peeters, *De bevoegdheidsverdeling en het recht van antwoord – Kanttekeningen bij het arrest van 28 mei 1991 van het Arbitragehof*, 1991-92 RW 481, 483-84; Marc Uyttendaele, *Fédéralisme et libertés fondamentales: la transparence administrative au regard de la réforme de l'Etat*, 1993 APT 96, 103.

by the end of that decade that 'fundamental rights protection' was no longer a *separate* matter[512]. Accordingly, there is quite some leeway in the texts[513], which does not render distinguishing so-called parallel competences with a textual basis from those without one an easy task.

Differentiating between *material* competences and *instrumental* competences[514], if this is possible at all[515], adds another twist to the analysis. Insofar as competences are coined as instrumental[516], they can be conceived of as accessory or complementary to the competence[517]. This also seems to be suggested by art. 6*bis*, §1 ('within the framework of their competences') and §2 SLIR. To that extent, these complementary competences could also be construed as more or less implied[518], notwithstanding the fact that they have been separately enshrined in the SLIR (albeit not under the general competence-conferring articles 4-6). In that case, there is no need to construe them as a *separate* matter[519]. However, some authors seem to have done exactly that, notwithstanding their instrumental nature[520]. This added layer of complexity just goes on to show the relativity of the concepts employed here[521], and how they might be hard to square with the most visible legal foundations, *ie* the competence-allocating texts.

More generally, the qualification of a specific norms (to be reviewed in light of the allocation of competences) is wrought with complexities. Even if there

512 CA No. 124/99 (Nov. 25, 1999) B.4.4 and No. 124/2000 (Nov. 29, 2000) B.4.2 (expressly and in general terms); *also see* CoS Advice, *Parl. Doc.* Flemish Parl. 1995 SS, Nos. 82/2 and 118/2 (pertaining to the *Carrefour* jurisprudence, which foreshadowed No. 124/2000).

513 *Compare* CA No. 55/2001 (May 8, 2001) B.4-B.5 (where the Court carves out again a residual competence for the federal state pertaining to express motivation of individual administrative acts, notwithstanding the fact that this competence could be easily construed as one guaranteeing fundamental rights). *Also see* Report (Van Hecke), *Parl. Doc.* Flemish Parl. 2000-01, No. 641/1 (with references); Alen, *supra* note 38, at p. 27-29; Velaers, de Grondwet en de Raad van State, *supra* note 13, at p. 223-27 (on the point of view of the CoS in this matter).

514 CA No. 24 (June 26, 1986) III.5.B.1 or CA No. 28 (Nov. 18, 1986) III.5.B.2.

515 Bribosia & Van Boxstael, *supra* note 13, at p. 100 (noting that it is not easy).

516 *Ie* to achieve the '*effet utile*' of a particular material competence; *cf.* Uyttendaele, *supra* note 13, at p. 462-63.

517 *See eg* Alen & Muylle, *supra* note 14, at p. 461 *et seq.*

518 *Compare infra* on art. 10 SLIR.

519 *Eg* CA No. 76/2000 (June 21, 2000) B.3.2.

520 *Eg* Bribosia & Van Boxstael, *supra* note 13, at p. 100.

521 *Compare* CA No. 76/2000 (June 21, 2000) B.3.2 and B.4.2-B.4.4 (where the Court seems to conceptually speak from both sides of its mouth, on the one hand stressing the parallel nature of the research competence, and on the other hand stressing the importance of determining the main point of the regulation at hand, concluding that the competence in this case is functionally limited (seemingly by the principle of proportionality)).

is some truth in Kant's famous adage that '[t]houghts without content are empty, intuitions without concepts are blind'[522], we have to make sure that the abstractions we rely upon in order to systematize our thoughts, do not linger away from the concrete (legal) reality we are dealing with. In other words, too rigid *analysis* and *synthesis* – I employ the words in their etymological sense, thus referring to phenomena like debates about whether a specific matter is 'a parallel' or 'a concurrent' competence (when it is clear that there is no general consensus on their meaning) – , might lead to reifications (arguably 'thoughts without content'[523]), and detract from the core issue at in competence matters, that is: 'who does what for whom'[524]. Accordingly, I do not intend this criticism to be (all too) radical, for we indeed need a vocabulary (and accordingly a conceptualization-as-idealization) to work with, and the rule of law itself as an "ideal" arguably relies on a more or less stable practice of communication[525]: it is merely a reminder not to loose track of the *real* legal[526] issues, nonetheless keeping in mind – both – that there is an 'insight' of legal scholars that 'when allocating competences, the most important point is to perspicuously distinguish different competence matters' *and* that this insight is flawed at the same time, since it relies on a wish to understand competence allocation in a Descartian deductive style, viz. *more geometrico*[527].

---

[522] IMMANUEL KANT, CRITIQUE OF PURE REASON 93 [A51/B75] (Norman K. Smith transl. 1985) (1781).

[523] *Compare* FRANCIS J. MOOTZ III, LAW HERMENEUTICS AND RHETORIC ix-x (2010) ('[l]egal theorists are far too quick to abstract from the legal practices in question to find more solid theoretical ground from which to assess the practices').

[524] Rimanque, *supra* note 140, at p. 68.

[525] *Eg* HART, *supra* note 109, at p. 126 ('[g]eneral terms would be useless to us as a medium of communication unless there were [...] familiar, generally unchallenged cases') and 152 ('though every rule may be doubtful at some points, it is indeed a necessary condition of a legal system existing, that not every rule is open to doubt on all points'); *also see supra* note 506.

[526] *Compare* LON L. FULLER, LEGAL FICTIONS 10-11, *also see* 107, 109-10 (1967).

[527] Peeters, *supra* note 188, at p. 73-75; Peeters, *supra* note 360, at c. 724-33 (discussing CoS advices on the basis of this premise). Especially in complex conceptual matters like this one, we should keep Polybius' *Histories* in mind, the translation of which French dramatist Philippe Néricault made proverbial in French (*'la critique est aisée, et l'art est difficle'*). Witness of that difficulty: ALEN *et al.* (including (!) Peeters), *supra* note 38, at p. 193-96 (criticizing dual federalism theory *more geometrico* themselves); *also see* Jan Gijssels, *Commentaren over de bevoegdheidsverdeling na de staatshervorming van 1980*, 1987 JURA FALCONIS 487, 496 (describing parallel competences by using the image of two standing beams on a graphic underground); *compare* Xavier Delgrange & Jean-Paul Keppene, *Convergences et divergences dans le contrôle constitutionnel de la non-discrimination et de l'union économique et l'unité monétaire* in L'UNION ÉCONOMIQUE, *supra* note 214, at p. 88 (where the hierarchy of rules is seen geometrically in relation to allocation of competences).

Turning to the case law, and trying to rebut the conceptual criticism brought about by these complexities, some would emphasize that the Court itself used the notion of parallel competences, already in 1986[528]. Even so, in line with what was mentioned before, this does not prove a whole lot, since some authors have interpreted this 'parallel' as meaning exactly the same as what have been called *divided* exclusive competences (in which a homogenous competence package is carved up over different competent legislatures)[529]. The difference only becomes important to the extent that consequences are drawn from the differentiation of concepts, and even then, one should remain careful: for instance, it is sometimes alleged that parallel competences (but not *divided* exclusive competences) are an exception to exclusivity[530]. Such a concept-construction in function of its results is somewhat uninsightful. It probably tries to denote that pertaining to, for instance, public financing of industry, the federation and the regions may both act, as they are both (independently and cumulatively) competent (whereas for divided exclusive competences, the '*competence area*' is carved up, and only one legislature is competent for a special aspect of each). This distinction, however – even if it might have some relevance in practice – turns out to be difficult to uphold, since it presupposes a *more geometrico* excavation of competence area (a process we denounced earlier). Depending on how one describes the *object* of competences (*eg* 'public initiative' or 'regional public initiative' or 'federal public initiative'), the competences can indeed be described as either parallel or divided exclusive competences[531].

We should conclude from the above that in light of the difficulties surrounding classification in terms of text and context (which find their basis in underlying theoretical and conceptual issues), and in light of a case law which is open to interpretation, we should be very careful not to conceive of the conceptual apparatus employed – and in this case: parallel competences – as a self-contained and self-explanatory rigid framework. The same observations seem to apply to concurrent competences, which we turn to next.

[528] CA No. 11 (Feb. 25, 1986) III.1.B.3 (as regards the public financing of industry, the competences of the federation and the regions are parallel).

[529] *See eg* CC No. 97/2011 (May 31, 2011) B.5.2 (on energy); *also see* Bribosia & Van Boxstael, *supra* note 13, at p. 105-06.

[530] *Eg* Vande Lanotte & Goedertier, *supra* note 13, at p. 967.

[531] *Also see* Poirier, *supra* note 207, at p. 282-84 (arguing that parallel powers might also warrant rules of conflict if contradictory obligations coincide). *Compare* Jan Velaers, *Social Federalism and the Distribution of competence in Belgium* in Social Federalism, *supra* note 45, at p. 146-48 (on whether, assessing both Nos. 33/2001 and 11/2009, 'social security', in the broad sense, is a parallel or a concurrent competence). *Also compare* Veys, *supra* note 358, at p. 136 n13 (distinguishing parallel powers in the strict sense from parallel powers in the broad sense).

94. Concurrent competences. Competence allocations have been coined *concurrent*, by and large, when a competence object may be regulated by different legislatures (but where a possible accumulation of legislative obligations may warrant a "rule of conflict"[532]). Here again, the concurrent nature of competences finds some support in authoritative texts[533]. Even so, the Court has generally not restrained from enunciating 'new' concurrent competences either. Pertinent examples of the latter (although, as with parallel competences, in this case textual support could also be construed or accounted for) are some areas in which the Court has established that the federal government remains competent to elaborate the general framework, which the federated entities (*within* their competence allocation[534]) may supplement, but must respect[535].

---

532 *Also see supra* note 369 and *infra* No. 95.

533 *Eg* art. 6, §1, IX, 3° SLIR (regions being competent to *apply* federal norms governing employment of foreign work forces) or art. 6, §1, VI (4) 1° SLIR (regions being competent to *supplement* and *apply* public tender rules; *but see* CA No. 79/92 (Dec. 23, 1992) B.4 (the federal competence is functionally limited to the goals of the EMU)). Moreover, the EMU itself, as (partly) enshrined in art. 6, §1, VI (3) SLIR, could be construed as special form of concurrent (framework) competence (Suetens & Leysen, *supra* note 316, at p. 51; Christine Vanderveeren, *Over leefmilieu en fiscaliteit in het raam van de economische en monetaire unie* (case note accompanying CA No. 47), 1988-89 RW 345). Much, again, depends on the formulation in the text (*compare* for instance *apply* with *supplement and apply* – *cf.* CA No. 79/92 (Dec. 23, 1992) B.4)), often read together with *travaux préparatoires*. Whereas during the first constitutional reform (1970), the concept of concurrent competences was not employed at all (CoS Advice, *Parl. Doc.* Senate 1979 SS, No. 261/1, Appendix II, at p. 31-32; cf. Peeters, *supra* note 38, at p. 272 n1 (with references)), in the 1988 round of institutional reform, it was explicitly recognized that sometimes reverting to concurrent powers would be necessary, at least 'on the explicit condition that the national government does not devoid or impede by its acting the exercise of community or regional powers' (CoS Advice, *Parl. Doc.* Chamber 1988 SS, No. 516/1, at p. 45; Peeters, *supra* note 38, at p. 272-75). In that sense, it has been pointed out the 'dogma of exclusivity' is something of the past (*eg* Suetens & Leysen, *supra* note 316, at p. 48-49; Uyttendaele, *supra* note 13, at p. 522, 526; Vanpraet, *supra* note 190, at p. 127 *et seq.* (who argues that the CoS and the Constitutional Court in several cases have deployed a double aspect doctrine, where it renders some 'exclusive' powers 'parallel' through cumulative application). We reached a similar conclusion above, albeit on (slightly) different and wider grounds (*compare* Stef Feyen, *supra* note 501). *Also see* André Mast, Overzicht van het Belgisch Grondwettelijk Recht 65 (9th ed. 1987). Even so, that does not mean that concurrent competences have not been generally frowned upon by Belgian scholarship (Popelier, *supra* note 45, at p. 98): even in 1988, they were still discussed as a 'problem' (Report (Cerexhe & Erdman), *Parl. Doc.* Senate 1988 SS, No. 405/2, at p. 14-15; *but compare* p. 20 ('most competences are concurrent')). Alen defends the idea of the possibility of severing two categories, in light of the consideration that 'the principle of exclusivity could only remain due to an evolution towards cooperative federalism' (Alen, *supra* note 38, at p. 35).

534 Therefore, arguably, the term *concurrent* competences might be out of place.

535 *Compare* Bribosia & Van Boxstael, *supra* note 13, at p. 71 *et seq.* (on how to construe the EMU)). *See further eg* CA No. 40 (Oct. 15, 1987) III.2.B.3 (whereas the federal government can prescribe fire protection rules which hold regardless of the destination of the premises, the Region may supplement these as regards elderly homes; *cf.* CA Nos 41 (Oct. 29, 1987)

95. (Full and limited) concurrent competences: clarifying concepts? Some authors have analytically distinguished between *full (integral)* concurrent competences and *more limited* concurrent competences (*eg* framework competences). The question – again – is: what can we learn from these concepts, either dogmatically, or more reflexively?

The only clear example in Belgian constitutional law of a full (integral) concurrent competence is said to be the autonomous fiscal competence[536]. In Belgium, fiscal law is held to prevail over fiscal decree[537]. But this does not hold without nuances. On the one hand, it has been argued that even here, the federal government is bound by the proportionality principle on the textual basis of article 170, § 2 Constitution[538]. On the other hand, 'rarely does the Court decide that the federal legislature has no reason to act'[539]. Dogmatically, the idea that the fiscal competence is a full (integral) concurrent competence accordingly does not counteract balancing, and the weighing (incorporating a more general assessment of the federal balance) can sometimes go so far so as to question the very meaning of concurrence.[540] At least it precludes that the norm enshrining the prevalence of the fiscal law over the fiscal decree can be applied *simpliciter*.

Especially as regards concurrent competences, quite some additional, though related theoretical controversy remains[541]. The controversy seems to hark back

III.2.B.3 and 49 (Mar. 10, 1988) III.2.B.2); CA No. 55/2001 (May 8, 2001) B.4-B.5 (the federal government is competent for determining the framework regarding formal justification of individual administrative acts; *but compare* CA No. 128/2001 (Oct. 18, 2001) B.17 (formal justification is not part of a matter conferred to Regions or Communities); *compare* No. 43/2002 (Feb. 20, 2002) B.6.2 (on public governance in light of different competence allocations).

536 Art. 170, § 2 Cons.

537 *See eg* No. 47 (Feb. 25, 1988) III.6.B.2; *also see* III.6.B.4 (regional taxing power is limited by the global conception of state); more recent confirmations hereof are *eg* CA No. 119/2007 (Sep. 19, 2007) B.4.7; CC No. 50/2011 (Apr. 6, 2011) B.57.2.1.

538 *See eg* Report (Lebrun & Duroi-Vanhelmont) *Parl. Doc.* Chamber 1988-89, No. 635/17, at p. 175; *also see* CA No. 66/2001 (May 17, 2001) B.3-B.5.1 or No. 85/2002 (May 8, 2002) B.14-B.15 (elaborating the rationale and the limits of federal power).

539 Popelier, *supra* note 45, at p. 111, referring to CA No. 85/2002 (May 8, 2002) B.16.1 *et seq.*

540 *Eg* CC No. 111/2012 (Sep. 20, 2012) B.12 *et seq.* (in depth review (both *in abstracto* as regards an exemption from taxes for the postal services (B.13.4) and *in concreto*, as regards the questioned exemption from a Regional tax on vacancies (B.14-B.15.2)) of the 'necessity' requirement, clarifying that federal taxes should be narrowly construed, since they limit the fiscal autonomy of the Regions (B.12), and deciding that the Postal Services could not be exempt from the latter tax, as the necessity of the exemption was not proved (B.15.2-B.16)).

541 Not only pertaining to their validity/adequacy within the Belgian system, which primarily rests on the principle of exclusivity (*see eg* Uyttendaele, *supra* note 13, at p. 471-72 (with references)), but also pertaining to their analytical elaboration and structuring (Suetens & Leysen, *supra* note 316, at p. 49 (noting the confusion)).

to the reflexive question whether either *full* or *limited* concurrent competences should be construed as *concurrent* at all, at least in the sense that pertaining to *concurrent* competences, there is a true antinomy, in need of resolution (through hierarchy, temporal application, *et cet.*). The (possibility of) antinomy seems to be central indeed to the idea of concurrence, which is why some authors have argued that concurrent competences are exceptions to the principle of exclusivity[542]. Again, this should be put in some perspective.

As regards *framework competences (limited concurrent competences)*, one could argue that these constitute a mere application of the principle of exclusivity, but primarily in a more 'vertical' way (whereas one authority remains exclusively competent for the framework, the other authority is exclusively competent for the application and elaboration thereof)[543]. In that case, again, the question of boundaries, both vertical and horizontal stands central to the inquiry. Abstract generalizations in this regard will by and large fail to explain the concrete practices of the Court[544].

As regards *full/integral concurrent competences* – which in this regard are also coined *alternative exclusive competences*[545] – one could argue that, insofar as a rule of conflict governing the alternation is part of the competence allocation, that exclusivity is still reached as a result. Whether one accordingly construes the alternative exclusive competences as *concurrent* or rather as *exclusive* competences, seems to depend on the spot upon which the focus is placed in the process of judicial reasoning[546].

These analytical problems aside, quite a lot *politically* may turn on the qualification of a specific competence[547]. What accordingly seems important

[542] *Eg* ALEN & MUYLLE, *supra* note 14, at p. 397 *et seq.* or VANDE LANOTTE & GOEDERTIER, *supra* note 13, at p. 967.

[543] *See* Peeters, *supra* note 188, at p. 71; ALEN & MUYLLE, *supra* note 14, at p. 400-402.

[544] *Cf. eg* CA No. 2/89 (Feb. 2, 1989) 2.B.3 or No. 79/92 (Dec. 23, 1992) B.3.c (the classical separation of powers distinctions (legislation / execution) are not as such transferable into the realm of federalism questions). *Compare eg* Popelier, *supra* note 45, at p. 100-01 and Suetens & Leysen, *supra* note 316, at p. 50-51 (refusing to subsume framework competences under concurrent competens) *to* PEETERS, *supra* note 38, at p. 281 (calling these a 'modality of concurrent competences').

[545] *Also see* CA No. 57 (June 2, 1988) IV.4.B.1 (where the Court still spoke of the national government's 'exclusive competence [...] to determine the exceptions')

[546] *See* BRIBOSIA & VAN BOXSTAEL, *supra* note 13, at p. 81-92; *also see* PEETERS, *supra* note 38, at p. 299 (speaking of the 'derogatory effect' of these competences); PLETS, *supra* note 47, at p. 61 (calling these competences virtual); *compare* Veys, *supra* note 358, at p. 137-40 (summarizing a similar debate in Germany on *Bundesrecht bricht Landesrecht* and art. 72 of the German Basic Law).

[547] *Compare eg* Velaers, *supra* note 155, at p. 302-303 (deeming the federal competence for

to remember is that the notion of concurrent competences offers the Court a way of construing competence allocation so as to reconcile the necessity of uniformity and diversity in a variegated manner[548]. Indeed, the notion serves as a tool for the Court, and not so much as a sterile concept which imposes a reality upon the allocation of competences which is unchangeable due to the *essential* or *necessary* features of the concept itself.

96. (Con)text as a tool. Consequently, it is hard to pin down exactly what is meant here by "(con)text" as an "incidental principle". The fact that the Court has determined that in interpreting the SLIR, it conceives of the competence allocation as different *matters*, does not make this task easier[549]. The characterization of competence allocation as *matters* (and not, for instance, explicitly as goals[550] or mere instruments), allows for the Court to construe the often polysemic language of the text with quite some discretion[551]. This is only in part mitigated by potential clarity in the *travaux préparatoires*, for instance in that they sometimes refer to existing legislation, which – in turn and as we noted[552] – brings about discretionary power by itself.

---

social security to be more 'concurrent') *to* Xavier Delgrange, *La Cour d'arbitrage momifie la compétence fédérale en matière de sécurité sociale*, 2001 RBDC 209, *esp.* 237 (deeming the federal competence for social security to be 'exclusive')). *Also see* Popelier, *supra* note 45, at p. 115 *et seq.* (arguing, from a broader autonomy protecting perspective, that concurrent competences cannot be isolated from other factors influencing allocation of competences; *but see eg* 3 André Alen, Handboek van het Belgisch Staatsrecht (Syllabusuitgave) 259 (2nd ed. 1997); Francis Delpérée & Marc Verdussen, *L'égalité, mesure du fédéralisme* in Le fédéralisme dans tous ses états: gouvernance, identité et methodologie / The States and moods of federalism: governance, identity and methodology 193, 199 (Jean-François Gaudreault-DesBiens & Fabien Gélinas eds. 2005) (first published in 2004 RBDC 289) ((relying on Robert A. Dahl, Democracy and its critics 197 (1989) and Wheare, *supra* note 131, at p. 10, 14, and) understanding the problem of necessary overlaps for which the concurrent powers of executive federalism might propose a solution (*ibid.* at p. 200-03), which – according to the authors – has not been adopted in Belgium (*ibid.* at p. 200)).

548 One could argue that this is the purpose of the 'whole' of federalism. Even if this is hard to deny, the *concurrent* competence construal offers a more tangible and direct way to reconcile the necessities of autonomy and unity, as it allows – through leeway qua qualification and elaboration – to set specific boundaries on an *ad hoc* basis (*cf.* CoS Advice, *Parl. Doc.* Chamber 1988 SS, No. 516/1, at p. 45; *also see* Uyttendaele, *supra* note 13, at p. 499-503).

549 *Cf.* Peeters, *supra* note 360, at c. 712.

550 *Cf.* CA 1/89 (Jan. 31, 1989) 8.B.4.

551 Rigaux & Renauld, *supra* note 16, at p. 70; *also see* Steven Vansteenkiste, De Bevoegdheidsverdeling in het Federale België. Het gezondheidsbeleid 57 (2001) (pointing out the link with the principle of proportionality); *compare* Peeters, *supra* note 38, at p. 313-14; *but compare* Peeters, *supra* note 360, at c. 725-26.

552 *Cf.* references *supra* notes 170-171.

Even if, in light of the values underpinning or postulated by the rule of law, the Court will not as such disavow the constraining power of the text, the entrenchment and embedding of this text in the broader context outlined – or at least referred to – here will effectively allow the Court employ the (con)text as a tool in structuring and ensuring an equilibrium perceived as adequate between the different interests of the entities. I do not analyze how to measure the adequacy of the equilibrium, nor will I elaborate how 'interests' should be understood here[553]. I merely criticize the extant forms of analysis, and offer a *general* framework which – I believe – would allow to solve many of the (strictly dogmatic and theoretical) problems (ex)posed here.

3.3.2 Proportionality

97. A more explicit dogmatic recognition of the search for equilibrium can be found in the principle of proportionality[554], which has been deployed both vis-à-vis material competences as, arguably, vis-à-vis territorial competences[555].

---

[553] Suffice it to say that some authors have indeed duly noted that the Court not only takes the interests of the (governmental) entities as such into regard, but that it also balances – perhaps implicitly – the interests of the addressees of the legislation under constitutional review (*eg* STORME, *supra* note 142, at p. 448-449). This all could result in some sort of osmosis between competence-related considerations and (broader) interest analysis (*ibid.* at p. 396 n515).

[554] On the principle of proportionality in general, *see* (dogmatically) *eg* ALEXY, *supra* note 3 and (from a more foundational perspective) *eg* DAVID M. BEATTY, THE ULTIMATE RULE OF LAW (2004) or FEYEN, *supra* note 110. A comprehensive analysis of the principle vis-à-vis Belgian constitutional court case law has not yet been undertaken, at least not directly (the literature on the principle of equality, which incorporates proportionality analysis, is vast, however). Even so, in this regard, the Belgian Courts seem inspired by the European Court of Human Rights (*see eg* SÉBASTIEN VAN DROOGHENBROECK, LA PROPORTIONNALITÉ DANS LE DROIT DE LA CONVENTION EUROPÉENNE DE DROITS DE L'HOMME: PRENDRE L'IDÉE SIMPLE AU SÉRIEUX (2001); *also see,* YOUNG BAR OF LIÈGE, LE PRINCIPE DE PROPORTIONNALITÉ EN DROIT BELGE ET EN DROIT FRANÇAIS (Acts of the Colloquim organized by the young bars of Liège and Lyon (Nov. 24, 1994) (1995)). Due to the ongoing complex debate regarding the issue, I will not delve into the analytical nature of the principle of proportionality, which has 'traditionally' been held to incorporate a *suitability*, a *necessity* and a *proportionality (sensu stricto) test* (*cf.* ALEXY, *supra* note 3, at p. 44 *et seq.*).

[555] Alen and Muylle distinguish here between completely exclusive competences on the one hand, and parallel or divided exclusive competences on the other hand, mentioning that as regards the first, the principle of proportionality can only be brought to bear insofar as the completely exclusive competence has a *repercussion* on the different government (*supra* note 14, at p. 402-403). Notwithstanding obvious interpretative difficulties with the concept of repercussion (*compare eg* CA No. 42/97 (July 14, 1997) B.10.2 *with* No. 114/2005 (June 30, 2005) B.8 and B.13-B.14 and CC No. 202/2009 (Dec. 23, 2009) B.13-B.14), theoretically, this assertion raises similar questions vis-à-vis material competences as we have raised vis-à-vis territorial competences.

Proportionality has been deemed to be 'inherent to any exercise of competences'[556], and accordingly is a heuristic device which constitutes for the Court yet another (indeed very useful) tool to ensure a federal equilibrium[557].

98. Proportionality and dogmatics. Classic dogmatic analysis situates proportionality review first and foremost on the level of the *exercise* of competences[558]. It is again somewhat remarkable that the Court here presupposes a rigid distinction between *having* a competence and *exercising* it. Even if – in light of the necessity of textual constraint and coherent categorization (proportionality analysis is deemed to be engaged as soon as the legislature was competent and *prima facie* remained within his competence allocation), and in light of the virtual nature of some competence conflicts – this analytical distinction might seem useful, one should be careful not to overinflate it, as it possibly regresses into reification and confusion then. It is probably correct to stipulate, as did Bribosia & Van Boxstael, that the principle of proportionality is 'the ultimate principle of interpretation of competences that serves as a last resort to fine-tune the lines of division – contributing to conjuring all dangers of concurrent competences – between the initiatives of the State, the Regions and the Communities'.[559] Such an assertion might not be able to provide concrete

556 *See eg* CC No. 31/2010 (Mar. 30, 2010) B.13 or No. 9/2011 (Jan. 27, 2011) B.8 (established jurisprudence since CA No. 27 (Oct. 22, 1986) III.3.B.3.1-III.3.B.3.4 (where the Court mentioned that 'proportionality is an element of the competence'); the quote has been used since No. 168/2004 (Oct. 28, 2004) B.5.3; *also see* No. 132/2004 (July 14) B.6.2 and No. 50/2011 (Apr. 6, 2011) B.10.1 (employing different phraseology)). *Also see* Popelier, *supra* note 45, at p. 106 ('reading into the provisions allocating competences'). *Compare generally* Peeters, *supra* note 38, at p. 566 *et seq.* (with a focus on CoS jurisprudence).

557 *Eg* Uyttendaele, *supra* note 13, at p. 953.

558 *Compare too* J. Öberg, *The Principle of Proportionality, federalism and judicial review in the law of free movement* in Deconstructing EU Federalism through competences 65 (Loïc Azoulai, Lena Boucon & François Xavier Millet eds. 2012) (applying a more 'realistic' inquiry into the principle, as applied by the COJ in the federal sense).

559 *Supra* note 13, at p. 186; *but compare ibid.* at p. 189 or Johan Vande Lanotte, *Brandpreventie of conflictpreventie* (case-note accompanying CA No. 40) 1988 RW 1010, 1016 (where it is (more inappositely) characterized as *ultimum remedium*). *Also see* Rimanque, *supra* note 392, at p. 87 (every competence-related form of reasoning implies interpretation of competence allocating rules against the backdrop of their coherence and the conception of state which has emerged from subsequent stages of institutional reforms). An example of the difficulties associated with the distinction is found in CA Nos. 4 and 6-10/95 (all Feb. 2, 1995) and No. 195/04 (Dec. 1, 2004) B.14.4-B.14.5 (where the federal power was arguably *founded* upon the EMU; *cf.* Alen & Muylle, *supra* note 14, at p. 407 n513). Even if one could argue that this was a special case (because of the concurrent nature of autonomous fiscality (*cf.* No. 4, B.5.3-B.5.4; No. 6, B.1.3-B.1.4; Nos. 7-10, B.2.3-B.2.4), and the Court's specific jurisprudence in this regard), it still remains the case that the federal measure laid out a policy pertaining to the environment and waste, which 'touches upon' (*raken / touchent [...] à / betreffen*) the regional competences (*cf. eg* No. 4 (Feb. 2, 1995) B.5.5; *compare however* B.5.6 (where the 'normal'

guidance, but it does usefully indicate how the principle of proportionality could and should be viewed as an attempt to (perhaps dogmatically[560]) reach beyond the confines of a more 'mechanic' (and) *more geometrico* form of jurisprudence. The principle performs a function akin to that of a safety valve, allowing to curb legislation that cannot be immediately dubbed as a competence transgression through use of other tools. Accordingly, the difference between a measure adopted by an entity *not having* a competence (which is therefore deemed unconstitutional) and a measure adopted by an entity *having* an (autonomous) competence, but exercising it in a disproportionate way (thus rendering it unconstitutional) is – in constitutional reality – a matter of degree, rather than a difference in kind.

Next to that (or perhaps better: because of that), key tenets of proportionality analysis can figure in other *tools*, such as the EMU or the implied powers. Or, more generally, as Constitutional Court Judge Luc Lavrysen has noted,

> [t]he principle of proportionality plays a role on different levels in the case law of the Court of Arbitration. It is employed as a touchstone in the framework of the case law on equality, it is brought up in the assessment of non-tariff measures impeding trade and it plays a role in the assessment of the question whether interferences with the freedom of trade and industry are justified or not. In the framework of the allocation of competences between the federal state, the regions and the communities, it plays a specific role. From the fact that strongly linked competences are divided between the federal state and several federated entities, the danger results that one legislature exercises his competences in a way that impedes the policy freedom of another. To limit these kinds of interferences, the Court of Arbitration has formulated a general

terminology is used)), and it seems for a large part justified by the 'necessity to outline a uniform framework that takes the economic union pertaining to environmental taxes into account' (*cf. eg* No. 4 (Feb. 2, 1995) B.5.7; in No. 195/2004 the Court added that the policies seemed complementary (B.14.6)). It is accordingly hard to deny that considerations which could be explained in terms of proportionality are deployed here in order to establish whether an entity indeed *has* a competence (rather than investigating the exercise thereof: *cf. eg* No. 4 (Feb. 2, 1995) B.5.8; *also see* CoS Advice, *Parl. Doc.* Senate 1994-95, No. 1239/1 (similar considerations pertaining to the Euro-vignette); *compare* CC No. 9/2011 (Jan. 27, 2011) B.2.2 (where a similar argument was presented) and CC No. 149/2010 (Dec. 22, 2010) No. B.4.2 (where the Court explains that the rationale for leaving at the federal level the competence for product norms is the free movement of goods).

[560] On why it could still be viewed as dogmatic, *see supra* No. 32.

> rule which every legislature, also the federal one, has to take into account in exercising its competences. No single government may, while laying out the policy which has been entrusted to it, take measures that go so far as to render the conducting of policies entrusted to other governments excessively hard or impossible. Proportionality is part of the competences[561].

3.3.2.1 Material

99. Material proportionality: the basics. Pertaining to material competences, the principle of proportionality has been dogmatically held to mean that when exercising their (autonomous) competences, the governmental entities should take care so as to not render the policies of other governments 'impossible or excessively difficult'[562]. Two examples can clarify this.

In 1992, the Court held that a provision in the Decree on manure, which delegated to the Flemish Government the power to limit the amounts of manure produced in case there is a real risk that the totality of manure produced in the Flemish Region cannot be disposed of in an ecologically justified manner, could have a direct repercussion on the federal agricultural competence. Even so, since the Flemish Decree itself limited this delegation to measures that do not hinder agricultural industries disproportionally, the Court did not find the exercise of the Region's environmental competence to be disproportionate[563].

More recently, in a case involving a decree regulating horse race betting, the Court held that, whereas the Flemish Government is competent to tax gambling[564] and regulate sports, and notwithstanding the fact that some Flemish policies might have repercussions on domains where the federal government is competent which are a result of the Flemish autonomy to choose the measures it deems appropriate to counter a negative socio-economic evolution, this

---

[561] Lavrysen, *supra* note 333, at p. 102-03.

[562] Established jurisprudence in this phraseology since CA No. 14/91 (May 28, 1991) B.3.3. Fairly recent examples include *eg* CC No. 175/2009 (Nov. 3, 2009) B.6.3, No. 29/2011 (Feb. 24, 2011) B.6.4 or No. 97/2011 (May 31, 2011) B.6.1. The Court, however, does not always mention it explicitly (*eg* CC 50/2011 (Apr. 6, 2011) B.10.1). *See already, eg* CA No. 54 (Jan. 11, 2006) III.6.B.12.c ('make it impossible for the State to conduct an efficacious policy in matters belonging to its competences'). *Also see* CA No. 2/89 (Feb. 2, 1989) 2.B.3. *Compare* CA No. 27 (Oct. 22, 1986) III.3.B.3.1-III.3.B.3.4.

[563] CA No. 55/92 (July 9, 1992) 5.B.7. The Court furthermore pointed out that it would be up to other jurisdictions to determine whether the exercise of the delegated authority (since this would constitute an executive measure) would be constitutional.

[564] More specifically, pursuant to art. 4, §1 SLFCR, to modify the rates, the tax base, and the exemptions of the gambling tax.

autonomy is confined by the principle of proportionality[565]. On the one hand, as the decree institutionalized a system of betting licenses, it fell outside the scope of the Region's authority, which was limited to regulating sports, and not the concomitant gambling[566]. On the other hand, insofar as the Region's authority relied on its taxing powers, the exercise of this authority was deemed disproportionate, as even the tax provisions sought to limit the discretion of the Federal Finance Minister in a matter that resorts under federal competences. If the Regions would in fact be regulating sports betting through the fiscal backdoor, this would render the exercise of this federal competence impossible or at least excessively hard[567].

100. General consequences of material proportionality? Obviously, further elaborating what this means is very hard to do in generalized terms which can provide guidance, for the question whether a certain policy is disproportionally impeded by another government's policy implies a reasonableness test[568], which renders the assessment largely *ad hoc* and dependent upon the factual predicates of a case. Even so, in certain areas, the principle of proportionality does seem to have a more *(sub-)rule-like* effect[569]. Accordingly, in cases pertaining to telecommunications sector[570], or more precisely its infrastructure, the Court has

---

565 CA No. 114/2005 (June 30, 2005) B.8.

566 The Court here relies on *travaux préparatoires* (*ibid.* B.10-B.11).

567 *Ibid.* B.13. The Court notes that the Regions cannot rely on implied competences here, because of the non-marginal nature of the repercussions (*ibid.* B.15.1). *Compare* CC No. 128/2011 (July 14, 2011) B.6-B.11 (where the petitioners complained that the federal government had overextended its reach in regulating sports betting, and the Court held that betting regulation is not a Community matter and that sports regulation is excluded from the federal betting regulation); CC No. 184/2011, 8 december 2011, B.7.3 (on using the 'financing of municipalities'-backdoor).

568 *Also see* Popelier, *supra* note 45, at p. 127-28 (pleading for prior impact assessments as benchmarks for judicial evaluation).

569 Even if that is the case, sometimes controversy might arise over which tool best captures a certain generalization (*compare* Feyen, *supra* note 32): *eg* pertaining to No. 55/2001 (May 8, 2001) B.5, *compare supra* note 513 (characterizing the express obligation as a limited concurrent competence (with nuances regarding residual powers)) *to* Popelier, *supra* note 45, at p. 107 (stressing how this is an application of the principle of proportionality). Fully elaborating the issue – if possible, in generalized terms – would require an analysis of the interaction of the tools, which falls beyond this book's scope.

570 *See eg* CA No. 132/2004 (July 14) B.6.2 ('[a]s a rule, the absence of cooperation in a matter for which the special legislature does not provide for an obligation thereto, does not violate the rules allocating competences. In this case, however, the competences of the State and the Communities regarding communications infrastructure, due to technological evolution, have become so interwoven that they cannot be exercised except through cooperation. It follows therefrom that the legislature by unilaterally regulating the competence of the regulator for communications, violates the principle of proportionality that is proper to every exercise of competences'). *Eg* confirmed in No. 128/2005 (July 13, 2005) B.6.2-B.6.4; No. 163/2006

inferred from the principle of proportionality a duty to cooperate[571]. Moreover, as the second example shows, the federated entities' fiscal autonomy is curbed[572] by the principle, to the extent the Court investigates the material allocation of competences as soon as the main goal of the fiscal measures lies in the non-fiscal repercussions of the measure.[573] Accordingly, the general norm of material proportionality can from time to time reproduce generalizable (indeed *(sub-) rule-like*) arguments: because of interaction with other tools, however, the guidance offered by these ('(sub-)rulified') standard remains limited indeed, thus again underlining how proportionality analysis remains tool-like by and large.

3.3.2.2 Territorial

101. Territorial proportionality: the basics. Arguably, "proportionality" requirements also limit the possible territorial scope of application of a given regulation: the Court has explicitly stated that in exercising its territorial competences[574], the federated entities cannot *hamper*[575] each other's competences.

(Nov. 8, 2006) B.3.1-B.4; No. 112/2011 (June 23, 2011) B.3.2-B.3.4 and No. 168/2011 (Nov. 10, 2011) B.21.2-B.22. *Also see* art. 30*bis* SLCC (*cf.* CC No. 84/2010 (July 8, 2010) B.14 *et seq.* (applying this vis-à-vis the obligation resulting from art. 6, §3 SLIR); CC No. 64/2009 (Apr. 2, 2009) B.14.3). *But compare* CA No. 178/05 (Dec. 7, 2005) B.13; CC No. 85/2008 (May 27, 2008) B.5 (the Court can only review the obligation to conclude cooperation agreements insofar as the principle of proportionality is violated) *with* CC 40/2012 (Mar. 8, 2012) B.5 (implying that the proportionality principle will be violated when an obligation rising out of article 92*bis* SLIR is infringed); *further see* Popelier, *supra* note 45, at p. 133-35 (fitting this within a broader federal Belgian picture); Alen & Peeters, *supra* note 361, at p. 74-79, *esp.* 76 (noticing that attention is shifting from allocation of competences and their description to the permitted amount of interference); Hélène Orban, *Les accords de coopération obligatoires – Les nouvelles obligations dégagées par la Cour Constitutionnel*, 2011 RBDC 3, 10 *et seq.* (on the judicially imposed duty to cooperate more generally).

[571] *See* Pascal Werner, *Télécommunication, radiodiffusion… et cooperation – La fin d'une saga politico-judiciaire?*, 2008 CDPK 150 (summarizing the case law).

[572] Next to the fact that it is curbed as an *integral concurrent* competence (*see supra* No. 95).

[573] *See eg* CA No. 31/92 (Apr. 23, 1992) 5.B.2 (the Regional legislature does not infringe federal material competences when taxing automatic leisure devices). *Also see* Nos. 4, 6, 7, 8, 9 and 10/95 (all Feb. 2, 1995) (on whether the federal government disproportionately impacts regional competences by an environmental tax). *Compare* CA No. 2/94 (Jan. 13, 1994) B.4.3 (pertaining to the Brussels agglomeration and housing). *Cf.* 1B Alen & Muylle, *supra* note 174, at p. 489. *See, generally* Plets, *supra* note 47.

[574] Or perhaps more precisely: 'that the territorial effects resulting from the exercise of these competences [cannot …]'.

[575] Some authors have noticed that the Court here deploys language which is different from the cases of material competences (*eg* Uyttendaele, *supra* note 263, at p. 975 *et seq.*). Even disregarding the fact that in No. 63/2005 (Mar. 23, 2005) B.10, the Court used 'hamper' in a case regarding material competence allocation, and notwithstanding the possibility that the Court indeed sought to differentiate between material and territorial competences in this regard (for

Due emphasis should be put, however, on the theoretical problems associated with this conceptualization[576].

102. A useful tool for the Court. The principle of proportionality thus figures as one of the standards according the Court a vast amount of leeway to assess particular circumstances in light of the requirements of a federal equilibrium. In that sense, it could be called empty (at least pertaining to *substance*), or a post-hoc rationalization of a decision, ultimately possibly relying on different grounds. The principle has become part and parcel of the Court's jurisprudence, and is particularly suited to solve cases on narrow grounds (because it allows to incorporate and balance many factual circumstances). Be that as it may, from a justificatory perspective, some more elaboration of the underlying premises of its deployment (in federalism cases) perhaps would not hurt[577].

---

instance because 'hamper' (*dwarsbomen* in Dutch, *contrarier* in French) might seem somewhat less strong as regards the effect than 'rendering impossible or excessively difficult', but perhaps more stringent as regards the intent (*see supra* note 460)), not a whole lot seems to turn on the semantics here (*compare eg* No. 18/89 (June 29, 1989) B.3.h or No. 7/90 (Jan. 25, 1990) 2.B.3 (where the Court employs 'does not infringe upon' for proportionality vis-à-vis material competences; *also see* CA No. 3/2006 (Jan. 11, 2006) B.4.1 (combining both))). Instead the question is first and foremost one of interpretation in light of specific factual constellation and given the nature of the underlying issues (*supra* No. 82 *et seq.*), generalizations are often spurious.

576 *Cf. supra* Nos. 82 *et seq.* Even if we have stressed the theoretical difficulties regarding *territorial* competence allocation, some similar considerations, next to these in Nos. 74 *et seq.* could be applied to *material* competences, at least if the principle of proportionality is here understood as a means of 'removing some prejudicial consequences' (*effects*) (Delpérée, *supra* note 401, at p. 593; *also see* Delpérée & Rasson-Roland, *supra* note 13, at p. 106 (proportionality ensures the federated entities' autonomy)) from the exercise of competences (*contra* (depending on the implications of the assertion) Uyttendaele, *supra* note 263, at p. 955 ('the Court implicitly, but radically, reconsiders the narrow character of the separations existing between the several competence blocks')).

577 *See* Stefan Sottiaux, *Het gelijkheidsbeginsel: langs oude paden en nieuwe wegen*, 2008-09 RW 690, 692-93 (offering similar remarks vis-à-vis the Constitutional Court's equality jurisprudence); *also see* Alen & Peeters, *supra* note 361, at 126 (arguing for a more principled approach by the Court in terms of proportionality); *compare* Willem Verrijdt, *Over toetsingscriteria en toetsingsintensiteit. Haalt het Grondwettelijk Hof de Straatsburgse standaarden?*, 2012 TBP 76 (approaching the issue quantitatively). Similar remarks have been made for other human rights jurisdictions (*compare eg* Gerhard van der Schryf & Stefan Sottiaux, *Methods of international human rights adjudication: Towards a more structured decision-making process for the European Court of Human Rights*, 31 Hastings International and Comparative Law Journal 115 (2008)). Even so, it is not entirely certain that the proposed clarification in terms of intensity of scrutiny is susceptible to analogous application in the field of federalism (some relevant reasons why are alluded to in Feyen, *supra* note 169, at p. 54-61; *compare* Jogchum Vrielinck, *De Grondwet aan het gezicht onttrokken*, 2013 TBP (forthcoming) Nos. 35-36 (from the viewpoint of the countermajoritarian problem in light of the rule of law)). Moreover, the more extensive elaboration of the judicial decision is primarily warranted from the perspective of *some* rule of law values, such as predictability, legal certainty, ... In light of some other values, which also might be deemed legally relevant, the flexibility of the approach could be applauded.

3.3.3 Federal loyalty

103. A competence allocating concept? The federal loyalty provision of the Constitution was explicitly inserted not to function as a competence allocating concept[578]. Be that as it may – arguably as an expression of a 'general principle' which is inherent to the federal structure[579] – the Constitutional Court has accepted 'federal loyalty' as an admissible argument in terms of which it may review legislation[580]. The meaning of the requirements set forth by 'federal loyalty', however, has not been entirely unequivocal. But by now: what would one expect?

In the *travel agencies case*, the Court for the first time explicitly and more elaborately expounded upon the meaning of the federal loyalty requirement. This requirement, the Court mentioned, obligates the different governments, when exercising their competences, 'not to disrupt the equilibrium of the federal construction as a whole; it pertains to more than merely exercising competences, as it indicates in which spirit that has to occur'[581]. The distinction between having and exercising competences being overinflated[582], this new turn of

---

[578] Art. 143, §1 Cons.; Constitutional Revision (Amendment), *Parl. Doc.* Senate 1991-92 SS, No. 100-27/7, at p. 3; Constitutional Revision (Amendment), *Parl. Doc.* Senate 1991-92 SS, No. 100-27/8, at p. 3. *Cf.* André Alen, *De federale loyauteit: ondanks alles, toch een bevoegdheidsverdelend concept?* in LA LOYAUTÉ – MÉLANGES OFFERS À ETIENNE CEREXHE 19, 22 (1997). *See eg* (more elaborately on the emergence of article 143 Cons.) Xavier Delgrange, *Le professeur, le sénateur et le juge face à la loyauté fédérale* in LA LOYAUTÉ – MÉLANGES OFFERTS À ETIENNE CEREXHE 97, 102-07 (1997) and Patrick Peeters, … *en de boer, hij ploegde voort… Een decennium lang federale loyauteit* in LIBER AMICORUM JEAN-PIERRE DE BANDT 889, 891-94 (2004). *Also see eg* (on how it is hard to distinguish between conflicts of interest and conflicts of competence), Alen, *supra* this note, at p. 27-29; Patrick Peeters, *Wijzigingen aan de bevoegdheden van de Staat, de Gemeenschappen en de Gewesten* in HET FEDERALE BELGIË NA DE VIERDE STAATSHERVORMING 25, 30 (André Alen & Louis-Paul Suetens eds. 1993); Marc Uyttendaele, *L'articulation des collectivités fédérées et la question de la sous-nationalité dans l'espace Wallonie-Bruxelles*, 2008 CDPK 284, 292.

[579] *Eg* Francis Delpérée, *A la loyale* in MÉLANGES OFFERTS À ETIENNE CEREXHE 113, 122 (1997); Sébastien Depré, *Les conflits d'intérêts : une solution à la lumière de la loyauté fédérale*, 1995 RBDC 149, 161 ; STORME, *supra* note 142, at p. 260-262. *See* Alen, *supra* note 578, at p. 36 (pointing out the irrelevance of article 143 Cons., as federal loyalty is a general principle). *But compare* Yves Lejeune, *Le principe de la loyauté fédérale: une règle de comportement au contenu mal define*, 1994-95 APT 233, 236 (emphasizing the need for judicial restraint) *with* STORME, *supra* note 142, at p. 264-65 (arguing that restraint is not necessary in this regard, due to a lack of political consensus and the need for an effective solution).

[580] CA No. 119/2004 (June 30, 2004) B.3.2-B.3.3. The issue was raised a lot earlier, sometimes in light of equality review (*eg* CA No. 34/96 (May 15, 1996) A.12.3; CA No. 62/96 (Nov. 7, 1996) B.4), sometimes specifically in light of competence jurisdiction (*eg* CA 12/96 (Mar. 5, 1996) B.4.1-B.4.2), but never explicitly declared inadmissible by the Court.

[581] CA No. 119/2004 (June 30, 2004) B.3.2.

[582] *Supra* No. 98.

phrase *a fortiori* did not seem all too intelligible as a signpost for ensuing case law[583].

104. Independent argument? Even so, the dogmatic question persisted whether the principle of federal loyalty provided an independent argument in constitutional adjudication. In earlier cases[584] the Court had often found reasons not to review provisions specifically in light of the requirement of federal loyalty.

In the *travel agencies case*, the Court seemed to equate the principle of federal loyalty to the principle of proportionality[585], in that it argued that both implied the same requirements.[586] Even so, in some recent cases regarding Flemish inspection of francophone schools on Flemish territory, the Court seems to have given the principle a specific meaning (apparently) aside from or beyond (mere dogmatic) proportionality. These school inspection cases[587] have been alluded to before and simplifiedly, they implied that the standstill standard enshrined in article 16*bis* SLIR[588], construed in light of some compromises during early

[583] For a recent, interesting attempt, *see* Anne-Cathérine Rasson, *Le principe du "vivre ensemble" belge: une épopée constitutionnelle*, 2012 CPDK 25 (who basically tries to (dogmatically) redeem the principle in light of its historical meaning for 'living together' in Belgium (thus also connecting it with other 'doctrines'), but also remarks that the Constitutional Court should develop 'less laconic, more adequate reasoning on the matter' (*ibid.* at p. 75)).

[584] *Eg* No. 62/96 (Nov. 7, 1996) B.4 (equivalent to equality review); No. 35/2003 (Mar. 25, 2003) B.19.9 (equivalent to equality review, read in light of still other constitutional provisions); CA No. 102/99 (Sep. 30, 1999) B.10 (equivalent to competence review). *Also see* CA No. 12/92 (Feb. 20, 1992) 1.B.10 (on the reasonable delay during which the federal government would have to take a measure regarding personnel).

[585] It could be noted that whereas in Belgium, a duty to cooperate emerged from the principle of equality, in Germany, the obligatory nature of that duty was the first and foremost reason for the Court to review legislation in light of an independent principle of federal loyalty. For a summary of the discussion in Germany, *see* Alen & Peeters, *supra* note 13, at p. 1145-47.

[586] CA No. 119/2004 (June 30, 2004) B.3.3 ('the exercise of the competence cannot render the exercise of other legislatures impossible or excessively difficult'). Moreover, the Court explicitly acknowledged that it read the principle of federal loyalty together with the principle of proportionality (*ibid.* B.3.3-B.3.4). This line of reasoning seemed to be confirmed in CA No. 146/2004 (Sep. 15, 2004) B.7.4 (proportionality review of a fiscal measure in corporate tax); CC No. 2/2009 (Jan. 15, 2009) B.3 and B.10 (proportionality review of immission standards for non-ionizing radition); No. 116/2009 (July 16, 2009) B.12 (proportionality review of a regulation regarding radio frequencies); Nos. 202/2009 (Dec. 23, 2009) B.17 and 31/2010 (Mar. 30, 2010) B.15 (proportionality review of a procedural innovation in a statute of limitations).

[587] *See supra* No. 86 (with accompanying notes). *Further see* Patrick Peeters, *De Opmars van het federale loyauteitsbeginsel voor het Grondwettelijk Hof* in Liber Amicorum Marc Boes 425 (David D'Hooghe, Kurt Deketelaere & Anne-Marie Draye eds. 2011).

[588] This *standstill* article, as applied in this case, reads as follows: '[d]ecrees, regulations and administrative acts cannot impinge upon the guarantees – existing at the time of entry into force of this article – enjoyed by Francophones in the [six peripheral communities] and by the

stages of state reforms, must imply that only French Community inspectors are allowed to inspect francophone schools in the municipalities with a special linguistic status. On the other hand, the Flemish government is principally competent to normatively regulate all other forms of control. Even so, because the schools are special and in light of the principle of mutual recognition, the Constitution constrains Flanders not to exercise any discretion in determining whether the deviations from development goals and final objectives which the decree foresaw anyhow would be allowed, insofar as the deviating goals and objectives were these of the French Community. It accordingly held that it would contravene the principle of federal loyalty if the Flemish government would cancel the schools' recognition or dock their allowances and subsidies if they were not afforded sufficient time to request deviations from the Flemish norms regarding development goals, policy objectives and educational plans[589]. Given the fact that the deviations in this regard had to be accepted by the Flemish Community[590], partially in light of the principle of mutual recognition, the principle of federal loyalty here supported a practical measure that avoided financial shocks in the educational system.

Given the highly specific nature of this case and the encompassing review standard (article 16*bis*)[591], it remains very hard to find any guidance in it. Perhaps after *the Butterfly Agreement*, which explicitly provides a legal basis for review of legislation by Constitutional in light of the principle of federal loyalty[592],

Dutch-speakers, Francophones and Germanophones in [other communities having special linguistic status']. The article was recently modified, implementing the sixth state reform (for elaboration, *see* Feyen, *supra* note 190, Nos. 25-30).

589 CC No. 95/2010 (July 29, 2010) B.42.2; No. 124/2010 (Oct. 28, 2010) B.39.2; CC No. 60/2011 (May 5, 2011) B.20.6.3.3. To that extent, the provisions of the decree were suspended / annulled (resp. at B.42.3, B.39.3 and B.20.6.4); *also see* the critical comments by Vanpraet, *supra* note 190.

590 CC No. 95/2010 (July 29, 2010) B.38.1-B.41.2; No. 124/2010 (Oct. 28, 2010) B.35.4-B.38.2; CC No. 60/2011 (May 5, 2011) B.20.6.1.2-B.20.6.2. It is striking that the Court in these considerations nowhere provided for an explicit constitutional rationale for this obligation. Arguably, on the basis of CC No. 41/2010 (Apr. 29, 2010) – *see supra* notes 458 and *esp.* 466 – one could argue that the principle of mutual recognition to which the Court refers is inherent in the EMU. However, in No. 41/2010 (*also see* 40/2012 (Mar. 8, 2012) B.7.1), the case directly pertained to taxi services, whereas here education is in play. The latter at least seems to have a more tenuous link with an economic union, even if, undoubtably, such a link could be construed, primarily in terms of access (*see eg* Koen Lenaerts & Piet Van Nuffel, European Union Law 162-63 (Robert Bray & Nathan Cambien eds. 3rd ed. 2011; *also see* Case C-73/08 (GC; Apr. 13, 2010) *Bressol et al.*, CC Nos. 12/2008 (Feb. 14, 2008) and 89/2011 (May 31, 2011) (on indirect discrimination on the basis of nationality in access to (para)medical education)).

591 *Compare supra* No. 86 (on the *exacting* nature of the review standard).

592 Butterfly Agreement, *supra* note 10, at p. 11.

things will change. But since the Constitutional Amendments pursuant to this institutional agreement have not been adopted yet, it is hard to predict what specific effect they will have on the Constitutional Court's jurisprudence. And it remains doubtful that the *travaux préparatoires* adjoined to the Constitutional Amendment will actually succeed in offering conclusive guidance to either the Constitutional Court itself, or – more importantly in our context – to scholars endeavoring to understand, explain or predict Constitutional Court case law.

3.3.4 Implied powers

105. Implied powers enshrined in the SLIR. Article 10 SLIR spells out that decrees can contain provisions in matters for which the federated entities are not competent, insofar as these are necessary[593] for the exercise of their competence. Accordingly, the federated entities[594] are provided with so-called implied powers or competences.

106. Dogmatic controversy. There has been a lot debate about the meaning of this article, and about the meaning of implied powers more generally[595]. Sometimes the controversy was about its meaning in relationship to article 19 SLIR[596]. Other times, the debate was focused on whether the implied powers provision constituted more of an interpretive principle than a new allocation of competence[597]. Even if recent case law points out that latter controversy

[593] *See* (on the history of this contentious concept) Geneviève Cerexhe, Les Compétences implicites et leur application en droit belge 137-54, 302-10 and 339-50 (1989).

[594] On the question whether also the federation may invoke implied competences, *see* Cerexhe, *supra* note 593, at p. 176-81 (with references). The Court of Arbitration seems to have answered this in the affirmative (*see eg* CA No. 90/94 (Dec. 22, 1994) B.15.6; CA No. 166/2003 (Dec. 17, 2003) B.3.8). This issue, however, cannot be understood if uncoupled from the problem of residual powers and the Court's competence to determine them (*also see* Bribosia & Van Boxstael, *supra* note 13, at p. 157), nor from the problem of how to conceptualize article 10 SLIR (*cf.* Velaers (Grondwet), *supra* note 13, at p. 827 and 824). *Compare too* CC No. 108/2010 (Sep. 30, 2010) B.7 (on executive implied competences).

[595] *See eg* Geoffrey R. Stone et al., Constitutional Law 73 (6th ed. 2009); *a fortiori* Uyttendaele, *supra* note 13, at p. 479 (calling the Belgian system irrational).

[596] *Supra* No. 70 (with further references). In fact, as becomes clear in Cerexhe's discussion (*supra* note 593), and in Uyttendaele's (*supra* note 13, at p. 504 *et seq.*), the area of implied competences is one of the most inchoate jurisprudential areas, primarily due to lack of coherence and theorization at a higher level. This remark goes for many of the tools discussed here, but vis-à-vis implied powers, this line of criticism is particularly powerful (both in light of Constitutional Court practice, as in light of the diverse modifications of article 10 and 19 SLIR; *cf. infra*, following paragraphs).

[597] *Compare* Rimanque, Gijssels & Peeters, *supra* note 388, at p. 226-27, 235, 242 or Cerexhe, *supra* note 593, at p. 133, 161 *et seq. to* Jean-Marie van Bol, *supra* note 171, at p. 638. On the debate (with further references), *see* Alen & Muylle, *supra* note 14, at p. 394-395; Bribosia & Van Boxstael, *supra* note 13, at p. 147-61; Peeters, *supra* note 38, at p. 428 *et seq.*;

was decided in favor of the latter construal[598], at least to the extent that article 10 SLIR indeed permits federated entities to venture into the forays of other entities[599], the theoretical questions linger, for instance about the boundaries between an interpretation and an excess of competences[600].

107. Implied powers and proportionality. From a less dogmatic perspective, the conditions set forth by the Court seem to be nuanced instances of the principle of proportionality[601]. Next to the necessity requirement, set forth in

---

Popelier, *supra* note 16, at p. 88-90; Uyttendaele, *supra* note 13, at p. 472-79, 504-13; Vande Lanotte & Goedertier, *supra* note 13, at p. 968-73; Velaers, de Grondwet en de Raad van State, *supra* note 13, at p. 822-27.

598 This should only partially be seen as a consequence of the (somewhat incoherent: *supra* note 321) legislative modifications of art. 19, §1 (1) SLIR; *cf.* Bribosia & Van Boxstael, *supra* note 13, at p. 150-55 (with references, albeit critical) or CoS Advice, *Parl. Doc.* Chamber 1988 SS, No. 516/1, p. 32, at p. 49. *Compare eg* No. 66 (June 30, 1988) 7.B (first regime) *to* No. 32/92 (Apr. 23, 1992) B.3.4 and B.3.6 (post-1988 regime) *or* No. 73/97 (Nov. 25, 1997) B.2.4-B.3.5 (post-1993 regime) *or* No. 91/2010 (July 29, 2010) B.3.3-B.3.7 (current post-2001 regime). Notwithstanding the exemplified 'regime' changes, it appears that the Court itself only deploys article 10 from the moment it has concluded that an entity has crossed upon another's turf. Whether this is the most adequate representation of how judicial interpretation really proceeds, is yet another question, purposefully left unanswered here (*compare eg* CC No. 9/2011 (Jan. 27, 2011) B.15-B.20 (not reviewing in light of article 10 SLIR) or Vanpraet, *Deelstatelijke administratieve rechtscolleges: enkele beschouwingen bij het arrest nr. 8/2011 van het Grondwettelijk Hof*, 2011 TBP 195, 200). Moreover, older regimes might be still relevant, given the *ratio temporis* application of constitutionality review (*see eg* CC No. 29/2011 (Feb. 24, 2011) B.4.4).

599 Even when the latter's competences are reserved by Special Law: *compare* CC 49/2003 (Apr. 30, 2003) B.7-B.8.5 (under the post 1993-regime) or CC No. 8/2011 (Jan. 27, 2011) B.8.5-B.8.10.3 (under the current regime) (on the possibility of deploying article 10 SLIR vis-à-vis the competences that art. 161 of the Constitution reserves to the federal legislature, the Court answered in the affirmative) *to* CA No. 25/97 (Apr. 30, 1997) B.9 (where the opposite result was reached; *also see* CA No. 124/2000 (Nov. 29, 2000) (not reaching the issue)). *See* Vanpraet, *supra* note 598, at p. 195 (the reservation follows from the Special Law, referring to the 1993 *travaux préparatoires*); *but see* Pas & Steen, *supra* note 320, at p. 39 *et seq.* (arguing that the reservation of art. 160 Cons. has a *constitutional* basis) *read together with* Vanpraet, *supra* note 598, at p. 199 (explaining how the regulation in No. 8/2011 has repercussions on the competence of the CoS, as established by art. 160 Cons).

600 It seems as if the border between both is indeed constituted not so much dogmatically (*compare* Cerexhe, *supra* note 593, at p. 167-68 for an example), but rather in relational terms. Accordingly, 'interpretation' here should be conceived of – in Dworkinian terms – as an interpretive concept, the boundaries of which can only be established through a more or less consistent practice (which in this (local) case, refers back to an interpretation of the 'necessity' requirement ex art. 10 SLIR). *Also see supra* note 499. *Compare eg* Peeters, *supra* note 38, at p. 561-76 (debating the distinction between the principle of federal loyalty as a principle of interpretation and as a legal principle per se, in light of the principle of proportionality).

601 *Eg* Bribosia & Van Boxstael, *supra* note 13, at p. 156 (the whole limit of the implied powers provision, is the principle of proportionality, which particularly is expressed in the need for possible differentiation); Vanpraet, *supra* note 190, at p. 112-113, 310, 341 (calling them

the text, and interpreted rather deferentially in the last decade[602], the Court reviews whether the regulation adopted under article 10 SLIR allows for a differentiated regulation by the other legislatures on the one hand, and whether its impact is merely marginal on the other[603].

Accordingly, not only the 'differentiated regulation'-prong (which seems to ensure indeed that the exercise of a different competence is not rendered impossible[604]), but also the 'marginal impact'-prong can be seen as a specific individuation of (a) proportionality (test), taking into account the effects of a particular regulation (a competence cannot be made excessively hard to exercise)[605]. Hence, one could argue that the implied competences are a mere application of proportionality review.

Conceptually, if one wants to uphold the distinction between *having* and *exercising* a competence[606], 'proportionality' functions as a bridge mechanism here, to ensure you can exercise what you do not have, insofar as you stay within the bounds of reasonableness, as construed by the Court[607]. Hereby, however, I do not imply operative unity of the principle of proportionality: as Lavrysen

---

each others 'conceptual mirror image' (*ibid.* at p. 480)). Even so, and notwithstanding its (contentious) emptiness, a certain conceptual unity – measured in terms of results – does *prima facie* seem to be aspired to, if not required, by rule of law values (*see eg* CA No. 114/2005 (June 30, 2005) B.13-B.16 (deploying both the principle of proportionality on its own, and in application of the article 10-criteria, reaching the same results, on the basis of by and large the same arguments)).

602 Since CA No. 189/2002 (Dec. 19, 2002) B.7, the Court has apparently relaxed its standard, so as to scrutinize the necessity requirement only marginally. *See eg* No. 49/2003 (Apr. 30, 2003) B.8.3. *Compare* CC No. 91/2010 (July 29, 2010) B.3.4-B.3.6 or CC No. 89/2012 (July 12, 2012) B.6.2 (where the legislature explicitly relied on art. 10 SLIR); *but compare* CC No. 57/2012 (May 3, 2012) B.13.3.3. One should also note that some authors have tried to capture some of the influence of European law through the prism of the implied powers (*see eg* Velaers & Vanpraet, *supra* note 388, at p. 207-209; *compare* CoS Adv. 45.835/1 on the Decree on Equal Opportunities, *Parl. Doc.* Flemish Parl. 2007-08, No. 1578/1, at p. 70).

603 Established jurisprudence since its application in CA No. 66 (June 30, 1988) III.13.B. *But see already* No. 7 (Dec. 20, 1985) III.6.B.2 (requiring a 'very tight nexus' between the main competence and the 'implied' competence under art. 10 SLIR, already mentioned the two additional requirements). A recent confirmation is found in CC No. 91/2010 (July 29, 2010) B.3.3-B.3.7.

604 *But compare* CA No. 36/2001 (Mar. 13, 2001) B.6.2 – explicitly connecting this requirement with EMU.

605 *Also see* CC No. 89/2012 (July 12, 2012) B.6.2 ('touching upon the essence itself of the federal government in re injection tariffs', in particular because the competence of the federal government to have energy tariffs reflect real costs is undermined due to a neutralization of its policies by a tariff exemption imposed for the growing market share of renewable energy).

606 *Cf. supra* No. 98.

607 *Compare* Popelier, *supra* note 45, at p. 108 (explaining how the conditions for implied powers ensure exclusivity).

noted[608], the principle plays different roles (in different forms of tests, relying on different legal provisions). Thus, it has been noted that implied powers could be conceived of as another form of "balancing" as well, notably as a compensation mechanism for the fact that the residual powers are reserved at the federal level[609]. As such, it can constitute a strong argument in favor of exercising certain competences, although generally a vastly un(der)determined argument *a priori*, the validity of which will always depend on the circumstances in play.

3.3.5 Economic and Monetary Union (EMU)

108. Establishment of the EMU. In Judgment No. 47, the Court operationalized the idea of the EMU in Belgian constitutional law, that is 'the institutional framework of an economy built up out of federated entities, which is characterized by an integrated market (economic union) and by a unity of currency (monetary union)'[610]. In this case, an action for annulment had been brought against a Walloon Decree that levied a tax on exporting water from the Region[611]. As the EMU implied 'free movement of goods and production factors amongst the federated entities of the State', which would render any autonomously imposed 'restriction' on free movement incompatible therewith (which was *a fortiori* the case for internal customs) a tax that had as its object the transferal of water was unacceptable as an internal custom, irrespective of the fact that it might have been grounded in an autonomous regional fiscal competence[612].

109. Enshrining the EMU as a transversal limitation. This principle was later enshrined in art. 6, §1, VI (3) SLIR[613] and arguably in some other provisions[614].

---

608 *Supra* note 561 and accompanying exerpt.

609 *Eg* Johan Vande Lanotte, *De impliciete bevoegdheden op een Belgisch spoor* in Zeven Knelpunten, *supra* note 126, at p. 88; Suetens & Leysen, *supra* note 316, at p. 58; *also see* Delpérée & Rasson-Roland, *supra* note 13, at p. 97-98.

610 CA No. 47 (Feb. 25, 1988) III.6.B.4-III.6.B.5.

611 Art. 32 Wall. Decr. (Oct. 7, 1985) pertaining to the protection of surface water against pollution, *BSG* Jan. 10, 1986. The tax was only levied on intra-state exportation of water (art. 32, §1) vis-à-vis those transporting the water (art. 32, §2), discounting the amount of imported water (art. 32, §2) and offering the possibilities for deviations in light of long term contracts for water supply (art. 32*bis*).

612 CA No. 47 (Feb. 25, 1988) III.6.B.4.

613 Even so, there was *some* textual support for it already in 1980 (*see* CA No. 47 (Feb. 25, 1988) III.6.B.4, referring to old art. 6, §1, VI, 3° and 4°). The extent of this textual support might be deemed relevant, first and foremost from an analytical perspective (*see eg* Bribosia & Van Boxstael, *supra* note 13, at p. 72-90 (elaborating a three-tiered reviewing structure in light of the EMU)).

614 *Eg* art. 9, §1, 9*bis* and 49, §§ 6-7 SLFCR.

If these legal provisions might have left quite a few questions open[615], the Court soon made clear that the EMU was a transversal limitation to any exercise of competences[616].

110. Scope of the obligations under the EMU. The EMU does not only pertain to customs measures or measures having equivalent effect, but also more broadly protects free movement of goods[617], persons[618], services[619] and

---

[615] Not only as regards the scope of the EMU (given its location under the Regional competence heading, plausibly or at least seemingly implying that it would not be enforced vis-à-vis Community measures), but also as regards its applicability, in the sense that the legislature had not set forth any further criteria for applying review in light of the EMU (*eg* Christine Vanderveeren & Jef Vuchelen, *Een Vlaamse fiscaliteit en de Belgische economische monetaire unie* in EEN VLAAMSE FISCALITEIT BINNEN EEN ECONOMISCHE EN MONETAIRE UNIE 25, 62-63 (Referates for the Flemish Symposium (Dec. 4-5, 1998)) (Christine Vanderveeren & Jef Vuchelen eds. 1998)).

[616] CA No. 12/89 (May 31, 1989) B.4 (implicitly: the special rules cannot fully and generally render the use of waste disposal grounds for waste originating in other Regions impossible, since this would violate the Belgian economic union); No. 32/91 (Nov. 14, 1991) 5.B.1.7 (explicitly: 'even if article 6, §1 (3) SLIR is framed in the Regional economic competences, it is valid as an express assertion of the will of the Special Legislature to enforce a uniform basic regulation of the organization of the economy in an integrated market'); No. 55/96 (Oct. 15, 1996) B.4.2.5; No. 34/97 (June 12, 1997) B.7.5; No. 51/98 (May 20, 1998) B.3.2; No. 128/2001 (Oct. 18, 2001) B.10; No. 121/2008 (Sep. 1, 2008) B.4 (all regarding environmental levies, and thus the fiscal competences of the Regions); No. 53/99 (May 26, 1999) B.6.2-B.6.3 (the EMU also holds vis-à-vis the Communities ('given the general goal of the provision'), at least insofar as it pertains to sports exercise as an economic activity), and vis-à-vis the French Community Commission (in its exercise of powers under art. 138 Cons.) (No. 119/2004 (June 30, 2004) B.2.2); André Alen, *De bevoegdheidsverdeling tussen de Staat, de Gemeenschappen en de Gewesten*, 1989 TBP 146; Rusen Ergec, *La réforme de l'Etat: les compétences économiques*, 1989 JT 143. *Also see* No. 55/92 (July 9, 1992) 5.B.8 (about the manure decree (prohibitive provisions) possibly violating freedom of trade) and No. 123/2010 (Oct. 28, 2010) B.5.2 (about the manure decree (fiscal provisions) possibly violating the EMU). *Compare* Nos. 4 and 6-10/95 (Feb. 2, 1995) (federal tax competence for environmental taxes is grounded the EMU; *cf. supra* notes 559 and 573); No. 146/2004 (Sep. 15, 2004) B.7.1 (discussed *infra*); CC No. 83/2010 (July 8, 2010) B.7 (regarding an inheritance tax; discussed *infra*).

[617] *Eg* CA No. 51/98 (May 20, 1998) B.3.1-B.3.6 or No. 146/2004 (Sep. 15, 2004) B.7.2. *See* No. 10/95 (Feb. 2, 1995) B.1.4 (discussed *supra* notes 559 and 573). *Also see* CA No. 33/91 (Nov. 14, 1991) 4.B.4.1 (lacking argumentation).

[618] *Eg* CA No. 107/05 (June 22, 2005) B.7 and B.8.2. This implies free movement for workers (*eg* CC No. 11/2009 (Jan. 21, 2009) B.7 *et seq.*; *also see* CA No. 51/2006 (Apr. 19, 2006) B.10.2-B.10.3 (implicitly)), and free establishment (free movement for self-employed persons) (*eg* CC No. 83/2010 (July 8, 2010) B.9; *compare* No. 139/2008 (Oct. 22, 2008) B.16.4 (relying on the European conception for free establishment)). *Compare* CC No. 50/2011 (Apr. 6, 2011) B.70-B.74.4 (referring the question to the COJ) or No. 16/2009 (Feb. 5, 2009) B.3 *et seq.* (relying on the European conception).

[619] *Eg* CA No. 56/96 (Oct. 15, 1996) B.6 *et seq.* or No. 119/2004 (June 30, 2004) B.2.4. *See* CC No. 56/2009 (Mar. 19, 2009) B.8 and CC 124/2009 (July 16, 2009) B.3. *Also see, eg* No. 29/96 (May 15, 1996) B.8.3; No. 73/98 (June 17, 1998) B.10.2 or No. 40/99 (Mar.

capitals[620]. Moreover, it can imply several other obligations, some of which may are enshrined in the Special Law. Accordingly, article 6, §1, VI (4) SLIR provides that the national government is competent to establish general rules relating to public tenders, consumer protection, corporate organization and maxima for corporate subsidies in the area of economic expansion (alterable only with the Region's consent). This competence can *only* be exercised in light of the goal of sustaining the EMU[621]. Other competence allocations (such as the federal 'exclusive' competence on price policy) find their obvious rationalization in the EMU[622], but they are nonetheless not expressly limited as means to ensure the EMU[623]. That demonstrates that the relationship between framework competences and the EMU can be somewhat complex, in that even if the EMU must be *respected* in any exercise of competences (and how this respect must be construed, in light of the requirements of the EMU, is yet another matter), in light of some specific competence allocations, the EMU must also be *strived* for[624].

Other (discrete) obligations have been judicially elaborated, such as the principle of mutual recognition[625]. The Court up till now has only explicitly recognized this principle once, so "elaboration" may be somewhat overstated. It held that

> a person who offers services on the territory of one of the federated entities and acts according to the applicable rules, is supposed to freely exercise that activity on the territory of any other federated entity of the State, unless that federated entity

30, 1999) B.12.3 (more implicitly). *Compare eg* No. 33/2004 (Mar. 10, 2004) B.11.4, No. 99/2010 (Sep. 16, 2010) B.4.8 *et seq.* or CC No. 128/2011 (July 14, 2011) B.13.4 *et seq.* (relying on the *European* conception).

620 *Eg* CC No. 83/2010 (July 10, 2010) B.9. *Also see* CA No. 67/2000 (June 14, 2000) B.3.1-B.3.5 (apparently explicitly connecting the Belgian interpretation of free capital movement with the European one). *Compare* No. 130/2005 (July 19, 2005) B.15-B.17 (planning to rely on a European conception alone) or CC No. 50/2011 (Apr. 6, 2011) B.54.1-B.54.4 (referring the question to the COJ). *Also compare* CC No. 143/2009 (Sep. 17, 2009) B.8 (considerations of free capital movements playing in the establishment of legislative intent in a "regular" equality review). On the relationship between free movement of capital, services and free establishment, *see* CC No. 50/2011 (Apr. 6, 2011) B.47.2 (referring the question to the COJ).

621 Explanatory Memo, *Parl. Doc.* Chamber 1988 SS, No. 516/1, at p. 10; *see eg* CC No. 9/2011 (Jan. 27, 2011) B.3.4.

622 Explanatory Memo, *Parl. Doc.* Chamber 1988 SS, No. 516/1, at p. 11.

623 *Cf.* Grégoire Brouhns, *L'union économique et l'unité monétaire: un principe juridique aux facettes multiples* in L'UNION ÉCONOMIQUE, *supra* note 214, at p. 49-50.

624 *Also see* Brouhns, *supra* note 623, at p. 46 *et seq.* (trying to fit the different competences into the old categories).

625 *Also see supra* notes 286 and 466.

> demonstrates that stricter rules must be enforced in order to serve a legitimate goal. The will to protect service providers located in the Brussels Metropolitan Region against competition by other market participants, for the sole reason that they are located in the Walloon Region or in the Flemish Region, is by definition incompatible with the principle itself economic and monetary union and could not conceived of as a legitimate goal[626].

The Court can probably find inspiration in the further elaboration of this principle in European law, as it is also crucial in European Single Market law, at least since the 1980 European Commission Communication on *Cassis de Dijon* and certainly after the 1985 White Paper on *Completing the Internal Market*, now generally enshrined in some directives[627]. Moreover, the principle is mostly conceived of 'as an alternative to EU legislative action operating primarily at the level of national administrations'[628]. However, immediate guidance is not offered by the European level: although one could argue that the principle has been recognized by the European judiciary, this recognition has sometimes occurred in ambiguous terms[629], and also seems to depend on the object regulation at hand[630]. Accordingly, the principle is not applied in a straightforward manner[631], and leaves quite a bit of leeway for the judge to play with.

---

626 CC No. 41/2010 (Apr. 29, 2010) B.5.3; *also see* the implicit confirmation in CC No. 40/2012 (Mar. 8, 2012) B.7.1.

627 *Eg* LENAERTS & VAN NUFFEL, *supra* note 590, at p. 263-66; PAUL CRAIG & GRÁINNE DE BÚRCA, EU LAW. TEXT, CASES, AND MATERIALS (5th ed. 2011) 809-13.

628 Kenneth A. Armstrong, *Mutual Recognition* in THE LAW OF THE SINGLE EUROPEAN MARKET. UNPACKING THE PREMISES 225, 226 (Catherine Barnard & Joanne Scott eds. 2002).

629 *See eg* Janssens & Hoornaert, *supra* note 466, 213-14; more elaborately on the ambiguity of the issue raised there, *see* ALEXANDRE NEMEL, LE PRINCIPE D'ÉQUIVALENCE OU DE RECONNAISSANCE MUTUELLE EN DROIT COMMUNAUTAIRE (Diss. doct., Université de Lausanne, 1995); *also see* VASSILIS HATZOPOULOS, LE PRINCIPE COMMUNAUTAIRE D'ÉQUIVALENCE ET DE RECONNAISSANCE MUTUELLE DANS LA LIBRE PRESTATION DES SERVICES (1999).

630 *Compare eg* Case C-110/05 (GC; Feb. 10, 2009) *Commission v. Italy*, para 34 (duty of mutual recognition for products produced in other member states, as an application of *Cassis de Dijon*; *also see* CRAIG & DE BÚRCA, *supra* note 627, at p. 659 *et seq.*) *with* Joined Cases C-316/07, 358-360/07, 409-410/07 (GC; Sep. 8, 2010), *Stoß*, para 112 (given the margin of appreciation and the lack of harmonization, there is not duty to mutually recognize betting licenses; *compare* CC No. 128/2011 (July 14, 2011) B.12 *et seq.*, referring to *Liga Portugesa* in B.14.1).

631 *See eg* Opinion A-G Mengozzi (Sep. 7, 2010) in Case C-382/08, *Neukirchinger*, § 68 (not imposing mutual recognition for transporation), unless some directives are at stake (*compare* Directives 92/61/EEC and 2002/24/EC, with a recent application in Case C-142/09 (Nov. 18, 2010), *Lahousse*, para 27). *See, generally,* Armstrong, *supra* note 628, at p. 228-52 or (even more broadly, from a political science perspective) the essays published in the special edition: 14 JOURNAL OF EUROPEAN PUBLIC POLICY (2007).

111. Right to free trade. More broadly even, the Constitutional Court views in the EMU a guarantee for the fundamental right to free trade. The Court in the last decade often connects this principle to article 7 of the famous *D'Allarde* decree, read in conjunction with articles 10 and 11 of the Constitution[632]. Generally, this right to free trade is reviewed only marginally, as the Court keeps emphasizing that it is not absolute[633]: the Court has subsequently held that the (right to) freedom of trade is only violated if 'it is restricted without any necessity and in a manner which is clearly disproportionate to the sought goal'.[634]. On the one hand, the scope of this freedom arguably exceeds that of the EMU[635]. On the other hand, it could be noted that even if the freedom has also been enshrined literally in art. 6, §1, VI (3) SLIR, a differentiation might be at hand in the sense that articles 10 and 11 of the Constitution seem to require comparability[636], whereas review under article art. 6 SLIR does not require that. Be that as it may, the Court explicitly held that a 'provision of law violating free movement of goods and services is *ipso facto* in violation of the freedom of industry and trade, and in violation of the principle of equality and non-discrimination'[637]. Therefore, the relationship between the EMU (in the institutional sense) and the right to freedom of trade is not easy to conceptualize. Delgrange and Keppene construe the EMU as a *guarantee* for freedom of trade[638]. But, the Constitutional Court seems to regard the EMU and freedom of trade, even if they are enshrined in the same provision, as different kinds of

[632] For the first time explicitly in CA No. 88/2004 (May 19, 2004) B.21-B.24; *see* CC No. 29/2010 (Mar. 18, 2010) B.6.1-B.6.4, B.33.2; *also see* CA No. 171/2006 (Nov. 21, 2006) B.9.1; CC No. 114/2007 (Sep. 19, 2007) B.8.1, B.10, B.31; No. 120/2008 (Sep. 1, 2008) B.10.1; No. 194/2009 (Nov. 26, 2009) B.4; No. 99/2010 (Sep. 16, 2010) B.6.2; *compare* CC No. 71/2011 (May 12, 2011) B.7.1 or CC No. 99/2011 (May 31, 2011) B.8.5.

[633] *See eg* No. 56/2011 (Apr. 28, 2011) B.8.2; *compare* B.12.

[634] *Eg* CC No. 29/2010 (Mar. 18, 2010) B.33.2; CC No. 99/2010 (Sep. 16, 2010) B.6.2. *Also see* Constitutional Amendment Proposition (Tommelein & De Croo) [treated twice before, in 2006-07 and 2007-08], *Parl. Doc.* Senate 2010 SS, No. 5-19/1 (arguing for a constitutionalization of the right).

[635] Implicit in an analytic reading of judgments such as CA No. 55/92 (July 9, 1992) 5.B.8; No. 42/97 (July 14, 1997) B.13.2; No. 124/99 (Nov. 25, 1999) B.5.3; No. 132/2005 (July 19, 2005) B.4.3 or 149/2010 (Dec. 22, 2010) B.8) and also apparent from considerations such as CA No. 29/96 (May 15, 1996) B.8.3 (arguing that *any* restriction on the freedom to act in general constitutes a restriction on freedom of trade); *but compare* No. 53/99 (May 26, 1999) B.6.4 (where the Court differentially construes the EMU as the freedom of trade, but where it earlier (B.6.2) made an opening for a connection with free trade, by pointing out that article 11 Cons. could be violated).

[636] *See eg* CA No. 55/92 (July 9, 1992) 4.B.3.

[637] CC No. 149/2010 (Dec. 22, 2010) B.11.

[638] *Supra* note 527, at p. 92.

review[639]. Even if the Court does not explicitly use this conceptual differentiation (and some of its case law argues quasi-explicitly against it[640]), it could be argued that whereas the EMU is first and foremost an institutional guarantee (*applicable* to the entities as such), the freedom to trade is an individual right, which is reviewed only marginally to the extent that no considerations of weighing institutional interests are in play[641]. Of course, the distinction cannot be made rigidly, and in fact, the (economic) considerations of individuals might become thoroughly relevant in the political tensions between federated entities. As such, the question of whether institutional considerations are in play becomes a question of intensity[642]. This, by and large, then, does not preclude the Court's contention that violating the *institution* guarantee *ipso facto* infringes upon the individual right. But this is a mere reconstruction of a number of cases, and the Court – in light of what has preceded and especially in light of what follows – has quite a bit of leeway in working with the EMU-provisions.

112. Conceptualization of the EMU (1): relationship with other tools. That is all the more so the case in light of the debate that has taken place about the right (theoretical and relational) conceptualization of the EMU. For instance, former Constitutional Court President Paul Martens raised the question whether the EMU is a concept or a principle[643].

Next to that, the relationship between the EMU and the Court's other tools has sometimes been emphasized and indeed questioned. Accordingly, the EMU has been connected with the concept of federal loyalty[644], or even with

---

[639] *See eg* CA No. 35/95 (Apr. 25, 1995) B.6.2-B.6.6; No. 88/2000 (July 13, 2000) B.3.2 (*a contrario*); No. 132/2005 (July 19, 2005) B.3 (*but compare* B.4.3); CC No. 2/2009 (Jan. 15, 2009) B.18-B.20.2 (although no real review here) *versus* B.21 *et seq*.; No. 87/2009 (May 28, 2009) B.6.2. *See* Velaers, de Grondwet en de Raad van State, *supra* note 13, at p. 757-763. *Compare eg* No. 135/2010 (Dec. 9, 2010) B.10.5.

[640] *See* No. 53/99 (May 26, 1999) B.6.4.

[641] *Compare eg* CA No. 55/96 (Oct. 15, 1996) (where the case is centered around institutional considerations) with cases like No. 29/96 (May 15, 1996) (where the interests of (private) entrepreneurs stood central) or No. 42/97 (July 14, 1997).

[642] *Cf.* Carl Schmitt, The Concept of the Political 37 (George Schwab transl. 1996) (1932) ('[e]very religious, moral, economic, ethical, or other antithesis transforms into a political one if it is sufficiently strong to group human beings effectively according to friend and enemy').

[643] Paul Martens, *Débats* (presided over by Jean-Paul Abraham) in L'Union économique, *supra* note 214, at p. 62 (according to him, principles have legal force, whereas concepts do not). According to Brouhns, there is no attribution of *concepts*, but rather of instruments (*ibid.* at p. 65: 'the list of exclusive competences of the national authority is nothing other than a list of tools that one has provided for the national authority in its quality as gardian of the economic and monetary union').

[644] *See* Alen & Peeters, *supra* note 13, at p. 1154; Delgrange & Keppene, *supra* note 527, at p. 90-91; *also see* CA No. 146/2004 (Sep. 15, 2004) B.4 *et seq.*

a (mere teleological) interpretative elaboration of the SLIR[645]. Interestingly, some see in the EMU an occasion for application of a more general principle of proportionality[646]. Surely there is something to that assertion, in the sense that applying the EMU principle sometimes requires the Court to rule upon the factual consequences of a certain provision, precisely in light of the balance it will have to strike between economic, monetary and other interests[647]. What seems clear from the start, is that the EMU is not *mere* 'proportionality': it also requires an assessment – and arguably this assessment is equally or more important – of whether an adopted measure constitutes a 'restriction' on economic or monetary union[648].

But matters are more complex than that. Formerly, whether there was a restriction was assessed in light of the principle of non-discrimination applied to nationality (where it could be argued that as soon as *nationality* was directly or indirect in play, proportionality analysis was incorporated into the review and accordingly part of the norm of discrimination). Nowadays, after *Dassonville*[649],

645 Alen & Peeters, *supra* note 13, at p. 1129.

646 *See eg* Vanderveeren & Vuchelen, *supra* note 615, at p. 60-61. *Also see* Delgrange & Keppene, *supra* note 527, at p. 72-73, 75-81 (noting that jurisprudence of the COJ transcends the principle of non-discrimination on the basis of nationality now, which however does not imply that the principle of proportionality is no longer employed). Jadot conceptually separates the review of competence allocation and of free trade (in light of the EMU), in the sense that the EMU review pertains to the exercise of competences, rather than to the possession thereof (Benoît Jadot, *La Communauté économique européenne, l'Etat, la Région et la protection de l'environnement*, 1988 JT 725, at p. 728; support can be found explicitly in the text or in the Explanatory memo, *Parl. Doc.* Chamber, 1988 SS, No. 516/1, at p. 7-8). Delgrange and Keppene note that this is a source of confusion (*supra* note 527, at p. 89), but argue that 'the economic union and monetary unity transcends the problem of competence allocation instead of being a modality thereof' (*ibid.* at p. 90). *Also see supra* No. 98. *Compare* CA No. 78/92 (Dec. 17, 1992) A.5.1 and B.5.1 (where the Court refuses to read together 10 and 11 Cons. and the EMU).

647 For a particularly clear application thereof, *see* CA No. 53/99 (May 26, 1999) B.6.4 (balancing the economic union from the perspective of sports clubs vis-à-vis the economic union from the perspective of individuals and the freedom of association); *compare* CA No. 35/95 (Apr. 25, 1995) B.6.5 (it is the primary responsibility of the legislature to balance economic interests with environmental interests). Notwithstanding theoretical dispute on the question of the conceptualization of the principle of proportionality, I *arguendo* accept that my formulation can and should be construed as an application thereof. The balance here of course stands central, but I mention the factual consequences primarily in light of the suitability and necessity requirement which are generally also thought to be part of the (broader) principle (*also see* Delgrange & Keppene, *supra* note 527, at p. 96-97).

648 *Also see infra* Ch. 5.2 (on how far this can go in European law).

649 *Cf.* Case 8/74 (July 11, 1974) *Dassonville*, para 5: '[a]ll trading rules enacted by Member States which are capable of hindering, directly or indirectly, actually or potentially, intra-Community trade are to be considered as measures having an effect equivalent to quantitative restrictions'; Lenaerts & Van Nuffel, *supra* note 590, at p. 218.

most authors argue (inspired European law[650]) that a showing of direct or indirect discrimination[651] is no longer required, and the assessment of what constitutes a restriction has accordingly become a separate prong in the test, which could imply that proportionality testing is not inherent to the norm anymore.[652] But overall clarity it still lacking, for instance because there is no (European) unanimity about the conceptualization of the test, especially after *Keck and Mithouard*: indeed, there is quite a bit of discussion over whether 'restrictions' go beyond measures that are either directly or indirectly discriminatory. Lenaerts & Van Nuffel seem to believe they do[653], and also Barnard sees evidence in case law for a broader 'market access' approach[654]. Graínne de Búrca, on the other hand, believes that the treaty 'post-*Keck*, seems to prohibit only measures which have directly or indirectly discriminatory effect'[655]. The debate is sometimes somewhat semantically spurious: if indirect discrimination is conceived of in a broad sense (accordingly widely construing the *effects* on the basis of which the differentiation is assessed), it can also incorporate 'restrictions' which are indistinctly applicable, at least so it seems[656]. However, it is far from conceptually solved, and indeed shows how the dogmatic categories worked with (restriction, discrimination, proportionality) are and remain subject of (theoretical and relational) debate[657]. Some have in that vein argued that the European language might imply a

---

[650] The Court is inspired by European law, for instance because it uses the "European language" (*eg* it speaks about *internal customs and measures having equal effect*, which can easily be traced back to art. 34 TFEU (*ex* art. 28)). More about this issue follows below.

[651] *Cf.* reference to Delgrange and Keppene, *supra* note 646.

[652] And should rather be conceived of as an exception – the problem seems analogous to the one discussed *supra*, in No. 98. *Also see* Delgrange & Keppene, *supra* note 527, at p. 75-81.

[653] *Supra* note 590, at p. 214-15, 225-228, *esp*. at p. 226.

[654] Catharine Barnard, The substantive law of the EU: the four freedoms 19 (2010), even if she leaves more room for interpretation (*ibid.* p. 97 *et seq., esp*. 137-38 and 162-65).

[655] *The role of equality in European Community Law* in The Principle of Equal Treatment in E.C. Law 13, 21 (Alan Dashwood & Siofra O'Leary eds. 1997).

[656] *See,* for further discussion, the papers presented at 'The Market State Project'-conference (Oslo, May 18-19, 2011) on the scope of European law, in particular Alina Tryfonidou, *What can the Court's response to reverse discrimination and purely internal situation contribute to our understanding of the relationship between the 'restriction' and 'discrimination' concepts in EU free movement law, esp.* at p. 15 *et seq.* (who offers a compelling systematizing argument taking into account recent case law) or Stefan Enchelmaier, *The reach of Free movement: restriction on the use of goods and services, esp.* lines 505-40 (on the differentiation between market access and discrimination, in light of recent case law on user restrictions), both available at http://www.jus.uio.no/ifp/forskning/prosjekter/markedsstaten/arrangementer/2011/free-movement-oslo/speakers-papers/speakers-pres.html (July 2, 2011); even so her section on 'passport movement' (p. 22-25) seems to be in need of updating since the Court's *McCarthy* (Case C-434/09 (May 5, 2011) para 52) and *Dereci* (Case C-256/11 (GC; Nov. 15, 2011) paras 59 *et seq.*) judgments.

[657] *Also see* Feyen, *supra* note 32.

"peculiar" understanding of proportionality. For instance, Vanderveeren argued that '[c]onsiderations of economic efficiency lie at the origins of the economic and monetary union. The institutional framework in which the functioning of the market is understood by government action, nonetheless is the result of a political rationality, for which economic rationality can be one of the possible directives in decision-making'[658]. This line of reasoning could warrant a wholly different understanding of the EMU, based solely on its wider goals, embedded in its specific context.

Accordingly, since quite a bit (dogmatically) can turn on the relationship between EMU and other tools, and because this relationship is problematic, the conclusion that the EMU affords the Court quite a bit of discretion is hereby reinforced.

113. Conceptualization of the EMU (2): European inspiration. Some would argue that the Court could still be constrained by European law, for it is clear that the Belgian EMU concept was thoroughly inspired[659] and probably will continue to be inspired[660] by its European counterpart. Accordingly, the (dogmatic) question was often posed whether the interpretations[661] of the Court of Justice and the Belgian Courts converge[662] (often presupposing and sometimes articulating that interpretations *should* indeed converge). The substance of

---

[658] Christine Vanderveeren *et al.*, De Economische en Monetaire Unie in de Belgische Staatshervorming. juridische en economische aspecten 24 (1987)). According to Vanderveeren and her co-authors, the EMU should be a check on exclusivity, from the perspective of 'economic efficiency', insofar as 'one can ascertain heterogeneity of preferences and absence of externalities' (*ibid.* at p. 36).

[659] Delgrange & Keppene, *supra* note 527, at p. 72 (pointing out that both its existence, and the aligned methodology are inspired by European law) and 81-87 (discussing the separate judgments). The text of art. 6, §1, VI (3) also seems to imply this, in that it refers to 'the general normative framework of the economic union and the monetary unity, as establish by or pursuant to a statute, and by or pursuant to international treaties'. *Also see eg* Brouhns, *supra* note 623, at p. 36-37; Jadot, *supra* note 646, at p. 728 (noticing how No. 47 was inspired by European law); van Ypersele, *supra* note 214, at p. 124-25.

[660] *See eg* Vanderveeren *et al., supra* note 658, at p. 49, 51, 53. *But compare* Delgrange & Keppene, *supra* note 527, at p. 83-87 (however, this contribution relied on early case law, especially CA No. 32/91 (Nov. 14, 1991) and No. 33/91 (Nov. 14, 1991), criticizing the lack of thoroughly reviewing the proportionality of the measure, as the Court of Justice would do it).

[661] I employ 'interpretation' *sensu lato* here to avoid having to deal with some of the theoretical difficulties associated with either conceptually elaborating the principle of proportionality (*compare supra* note 498).

[662] And should be distinguished from the issue of *why* they either converge or not, and the issue of *justification* of possible convergence/divergence (*see* further Vanpraet, *supra* note 190, at p. 191 *et seq.; also see supra* note 630).

the issue is discussed further on; here, we merely wish to point out that the constraining power of European law is far from self-evident.

For instance, the question *whether* there is convergence necessarily raises further questions: is there a convergence in outcomes, or rather in the stipulation of the criteria for applying the rule / principle? Or is it rather the case that due to a different interpretation of the criteria deployed for the application of a rule, that the outcomes converge, notwithstanding relevant factual distinctions? Accordingly, the question of convergence raises issues of differentiation between fact and law, of the proper use of analogy in legal discourse, and more broadly, issues of legal interpretation as such. To give but one example: Vanderveeren has argued that there is a greater degree of market unity in Belgium than there is in Europe, due to a strong trans-regional interlocking of the economy[663]. Now one could ask the question whether in light of the norm incorporated in the EMU, this should be conceived of as a (relevant) factual difference, warranting a different outcome, or rather as an unimportant factual difference, warranting convergence in terms of results, or perhaps that indeed the norm itself is different, or perhaps the interpretation – for instance, because it is deferential towards assessing the necessity requirement under the principle of proportionality – thereof by the Constitutional Court (or Court of Justice, for that matter). Because I do not want to open that Pandora's box here, I leave questions pertaining to the issue more generally aside, in spite of my full acknowledgment of its importance[664]. What I merely wished to point out here, is that dogmatic thinking about the EMU (also in light of the relationship with European law) runs into enormous difficulties.

114. Implications of the EMU. If only for that reason, it certainly lies well beyond the scope of this book to examine the *substantive* implications of the EMU in different policy areas, either in Belgium[665] or Europe[666]. Even so, an example might help to clarify the sense of the Constitutional Court's reasoning.

---

663 Vanderveeren et al., *supra* note 658, at p. 63.

664 Somewhat further on these issues, *see* Feyen, *supra* note 32.

665 Although there have been several important books and articles written on the Belgian EMU (next to these already mentioned, *see eg* Franklin Dehousse, L'union économique et monétaire (CRISP theme number 1995)), I am not aware of any work that more or less exhaustively elaborates the substantive policy elaborations from a legal perspective in Belgium. Perhaps, of course, it would be hard to either create such a work coherently or exhaustively. For certain policy areas, however, there have been analyses on the question of the EMU's reach (*see eg* Plets, *supra* note 47 (on fiscal policy)).

666 *See, generally,* Barnard, *supra* note 654.

In case number 146/2004, an action for annulment was brought against a federal law reforming corporate taxes, lamenting the preclusion of deduction of autonomous regional (environmental) taxes as business costs.[667] The petitioners argued that because the environmental taxes in Flanders are generally higher, the Federal Government tried to accomplish its corporate reform primarily at Flanders' expense, which they deemed to be incompatible with 'the equal protection of the EMU'[668]. The Court did not accept this argument, since the petitioners had not shown how the law could infringe upon the EMU[669]. The Court emphasized that the fact that a federal regulation might have an impact or even a hortatory effect vis-à-vis the Region did not by itself establish a violation of the EMU[670].

Moreover, by and large, the Court is quite lenient in its EMU review. Only when regulations can be construed as customs duties or charges having equal effect, or when the obstruction to free trade becomes patent[671], the Court will more readily enforce article 6, §1, VI (3) SLIR. Accordingly, when the Court has to weigh the interests of the economy vis-à-vis other interests, it grants the legislature quite a bit of leeway in its judgments[672].

---

667 CA No. 146/2004 (Sep. 15, 2004). *See* Marc Delanote, *De aftrekbaarheid van regionale heffingen onder grondwettelijk recht*, 2005 Lokale en Regionale Belastingen 32, 42-43 (critical due to lack of depth).

668 CA No. 146/2004 (Sep. 15, 2004) A.5.1, A.5.3, B.6.

669 CA No. 146/2004 (Sep. 15, 2004) B.7.2.

670 CA No. 146/2004 (Sep. 15, 2004) B.7.3.

671 *Also see* CA No. 107/2005 (June 22, 2005) B.8.2 ('[e]ven if the existence of a economic union first and foremost implies free movement of goods and production factors, it also implies free movement of persons between the federated entities of a state').

672 On the whole, the line of cases for which the assertion I make here goes, is incomplete (I discuss here the cases in which art. 6, §1, VI (3) SLIR is in play), to the extent that sometimes, the Court does not expressly invoke art. 6, §1, VI (3) when it is nonetheless seeking to protect the four freedoms, certainly in a European perspective.
See CA No. 32/91 (Nov. 14, 1991) 5.B.1.8-5.B.1.9 (tax regarding the disposal of waste does not violate due to reasonable justification); No. 55/92 (July 9, 1992) 5.B.8 (some inventarization duties for farmers pertaining to manure are not unreasonable); No. 78/92 (Dec. 17, 1992) (the Court sounds somewhat confused here); Nos. 4-10/95 (Feb. 2, 1995) (discussed, *int. al. supra* note 559); No. 35/95 (Apr. 25, 1995) B.6.5 (it is not unreasonable for a legislature to want to decelerate gravel exploitation); No. 29/96 (May 15, 1996) B.8.4 (applying noice nuisance controls to construction which effectively renders construction factually impossible violates the EMU); No. 55/96 (Oct. 15, 1996) B.4.2.6 (an environmental tax that was qualified as a charge having equal effect was judged to be unconstitutional); No. 56/96 (Oct. 15, 1996) B.7.2-B.7.3 (obligating a taxi who starts driving in Brussels to obtain a licence does not constitute a violation); No. 34/97 (June 12, 1997) B.7.5-B.7.7 (an environmental tax was qualified as a charge having equal effect and judged to be unconstitutional); No. 42/97 (July 14, 1997) B.13.2-B.13.3 (the legislature's legitimate goal to limit a specific regime to family businesses justified a prohibition to take on a certain corporate form and a specific property

regime); No. 81/97 (Dec. 17, 1997) B.5.5-B.5.6 (allowing entities who technically engrave waste to expropriate is not a clear violation of the EMU); No. 51/98 (May 20, 1998) B.3.4 (an environmental tax was not qualified as a charge having equal effect as customs duties since there was no disproportionate impact, and therefore no violation); Nos. 73/98 (June 17, 1998) and 40/99 (Mar. 30, 1999) (establishing merely directive rental prices does not constitute an infringement in the EMU); No. 53/99 (May 26, 1999) B.6.4 (the economic disadvantages for one group are offset by the advantages of another, read together with the principle of free association); No. 124/99 (Nov. 25, 1999) B.5.4.1-B.5.5.2 (the Flemish legislature struck a justifiable balance between exclusivity of contracts and right to free news gathering); No. 67/2000 (June 14, 2000) B.3.2-B.3.3 (the free movement of capital can be offset by a general interest, like the fiscal and residential one here); No. 36/2001 (Mar. 13, 2001) B.4.2-B.6.2 (the federal competence to prohibit tobacco advertising can ground itself in the EMU, and precludes the Walloon government to create a transitional regime not federally foreseen); No. 128/2001 (Oct. 10, 2011) B.12 (an environmental tax was qualified as a charge having equal effect and judged to be unconstitutional); No. 69/2004 (May 5, 2004) B.15.2-B.15.4 (an environmental levy does not violate the EMU since it applies irrespective of origins of the waste and coordinates with other possible levies); No. 119/2004 (June 30, 2004) B.2.3-B.2.4 (for Francophone travel agencies, the new regulation expanded its economic freedoms, but for Flemish, the lack of expansion was justified in terms of material and territorial competences); No. 146/2004 (Sep. 15, 2004) (discussed *supra* No. 114); No. 195/2004 (Dec. 1, 2004) B.14.4-B.14.6 (*supra* note 559); No. 107/2005 (June 22, 2005) B.9.2-B.9.5 (a very high succession tax imposed by the Regions does not violate the EMU inasmuch it does not *necessarily* lead to delocalization of the tax base and because it finds legal support in the SLFCR); No. 132/2005 (July 19, 2005) B.5.1-B.5.5 (a legislature may determine that a crematorium must be run as a public service, in the sense that its core duties are fully regulated); No. 51/2006 (Apr. 19, 2006) (discussed *infra,* on the care insurance); CC No. 121/2008 (Sep. 1, 2008) B.5.1-B.5.3 (an environmental tax was not qualified as a charge having equal effect as customs duties since there was no disproportionate impact, and therefore no violation); No. 2/2009 (Jan. 15, 2009) B.21-B.22.2 (the limitations set forth due to immision norms are not disproportionate to the goal in light of freedom of trade); No. 11/2009 (Jan. 21, 2009) (discussed *infra,* on care insurance); No. 87/2009 (May 28, 2009) B.17-B.19 (obligating a transport company to coordinate and integrate bus traffic in the capital to end proliferation of bus lines does not infringe freedom of trade of several transport companies) ; No. 41/2010 (Apr. 29, 2010) B.5.3 (if licences used are mutually recognized, there is no violation of the EMU); No. 83/2010 (July 9, 2010) (discussed *infra,* on inheritance tax); No. 123/2010 (Oct. 28, 2010) B.5.2-B.6 (a disproportionate levy on animal manure infringes the EMU, no matter whether it is construed as a customs duty or as a charge having equal effect); No. 149/2010 (Dec. 22, 2010); *also see* No. 47 (discussed *supra*); No. 12/89 (May 31, 1989) B.4 (where the Court set some conditions but could not rule on the matter (of waste sites) in depth since there was a delegation to the Executive).

3.4 Interaction in the Constitutional Court's toolbox

115. Interaction: a delicate, avoided subject. I will not describe in the abstract how the aforementioned, distinct tools can interact. That is in fact one of the main reasons why I chose to call the different interpretative forms of argument *tools*.

I here disregard the 'original' distinction between forms of arguments having a textual basis or not, as I do not want to enter in the abstract debate between 'originalism' or 'textualism' and the 'living Constitution' (understood materially here, in light of deconstitutionalization, and disregarding conceptual difficulties underlying these terms). To a large extent in Belgium, this debate – on a level of high abstraction - has been solved in favor of the latter stance anyhow[673]. This, however, does not mean that the relationship between the 'living elements' (principles, values, …) and the text itself are undiscussed: in fact, much of debate on constitutional matters can – I believe – be described in exactly those terms. That for me constitutes sufficient reason not to further discuss the issue here (although it does undergird some of what follows).

But even if a *tool*-like conceptualization of constitutional argumentation allows for a better explanation of the case law, the question remains whether it can also succeed in predicting case law. In order to that, one would have to find regularities within the relationships amongst the different tools, in order to more fully understand their interaction (however, without reifying them). Some of the interactions have been summarily or tangentially alluded to above.

For instance, we discussed shortly whether the principle of federal loyalty imposes different constraints than the principle of proportionality on legislative decision-making. Moreover, it could be asked whether the entirety of *non-textual* constraints could not be captured under the heading of federal loyalty[674]. Moreover, in several footnotes above, I alluded to possible interactions (either implicitly, or explicitly). Sometimes I refer explicitly to authors, who elaborate these interactions[675]. Other times I offer alone-standing argument, such as the argument why it is not always easy to distinguish between concurrent

[673] *See eg* Alen & Peeters, *supra* note 13, at p. 1124-25; Francis Delpérée, *La vie de la Constitution*, 1980 Annales de Droit de Louvain 123, 128-29.

[674] *See eg* Delgrange & Keppene, *supra* note 527, at p. 90; Storme, *supra* note 142, at p. 267-68 (equating EMU with federal loyalty).

[675] *Eg* Peeters, *supra* note 38, at p. 561 *et seq.*, on the interaction between federal loyalty, proportionality and the concept of interpretation.

and parallel competences[676]. Some interactions have moreover been subject of intense scholarly debate, for instance the interaction of reserved competences and implied competences (article 19 SLIR)[677].

However, discussing these interactions comprehensively here, if possible, would only take up a lot of space. Actually trying to settle the discussions might even be sheer impossible[678].

116. Competence and rights jurisdiction: a myriad of interactions. One (abstract) interaction in particular though, in light of what is to come, seems particularly thought provoking. Up till now, I have explained how the Belgian allocation of competences cannot be discussed separately from the broader institutional framework in which this allocation of competences has come about. Moreover, I have pointed out several ways in which rights jurisdiction and competence jurisdiction are entangled indeed[679]. In what follows, I will revisit this issue in some more depth and tailor it to what follows on European law.

We already mentioned that even if the Court upholds the possibility of *conceptually* separating the kinds of review[680], it acknowledges the entanglement explicitly.

[676] *See eg supra* No. 68.

[677] *Also see* Bernard Haubert, *Les pouvoirs implicites ou les creux de la réforme institutionnelle,* 1985 APT 290 ; Vande Lanotte, *supra* note 609.

[678] Which does of course not undermine the validity of the discussions about them.

[679] *Supra* Nos. 61 and 62.

[680] *Eg*, it is established jurisprudence of the Court, even if there have been some deviations (*eg* CA No. 23/92 (Feb. 4, 1992) B.16 *et seq.*), that in principle, the Court first reviews legislation in light of its conformity with the rule allocating competences (established jurisprudence since CA No. 30/92 (Feb. 4, 1992) 5.B.2). This, of course, does not mean that the separation in the Court's jurisprudence is rigid, but rather implies that the Court at least acknowledges a *conceptual* possibility of separating the kinds of review. *Also see* art. 142 Cons. *juncto* art. 1 and 26 SLCC. Apparently more rigidly, *see* CA No. 35/2003 (Mar. 25, 2003) B.9.1 and B.9.3 ('provisions regarding competences of Communities and Regions cannot – in their nature – directly affect the individual situations of citizens, since they are directed to the Communities and Regions'). Even if such a contention is not entirely bereft of truth (*see supra* No. 111 (on the distinction between the EMU, arguably vis-à-vis the entities, and the freedom of trade, as an individual right); *compare infra* note 261), matters are certainly somewhat more complex than this. On the one hand, the principle of equality (in the Constitution itself) could be said to be directed to the government itself as well, not having any 'direct' consequence for individuals. Moreover, it is clear that even seemingly neutral *fundamental rules* – as the Court apparently perceives the rules governing the allocation of competences – may exert influence in concrete situations (*see eg* Duncan Kennedy, *The Stakes of Law, or Hale and Foucault!* in Sexy Dressing etc. Essays on the Power and Politics of Cultural Identity 83, 84-111 (1993) (explaining how seemingly neutral fundamental rules (*eg* of property) can have effects on the determination of the distribution of income in terms of the bargaining power of different classes and individuals - Kennedy here is influenced by Hale, whom he is

For instance, in a 2003 case it considered that '[t]he question pertaining to a possible violation of the principle of equality cannot be examined without taking into account the division of competences between the State and the Regions as regulated by the Constitution and the laws on institutional reforms'[681]. As a further instantiation thereof, in the context of a review of (special) legislation in light of the principle of equality, it endorsed the legitimacy of justifications that appeal to larger context of the 'essential principles underlying the Belgian State'[682]. The Court has explicitly recognized the fact that it should take into account this sort of principles, when it added to its 'equality refrain' the clause that it takes the existence of a justification must be assessed in light of not only the objective and the consequences of the measure, but also in light of 'nature of the principles valid at hand'[683]. It has further been noticed that some important federalism-related (communautarian[684]) judgments (in the broad sense of having to do with the tensions between the different Belgian sociological communities) are not dealt with on the (narrow) allocation of competences grounds. For instance, even if the now infamous Brussels-Hal-Vilvorde judgment[685] is unquestionably related to the Belgian communautarian issues[686], the ground

discussing, and Hohfeld's (*cf. infra* note 1028) thoughts on permission); *compare supra* No. 98). Conceptually, the distinction is not wholly useless, but one should pay attention to how and when it is best used. To the Court's defense perhaps, in the example it was used to assess the *legal* meaning of 'directly affect' in terms of admissibility requirements.

681 CA No. 119/2003 (Sep. 24, 2003) B.3.1. *Also see* 102/99 (Sept. 30, 1999) B.9.4. (more implicitly: '[t]o the extent that the argument complains about the factual consequences resulting from the law – which are dispute by the Cabinet – in order to justify the exaggerated character of the prohibition in question, this argument in reality takes the provisions to impinge upon the principle of proportionality, violating articles 10 and 11 Cons.'). *Compare* CA No. 146/2001 (Nov. 20, 2001) B.5.5 *with* CA No. 164/2006 (Nov. 8, 2006) B.6.2) (on economic help for particular sectors in which the legislatures are competent, in casu agriculture). *Also see* BRIBOSIA & VAN BOXSTAEL, *supra* note 13, at p. 161 *et seq.* or PEETERS, *supra* note 38, at p. 211.

682 *Cf.* CA 18/90 (May 23, 1990) B.9.1-B.9.2 (on the 'Pacification Law'); CA 26/90 (July 14, 1990), 6.B.7-6.B.8, 7.B.2 (on European elections); CA No. 35/2003 (Mar. 25, 2003), B.13.4-B.13.5, B.14.2 (on the 2001 Special Law on State Reform); CA 35/2004 (Mar. 10, 2004) B.4.1-B.4.2 (on art. 5*bis-ter* SLBI) (granting the (special) legislature a large margin of appreciation). *Compare* art. 16*ter* SLIR, 5*bis-ter* SLBI, 7*bis* SLBI and 16*bis* SLIR (where the distinction is apparently far less clear as well) in light of CA No. 35/2004 (Mar. 10, 2004) B.4.1 (relationship between 5*ter* SLBI and art. 10 & 11 Cons.) and CA No. 17/2007 (Jan. 17, 2007) B.14 (applicability to the federal government).

683 Established jurisprudence, *see eg* CA No. 18/91 (July 4, 1991) B.3 *or* CA No. 25/94 (Mar. 22, 1994) B.3.

684 On a more historical explanation of 'communautarian', *see eg* HUYSE, *supra* note 126, at p. 58 *et seq.*

685 CA No. 73/2003 (May 26, 2003).

686 *Ibid.* B.9.5.

for the holding of unconstitutionality in this case was primarily the principle of equality and non-discrimination[687]. This is the case for most of the judgments that were conceived in media and scholarship as important[688], even if they were federalism-related or if they had a clear communautarian impact.

117. Discrimination, differentiation and federalism-based or constitutional reasons. Moreover, the Court has constantly recognized that differences in treatment resulting from the separate policies of federated entities could not by themselves establish a discrimination, since the differentiation was justified by the constitutionally entrenched autonomy of the federated entities[689]. Most of the time, conceptually, the Court has argued that the situations are not comparable, and therefore not amenable to equality review[690]. Other times[691] it has employed formulations allowing room for more conceptual and structural questions, and in recent cases, it seems to go with the reasoning that such a distinction can 'by itself not be deemed to violate articles 10 and 11 of the

---

687 *Ibid.* B.6, where the fourteen discrimination grounds are described; *also see* B.9, which constituted the most 'salient' issue in terms of media attention.

688 *See* Luc Théry and Nicolas Dupont, *Wetenschappelijke en statistische analyse van de weerklank van de uitspraken van het Hof. Welke arresten en welke thema's beroeren de doctrine en de publieke opinie? Une analyse scientifique et statistique de l'écho des arrêts de la Cour. Quels arrêts et quels thèmes touchent la doctrine et l'opinion publique?* 2010 CDPK 328. *Also see eg* Alen & Muylle, *supra* note 14, at p. 247-249 and 364; CA No. 90/94 (Dec. 22, 1994).

689 This is established jurisprudence. *See eg* CA No. 35/1995 (Apr. 24, 1995) B.12.2; CA No. 190/2005 (Dec. 14, 2005) B.4.7; CC No. 63/2010 (May 27, 2010) B.3; Paul Martens, *Le rôle de la Cour d'arbitrage dans l'édification du federalism en Belgique*, 2003 RBDC 3, 5; Popelier, *supra* note 16, at p. 104 *et seq.*; Rigaux & Renauld, *supra* note 16, at p. 61-63 (with references); Vande Lanotte & Goedertier, *supra* note 13, at p. 361 *et seq.* and 1003-04; Velaers & Vanpraet, *supra* note 388, at p. 212. *But compare* CA No. 120/98 (Dec. 3, 1998) B.3.4 ('[t]he circumstance that the French Community has not yet legislated here cannot liberate the Court from analyzing the argument to the extent that it can be interpreted in the sense that the provision in question has discriminatorily violated the obligation to take the European Directive into account, whereas the other Communities are bound by that obligation') (*in comparison with* B.4). It should be noted, however, that No. 120/98 has been generally conceived of as an exception or an aberration in the Court's jurisprudence (*eg* Popelier, *supra* note 45, at p. 104; Vanden Heede & Goedertier, *supra* note 226, at p. 264; *compare* Vansteenkiste, *supra* note 551 (who does not mention it as an aberration)).

690 *See eg* Dajo De Prins, Stefan Sottiaux & Jogchum Vrielink, Handboek Discriminatierecht 254-55 (2005); *also see* Valérie Flohimont, *Comparaison et comparabilité dans la jurisprudence de la Cour constitutionnelle: rigueur ou jeu de hazard?*, 2008 RBDC 217, 224-25; Dirk Vanheule, Amerikaanse modellen van grondwettigheidstoetsing toegepast op de rechtspraak van het Arbitragehof over de artikelen 10 en 11 van de Grondwet 328-31 (diss. doct. Antwerp University 2001).

691 For further references, *see supra* Nos. 61-62.

Constitution'[692]. It is thus hard to see a clear line in this form of reasoning[693]. That clear line is moreover more generally lacking vis-à-vis the applicability of the comparability test, not the least because this test already presupposes some judgment on the merits[694]. The assessment of comparability can indeed only occur within a contextual and purposeful frame of reference, the determination of which is by and large a political exercise, or at least made within a particular social constellation, infused with normative assumptions, begotten from different sources, for instance the legislature's objective[695].

All this, according to standing doctrine, does not preclude groups as such from relying on the equality provision[696]. That includes municipalities or provinces[697], but also the Communities, Regions and the Federal State[698]. In a 1996 case, for instance, the Court compared the State (that was exempt as an employer from paying social security contributions) to the Regions and Communities, but concluded that there was in this case a connection to the exclusive competences of the federal State[699]. A year later, the Court investigated the constitutionality of a SLIR-provision namely article 87, §§ 2 and 4, but concluded that the possible differences in treatment find their legal basis in the Constitution, in which case they cannot be compared efficiently[700]. More generally, the Court seems to sometimes ground its argument in the fact that it cannot doubt the choices of the Constitutional framers[701] or in the fact that the *framers of the Constitution* have left a measure

---

692 *Eg* CC No. 151/2007 (Dec. 12, 2007) B.13.3; No. 3/2010 (Jan. 20, 2010) B.26; *compare* CC No. 63/2010 (May 27, 2010) B.3 (ecliptic).

693 *Contra* Geert Goedertier, *De Gemeenschappen en Gewesten als houders van de rechten die in de artikelen 10 en 11 van de Grondwet zijn gewaarborgd*, 1997-98 RW 1384, 1386 (who argues that a rule allocating competences contained in special legislative provisions cannot be reviewed in light of the differences it creates).

694 *Eg* Rimanque, *supra* note 278, at p. 6, 8; Flohimont, *supra* note 690, at p. 220-21, 229-30; *but compare* Scott Brewer, *Exemplary reasoning: semantics, pragmatics, and the rational force of legal argument by analogy*, 109 Harv. L.R. 923 (arguing for the existence of 'analogy-warranting rules').

695 Flohimont, *supra* note 690, p. 230-32, with references.

696 *Eg* Velaers, De Grondwet en de Raad van State, *supra* note 13, at p. 70-71.

697 *Eg* CA No. 13/91 (May 28, 1991) 4.B.2 or CA No. 31/91 (Nov. 7, 1991).

698 *Eg* CA No. 62/96 (Nov. 7, 1996) and CA No. 78/97 (Dec. 17, 1997).

699 CA No. 62/96 (Nov. 7, 1996) B.3.2; *compare* CA No. 65/2005 (Mar. 23, 2005) B.7.2; *cf.* Flohimont, *supra* note 690, at p. 225.

700 CA No. 78/97 (Dec. 17, 1997) B.4.

701 *Also see* CA No. 47/2006 (Mar. 22, 2006) B.6 (on the regime in art. 25 Cons.) or CC No. 44/2011 (Mar. 30, 2011) B.16 (on the applicability of art. 159 Cons. in the context of administrative courts); *compare* Paul Van Orshoven, *De onrechtmatige Grondwet* in Liège, Strasbourg, Bruxelles, *supra* note 27, at p. 989 *et seq.* (contemplating the idea of an

of discretion to the special legislature[702]. Even so, these choices are not always as unequivocal as the Court sometimes suggests.

In the broadest conceptual sense, one could argue that 'proportionality' – here as a shorthand considerations of reasonableness – is not only comprised in allocation of competence, but also sometimes vice versa. This, given the emptiness of the principle of proportionality, is perhaps a statement lacking sufficient analytical clarity, or even a reification. However, it does make clear that arguments which are deemed primarily relevant in either equality or competence jurisdiction, might be relevant in the other jurisdiction as well, notwithstanding how they have been specifically affixed in the *dogmatic structure* the Court has built up[703]. As such, proportionality should be deemed to be metonymic for *reasonableness*. This still does not imply a whole lot, since it does not explain – *arguendo* that the 'structures' of equality[704] are in fact an adequate representation of how judicial review in light of equality works – where the *reasonableness* requirement comes in within the structure. It can be imagined to come in at different 'levels'[705]. Indeed, we are still talking about 'realities that are often hard to grasp and certainly to put in a legal perspective'[706]. An argument could even be developed in which the fact that reasonableness operates on different levels vis-à-vis the structure is believed to imply the very deterioration of the structure itself. Taken to its/this extreme, this seems to go too far[707].

At any rate, the concrete intricacies and complexities established by this admittedly broad and conceptually imperfect interaction fall beyond the scope of this book[708]. Metaphorically, one could proffer that if the jurisprudence about

unjustified constitution); *also compare* (interestingly with reference to a new form of European federalism) Pas, *supra* note 139, at p. 134-137 ('formal equality will always diminish, but his is the essence of federalism' (*ibid.* at p. 136)).

702 *Eg* CA No. 24/98 (Mar. 10, 1998) B.10-B.11, on the different treatment of Brussels. *Compare* CoS No. 45.858 (Jan. 28, 1994) (similarly on municipal autonomy).

703 *Eg* as a consideration of *non-comparability* or as a consideration of *justification* of an establishedly comparable difference in treatment.

704 *Also see supra* note 237.

705 For some European reflections, *see* Elke Cloots, *The European Court of Justice and Member State Federalism: Balancing or Categorisation?* in Federalism, *supra* note 32, at p. 322 *et seq. Compare* Dworkin, Justice in Robes, *supra* note 62, at p. 5 *et seq.* (elaborating the doctrinal concept of law in different stages).

706 Paul Tapie, *Introduction to* Uyttendaele, *supra* note 13, at p. 9.

707 Especially in light of the rule of law values which we further discuss.

708 In a more extra-judicial setting, the relationship between rights and federalism has been widely discussed (*see eg* the contributions in Federalism and Rights (Ellis Katz & G. Alan Tarr eds. 1996)). Elaborating this again would drag us into a debate on either jurisdictional questions (from a federal perspective) (*see eg* Aida Torres Pérez, *The Dual System of Rights Protection in*

allocation of competences *sensu stricto* is a toolbox, then the interaction of this federalism-toolbox with the constitutional rights jurisprudence would be a construction site in motion[709]. Walking across this site, one runs into different debates, cases, or other scattered examples of interaction. This includes but is not limited to the whole debate in the 1980s (when the Court was not yet formally empowered to review norms in light of anything but the rules governing the allocation of competences), regarding the inclusion of other constitutional norms in the judgments[710], or the occasional reliance by the Court on similar or the same justifications in order to renounce both competence and equality

the European Union in Light of US Federalism in FEDERALISM, *supra* note 32, 110 *et seq.*), or political philosophy (*compare eg* I GEORGE SCELLE, PRÉCIS DE DROIT DES GENS: PRINCIPES ET SYSTÉMATIQUE. LE MILIEU INTERSOCIAL 188 (1932) *with* RAYMOND ARON & ALEXANDRE MARC, PRINCIPES DU FÉDÉRALISME 19 (1948) (discussing the relationship between rights and federalism from a more theoretical perspective)), or at least into a discussion about minority rights (*see eg* the different contributions on 'Theme 2', in FEDERALISM: TURNING DIVERSITY INTO HARMONY, *supra* note 188, at p. 56-68). Sometimes these debates have been redeemed in legal doctrine (*see* BRIBOSIA & VAN BOXSTAEL, *supra* note 13, at p. 161 *et seq.*; PEETERS, *supra* note 38, at p. 198 *et seq.* (on how, from a Kelsenian perspective, the distinction between rights and federalism issues is somewhat artificial)) or G. Alan Tarr, *Constitutional Theories and Constitutional Rights: Federalist Considerations*, 22 PUBLIUS 93, 103 *et seq.* (1992) (a criticism of how Dworkin's cannot account for structural considerations in the elaboration of rights), or even arguably in case law (*see* the very holistic reasoning (I am not judging its intrinsic soundness) proposed in CC No. 93/2009 (Feb. 18, 2009), which was not followed by the Court (I mean *holistic* here *not* in the sense of *eg* Eric Lancksweerdt, *Een holistische aanpak in het publiek recht*, 2012 TBP 420-421); *compare see* ECtHR Nos. 1474/62, 1677/62, 1691/62, 1769/63, 1994/63 and 2126/24 (July 23, 1968) *Case "relating to certain aspects of the laws on the use of languages in Belgium" v. Belgium* (*Belgian Linguistics Case*) and ECtHR No. 9267/81 (Mar. 2, 1987) *Mathieu-Mohin Clerfayt v. Belgium*, as more widely discussed, for instance by CLEMENT, *supra* note 197, at p. 824 *et seq.* *Also compare* ANDRÉ ALEN, POGING TOT EEN JURIDISCHE BEGRIPSOMSCHRIJVING VAN UNITARISME, CENTRALISATIE, DECONCENTRATIE, DECENTRALISATIE, REGIONALISME, FEDERALISME EN CONFEDERATIE 65 *et seq.* (1975); Delpérée & Verdussen, *supra* note 547; UYTTENDAELE, *supra* note 13, at p. 369 *et seq.* and UYTTENDAELE, *supra* note 263, at p. 872-903 (all on the 'equality' of the constitutive entities of the Belgian federal state).

[709] *Also see* RIGAUX & RENAULD, *supra* note 16, at p. 81-82 (with references, on the 'emptiness' – borrowed from Westen's famous article in 95 HARV. L.R. 537 (1982) – of the concept of equality, as employed by the Constitutional Court after *Biorim*). *Compare* Jean-Claude Scholsem, *L'égalité devant la Cour d'arbitrage* in LIBER AMICORUM PROF. EM. E. KRINGS 777 (1991) ('it is difficult, nearly impossible, for any court to adjudicate in matters of equality, always following in all the case, the same intellectual path in a way that could be called mechanical'). Accordingly, the authors of the 'standard work' on equality in Belgium admit that 'there are few areas of law in which there is so much discord regarding the content and scope of the applicable rules' as in the equality area (DE PRINS, SOTTIAUX & VRIELINK, *supra* note 690, at p. xxxv).

[710] *See eg* PEETERS, *supra* note 38, at p. 203-13; Karel Rimanque, *Het vraagstuk van de rechterlijke toetsing van wetten en decreten aan de Grondwet: kritische bedenkingen bij een heilsverwachting* 1986-87 JURA FALCONIS 561; VELAERS, VAN ARBITRAGEHOF TOT ..., *supra* note 13, at p. 133 *et seq.*; *compare* RIGAUX & RENAULD, *supra* note 16, at p. 63 *et seq.* (on how these considerations might still be relevant now).

arguments[711]. Also, in 1998, the Court once reframed arguments of territoriality to fit is equality test[712] and more recently, the Court even reformulated a question pertaining to competence allocation into one pertaining to equality[713]. More complexly, in a 2010 case, it was argued that the provision of the arms law violated either the rules allocating competences or the principle of equality, depending on the interpretation (the Court dismissed the argument, first dealing with the competence argument, and further on dismissing the equality argument on the basis of federated autonomy)[714]. However, without relying on a very general concept of proportionality here[715], it is hard to bring all these interactions under one conceptual or analytical category that fits (and justifies) the cases under review.

118. Rule of law values. Be that as it may, since the view on the Court's jurisprudence I propose here is not *radically realist* (in a technical jurisprudential sense[716]), we have to take some 'rule of law'-values into account in unfolding

---

711 *Eg* CA No. 32/91 (Nov. 14, 1991); CC No. 202/2009 (Dec. 23, 2009) B.14; 31/2010 (Mar. 30, 2010) B.14; No. 89/2010 (July 29, 2010) B.13.1 *juncto* B.19.

712 CA 128/98 (Dec. 9, 1998) B.16.1-B.16.7.

713 CC 41/2010 (Apr. 29, 2010) A.2.2.

714 CC No. 3/2010 (Jan. 20, 2010) B.17 *et seq.*

715 *Cf.* the one elaborated *supra* in this No. (in the paragraph starting with '[i]n the broadest conceptual sense').

716 Let us call a *radically* realist view on law the view often thought espoused by the Scandinavian realists. Often reference is made to Alf Ross (*supra* note 440), who indeed seeks to 'carry in the field of law, the empirical principles to their ultimate conclusions' (*ibid.* at p. ix), and starts from the premise that there are 'no inner criteria that determine where the doctrinal study of law ends' (*ibid.* at p. x). For some it follows from this that such a radically realist view fails to take into account the pervading sense of obligation felt by legal officials. This is what Hart called the 'internal point of view' into account (Hart, *supra* note 109, p. 133 *et seq.* and Herbert L.A. Hart, *Scandinavian Realism* in Essays in Jurisprudence and Philosophy 161 (1983); *also see* Leiter, *supra* note 72, at p. 4, 190-191): it is, in other words, a normative attitude of participants of the legal process, namely one of acceptance of the legitimacy of the rules and obligations (Hart, *supra* note 109, at p. 86). Leiter argued that in also thinking that American legal realists made a similar mistake (*ie* adhering to conceptual rule skepticism), Hart went awry (*supra* note 72, at p. 69 *et seq.*). It is unsure whether this is a fair characterization of Ross, since he was well aware in On Law and Justice of a 'point of view of [...] consciousness of the rules' (*supra* note 440, at p. 13), and he argued that 'directives are felt by each player [in his chess analogy] to be socially binding' (*ibid.* at p. 14), thus criticizing a mere 'behaviourist angle' (*ibid.* at p. 15; *also see* p. 37 *et seq.*; *but compare* at p. 30 *et seq.* ('these systems are facts' (*ibid.* at p. 31) or '[t]he instruction to the private individual is implicit in the fact that he knows what reactions on the part of the courts he can expect' (*ibid.* at p. 33)), but that is of lesser importance here. Also of lesser importance is that the view on the 'internal point of view' espoused by Leiter (and upon which we rely here to construe the notion of radical realism), is not generally accepted (*see eg* Scott J. Shapiro, *What is the internal point of view?*, 75 Fordh. L. Rev. 1157 (2006) (who argues against the methodological implications)).

the Court's jurisprudence[717]. We already *have* taken them into account in this chapter, be it either through presupposition, or in an implied way (for instance talking about (con)textual constraints). Here, however, I want to explicitly underline their importance. In what follows, no full theorization of what rule of law values are will be found, however. First, a full theorization would require some substantiation of them within a broader theory[718], which lies beyond the scope of this work. Moreover, it is uncertain whether such a broader theory is either warranted, or whether it offers a suitable interpretation of the practice of the Constitutional Court. [719] Relatedly, in order to work out a broader theory comprehensively – and in light of what has been said above about the toolbox conceptualization of the Court's case law – the interaction between rule of law values and the toolbox (instrumental) approach of the Court would have to be (fully) theorized: this goes beyond the scope of this work, my capabilities and perhaps conceptual possibility itself.

What we do want to stress is the importance of rule of law values for a theory of constitutional prudence. Such a theory indeed need not be comprehensive (in the sense of fleshing out all relationships, distinctions and implications), because everyone can recognize that rule of law values, notably text, precedent and coherence, have all been argued, be it in various mutual relationships and with variegated levels of enthusiasm and conviction, to be crucial in limiting the instrumentalizing capabilities of judges. Even if that basic insight is relatively easy to apperceive, this does not mean that it is smoothly operationalized, even without (or perhaps because of a lack of) a comprehensive theory.

119. Rule of law values: initial issues with operationalizing. Accordingly, operationalization of rule of law values in *text, precedent* and *coherence* runs into some very basic difficulties at the outset, especially taking into account the

[717] The opposition between the instrumental line of reasoning (in the sense of judicial fiat) and 'reason' (embodying the constraining power of law) has a long history: *see eg* Lon L. Fuller, *Reason and Fiat in Case Law*, 59 HARV. L.R. 376 (1946).

[718] For instance answering whether our proposed study perceives the rule of law values as for instance internally (socially) binding, though not legally binding as such but nonetheless relevant in legal exposition, *or* externally (legally) binding, though open to interpretation and defeasibility, *and so on.* Of course, a coherent theory about the relationship between rule of law values and tools will depend on taking a stance on these issues. However, as we mentioned, what we offer is not a full-fledged theory, but just a *model* to show how to incorporate more instrumental / pragmatic forms of reasoning into legal inquiry (or at least: common inquiry by constitutional lawyers).

[719] Compare Sunstein's perspective of law as incompletely theorized (*see eg* his ONE CASE AT A TIME: JUDICIAL MINIMALISM ON THE SUPREME COURT (2001)); *compare* Van Drooghenbroek, *supra* note 393, at p. 250-251 (who argues that the Constitutional Court indeed could be seen as to engage in a practice of decisional minimalism); *further see infra* note 1038.

instrumental mode of thought of the Constitutional Court. As such, these rule of law values cannot be said to be dispositive, because they certainly do not take away the discretion accorded to the Court. Instead, they (can) present themselves in a relationship of *tension* with the Court's more instrumental approach.

As regards the text, first, we should emphasize that a *realist* line of jurisprudence basically contends – as we saw – that the constraining force of texts on judges is highly overestimated[720]. Even if that is the case, they did not generally[721] deny that rules – some caricatures or provocations notwithstanding[722] - indeed mattered. Accordingly, I am convinced that the Belgian constitutional law judges take the written law seriously; but at the same time, I note that the open textured nature[723] (and even more so the open structure which we alluded to earlier) of the law *does* grant judges quite a bit of leeway. Even if the position described here cannot be deemed to be *radically realist*, I take no *jurisprudential* position here on how the meaning and relevance of a particular text must be assessed in general. Rather, I focus on the practical issues – *ie* the relationship between European law and Belgian Constitutional Court jurisprudence – further on.

As regards precedent, some initial difficulties arise in the sense that the traditional continental theory of law does not consider precedent to be a formal source of law. This, however, should be starkly relativized.[724] Even if there are still substantial differences between doctrines of precedent (*stare decisis*) in

[720] Even if it is the case that many American legal realists constructed their arguments in the context of US private law, which was predominantly governed by the *common law* – and thus, by implication, could be categorized as *precedent* – (some of) their arguments can be extrapolated to cover written norms too. This is the case because generally text and precedent are not always easily distinguishable (*also see infra* No. 120), for instance in the sense that reasoning on the basis of a holding presupposes at least an implicit 'textualization' of a rule.

[721] Some authors, like Brian Leiter, see exceptions in the statements of writers like Jerome Frank, who pervasively stressed the importance of the individual judge (*eg supra* note 72, at p. 110-111).

[722] For instance LLEWELLYN, who called the rules mere 'pretty playthings' (LLEWELLYN, *supra* note 67, at p. 7), and not only in the same book, but also more explicitly later, fully recognized the constraining power of rules (*eg* LLEWELLYN, *supra* note 81).

[723] Even if I rely on Hart's notion here (*supra* note 109, at p. 134-135), I do not necessarily accept Hart's concomitant distinction between core and penumbra of rules, implying that discretion was often very limited (*ibid.* at p. 141-147 and 272-273) . I moreover disregard the jurisprudential debates that have surrounded this notion of open texture, like the Hart/Fuller-debate, but also broader debates about the indeterminacy of law.

[724] *Eg* CC No. 125/2011 (July 7, 2011) B.5.1 (*et seq.*). *See* Neil MacCormick & Robert S. Summers, *Further General Reflections and Conclusions* in INTERPRETING PRECEDENTS 531-32 (Neil MacCormick & Robert S. Summers eds. 1997). *Also see* Marc Bossuyt, *De invloed van de rechtspraak van het Grondwettelijk Hof op de evolutie van het recht*, 2011-2012 RW 382, 386.

the common law countries and in (continental) Europe[725], convergence has been noted[726]. In that light, it will be assumed that even if some changes in jurisprudence have occurred throughout the years, the Constitutional Court will not (or at least should not) adapt its jurisprudence without reason[727]. At the same time, implicitly or explicitly, the Court can distinguish and indeed even overrule its own case law, again rendering precedent as a rule of law value relative in nature.

As regards coherence, some scholars have vehemently denounced this requirement as a rule of law value, for instance because it is believed to be neither a sufficient, nor a necessary condition for justification[728]. Even so, many judges, and more importantly scholars[729], find it to be of great importance, and indeed partly presuppose the value (in that dogmatics aspires to systematize). *Pace* Dworkin, this does not mean that 'coherence' is an unequivocal concept excluding a sense of judicial discretion.[730] Rather, coherence can serve in different ways in a judicial argumentative structure, not only as a means of ensuring the intelligibility and stability of the rule of law itself, but also as an instrument (*tool*), that can be geared towards various ends, some of which are not necessarily part of Law's 'inner Reason'.

---

[725] *Eg* URS PETER GRUBER, METHODEN DES INTERNATIONALEN EINHEITSRECHT 275-328 (2004); *but compare* CATHERINE VAN DE HEYNING, FUNDAMENTAL RIGHTS LOST IN COMPLEXITY 158 *et seq., esp.* 171- 81 (diss. doct. Antwerp University 2011) (on the erga omnes effects of ECtHR law).

[726] *Eg* Mauro Cappelletti, *The doctrine of stare decisis and the civil law: a fundamental difference or no difference at all?* in FESTSCHRIFT FÜR KONRAD ZWEIGERT ZUM 70. GEBURTSTAG 381 (Herbert Bernstein *et al.* 1981) or more recently Frank Emmert, Stare Decisis: *A Universally misunderstood idea*, 6 LEGISLPRUDENCE 207 (2012).

[727] *Compare* the contributions by Maurice Adams (whose focus lies on private law) and Sébastien Van Drooghenbroeck (who focuses on judicial independence more broadly, but from the perspective of public law) in THE BELGIAN REPORTS AT THE CONGRESS OF UTRECHT OF THE INTERNATIONAL ACADEMY OF COMPARATIVE LAW 47 *et seq.* and 521 *et seq.* (Eric Dirix & Yves-Henri Leleu eds. 2006). *Also see* art. 9 SLCC (*erga omnes* power for judgments granting annulment, *inter partes* power for judgments declining to annul), art. 26, §§ 2-4 and 29, § 2 SLCC (on the duty of judges to refer for preliminary rulings); CA No. 18/91 (July 4, 1991) B.9 or CC No. 125/2011 (July 7, 2011) B.5.1 (even in preliminary proceedings, the Court takes into account the *precedential* repercussions of its judgments).

[728] Joseph Raz, *The relevance of coherence*, in ETHICS IN THE PUBLIC DOMAIN. ESSAYS IN THE MORALITY OF LAW AND POLITICS 277, 282-86 (revised ed. 1994).

[729] This also holds for a lot of scholars theorizing about the law, *eg* DWORKIN, *supra* note 99, at p. 83 *et seq.* (still calling it 'articulate consistency'; in his later works, he refers to the broader concept of '*fit*' (*eg* RONALD DWORKIN, LAW'S EMPIRE 67 (1986)) or MACCORMICK, *supra* note 98, at p. 152-94.

[730] *See* Stefano Bertea, *The Arguments from Coherence: Analysis and Evaluation*, 25 OXFORD JOURNAL OF LEGAL STUDIES 369 (2005).

120. Further difficulties: a complex relationship. This last remark comes to show that the distinction between rule of law values and tools should not be conceived of as a pure dichotomy, and that the relationship between both is complex and multi-leveled. The same moreover goes for different rule of law values themselves, which are closely intertwined in different ways. For instance, the fact that court opinions might exert a (*de facto* or *de jure*) precedential value could be deemed to be an instance of a broader coherence theory[731]. On the other hand, Raz notes – in the context of the relationship between a text and coherence, and here he is probably right, at least that seems to be the case in Belgium[732] – that 'if the set of principles one is considering represents the dictates of authority, they mail fail to cohere and yet be valid because the authority is a legitimate one with power to bind its subjects'[733]. Conversely, coherence can function as an underlying *method* of interpretation, which – in a positivistic system – does not always obtain results that cohere, but can nonetheless ensure a 'rule-governed consistency' as a hermeneutical aspiration[734].

121. Two un(der)articulated premises on the rule of law. In light of this complexity, it should by now by clear that it is not this book's aspiration to give a full – let alone jurisprudential – account of what 'rule of law'-values are, how they relate to instrumental reasoning, and how they are intertwined amongst themselves. There are, however, two as of yet unarticulated premises in my own account, which I would like to elucidate for the sake of clarity.

The first premise is that the rule of law is an important value, which implies that judges *should* be to some extent constrained in their decision-maker power. Few would disagree with me that this is indeed the normative foundation of the rule of law in a democracy. The second premise is somewhat more contentious, in that it is presupposed here that this constraining function of the rule of law is adequately translated in terms of a set of (admittedly complex, diverse and variegatingly intertwining) values, which I call rule of law values[735]. The three values relied upon here are certainly not the only ones underlying the notion of or implicated by the rule of law, but they are important ones indeed.

---

[731] *See eg* S.L. Hurley, *Coherence, Hypothetical Cases, and Precedent* in Exploring Law's Empire. The Jurisprudence of Ronald Dworkin 69 (Scott Hershovitz ed. 2006).

[732] *Cf.* Feyen, *supra* note 169, at p. 54 *et seq*.

[733] Raz, *supra* note 728, at p. 298.

[734] Mootz, *supra* note 523, at p. 4.

[735] Even if for some this is second-order reasoning, as some rule of law values are thought to constrain as exclusionary reasons. We make no judgment on the issue of the nature of rules here, except to say that if they (or other rule of law values) are indeed exclusionary reasons (Raz / Schauer), they must be defeasible (by other rule of law values), or at least adapatable to cohere with or be somehow made to live with other rule of law values (or what are construed as such).

They are important because not only do these values exemplify how the rule of law has been historically understood, but also – even more importantly – they embody what the rule of law has come to mean in the legal process nowadays. Plato already can be read as delineating the idea of a rule of law in terms of a form of textuality and coherence[736] and more recent (classic) statements of the rule of law also imply an adherence to text, precedent and principle[737]. These contentions should of course be embedded in a broader institutional framework[738], understood against the background of unarticulated principles[739], and within a broader political structure striving for a law that works[740]. In this regard, I acknowledge fully that invoking 'rule of law'-values is to some extent avoiding an important part of the debate. Moreover, it has been stressed before that this 'rule of law'-values approach is selective, and surely under-theorized (leaving ample room for interpretation). However, it does point in a direction that seems more fruitful than engaging the problems of constitutional interpretation (*sensu lato*) from a dogmatic angle, since that often relies on tacit, though disputable assumptions associated with the rule of law (in forms of interpretive methods, or presupposed requirements). To some extent, in law, of course the rule of law values must constitute a benchmark against which the appropriateness and practice itself of judicial review must be measured. However, given that the rule

[736] *Eg* REPUBLIC 176 *et seq.* (484b *et seq.*) (C.D.C. Reeve trans. 2004) (with 'truth' as the overarching coherence requirement (*see esp.* 178 (486a)), even if few would now agree that his philosopher-king of Kallipolis would be the best incarnation thereof). Aristotle was more dismayed about the written rules (THE POLITICS 111 (1286a). (Carnes Lord trans. 1984)), but nonetheless fully acknowledged the constraining power of the idea (*ibid.* at p. 103 (1282b)).

[737] *See* DICEY, *supra* note 215, 110 *et seq.*; FULLER, *supra* note 60, p. 31 *et seq.* (with an emphasis on the generality and promulgation of the laws, but also on coherence).

[738] *See eg* Raz, *supra* note 60, *passim*. Institutional here not only refers to the different entities of federalism, as it often has throughout the book, but also to the institutional structure embedded in the separation of powers (*cf.* SHAPIRO, *supra* note 37, at p. 33-34).

[739] *Compare eg* RENÉ FOQUÉ & A.C. 'T HART, INSTRUMENTALITEIT EN RECHTSBESCHERMING. GRONDSLAGEN VAN EEN STRAFRECHTELIJKE WAARDENDISCUSSIE 145 (1990) (further elaborating the problem of instrumentalization, focusing on criminal law) or René Foqué, *De crisis van het juridisch fundamentalisme (sic). Instrumentaliteit en rechtsbescherming in het licht van Scholtens beschouwingen* in RECHT, BESLISSING EN GEWETEN. BESCHOUWINGEN NAAR AANLEIDING VAN PAUL SCHOLTEN 223 (A. Ellian, T. Slootweg & C. Smith eds. 2010) (from a more abstract perspective, comparing Paul Scholten to Carl Schmitt, where instrumentalism is defined as a 'denial of the value orientations which define and characterize a legal order from within' (*ibid.* at p. 223)) *to* (for a criticism of the concept of instrumentality) Cees Maris, *Wat is instrumentaliteit* in LIBER AMICORUM RENÉ FOQUÉ 85, 91-93 (Marie-Claire Foblets, Mireille Hildebrandt & Jacques Steenbergen eds. 2012) (who shows the connection to deeper politico-philosophical issues).

[740] *See eg* MARK V. TUSHNET, TAKING THE CONSTITUTION AWAY FROM THE COURTS (1999) (offering some pragmatic examples of problems) (on the interpretive nature of legality).

of law (legality) is an interpretive concept[741], it seems more prudent not to rely on tacit generalizations that bear a direct influence on the problems at hand.

Although the issue will remain incompletely theorized, some further theoretical reflections or at least presuppositions regarding the relationship between rule of law values and the toolbox of the Constitutional Court will emerge from what follows. First, however, I will discuss the relationship between European law and the Constitutional Court from a more classic, dogmatic angle.

[741] DWORKIN, JUSTICE IN ROBES, *supra* note 62, at p. 140 *et seq*.; *compare* SHAPIRO, *supra* note 37, at p. 16-18 (attempting to refomulate the issue in terms of analytical, conceptual analysis).

4.

European influence on Constitutional Court case law

4.1 Preliminary observations

122. A kaleidoscopic, colorful reality without a central theory. Many authors have delved into the 'colorful reality'[742] of the relationship between European law and the Constitutional Court. A whole array of questions has been raised, and often treated from different angles or perspectives[743].

Not so long ago, scholars[744] usually discussed the relationship between international law and national (constitutional) law in light of the jurisprudence of the Court, generally comparing the European 'primacy' perspective, as elaborated in *Costa*[745] and *Internationale Handelsgesellschaft*[746], with the Constitutional Court case law since the *Lanaken* judgment[747], where the Court,

---

[742] Jan Wouters & Dries Van Eeckhoutte, *Epiloog. Doorwerking: een kleurrijke realiteit*, in DOORWERKING , *supra* note 226.

[743] *Cf.* Piet Van Nuffel, *Doorwerking van Europees Gemeenschapsrecht in de Belgische rechtsorde*, in DOORWERKING, *supra* note 226, 337 *et seq.* (explaining how the question of penetration is much more complex than the mere question of primacy); *also see* Willem Verrijdt, *Het Grondwettelijk Hof en het Unierecht: over een constitutioneel pluralism en rechterlijke dialoog* in DE INVLOED VAN HET EUROPEES RECHT OP HET BELGISCH (PRIVAAT)RECHT 41 (Vincent Sagaert, Ilse Samoy & Evelyne Terryn eds. 2012) (trying to capture the relationship from the viewpoint of constitutional pluralism).

[744] Some standard references in Belgian scholarship include the reports of the 2005 Symposium DE VERHOUDING TUSSEN HET ARBITRAGEHOF, DE RECHTERLIJKE MACHT EN DE RAAD VAN STATE (Alex Arts, Ivan Verougstraete & Robert Andersen eds.); André Alen, *De hiërarchie der rechtsnormen* in STAATSRECHT (THEMIS CAHIER 36) 11 (André Alen & Paul Lemmens 2006); Bribosia, *supra* note 233, at p. 35 *et seq.*; Philippe Brouwers & Henri Simonart, *Le conflit entre la Constitution et le droit international conventionnel dans la jurisprudence de la Cour d'arbitrage*, 1995 CAHIERS DE DROIT EUROPÉEN 7; Jan Delva, *De impact van het Europese verdragsrecht op de rechtspraak van het Arbitragehof – Een poging tot kritische doorlichting*, 50 TBP 637, 638-639 (1995); Patricia Popelier, *De visie van het Grondwettelijk Hof op de verhouding tussen de Grondwet en het internationaal recht : een discussie op gang gebracht door het arrest van het Grondwettelijk Hof nr. 26/91,* 2007 CDPK 227; Vanden Heede & Goedertier, *supra* note 226; JACQUES VELU, CONTRÔLE DE CONSTITUTIONNALITÉ ET CONTRÔLE DE COMPATIBILITÉ AVEC LES TRAITÉS (Discourse by the First A-G during the solemn inauguration of the Court of Cassation of Sep. 1, 1992) 201 *et seq.* (1992). *Also see* Patricia Popelier, *Prejudiciële vragen bij samenloop van grondrechten. Prioriteit voor bescherming van grondrechten of voor bescherming van de wet?* 2009-10 RW 50 (trying to show how the debate has been recharacterized in terms of precedence of *Courts* and see particularly, references at p. 59-60, *but compare (showing that the debate is ongoing)* Marc Verdussen, *La Cour Constitutionnelle, partenaire de la Cour de Justice de l'Union Européenne*, 2011 RBDC 81, 85 *et seq.* (in terms of traditional primacy, but also emphasizing dialogue)). Some further references are available in Stef Feyen, *Verdragsrechtelijke inwerking. Enkele overwegingen omtrent de inwerkingsmechanismen in de Belgische rechtsorde en hun rechtstheoretische grondslag*, 2008 CDPK 166, *esp.* 179 *et seq.*

[745] Case 6-64 (June 15, 1964).

[746] Case 11/70 (Dec. 17, 1970).

[747] CA No. 26/91 (Oct. 16, 1991).

notwithstanding the utterly monistic jurisprudence of the Belgian Court of Cassation[748], held that it can (contentiously) review legislation approving treaties, partly relying on specific provisions in the SLCC on European law[749].

Next to that, focus was laid on how European law substantively influences Belgian (constitutional) law[750] and still others discussed the relationship in terms of what could be called procedural effects[751]. In the framework of EMU we ourselves already hinted at the fact that international law does occupy a prominent place in the Court's jurisprudence.

All these different perspectives could be deemed, or at least *made* relevant in the course of examining whether European law influences the case law of the Constitutional Court. However, no credible and readily deployable general and coherent theory of the influence of European law on the jurisprudence of the Court exists, at least not from the viewpoint of the Constitutional Court's reasoning and case law (some call the Court's jurisprudence incoherent[752], others go for the more polite 'nuanced'[753]).

As regards the influence of European law on federalism, confusion seems to be the rule rather than the exception too: on the one hand, the reciprocal neutrality between European law and the internal allocation of competences is

748 Cass. (May 27, 1971) *Franco-Suisse Le Ski / Smeerkaasarrest*, 1971 Arresten van het Hof van Cassatie 959, with a conclusion by Walter J. Ganshof van der Meersch and 1971 Pasicrisie 886; *also see* No. P.04.0849.N (Nov. 9, 2004) *Flemish Block Case*; Nos. P.04.0644.N and P.04.1127.N (both Nov. 16, 2004).

749 *See, esp.* art. 3, §2, art. 26, §1*bis* and §4 (*also see supra* note 226).

750 The standard reference, focusing on private law, is De Invloed van het Europees recht op het Belgisch recht (Postuniversitaire Cyclus ed. 2003). *Also see* Kamiel Mortelmans, De invloed van het Europees Gemeenschapsrecht op het Belgisch economisch recht (1978). However, these works fall under the exclusions postulated in my introductory chapter.

751 *See eg* Courtoy, *supra* note 15, at p. 345-47 (asking question about the binding force of preliminary rulings to the Court of Justice).

752 *Also see eg* Velu, *supra* note 744, at p. 138, 203-207 (criticizing both the law and the jurisprudence, or at least No. 26/91).

753 Vanden Heede & Goedertier, *supra* note 226, at p. 261 (here on the specific topic of reviewing laws and decrees transposing directives). Further on, the authors do hesitatingly call the Court's handling of international law 'ambiguous' (*ibid.* at p. 293), at the same time emphasizing the Court's feel for pragmatic solution (*ibid.* at p. 294); *cf.* Delpérée, *supra* note 401, at p. 688 (with some further references). Others note that Court seems 'stricter' when it reviews legislation in light of European law, because the latter's provisions are thought to be more specific than the constitutional provisions (Verrijdt, *supra* note 743, at p. 54-55). Verrijdt does a remarkable job in explaining Constitutional Court case law in light of a coherent and 'unifying' theory of constitutional pluralism, but we discussed above (*supra* No. 17) to which extent our way of understanding diverges from this theory.

often emphasized[754], but on the other hand, many authors recognize that this neutrality, borne out by a principle of constitutional autonomy, is relativized in certain ways. Although the latter relativization is noticed, it is generally not captured through the lens of an overarching theory, but rather construed as an 'indirect weight' attached to European law in respect of Belgian federalism[755]. All in all, the discourse about the relativization remains confused, or at least convoluted, from the perspective of the Belgian Constitutional Court[756].

123. Our proposed theory: European law as a tool. In light of what has preceded, I will investigate whether and to what extent European legal concepts, doctrines et cetera, too, can be construed as a tool in the Constitutional Court's toolbox regarding federalism. This 'methodological' approach is likely to produce some form of inner coherence (although no full-fledged theory). Within the greater scheme of problems associated with the relationship between European law and the Constitutional Court, what follows might fail to grasp certain aspects of the relationship, but sets out to first and foremost create a framework of thinking.

---

[754] Art. 4 (2) TEU; *see* ECJ Case 230-78 (Sep. 27, 1979) *Eridania*, para 34; Case C-428/07 (GC; July 16, 2009) *Horvath*, para 58. This has been generally coined the 'regional blindness' of EU law by Weatherill (*The challenge of the Regional Dimension in the European Union* in THE ROLE OF THE REGIONS AND SUB-NATIONAL ACTORS IN EUROPE 1, 1 (Stephen Weatherill & Ulf Bernitz eds. 2005)).

[755] *Eg* Van Drooghenbroeck, *supra* note 393, at p. 255 ('Europe 'weighs', not directly, but indirectly, on the reform of state'); *see* Popelier, *supra* note 11, at p. 20-22 (generally distinguishing integrating and disintegrating forms of influence); *also see* VANPRAET, *supra* note 190, at p. 371-372 (who points out the influence on the legislature, in framing the allocation of competences pertaining to insurance measures); *compare eg* Koen Lenaerts & Nathan Cambien, *Regions and the European Court: giving shape to the regional dimension of the Member States*, 35 EUROPEAN LAW REVIEW 609 (2010) (who stress the need for a delicate balance in practice, notwithstanding the theoretical neutrality).

[756] *Compare infra* Ch. 5.3. *Compare also* Van Drooghenbroeck, *supra* note 393, at p. 256: this author points out that sometimes because of European integration, 'differentiation' (as a condition for the exercise of implied powers) becomes impossible in the case law of the Constitutional Court. This is a typical doctrinal redemption of European case law, which – however – can hardly be generalized as *such* (*compare infra* note 974 and accompanying text). At the same time, Van Drooghenbroeck recognizes that the influence of European law is 'of a truly structural, and not merely punctual nature' (*ibid.* at p. 256), and thus recognizes the complexity thereof (*see ibid.* at p. 258 *et seq.* (both describing the complexity of the influence, and recognizing the need for 'pragmatism in opposition to constitutional orthodoxy', with further references to writings by PALLEMAERTS & TULKENS and several CoS advices which are interesting in this regard)). Another attempt to 'doctrinally' capture the influence is Patricia Popelier & Werner Vandenbruwaene, *The subsidiarity mechanism as a tool for inter-level Dialogue in Belgium: on "Regional Blindness" and Co-operative flaws*, 7 EUCONS 204, 216 *et seq.* (2011) (pointing out the difficulties of applying the (European) principle of subsidiarity in a federal system based on exclusivity).

124. A one-sided theory? In fact, it *will* (intentionally) fail to grasp certain aspects, and these aspects could even be deemed to be, or at least made to be important.

It could be argued, for instance, that the question regarding the implementation of European law is constitutionally very relevant. In fact, probing this issue would probably be one of the most easily discernible ways to answer the question of how European law can influence the allocation of competences in general[757]. In that sense, one would have to investigate the *ad hoc* (and comparatively heavily conditioned[758]) substitution mechanism that the Belgian legislature has introduced for cases where the federated entities fail to live up to their task to suitably implement EU law. Even if the issue stands central in case law of constitutional courts of other jurisdictions[759], it arguably does not occupy an

[757] *See eg* Report (De Gucht), *Parl. Doc.* Chamber 1986-87, No. 20-739/1 (on state aid).

[758] *See, esp.* art. 169 Cons. *juncto* art. 16, §3 SLIR ('when the State has been condemned by an international or supranational judicial organ due to the infringement of an international or supranational obligation by a Community or a Region, the involved Community or the involved Region may be substituted by the State, to execute the dictum of the judgments', if and only if the federated entity has been notified by the federal government, notwithstanding urgencies, at least three months in advance and has been involved in the international or supranational proceedings. Moreover the cooperation agreement on this issue imposes extra obligations in terms of representation of the federated entities before the Court of Justice). On this issue *see eg* Frank Ingelaere, *De Belgische deelstaten en de Europese Unie*, in INTERNATIONALE BETREKKINGEN, *supra* note 434, at p. 180-83; Michel Struys, *La mise en oeuvre des obligations découlant du droit européen (la Belgique fédérale dans l'Europe fédérale)* in LA BELGIQUE FÉDÉRALE 483, 486-95 (Francis Delpérée ed. 1994); Jan Velaers, *supra* note 434, at p. 63-68 (with some further references, also to ECJ jurisprudence), *esp.* 66-68 (comparing with some other regimes, and arguing that the mechanism is impracticable); Jean Victor Louis & André Alen, *La Constitution et la participation à la Communauté européenne*, 1994 REVUE BELGE DE DROIT EUROPÉENNE 81, 102-03; Vuillermoz, *supra* note 42, at p. 668-83. *Compare* (noting the date of these contributions) Godelieve Craenen, *De bevoegdheid van de Gemeenschappen en Gewesten in internationale aangelegenheden* in 1 LIBER AMICORUM FRÉDÉRIC DUMON 711, 721 (1983) or Koenraad Lenaerts, *The application of the Community Law in Belgium,* 23 COMMON MARKET LAW REVIEW 253, 259-60 (1986) (arguing that the federal government should be allowed to intervene on the basis of its exclusive foreign relations power in order to impede a violation by federated entities of the duty to apply Community Law, with reference to ECJ case law) *to* VELAERS, VAN ARBITRAGEHOF TOT ..., *supra* noot 13, at p. 253 (one excess of competences cannot lead to an encroachment of the federation upon autonomous federated competences).

[759] Vuillermoz (*supra* note 42, at p. 510 *et seq.*) has treated the issue for Spain and Italy in depth, but declined to do so for Belgium, lacking any interesting Constitutional Court case law (*compare ibid.* p. 476-85: on the legislative framework). This 'decline' should be relativized (*ibid.* p. 580), in that Vuillermoz asserts that European law does play a role in determining the competent authority on the Belgian level, in the sense that the need for 'effet utile' influences the determination. Even if Vuillermoz devotes an entire subsection to the matter (*ibid.* p. 579-91), I will decline to so, for two reasons: I believe that the issue relates first and foremost to the *substantive* outcome of particular cases (also in terms of a political need for cooperation

important place in Belgian Constitutional Court case law. It could be imagined that it occupies a central place (and was therefore not yet excluded earlier[760]), and perhaps will do so in the future[761]. Accepting for instance the fact that during substitution, the state must take into account the duties accruing from federal loyalty or proportionality[762], it is not farfetched to imagine that a Community would fight a federal (legislative) measure in the Constitutional Court[763]. But the mechanism has up till now never been deployed, which, conversely, has not precluded a fierce debate by Belgian constitutional scholars on the matter[764]. Be that as it may, I would contend that it is not stretch to say that Court itself has barely touched upon the issue 'directly'. The Court has always held that 'the transposition of a European Directive can only occur taking the rules governing the allocation of the distinct competences to the State, the Communities and the Regions'[765]. Therefore, the question of influence of European law on the Belgian constitutional court case law does not as such arise, at least not within the contours of the perspective set out above[766].

– *ibid.* p. 591 *et seq.* and Pascal Gilliaux, Les Directives européennes et le droit belge 9-14 (1997)) and can hardly be construed as a *structural* feature of influence (*cf. supra* Ch. 1.2; *also see* Vuillermoz, supra note 42, at p. 585 ('utilized less constantly and less profoundly')). Moreover, to the extent that it could be construed as a structural feature, I discuss the matter (at least implicitly) under my section on autonomous concepts (*see ibid.* p. 586; *also see ibid.* p. 412 *et seq.*). More broadly (not limited to Constitutional Court jurisprudence), this issue could be construed as one in which another rule of law value, *ie* the necessity for effet utile on a European level, interferes within the Belgian sphere of competences (*compare* Vuillermoz, supra note 42, at p. 582-85).

760 See *supra* Ch. 1.

761 *See* Butterfly Agreement, *supra* note 10, at p. 43-44 ('[t]he federal government will have a right to substitute a Community or a Region in cases where they do not abide by the obligations set forth by the UN Framework Convention on Climate Change, or one of its Protocols); *compare Parl. Doc.* Senate 2007-08, n° 4-602/1, at p. 3-4, 8, 36-43, 59-60 (earlier proposal to the same effect, but also envisaging the case when Regions were implementing *European law*, which might have been dropped after a rather critical assessment by the CoS (4-602/2, p. 34-35); *also see* Van Drooghenbroeck, *supra* note 393, at p. 257).

762 Report (Gehlen & Van der Maelen), *Parl. Doc.* Chamber 1992-93, No. 798/3, at p. 7.

763 *Cf. ibid.* at p. 2.

764 *Compare eg* André Alen, *De externe autonomie of de Gemeenschappen en de Gewesten in Europa en de wereld* in Vlaanderen op een kruispunt, *supra* note 38, at p. 241 (pleading for alleviating the condition) *with* Michel Melchior, *Constitution et organisations internationales. Le problème de la supranationalité* in Le nouveau droit constitutionnel (Acts of the 2nd mondial congress on constitutional law, Paris & Aix-en-Provence, Aug. 31 – Sep. 5, 1987) 321, 334 (Centre interuniversitaire de droit public ed. 1987). *Cf.* Vuillermoz, supra note 42, at p. 482-83 (how problems are not merely imaginary).

765 *Eg* CA No. 109/2000 (Oct. 31, 2000) B.4.1

766 *Cf. supra* Ch. 1.

Next to that, there are other ways to defend the position that European law thoroughly invades the way the allocation of competences in the implementation of European law is arranged, not merely *substantively*[767], but also more structurally, which we do not discuss in depth. These could be coined cases of indirect structural influence. The 'indirect structural influence' – for lack of a better name – can best be illustrated with reference to a concrete example. In Case No. 54 the question arose whether a Region can regulate using environmental effect reports. The Constitutional Court judgment could be read as asserting that the Region could do so, *since* it was implementing European law. The Court reasoned that given that Regions are competent for building permits and that building permits come within the ambit of article 1 of Directive 85/337/EC, it is the case that this Directive requires an environmental effects report in respect of this permit. 'Therefore'[768], the Region can obligate such an effects study, *however* limited to the areas of its competence. The question of course remains whether and to which extent one can truly speak of influence in this case, for reasons related to the ones stipulated above[769]. Some other examples might include similar instances of what one could coin to be *indirect* influence[770].

For Vuillermoz, Case No. 6/97[771] is of great importance in the assessment of the relationship between European law and Belgian federalism, in particular as regards the question of which authority is in charge of implementing European directives[772], because the Belgian Constitutional Court referred a case under competence jurisdiction to the Court of Justice for a preliminary ruling on the meaning of mutual recognition of doctors' diplomas. In fact, he calls it 'a veritable revolution'[773], which we can agree with, but only in an institutional sense (referring to the Court of Justice[774]), or perhaps in a substantive sense (limited to

767 *See supra* Ch. 1.

768 CA No. 54 (May 24, 1988) 6.B.12.c ('derhalve'/ 'dès lors').

769 *Cf. supra* Ch. 1.

770 *Compare eg* CC No. 1/89 (Jan. 31, 1989) with CC No. 19/97 (Apr. 15, 1997), as discussed in Vuillermoz, *supra* note 42, at p. 585-586. *Also see infra* Ch. 1.2.

771 CA No. 6/97 (Feb. 19, 1997).

772 Vuillermoz, *supra* note 42, at p. 545 (*also see* n879 there) (it is here, according to this author that one can 'appreciate the real impact of (European) legal integration on the state structure and the complexity stemming from the partitioning of competences between the central state and the regional entities' (*ibid.* at p. 546)).

773 Vuillermoz, *supra* note 42, at p. 585 and 586.

774 It has been noted that the Belgian constitutional court right now is the 'most eurofile' Court in Europe, for instance because of the amount of preliminary references (*see* David Keyaerts, *supra* note 248, at p. 55). *Also see* Monica Claes, The National Court's Mandate in the European Constitution 641 (2006) (describing the Belgian Constitutional Court as 'the least protective and most *communautaire* of all constitutional courts'). On the other hand, it

the issue of doctors' diplomas). For Vuillermoz, however, it is important because the case shows how the Constitutional Court will align itself with European concepts, which can result in shifts in competence allocation[775]. That might be a correct conceptualization in this case, but he seems to go to far in generalizing that this generally leads to a 'sort of subordination of Belgian law to [European] law'. I refer not only to my subsequent sections on 'autonomous concepts'[776] and 'evacuation'[777] to disavow the generality of such a claim, but also rely on the other preliminary rulings to the Court of Justice, which first, did not *generally* involve issues of (Belgian) competence allocation[778], and second, do not indicate that my own structure cannot account (more representatively) for these cases.

has been noted that in *implementing* Union law, Belgium nowadays figures at the bottom of the European class, possibly because of complicated internal decision-making processes (*België is de slechtste leerling van de EU-klas,* DeRedactie.be (Feb. 19, 2013), http://www.deredactie.be/permalink/1.1553126).

775 Vuillermoz, *supra* note 42, at p. 585 *et seq.*

776 *Cf. infra* Ch. 5. One should further mention CC No. 75/2012 (June 14, 2012) here, about a Flemish Decree of 10 December 2010 regarding private placement services, which implemented both the Bolkenstein-Directive and the ILO Convention No. 181. The Decree was fought and it was argued that in defining the concept 'posting' (of workers) and 'temporary agency work' in deviation from federal law, the Region infringed upon the federal competence regarding employment law. The Flemish legislature was held to have overstepped the bounds of its competence (B.12) and could not rely on implied competences to regulate the matter for lack of necessity and and marginal impact (B.13.1-B.13.2), but importantly, the Court considered that the Belgian division of competences (and especially the concept of private employment agency) does not (have to) align itself with ILO Convention No. 181 (B.10; *and see Parl. Doc.* Flemish Parl. 2009-10, No. 641/1, at p. 11-12 (with reference to Directive 2008/104/EG on temporary work agencies)), but is interpreted conform the *travaux préparatoires* (B.11).

777 *Infra* Ch. 4.3.1; *cf.* the cases on the Flemish decree on land and buildings policy, CC Nos. 49/2011 and 50/2011 (both Apr. 6, 2011).

778 *See* the Birds Directive Cases (CA No. 139/2003 (Oct. 29, 2003) B.11.2; 28/2005 (Feb. 9, 2005)); the European Arrest Warrant Cases (CA/CC Nos. 124/2005 (July 13, 2005);128/2007 (Oct. 10, 2007);128/2009 (July 24, 2009) and 28/2011 (Feb. 24, 2011)); the Laundering Cases (CA/CC Nos. 126/2005 (July 13, 2005) and 10/2008 (Jan. 23, 2008)); the Access to Higher Education Cases (CC Nos. 12/2008 (Feb. 14, 2008) and 89/2011 (May 31, 2011)); the Universal Services Cases (CC Nos. 131/2008 (Sep. 1, 2008) and 7/2011 (Jan. 27, 2011)); the Gender Equality in Insurance Cases (CC Nos. 103/2009 (June 18, 2009) and 116/2011 (June 30, 2011)); the Aarhus treaty Cases (CC No. 30/2010 (Mar. 30, 2010) and 144/2012 (Nov. 22, 2012)); the bio-fuel case (CC No. 149/2010 (Dec. 22, 2010)); the Environmental Effects cases (CC No. 133/2010 (Nov. 25, 2010) and 95/2012 (July 19, 2012)); the Radio Frequency levy case (CC No. 110/2011 (June 16, 2011)); the Elderly Housing Case (CC No. 10/2012 (Jan. 25, 2012)), the Green Certificate Case regarding wood (CC No. 54/2012 (Apr. 19, 2012)), the private detective case regarding data protection (CC No. 116/2012 (Oct. 10, 2012)) and Closing Day Case (CC No. 119/2012 (Oct. 18, 2012)). The Care Insurance saga is a special instance, discussed below, as are the Flemish decree on land and buildings policy cases, also discussed below. They do not pertain to competence allocation *sensu stricto,* as was the case in Vuillermoz' example, but do have an important meaning for Belgian constitutional case law regarding federalism (because of an explicit *communautarian* dimension).

Indeed, the 'terminology of [European] law'[779] is *an* explanatory variable, but certainly not one that allows generalizations such as the one Vuillermoz inferred, and for that reason, we eschew the use of the notion of structural influence in the cases discussed by him.

More judgments could be 'interconnected'[780] in order to establish some tenuous sort of (non-structural) 'influence'. However, my arguments here work *mutatis mutandis* vis-à-vis all of them, which does not mean that my account can necessarily catch the entire 'colorful reality' of allocation of competences. It does mean, however, that I believe that my structure more adequately represents how and particularly why European law exerts an influence, at least understood from the particular perspective I adopted, that is the perspective of the Belgian Constitutional Court in action.

125. Methodological pragmatism within principled borders. On the other hand, even if the methodological limits I have set myself help to structure the following thoughts, to some extent I do need to elaborate some more on case law of Constitutional Court which does not directly pertain to its competence jurisdiction, exactly because of the fact that the equality jurisdiction and the competence jurisdiction interact and procure results which are relevant in terms of the question asked here. Even so, if the general influence of European law on the Belgian Constitutional Court's case law is relevant, I will not discuss it at length, partly due to its complexity and the concomitant difficulties to theorize the issue, and partly due to sheer amount of case law which involves European law in one way or another.

Moreover, there might be other ways in which European law is construed or employed as a tool in the jurisprudence of the Constitutional Court, which I refrain from discussing separately or dealing with at all, either because the conceptualization-as-tool to my mind is too tenuous, or because for the sake of analytic clarity it will be more productive to focus on one case. Accordingly, some methodological pragmatism on my account seems in order, at least within the more or less *principled* boundaries I have set myself above.

[779] Vuillermoz, *supra* note 42, at p. 588; *also see* Report (Caluwé *et al.*), *Parl. Doc.* Senate 1998-99, No. 1-1333/1, at p. 818-32.

[780] *See eg* Vuillermoz, *supra* note 42, at p. 587-88, *esp.* n1093.

4.2 European law and the Constitutional Court

126. European influence on laws and the Constitution: the issue of primacy. European law first and foremost penetrates Belgian constitutional law via articles 10 and 11 of the Constitution – provisions enshrining a principle which has a *general* scope according to the Court – on which petitioners may rely to invoke specific norms of European law[781]. Accordingly, Belgian laws have been reviewed in terms of their conformity to different directives, or to the European constitutive treaties[782]. Early on, the Court recognized explicitly that European law obligations prevail over *legal* obligations in Belgium[783]. Vis-à-vis such legislative measures, European law can play in different and complex ways[784]. Sometimes the boundary between different forms of invoking European law becomes shady. For instance, when the Court argues that a differentiation might be justified, and mentions that a Directive does not oppose phasing in the legislative reforms[785], this could be construed, depending on text and context, as a *review* in light of European law, or as a mere deployment of European law as a justificatory mechanism within the bounds of review. In this context, mention should also be made of the so-called technique of conform interpretation[786], which, then again, cannot always be deployed[787]. Moreover, the question when a norm conflict arises and what its implications could be, rises again here[788].

---

[781] On which norms can be usefully invoked, *see* Vanden Heede & Goedertier, *supra* note 226, at p. 257 *et seq*. The authors here conclude that the Constitutional Court employs a wide interpretation of the concept of (analogous) *rights and liberties*, so that not only treaty provisions can be invoked, but even directives. In terms of invocability, they conclude that the classic limitation to 'rights and liberties' has lost its relevance (rendering the principle accordingly 'empty'). *Also see* Rusen Ergec, *La Cour constitutionnelle belge et le droit européen* in MÉLANGES EN HOMMAGE À GEORGES VANDERSANDEN. PROMENADES AU SEIN DU DROIT EUROPÉEN 167-173 (2008).

[782] Some examples can be found in the footnotes in the preceding section. *Compare* CC No. 142/2011 (July 27, 2011) B.6.1-B.6.2 (the Court does not review differences in treatment stemming from regulations); *but compare* CC No. 142/2012 (Nov. 22, 2012) B.9.3 (no review of measures preceding the adoption of laws, not even in light of European Directives).

[783] This is generally accepted (*see eg* CC No. 128/2010 (Nov. 4, 2010) B.8.3).

[784] *See eg* Vanden Heede & Goedertier, *supra* note 226, at p. 260-61 (European law functioning as a justification for a distinction made which is reviewed in light of art. 10-11 Cons.).

[785] *Compare* CA No. 10/95 (Feb. 2, 1995) B.3.5 (in light of Directive 85/339/EC, on environmental tax) *with* CA No. 6/99 (Jan. 20, 1999) B.6 (in light of Directive 79/7/EEC, on gender differences in early pensions).

[786] *See eg* CA No. 96/2002 (June 12, 2002) B.2.4; *also see* CC No. 95/2008 (June 26, 2008) B.50.

[787] *Eg* CC No. 55/2011 (Apr. 6, 2011) B.2.

[788] Vanden Heede & Goedertier, *supra* note 226, at p. 261-65 (on how to review legislative measures which implement Directives).

These problems notwithstanding, as the system of competence allocation in Belgium generally finds its legal basis in the Constitution[789], the question has arisen whether and how European law should, can or will take precedence in that case. Without having to answer this question of primacy at length, one can say that the Court has adopted an ambiguous position, which harks back to the debate we alluded to above[790]. To resume but one example: while the Court has engaged in reviewing the constitutionality of laws that either approve treaties or implement European law, it at the same time does not refrain from referring cases for preliminary rulings to the Court of Justice[791], the rulings of which it implements more or less vigorously, even if they stand in tension with constitutional requirements[792]. Notwithstanding the conceptual difficulties that

---

789 Adding an additional layer of complexity, the competences of the Regions have been by and large determined by Special Law, which may be reviewed in turn as to its constitutionality, and accordingly, in light of European obligations which protect rights and liberties as well. *Supra* note 466 and *infra* note 1107.

790 On the Court's *Lanaken* jurisprudence (*cf. supra* notes 747-749).

791 *See supra* note 778, offering further references in this regard.

792 Difficult interpretative issues have arisen in this regard. *Compare eg* Stef Feyen, *Zorgen voor morgen: implicaties van het arrest van het Grondwettelijk Hof over discriminaties in de Vlaamse Zorgverzekering*, 2009 TBP 169, 173-74 (arguing that Belgian Care insurance case was an example of how the Constitutional Court recognized the primacy of European law) *to* Velaers & Vanpraet, *supra* note 388, at p. 207-08 (who argue that the Court did not recognize primacy, but only interpreted it conform EU law, and stress how the Court tries to hold on as much as possible to the Belgian requirements of territoriality). Of course, I could – by way of reply – state that the fact that the Court differentiates between two sorts of outcomes is the evidence *par excellence* that European law has precedence – at least *within its material sphere*. All depends on characterization though, from an analytic perspective. If I want to "prove" that European law *precedes* constitutional law in terms of a norm conflict, that would require me to establish that the the *place of residence requirement* (instead of *lex loci labori*) *necessarily* and *logically* followed from the Constitutional provisions, so as to give rise to mutually exclusive obligations (notwithstanding the possible integration thereof in terms of pluralism). Given the fact that there is wide debate on how to characterize connecting factors (*compare supra* notes 442 and 447), this would be hard to do. However, the devil is in the details: for instance, one could also see a norm *conflict* in a clear constitutional permission vis-à-vis a European *obligation*. I am not talking about a permission that is implicit – although some theorists like Hohfeld and Duncan Kennedy would disagree about the relevance thereof – but rather the explicit permission granted by the Constitutional Court (which – in traditional Belgian scholarship – merely interprets the Constitution, and therefore expounds what is already in the text, even if we all know that is not the whole truth) in case No. 51/2006 (relying on *constitutional* arguments here). The devil accordingly seems to lie in the 'even if we all know that is not the whole truth', and in turn the question becomes one of *constitutional interpretation* and *institutional competences*, for one could also respond that the Constitution itself was 're-interpreted' (and in traditional doctrine, this means: authoritatively *interpreted*) (*cf.* Elke Cloots, *Germs of Pluralist Judicial Adjudication:* Advocaten voor de Wereld *and Other References from the Belgian Constitutional Court* 47 COMMON MARKET LAW REVIEW 645, 667 (2010); *also see eg* Cass Sunstein & Adriaen Vermeule, *Interpretation and Institutions*, 101 MICHIGAN LAW REVIEW 885 (2003) (lamenting the uni-dimensional focus of interpretative

arise through this ambiguity, the Court has formally held that European law does not in principle interfere with the allocation of competences[793].

127. European law as a (precarious) tool that allows to partly set aside conceptual and theoretical issues. This drags us in quite a conundrum: where the Court itself denies any interference (*in principle*) of European law within the allocation of competences, the broader theoretical framework on the relationship between EU law and constitutional law is ambiguous at best, notwithstanding innovative doctrinal attempts to account for the case law[794]. Hence, even within the case law of the Court, it will be hard to assess the concept of influence, because preliminary conceptual and theoretical questions are often left open by the Court itself[795]. Here the concept of a tool comes in again. European law, so I argue, can be best conceptualized as a *tool* the Court deploys in different circumstances and as an answer to a variety of (concrete) problems.

---

methodology commentaries)). *See, for a similar, though distinct line of argumentation,* Feyen, *supra* note 32. The issue exposed here makes clear again how dogmatics can run in circles, because of a lack of explication of its own presuppositions: insofar as Velaers and Vanpraet go to the intention-process (if that would exist) of the Constitutional Court, they are probably right; however, that is going beyond a traditional dogmatic approach, or at least lifting it to a different level of abstraction (which on the one hand should be applauded, but on the other hand means that they have been talking past my point). *Adde* CC No. 144/2012 (Nov. 22, 2012) B.13 (where the Court expanded its own jurisdiction (which was *constitutionally* confined, as well as by the special laws – B.9.3) so as to include review of the acts preceding the adoption of a legislative measure).

[793] *Eg* CA No. 70 (Dec. 14, 1988) III.B.8 ('when the Court invalidates provisions of a decree which – violating the constitutional allocation of competences – take over or implement treaty provisions, it does not infringe upon the treaty itself or the precedence of the treaty on the basis of the hierarchy of legal norms'); *see* CA 109/2000 (Oct. 31, 2000) B.4.1 ('the transposition in the Belgian legal order of a European Directive must occur with respect for the rules determining the respective competences of the State, the Communities and the Regions'); *also see* CA No. 139/2003 (Oct. 29, 2003) B.11.2 ('it is not necessary to adjudicate upon the scope of Directive 79/409/EEC to describe the competence of the Walloon Region'). *Compare* CA No. 47 (Feb. 25, 1988) III.3.B.c (on the three competent levels vis-à-vis the environmental competence). *Cf.* Vanden Heede & Goedertier, *supra* note 226, at p. 266; Piet Van Nuffel, *Het Europees recht in de rechtspraak van het Arbitragehof. Prejudiciële vragen, te veel gevraagd?* in 20 Jaar Arbitragehof, *supra* note 281, at p. 40; Vuillermoz, *supra* note 42, at p. 476-85.

[794] *See eg* Cloots, *supra* note 792, at p. 664 *et seq.*; Popelier, *Prejudiciële vragen, supra* note 744, et p. 59 *et seq.* (all pleading in terms of increased dynamics (dialogue and mutual respect as aspects of constitutional pluralism)).

[795] *Also see* Elke Cloots, *Het Grondwettelijk Hof en de toetsing van secundair Unierecht aan fundamentele rechten* in Leuvense Staatsrechtelijke Standpunten 17, 51-52 (André Alen & Jeroen Van Nieuwenhove eds. 2008) (concluding that the Constitutional Court is unclear on the issue and does not theorize it enough).

On the one hand, I offer different examples of how the Court instrumentalizes European law in the context of federalism: it can be deployed in order to help the judges decide upon cases (or exactly not to decide upon them, as will become clear). As such, European law seems to *streamline* constitutional reasoning. On the other hand, European law is a precarious tool, especially in light of rule of law values. These rule of law values set certain limits to the instrumentalization by the Constitutional Court[796], and in light of these limits, European law can become problematic in light of Belgian federalism and fail to live up to the aspirations of streamlining. This is not new. Rule of law values, as we have seen, can produce tension within the (internal Belgian) constitutional toolbox itself[797].

My point here is twofold. On the one hand that European law sometimes fails to fulfill its tool-like function because of certain rule of law values. On the other hand, but this point is framed more tentatively, I offer several reasons why the already existing tension between rule of law values and the more instrumental approach might be exacerbated by European law.

[796] Arguably the distinction between European law as an instrument, and the limits thereof, to some extent presupposes a direction the Constitutional Court pledges to go. Even if this is the case, the distinction is nonetheless not wholly arbitrary, in the sense that in the case of instrumentalization, the Court seems to deploy European law in general – or at least that often seems to be a viable intuition – in order to deflate communautarian rivalries within the Court. As such, the category of 'evacuating' could be construed more broadly.

[797] *Supra* Nos. 120-121.

4.3 European law as a streamlining tool

4.3.1 European law as a (quasi) political tool for evacuation of conflict

128. Leeway in interpretation when it comes to references. In a first – arguably more political – sense[798], European law is sometimes invoked by the Constitutional Court to allow for an evacuation of federalism-related conflicts. As such, the judges of the Constitutional Court decide to revert a federalism-related issue upon which they are intensely divided to the Court of Justice, or resort to specifically European arguments to alleviate internal tensions[799].

I mean 'intensely divided' here in a *communautarian* sense, and not primarily in the sense of the requirements of doubts in conformity with the European *CILFIT* case law, although these are not necessarily unrelated. For the purposes of this section, I recognize that the Constitutional Court does explicitly take *CILFIT* into account from time to time[800]. Even so, I would like to stress that interpretative question about the extent of the duty to refer still exist, certainly

[798] Which might even be construed more broadly then I do here (*cf. supra* No. 16). Even if the European option might be problematic in light of the requirements of article 57 SLCC (of course, depending on the reasoning and the rationale), I will not discuss this issue here. For some normative arguments in this regard, nonetheless also presupposing the leeway, *see* Verrijdt, *supra* note 743, at p. 74-77 (who concludes that the Court is 'very respectful of the judicial dialogue' and indeed 'eurofile' (*ibid.* at p. 77); *cf. supra* note 774).

[799] This second case will sometimes overlap with what is written further in this section. For instance, it could be argued that in imposing a cooperation duty on the basis of European law arguments, the Court relied on European law to split the difference between competing national positions.

[800] *Cf.* Claes, *supra* noot 774, 426-427; Keyaerts, *supra* note 248, at p. 60-61. For the first time, it did so in CA 151/2003 (Nov. 26, 2003) B.23.2-B.24, and since then, it has *explicitly* reviewed its own duty to ask for a preliminary reference at least sixteen times (CA No. 92/2006 (June 7, 2006) B.10-B.13 and B.21-B.25 (no reasonable doubt as to its meaning); No. 139/2006 (Sep. 14, 2006) B.31-B.34 (applying the rule of reason); CC No. 121/2008 (Sep. 1, 2008) B.15.2-B.15.3 (deviating from a classification in a Framework Directive not deemed relevant); No. 99/2010 (Sep. 16, 2010) B.4.12 (applying the rule of reason); No. 128/2011 (July 14, 2011) B.31-B.32.2 (having conducted proportionality review itself); No. 180/2011 (Nov. 24, 2011) B.11.1 – B.13.9 (checking itself how a form of differentiation within the Belgian health care system can square with Directive 79/239/EEC); No. 40/2012 (Mar. 8, 2012) B.8.4-B.11.2 (conducting proportionality analysis itself, taking mutual recognition into account) and 161/2012 (Dec. 20, 2012) B.5-B.15 (a case in which the European Commission in fact intervened (in the sense of the Court of Justice jurisprudence in C-429/07), but where the Court refused to refer to the Court of Justice as it interpreted the European competition rules, as applied to the interpretation of a legal provision, itself), eight occasions of which it actually referred to the Court of Justice (Nos. 51/2006; 12/2008; 30/2010; 133/2010; 49-50/2011; 110/2011; 10/2012); *compare* CC No. 84/2010 (July 8, 2010) and No. 131/2010 (Nov. 18, 2010) B.9.2-B.9.3).

when only the *interpretation* of Union law is in play[801], and that political considerations might play a role in deciding whether or not to rely on European law. Moreover, the cases on which we focus here do not adequately reflect the broader impact of the issue, since in many cases, the Court does not explicitly refer to *CILFIT*, but just (arguably sometimes wrongly) applies it[802].

One example to clarify this point about interpretative leeway is a 2006 case on emission rights[803]. There, the Court had to decide whether or not to refer the following question to Luxembourg: is the distinction Directive No. 2003/87/EC makes between different industries, in terms of their rights regarding emissions, discriminatory or not? The Court argued here that because the distinction the Directive drew was of a facultative nature, that

> because [...] the Directive does not proscribe the Walloon legislature in any way to extend the scope of the regulation regarding greenhouse emissions to other activities and that therefore it could not be at the basis of the grieves formulated in the first argument [...], referring a question to the Court of Justice [is unnecessary] since the question is irrelevant.[804]

Of course, this line of argumentation is not entirely bereft of any logic. Nevertheless, could one reasonably deny that the distinction made between the different industries, and in which for one of the industries the regulation was obligatory, whereas for the other industries it could have been made obligatory, did not constitute the underlying reason for the difference in treatment at all? It could indeed by argued that the decision-making authority resided with the Walloon government, but the *objectivity*, *pertinence* and *proportionality* of the difference in treatment nonetheless directly originated from the European level, as there the *distinction*, in the sense of *difference in treatment* was first proposed. In this sense, the obligations the Court is bound by to refer to the Court of Justice for a preliminary ruling are at least open to quite a bit of

801 *Compare* CC No. 103/2009 *juncto* No. 116/2011 in light of the Court of Justice's *Foto-Frost* jurisprudence. *But compare* ECtHR Nos. 3989/07 and 38353/07 (Sep. 20, 2011) *Ullens de Schooten and Rezabek v. Belgium*, paras 55 *et seq.* (where the Court found itself competent to adjudge the question whether a preliminary question had to be referred to the Court of Justice, not so much as a question by itself (para 57), but rather in the context of article 6 ECHR (para 58)).

802 *Eg* CC No. 90/2011 (May 31, 2011) B.13.5; CC Nos. 54/2012 (Apr. 19, 2012) B.10.1-B.10.4; 116/2012 (Oct. 10, 2012) and 119/2012 (Oct. 18, 2012) B.5.2-B.5.4.

803 CA No. 92/2006 (June 7, 2006).

804 *Ibid.* B.13.

interpretation[805]. This is just one example, however, pointing out the difficulties for the issue of interpretation, and it is less relevant on other accounts, as in this case, no communautarian issues had arisen, since the Flemish and the Walloon government pleaded side by side[806].

129. Evacuation of (communautarian) conflict. In a set of recent cases on the Flemish decree on land and buildings policy the Court openly conditioned part of its holding on the outcome of a ruling of the Court of Justice. In these cases, one of the questions referred to the Court of Justice was whether making the transfers of land and constructions subject to the condition that there exists a sufficient tie between the prospective buyer or tenant and the relevant municipality would be contrary to the requirements of the European fundamental freedoms[807]. Of course, in a sense, every preliminary question referred to the Court of Justice conditions the holding of a case, but what seemed peculiar here, is that the Court tried to solve a question with an obvious communautarian dimension[808] by relying on European law provisions that – at first sight – have a mere tangential relationship with the communautarian issue[809]. As such, it could be argued that the Court indeed evacuated a potential communautarian conflict by using European law as a (reference) tool.

805 *Compare* to the arguments made by the parties: *ibid.* A.8.1-A.8.2 (which plainly seem wrongly formulated).

806 *Ibid.* A.10.1.

807 CC No. 50/2011 (Apr. 6, 2011) *dictum* (twelfth question); No. 49/2011 (Apr. 6, 2011) *dictum*.

808 *See* CC No. 49/2011 (Apr. 6, 2011) B.11 *et seq.* and No. 50/2011 (Apr. 6, 2011) B.64 *et seq.* (*compare* B.7.2, B.42.2, suspending proportionality review). It should be noted, however, that the Court here did answer some competence-related questions in light of the federal competence in civil law and the federal fiscal competence (*cf.* No. 49/2011 (Apr. 6, 2011) B.9.2 and No. 50/2011 (Apr. 6, 2011) B.10.1-B.10.3). Accordingly, it could be argued that it was exactly the non-federalism-related issue that was referred to the COJ. However, as we already noted, this conclusion does not necessarily stand, and the Flemish decree on land and buildings policy, precisely because it is an example of far-reaching use of Flemish autonomy, *must have* – reasonably interpreted (and at least for the part 'living in your own region') – caused communautarian tensions, also in the Court. I do not insist on describing the whole dynamic of these tensions, but is it so inconceivable that through a symbolic of antagonism, a certain piece of legislation can come to be perceived as a bulwark of autonomy all by itself, thus inducing communataurian dissension?

809 It should be noted that in his opinion on the issue (Opinion A-G Mazak (Oct. 4, 2012) accompanying Joined Case C-197/11 and C-203/11 (*Libert*)), the Advocate General partly referred the most ardent *communautarian* issue back to the Constitutional Court, in the sense that he clarified that the Constitutional Court would have to decide upon the issue depending on the interpretation of the purpose of the measures (*see* § 34: on whether it was a socio-economic, or 'Flemish-protective' measure), without however, leaving the Court (too) much leeway (because he argued that even if the purpose of the measure was socio-economic, the measure was disproportionate, not being an appropriate means to achieve the goal (§§ 35 *et seq.*)).

Admittedly, arguing that a case contains contentious federalism-related issues and is then referred to the Court of Justice, does not amount to "evacuation". Some will for instance argue that the parties here invoked European law, so that the Court was in fact obligated to refer for a preliminary ruling. This inference, however, will not work. Even if the parties invoked European law, this does not necessarily obligate the Constitutional Court to refer for a preliminary under the *CILFIT*-principles. Even if there is a legal obligation upon the Court to refer to the Court of Justice as soon as there is doubt about the interpretation of European law, the Court can still deploy different *tools* to (legally?) by and large avert the reference[810]. I, on the other hand, would argue that the 'evacuation hypothesis' offers one of the most plausible explanations for it [811], especially because it offers an adequate explanation of the (conjectured) communautarian divisions within the Court.

130. The evacuation hypothesis nuanced. However, at least four caveats are in order here.

The most important one is probably that my assertions here are by and large of a speculative nature (more conjecture than proof). Indeed notwithstanding some conceptual confusion in this regard[812], art. 108 SLCC clearly determines that 'deliberations are secret'. [813] Therefore, we cannot possibly (adequately[814]) verify on which issues the judges were divided and on which they were not. Even so there is good reason to believe that judges do divide on specific communautarian issues. In fact, institutionally, this has been presupposed in the Special Law on the Constitutional Court[815].

Accordingly, it should be noted that the *travaux préparatoires* at several points make clear that some provisions of the SLCC rest upon an assumption that communautarian division might arise[816]. This does not mean that there are no

[810] *Eg* (re)characterization of the linguistic duties in the Habitational Code Case (*infra* No. 131).

[811] *See* (hypothesizing) Keyaerts, *supra* note 248, at p. 55-56; *also see eg* Karel Vervoort, *Tussenarrest in juridische procedure decreet grond-en pandenbeleid*, VOKA News (June 16, 2011), available at www.voka.be (July 4, 2011).

[812] *See eg* Wanda Mastor, Les opinions séparées des juges constitutionnels 715 (2005).

[813] *Also see* art. 777 *et seq.* Belgian Judiciary Code (embodying the general rule in Belgian jurisprudence).

[814] If that is ever conclusively possible indeed: *see supra* note 298.

[815] *See* art. 31 *et seq. juncto* art. 54 *et seq.* SLCC (determining the composition and the functioning of the Court, and more precisely, which judges will be assigned to which cases). *Also compare* Feyen, *supra* note 67, at p. 268 *et seq.*

[816] *See eg* Report (Herman-Michielsens & Lallemand), *Parl. Doc.* Senate 1981-82, No. 246/2, at p. 192 *et seq.*; Report (Michel-Tant), *Parl. Doc.* Chamber 1982-83, No. 647/4, at p. 47; Amendment (Vanden Bossche), *Parl. Doc.* Chamber 1982-83, No. 647/5, at p. 15-16 and *very*

different – or perhaps it is better to say: interrelated, though distinguishable – justifications for these provisions, such as, for instance, the dispute resolving function of law as such[817]. Nor does it mean that *travaux préparatoires* as such necessarily inform well about the current structure and tasks of the Court[818]. Nor, finally, does this institutional presupposition impede the Court from being characterized as a Court of *law*, a characterization most authors nowadays would agree with, basically relying on its judicial function, the judicial procedures followed, the public nature of the treatment of problems and the guarantees for judicial impartiality[819], although not so much may in fact turn on the *characterization* or *abstract conceptualization* of the institution.

Keeping that in mind, because of dangers associated with a split vote, in which case the President casts the decisive one (knowing that the Presidency changes linguistic sides each year)[820], it does not seem implausible to contend that European law could potentially serve as a way out, primarily through preliminary references to the Court of Justice. In light of the fact that the Court did not sit *en banc* in all cases referring issues to the Court of Justice – in fact, only in the latest cases, the Court apparently often adjudicates *en banc*[821]– these contentions could perhaps be extrapolated to cover also regular sessions of the Court (7 judges), in which case the swing vote, if necessary, still belongs to the

clearly Jean-Luc Dehaene, *Integral Report* Senate (Apr. 27, 1983) No. 53, at p. 1813 (dissenting opinions would 'allow for the communautarian tensions which surely also might exist in the Court, to exteriorize').

817 *Eg* Paul Ricoeur, Le Juste 185 (1995) (distinguishing the short term finality of judging (dispute resolution) from the long term finality, which is – by and large – contribution to the public peace).

818 *Cf.* Martens, *supra* note 689, at p. 4 (explaining how the Court was an unwanted – albeit necessary – child at the time of federalization).

819 *See eg* André Alen & Frank Meersschaut, *Het Arbitragehof, (nog steeds) een grondwettelijk hof in wording*, 1989 TBP 211, 213-14; Jan Delva, *Staatsrechtelijk profiel van het Belgisch Arbitragehof*, 1991 TBP 69, 77-78.

820 Cases can be referred to a the Court *en banc* (normally 12 judges), by either the French of the Dutch President of the Court (art. 56 (2) SLCC), in which case the vote of the President in function can become the swing vote (art. 56 (3) SLCC). The function of President of the Court alternates each year (art. 54 SLCC), in function of linguistic groups. By and large, the system construed in the law has been built to enforce as much parity as possible (*also see* art. 55, 58, 59 and 60 SLCC).

821 *See* both European Arrest Warrant Cases (No. 124/2005; No. 128/2009), the Care Insurance Case (No. 51/2006), the Bressol case (No. 12/2008), the *Base* case (No. 131/2008), the Gender Equality in Insurance Case (No. 103/2009), the Aarhus Treaty case (No. 30/2010), the Environmental Effects case (No. 133/2010), the biofuel case (No. 149/2010), the Flemish decree on land and buildings policy cases (Nos. 49-50/2011) and cell phone licences case (No. 110/2011).

linguistic group of the President in function[822]. Even so, this is not necessary, as I nowhere contend that *every* referral to the Court of Justice is best understood in terms of evacuation.

A second caveat pertains to the limited area in which such evacuation is possible. This is due to several factors, including the (principally limited) material scope of Union law. Accordingly, in some cases where the vote is tied, the European option will not be immediately available[823]. However, as any student of European law knows, the *material* scope of this legal order is *potentially* quasi-unlimited[824], and *in fact* now very far-reaching[825].

Third, there seem to be some cases where European law might have been deemed relevant, but where the Court nonetheless refused to 'enter into a dialogue' with Luxembourg[826]. For instance, in the case regarding the Flemish habitational code, the Court refused to refer for a preliminary ruling[827]. The Court essentially held that it did not have to investigate whether the measure here (an obligation imposed to strive to learn Dutch[828]), constituted a restriction on free movement of workers, since it certainly complied with all the conditions set forth to justify such a restriction[829]. It is uncertain, however, whether European law really warrants such a conclusion, especially in light of *Groener*'s[830]

[822] *Cf.* art. 55 *juncto* 59 SLCC.

[823] *Compare* Opinion A-G Mazak (Oct. 4, 2012) accompanying Joined Cases C-197/11 and C-203/11 (*Libert*), § 23.

[824] Compare to the American doctrine on federalism, which, during much of the 20th century, was held to be non-existent in the sense that all or most Congressional powers were accepted.

[825] Out of numerous references, I could mention an early classic, *ie* Joseph H.H. Weiler, *The Transformation of Europe*, 100 YALE L.J. 2403 (1990-91) (describing the evolution up till the Maastricht treaty). *Also see infra*, in light of, for instance, CA No. 92/2006 (June 7, 2006) B.10 *et seq.*

[826] There are probably cases where European law could have served *within* the (closed) decision-making process as well in order to deflate communautarian tension, but it seems to me to be *too* speculative to assess whether and to which extent a compromise could have impeded its use. See for some other (legal and institutional (*see*, especially his No. 7 *et seq.*)) factors playing, also pointing out the relevance of the much-discussed *Melki* jurisprudence (*see* his No. 29 *et seq.*) and some Habermasian normative presuppositions of a dialogue (*see* his No. 5 *et seq.*), Verrijdt, *supra* note 743.

[827] CC No. 101/2008 (July 10, 2008) B.42.2 *et seq. Also see* CC No. 104/2007 (July 12, 2007) (suspension).

[828] Which perhaps was not intended to destabilize federal relationships, but could surely be anticipated to have done that (and was thus undoubtedly communautarian, at least in impact); *compare supra* notes 460 and 684.

[829] CC No. 101/2008 (July 10, 2008) B.44.2.

[830] Case 379/87 (Nov. 28, 1989).

progeny[831]. The 'more political' reason there was – probably – that an internal compromise had been made about how to interpret the linguistic requirements in the Flemish code, and accordingly, a reference was no longer necessary, or even warranted for that matter, as the European Court of Justice could in that case possibly destabilize the (presupposedly fragile) compromise[832].

That, fourthly, does not imply in turn that when a Belgian compromise has been reached, that European law has lost all of its relevance. Quite to the contrary, to the extent that European law fortifies or undergirds such a compromise, the Court can indeed invoke it. This for instance seems to be the case in Judgment No. 33/2011 or in the radio-communication cases[833], where European law was deployed in order to reinforce the cooperation duties imposed upon autonomous entities.

131. Explanation, though no conclusive evidence. More generally, it would be tenuous to unduly generalize the point I am making here. I do not mean that whenever there is internal division in the Court and it has the chance (meaning that it is not 'impeded' by an internal compromise), it will pass the buck to Europe[834]. In fact, many other considerations can be in play here[835]. To mention

---

[831] Not restricted to art. 3 (1) of Regulation No. 1612/68; *see eg* case C-281/98 (June 6, 2000) *Angonese*; case C-168/98 (Nov. 7, 2000) *Haim* and the Commission's Communication of Dec. 11, 2002 on language requirements. *Also see* Eva Brems, *Vlaamse taalvereisten getoetst aan internationale mensenrechtenverdragen* in TAALEISEN JURIDISCH GETOETST 1, 8-10 (André Alen & Stefan Sottiaux 2009) (lamenting the fact that the Constitutional Court does not enter into a dialogue with international courts and bodies). Some other examples are mentioned in Van Nuffel, *supra* note 828, at p. 38-47. *For some recent reflections, see* the Opinion of A-G Mazak accompanying *Libert* (mentioned *supra* note 823) or those of Opinion of A-G Jääskinen (July 12, 2012) accompanying Case C-202/11 (*Las*) § 27 *et seq*., or more generally (and broadly), Elke Cloots & Stefan Sottiaux, *EU Law and Language Regulation in (Quasi-)Federal Member States*, in FEDERALISM, *supra* note 32, at p. 287 *et seq.*

[832] *See* Evelyne Maes, *Vlaamse Wooncode: Grondwettelijk Hof slaat en zalft*, JURISTENKRANT (Sep. 17, 2008) p. 5 (emphasizing how both 'parties' won on some essential, though different points). *Compare* Emmanuelle Jouannet, *La Motivation ou le Mystère de la boîte noire* in LA MOTIVATION DES DÉCISIONS DES JURIDICTIONS INTERNATIONALES 251, 270 (Hélène Ruiz Fabri & Jean-Marc Sorel eds. 2008) (arguing that ther Court's motivation should not be perceived in 'an angelic fashion').

[833] Discussed *infra*. *Also see* CC No. 76/2012 (June 14, 2012).

[834] Passing the buck to Europe could sometimes even be interpreted more widely, in the sense that the Court will leave the determination of the concrete European requirements to the judge *a quo* (for a recent example, albeit not in a federalism-related case), *see* CC No. 118/2012 (Oct. 10, 2012) *esp*. B.6.1.

[835] It has furthermore been upheld that, from a comparative perspective, '[t]he position of the Belgian *Arbitragehof* may be more co-operative than that of the other constitutional courts, but its final position on several issues is not entirely clear' (CLAES, *supra* note 774, at p. 8; *see* Keyaerts, *supra* note 248, at p. 53-56; *compare supra* note 774).

but two, very abstract underlying questions: the answer to the question whether a preliminary reference will be made is prejudiced upon the answer to hard theoretical (indeed even dogmatic) questions, such as the place of European law in the hierarchy of norms, or questions pertaining to the relevance of European law considerations, which in turn presuppose answers to even more difficult questions. The Court here seems to sidestep having to answer these difficult theoretical issues. Moreover, one cannot forget that – also from a political perspective – the Court, when passing the buck to Europe, to some extent curtails its own decision-making power. It seems it will be unlikely to do so, if its own conception of the rule of law[836] viewed in light of its self-understanding as political pacifier and court of law with a specific function, do not impose a duty of some kind to have Europe interfere. Then again 'interference' should be qualified, as, for instance in the Flemish decree on land and buildings policy case, the Court does deploy quite a bit of European law reasoning, but it deploys it *itself* (and does not refer to the Court of Justice).

Even so, that does not undermine the point that from time to time, the European Court of Justice has been instrumentalized as an evacuation route for divisive communautarian issues and that this political instrumentalization has independent explanatory value.

132. Possible problems with the rule of law. Even if the Court often succeeds in pacifying issues – arguably its primary function –, it should be noted that its behavior here is prone to jeopardize some of the rule of law values it intends to uphold[837]. Moreover, even if the compromises are more or less 'silent', an emerging pattern of their possible inconsistencies in terms of referral could have adverse effects or at least produce certain externalities, which – *arguendo* that pacification might be the Court's first function[838] – could in the long run undermine the very pacifying function the Court intends to fulfill[839].

---

[836] Here, in particular, art. 19 (3) b TEU and art. 267 TFEU.

[837] *Also see* Van Nuffel, *supra* note 828, at p. 38-47 (primarily focusing on the amount, but also implicitly criticizing the Court for inconsistency – reformulated in terms of the Court's interpretation of *CILFIT*); Piet Van Nuffel, *Prejudiciële vragen aan het Hof van Justitie van de Europese Unie: leidraad voor de rechtspraktijk na het Verdrag van Lissabon,* 2009-10 RW 1154. *But compare supra* note 313 (implying that the Court might have taken these values into account). *See generally* Marc Verdussen, Les douze juges. La légitimité de la cour constitutionnelle 65 *et seq.* (2004).

[838] *Compare* François Ost, *Juge-pacificateur, juge-arbitre, juge-entraîneur. Trois modèles de justice* in Fonction de juger et pouvoir judiciare. Transformations et déplacements 1, *esp.* 44 *et seq.* (Philippe Gérard, François Ost, Michel van de Kerchove eds. 1983).

[839] Arguably the Court will loose some of its legitimacy if it openly politicizes. The inconsistencies are prone to politicize its role, or at least to enhance perception of politicization. Accordingly, the concealing terms in which the Court speaks might be construed as delegitimating in the

4.3.2 European law as an argumentative tool in the context of the EMU

133. The EMU: convergence? More subtly – and arguably more 'legally'[840] – the Court has deployed European law as a tool in its rendition of the Belgian Economic and Monetary Union (EMU). We already established that the Court's exposition of the EMU was much inspired by European law, but the question remained whether and to which extent there was convergence between the interpretations of the European Court of Justice and those of the Constitutional Court in this regard[841].

134. Prior theoretical questions. Even if some authors have bemoaned the Court throughout the nineties for reading the Belgian EMU provisions in tension with European law requirements[842], at least two priors should be considered.

The first preliminary evaluative question to be answered would be whether there is a need for convergence. As implied above[843], I will not discuss this question at length, as it presupposes, amongst others, complex economic arguments which I have the time nor the capacity to fully develop[844]. Nonetheless, an

---

long run. The argument is not implausible. This opens up a large space for debate, for instance in terms of legitimacy (*see eg* Hugues Dumont, *Le contrôle de la constitutionnalité des lois et des décrets en Belgique: fonction juridictionnelle ou politique,* in Fonction de juger, *supra* note 838, at p. 71 *et seq.* or Verdussen, *supra* note 837), or in terms of political effects (*compare* Tushnet, *supra* note 740), or in terms of broader social and political issues, the complexity of which precludes us from making any further comments here.

840 Even if this is not the time or place to start distinguishing between the 'legal' and the 'political' realm in conceptual terms.

841 *Cf. supra* No. 113. *See more extensively* Feyen, *supra* note 32, at p. 396 *et seq.* (explaining further difficulties in light of comparison, first in terms of application of the EMU, noting a possible divergence between *structural* and *substantive* convergence, and afterwards in terms of unarticulated premises).

842 *See eg* Delgrange & Keppene, *supra* note 527, at p. 91 *et seq.*; van Ypersele, *supra* note 214, at p. 126 *et seq., but compare ibid.* at p. 137-42 (arguing for a broad self-imposing form of European law). *Also see* Michel Melchior & Pierre Vandernoot, *Contrôle de constitutionnalité et droit communautaire derive,* 1998 RBDC 17, 24-25 ('one could not imagine indeed that the national requirements in these matters would be more leniently conceived of than those prevailing at the [Union] level'). *Compare* Herwig Verschueren, *Social Federalism and EU law on the free movement of persons* in Social Federalism, *supra* note 45, at p. 222 (arguing from a European perspective, which actually constitutes, in this case, a different argument). *Compare supra* Nos. 112-113 in light of *infra* Ch. 5.

843 *Supra* No. 113.

844 Often these economic arguments themselves are again liable to be criticized, for instance on ideological grounds. As such, it has been argued that in recent cases like *Mangold* (C-144/04), *Commission v. Austria* (C-147/03; *compare* C-73/08 (GC; Apr. 10, 2010) *Bressol*), *Watts* (C-372/04) and *Viking & Laval* (Cases C-438/05 and C-341/05) the Court has become a true

eclectic example[845], such as Vanderveeren's *et al.*, that it would not make sense to allow industrial and commercial property considerations to play as a Belgian justification vis-à-vis restrictions against the EMU (which considerations *are* allowed in European law[846]), makes clear that it is not wholly self-evident that interpretations of the Court of Justice and the Constitutional Court should converge[847].

Even prior to the question about *why* they should or could either converge or diverge, comes the conceptual issue of what convergence would consist in. That, in turn, depends not only on the level of abstraction at which convergence is pondered about[848], but also on several hotly debated theoretical issues, such as the scope of European Union law, or the conceptualization of primacy of European law[849]. For instance, if some theories of constitutional pluralism are right in contending that the European legal order solves problems which are *different* from problems solved by the constitutional order, then the question of primacy does not come up, and one would first have to argue that there is an analogy

engine of 'turbo-capitalism' (I borrow the language and point from Reich, Norbert Reich, *How proportionate is the proportionality principle* (paper presented at the conference 'The Market State Project', Oslo, May 18-19), available at http://www.jus.uio.no/ifp/forskning/prosjekter/markedsstaten/arrangementer/2011/free-movement-oslo/speakers-papers/speakers-pres.html (July 2, 2011), at p. 2), and published in THE EUROPEAN COURT OF JUSTICE AND THE AUTONOMY OF THE MEMBER STATES 83, 84 (Hans-Wolfgang Micklitz & Bruno de Witte eds. 2012).

845 *See* more generally *supra* about political rationality (*supra* note 658, and accompanying text).

846 *Cf.* art. 36 TFEU (*ex* art. 30 TEC). In some sense, they argue that the rationale is not so far from European law indeed, as *Cassis* precludes justifications on the basis of art. 36 TFEU in cases where harmonization has taken place: in Belgium, the regulation of industrial and commercial property is regulated at the federal level (VANDERVEEREN *et al., supra* note 658, at p. 51-52). This in turn underlines that *convergence* can mean different things: one can converge on structures of tests, argumentative structures, outcomes, ... (*see following paragraph*). Further on, however, Vanderveeren *et al.* also rely on purely empirical differentiations (*eg* the stronger trans-regional interlocking of the economy, warranting a different treatment in terms of industrial economic policy – *ibid.* at p. 63 *et seq.*). *Compare ibid.* at p. 101 ('in terms of its content, European law is part of the normative framework of the Belgian EMU').

847 VANDERVEEREN *et al.*, *supra* note 658, at p. 51-52. *Also see* Velaers & Vanpraet, *supra* note 388, at p. 211.

848 Feyen, *supra* note 32, at p. 398 *et seq.*

849 *Also see* Feyen, supra note 32, at p. 399. *Cf.* Tryfonidou, *supra* note 656, at p. 10 *et seq.* For some recent elaborations in the field of free movement of persons, in light of the cases *Ruiz Zambrano* and *McCarthy*, *see* Thomas Bombois, *La Citoyenneté européenne appliqué aux situations purement internes: portée et enjeux des arrest* Zambrano *et* McCarthy, 2011 JURISPRUDENCE DE LIÈGE, MONS ET BRUXELLES 1227, 1234 *et seq.*; Koen Lenaerts, *EU Federalism in 3-D* in FEDERALISM, *supra* note 32, at p. 31 *et seq.;* or Valérie Verbist, *De invloed van het Unieburgerschap op zuiver interne situaties,* 2011-12 RW 510. *Also see* Case C-256/11 *Dereci* (GC; Nov. 15, 2011) paras 59 *et seq.*

between the problems addressed by both orders in order to discern whether there is *überhaupt* possibility of convergence or not. However, notwithstanding the answer to these theoretical questions, is has become clear– and few would disagree, I think – that problems can be construed as analogous and that the legal orders at least in that sense intertwine[850].

We can sidestep the issue over whether convergence should be construed and whether it is a constant in the Belgian case law[851] by claiming that sometimes

---

850 Which in turn does not mean – starting from dogmatic premises – that convergence does not presuppose a distinction between legal orders, for if there were no such difference, convergence would be a mere instance of application. Convergence thus presupposes the existence of purely internal situations, principally not governed by EU law (*cf.* Feyen, *supra* note 32, at p. 399).

851 Most believe it is not, certainly after the Care Insurance Judgment (*eg* Velaers & Vanpraet, *supra* note 388, at p. 210-11; *compare* Verschueren, *supra* note 842). Accordingly, I do not answer the question here whether European law *obliges* the Belgian Court to construe the EMU completely in line with the criteria of European law (para 40 of Case C-212/06 suggests otherwise), nor whether a specific interpretative methodology would oblige the Court to interpret – as an obligation under Belgian law – the EMU requirements fully in line with European criteria (in that case, the Belgian Care insurance case could be deemed problematic – although not entirely unjustifi*able* – even if not justified explicitly in these terms, *ie* the possible hierarchical relationship between the principle of territoriality and the EMU – *eg* Isabelle Buelens & Frank Judo, *Rechterlijke dialoog over de zorgverzekering: het Luxemburgse arrest van 1 april 2008,* SOCIAALRECHTELIJKE KRONIEKEN 2009, 185, 193; Feyen, *supra* note 792, at p. 174-75 ; Velaers & Vanpraet, *supra* note 388, at p. 211). *Also see* BRIBOSIA & VAN BOXSTAEL, *supra* note 13, at p. 32-33. On the consequences of a construal, *see* BRIBOSIA & VAN BOXSTAEL, *supra* note 13, at p. 32-33: here, the authors distinguish between two interpretations. A first interpretation, according to which every infringement of Union law is an infringement of the rules allocation competences ('[i]t should finally be noticed that the Regions, like the State and all other public authorities, remain subject to international treaties, also in the economic sphere' (*Parl. Doc.* Chamber, 1988, No. 516/1, at p. 12)) would imply that, for instance, when a Flemish Region would levy an export tax on waste transgressing Belgian borders, this would violate Union Law, and *therefore* the Constitutional Court could invalidate it (Van Ypersele, *supra* note 214, at p. 131-136). According to Bribosia and Van Boxstael, this would go beyond the text, which guarantees an exercise by the Regions of competence taking into account the Belgian Economic and Monetary Union (BRIBOSIA & VAN BOXSTAEL, *supra* note 13, at p. 33). They offer no arguments however, and the text of art. 6, §1, VI, 2nd clause, 2°, 2nd clause since 1988 only mentions 'keeping the general normative framework of the economic union and the monetary unity into account, as established by or through the law, and by or through the international treaties'. They see a second interpretation, according to which respect for the Belgian EMU, requires Union law to be applicable to intra-etatic Belgian relations ('many of them, such as the treaties regarding the Belgian-Luxembourg Economic Union, the Benelux, the European Communities, and the International Monetary Fund, contribute to limit the scope of the economic union and the monetary unity' (*Parl. Doc.* Chamber 1988, No. 516/1, at p. 12)). This latter interpretation would imply that, for instance, when a Flemish Region would levy an export tax on waste transgressing *Flemish* borders, possibly this could violate the EMU (*cf.* C.A. No. 32/91 (Nov. 14, 1991) 5.B.1.9 possibly read together with C.A. No. 27/90 (July 14, 1990) (rejecting the suspension petition) (upholding an environmental levy of 350 Belgian francs for every ton of waste picked up in the Flemish region, and exported outside

European law functions as a tool in order to further construe the requirements of Belgian law, at least from the viewpoint of the Constitutional Court.

135. An example: inheritance tax exemption. That could be illustrated by a Belgian case involving an inheritance tax exemption[852]. This case originated in a Flemish decree that introduced an exemption from inheritance taxes relating to family undertakings. The exemption was available only if the undertaking employed, in the three years preceding the date of death of the deceased, at least five workers in the Flemish Region. The Court of Justice found that this condition amounted to 'indirect discrimination'[853], incompatible with the freedom of establishment, as it provided for a difference in treatment between taxpayers on the basis of the place of employment. The Belgian Constitutional Court was called upon to decide whether the decree passed constitutional muster, this time under the Belgian EMU in 2010[854].

The Court first reiterated that a mere discrepancy between regional inheritance tax rates, which arguably might have an influence on the behavioral pattern of taxpayers, did not, as such infringe on the Belgian EMU[855]. However, so the Court continued, this decree restricts or renders more difficult the investment in corporations which do not at least employ five employees in the Flemish Region, since the consequences of an inheritance tax regulation are taken into account in investment decisions. This amounted to a restriction on the freedom of establishment and the free movement of capital. In the Court's opinion, this

it to be burnt, as it was deemed necessary to conduct a global policy and allowed insofar as it only lifted the existing fiscal immunity for exports)), but the relationship with EU law is less clear, since European law does not in effect govern internal relations. *See* Van Ypersele, *supra* note 214, at p. 137-142 and 145-146. *See, more generally (and indicating the limits of these abstractions),* Feyen, *supra* note 32, at p. 399 (*et seq.*).

852 CC No. 83/2010 (July 8, 2010).

853 Case C-464/05 (Oct. 25, 2007) *Geurts & Vogten*, paras 16 (only on the basis of freedom of establishment), 20 and 22. *Also see* Opinion A-G Kokott (Feb. 15, 2007) accompanying Case C-464/05 (who relentingly argued this case only on the basis of free establishment – *cf.* §§ 22 *et seq.*). *See further* Feyen, *supra* note 32, at p. 402.

854 It should be noted that the decree was modified by Fl. Decree (Dec. 21, 2007) on measures accompanying the 2008 budget, *BSG* Dec. 31, 2007, with an *errandum* in *BSG* Oct. 9, 2008, adding some extra conditions to the exemption, and abolishing the criterion of employing employees in the Flemish Region, as a reaction to Case C-464/05 (Oct. 25, 2007) *Geurts and Vogten*; *see* Amendment, *Parl. Doc.* Flemish Parl. 2007-08, No. 1368/6, at p. 5-6. The Constitutional Court had to judge upon the constitutionality of the decree as it stood before this amendment (*cf.* CC No. 83/2010 (July 8, 2010) B.1). However, this does not exclude that the modification itself arguably, at least implicitly, formed part of the reasoning of the Court (*ibid.* B.3). In fact, it has done so analogously in other cases as well (*see eg* CA No. 4/95 (Feb. 2, 1995) B.5.8).

855 CC No. 83/2010 (July 8, 2010) B.8.

restriction could not be justified, because – relying on *Geurts & Vogten*[856] – the argument based on employment and business survival did not succeed, since the condition in question was not necessary to attain that goal[857].

136. European law as a tool. Accordingly, in this case, the Court seemed to be interpreting the Belgian EMU requirement in line[858] with European law requirement. It in fact extrapolated European considerations, which normally play between member states[859], to the federated entities as such, and explicitly relied on European law to justify this operation. As such, European law also seems to be the primary ground of distinction between the situation which the Court described as normal (*ie* diverging rates), from the situation which was proscribed here[860].

4.3.3 European law as an argumentative tool reinforcing cooperation

137. Reinforcing cooperation: a function of proportionality review. European law not only functions as a possible tool for in the arguments pertaining to the EMU as such; it has also been deployed by the Court to reinforce or reach[861] its conclusions on the basis of the principle of proportionality, thus streamlining its reasoning.

---

856 On the difference in arguments (in light of the question of convergence and the presupposition of different legal orders), *see* Feyen, *supra* note 32, at p. 403.

857 CC No. 83/2010 (July 8, 2010) B.9.

858 If not in terms of justification then at least in terms of structure and results (*compare supra* Nos. 112 and 134).

859 *Compare infra* on Care Insurance (*cf.* Feyen, *supra* note 32, at p. 400-402 and 403-404). *Also compare* Alina Tryfonidou, *Resolving the reverse discrimination paradox in the area of customs duties: the* Lancry *saga*, 22 European Business Law Review 311, *esp.* 321 *et seq.* (2011) (explaining how the COJ broke through the purely internal rule in case of custom duties in order to avert reverse discriminations, but actually relied on the wrong article to do so) or the progeny of the *Knoors* judgment (Case 115/78); *cf.* Tryfonidou, *supra* note 656, at p. 10 *et seq.*

860 Which, according to the Court of Justice, renders itself competent to adjudicate upon the (formerly 'purely internal') issue (Joined Cases C-297/88 and C-197/89 (Oct. 18, 1990) *Dzodzi*, paras 36-42, *esp.* 37; Case C-280/06 (GC; Dec. 11, 2007) *Autorita Garante della Concorrenza e del Mercato*, para 19-29, esp. 21). Nonetheless, *see* Case C-48/07 (Dec. 22, 2008), *Les Vergers du Vieux Trauves SA*, para 27 (which boundaries the national legislature has set to the application of Community law to internal situation, is a matter of national law, but as regards Union Law, the national judge, to the extent that the national law made reference to Community law, cannot deviate from the interpretation by the Court). *Cf.* Case C-310/10 (July 7, 2011) *Agafiței*, paras 38-39, 46-47. *Compare, then again,* Feyen, *supra* note 32, at p. 403-404.

861 On the relevance and adequacy of the distinction, *see supra* introductory chapter. *Also see* Orban, *supra* note 570, 19-20.

In resolving the so-called telecommunications saga[862], the Court for the first time used the principle of proportionality in order to impose a duty to cooperate on autonomous federated entities.

138. Administrative control on aircraft operators and the European argument. In a 2011 case[863], this move was more or less re-enacted. The Court in this case held that the Flemish legislature is not competent to regulate greenhouse gas emission allowance trading in the field of aviation. More precisely, a Flemish decree regulated the administrative control on several aircraft operators for which Belgium, according to Directive 2003/87/EC is the administering Member State and determined that the effective control will be conducted by the Region which is confronted with the highest amount of carbon dioxide emissions. It furthermore established that allowances would be allotted to the Flemish Region for all flights departing from airports located on Flemish territory and for all flights landing on such airports, on the condition that these flights do not depart from a member state of the EU[864]. In practice, the decree meant that the revenue generated by the ever increasing *auctioned* part of the allowances would flow to the Flemish government, which would have to be combined with the fines the Flemish government could impose on aircraft operators not fulfilling their duties to surrender the allotted allowances. Notwithstanding the fact that the Flemish Region is in principle competent to regulate the reduction of greenhouse gas emissions pursuant to its environmental powers[865], it can only regulate this on Flemish territory[866]. Although Directive 2003/87/EC sets forth Belgium as the relevant administering authority and Flanders did not legislate matters for which Belgium as such was not competent[867], the territorial criterion it employed, irrespective of whether it was inspired by article 18 of the Directive itself[868], would result in the Flemish Region exercising competence vis-à-vis emissions which 'only very partially occur in [Flemish] Regional airspace'[869].

[862] *Cf.* Werner, *supra* note 571. *Also see supra* No. 100. *Further see* Butterfly Agreement, *supra* note 10, at p. 46 (constitutionalizing Constitutional Court jurisprudence).

[863] CC 33/2011 (Mar. 2, 2011).

[864] Art. 20*bis* Fl. Decr. (Apr. 2, 2004) as inserted by art. 4 Fl. Decr. (May 8, 2009); *cf.* CC 33/2011 (Mar. 2, 2011) B.2.1; *also see* B.2.2 for other duties under the new decree.

[865] CC 33/2011 (Mar. 2, 2011) B.4.1-B.4.4.

[866] *Ibid.* B.5. *Cf. supra* No. 97 *et seq.*

[867] CC 33/2011 (Mar. 2, 2011) B.6.1-B.7.

[868] *Nota bene:* the Court mentions art. 18*bis* (CC 33/2011 (Mar. 2, 2011) B.8.1), but it probably means article 18*a* (1) (b), as inserted by article 2 of Directive 2008/101/EC (*OJ* (Jan. 1, 2009) L 8/14) ('greatest estimated attributed aviation emissions from flights performed by that aircraft operator in the base year').

[869] CC 33/2011 (Mar. 2, 2011) B.8.1-B.8.2.

There was a problem according to the Court, not only because of the limited size of Flanders and the scantly developed interregional aviation. More importantly, it relies on the argument that 'the combination of the fact that there may only be one administering authority per aircraft operator [the European requirement] and the criterion of article 20*bis* of the [Flemish] Decree, brings about that emissions of certain flights which exclusively fly across other regions or member states of the European Union, fall within the scope of the Decree in question as soon as these flights are operated by an aircraft operator which would fall under the competence of the Flemish Region, applying the criterion in question'[870]. For those reasons, the decree violates the principle of exclusive territoriality[871].

The Court could have stopped here, and invalidated the decree for this reason alone[872]. However, it considered in B.10.2:

> As a rule, the absence of cooperation in a matter for which the special legislature does not foresee an obligation [to cooperate], does not constitute a violation of the rules allocating competences.
>
> Here, however, the competences of the federal State and the Regions are interlaced to the extent that they can only exercised in joint cooperation, due to, on the one hand, the European necessity that there might be only one administrative authority per aircraft operator, and, on the other hand, the principally trans-regional nature of the flight emissions caused by planes landing or departing in one region. A cooperation agreement will moreover render it possible, following the example of Directive 2003/87/EC, to involve the federal aviation authorities in the application of the system.

870 *Ibid.* B.8.1.

871 CC 33/2011 (Mar. 2, 2011) B.8.2.

872 The case would have been a lot less interesting from a European perspective, because the relevance of European law in the testing here would only be circumstantial, or indirect at best. I do not theoretically clarify the distinction I make here between 'direct', 'indirect' or 'circumstantial' influence (*compare supra* Ch. 1.2). Suffice it to say, however, that it would not be farfetched to argue that in some cases European law has at least circumstantially and perhaps indirectly influenced the Court's proportionality reasoning, in terms of territorial scope read in conjunction with a cooperation duty *c.q.* possibility, in competence jurisdiction. *See eg* CC No. 2/2009 (Jan. 15, 2009). An argument could even be made that European law 'influences' in many cases, but the argument to establish that influence would become all the more strenuous, in the sense that more theoretical issues would emerge (*cf. supra* Ch. 4.1-4.2), and tangential, in the sense that it would not *immediately* necessarily pertain to territorial scope or even a duty to cooperation.

Afterwards, the Court of Justice confirmed the validity of the Directive[873], and the Constitutional Court was again confronted with a case, in which the Federal Government sought to annul a Walloon Decree seeking to transform the Directive into Belgian (Walloon) law, using quasi-identical territoriality criteria. It upheld its earlier reasoning[874], this time urging the respective government to come to a cooperation agreement very quickly.[875]

139. Comparing with the telecommunications cases: dogmatics falling short. These cases accordingly seem to be in line with the communications cases, but one could wonder whether there was European influence in the telecommunications cases too.

True, there were important differences between the 2011 case and the telecommunications cases. A first relevant difference between the telecommunications line of cases and No. 33/2011 lies in the (*extra*) influence European law had in case 33/2011 in assessing whether the consequences of the invalidated legislation should be maintained. Whereas this question was not influenced by European law in the telecommunications cases[876], in No. 33/2011 European law played a mentionable role, as the Court here maintained the consequences of the invalidated decree in order to 'render Belgium capable to further execute the [...] Directives'[877]. Surely another relevant difference lies in the way the competences are interwoven in the different cases. Whereas in the communication cases, the interwoven nature had to do with several technical factors, the reason why in 33/2011 the competences were interlaced was primarily territorial[878]. A third possible difference might lie in the fact that the European Directive[879] in Case 33/2011 was primarily a modification of Directive 2003/87/EC, which executed an international treaty itself, that is the Kyoto Protocol[880]. Finally, one should note that some of these cases involve Decrees and Laws transposing Directives[881].

---

[873] Case C-366/10 (Dec. 21, 2011), *Air transport Association of America.*

[874] CC 76/2012 (June 14, 2012) B.9.1 and B.11.2.

[875] CC 76/2012 (June 14, 2012) B.12 and dictum, second indent.

[876] *See* CA No. 132/2004 (July 14, 2004) B.7.1-B.7.2; No. 128/2005 (July 13, 2005) B.6.6-B.6.7 and No. 163/2006 (Nov. 8, 2006) B.12.

[877] CC No. 33/2011 (Mar. 2, 2011) B.11.

[878] CC 33/2011 (Mar. 2, 2011) B.5 *et seq.*

[879] Directive No. 2008/101/EC.

[880] On why it might be deemed a *relevant* difference, see the reference made by the High Court of Justice Queen's Bench Division in Case C-366/10 (*The Air Transport of America*) on arguments of international law influencing the validity of the Directive.

[881] *Eg* Case No. 33/2011 – *cf.* Explanatory Memo, *Parl. Doc.* Flemish Parl. 2008-09, No. 2184/1, at p. 2). This is not a constant, however (*see eg* No. 112/2011 (July 23, 2011)).

All these distinctions notwithstanding, one could argue that European influence was in play in the telecommunications cases too[882]. Recital 5 of the Framework Directive on Electronic communication networks[883] indeed considers that '[t]he convergence of the telecommunications, media and information technology sectors means that all transmission networks and services should be covered by a single regulatory framework'. It is after the adoption of this Directive that the Constitutional Court's jurisprudence on the cooperation duties emerged. The Court was surely aware of this Directive, because it came across it[884]. In fact, it mentioned the European provisions explicitly in its argumentation[885].

Two issues remain unsolved, however, reminiscent of some the theoretical difficulties we pointed out in the concept of influence.

First, the convergence in terms of infrastructure of telecommunication and radiodiffusion is first and foremost a *factual* matter. The fact that Europe, in a recital of a Directive, makes a factual assertion – notwithstanding the fact that it draws a *legal* consequence (need for a single regulatory framework) from that fact – does not seem to be a case of performative language use (in the Austinian sense[886]). Accordingly, the fact is not (institutionally) created by Europe, so one could wonder how it could influence Belgian law[887].

Moreover – implicitly accepting that the need for a regulatory framework does indeed give rise to a (legally operative) fact (in the sense of 'obligation') – the question remains whether the Constitutional Court would have come to the same conclusion if the Directive was not adopted, or if Europe had not existed[888].

---

882 *Also see* Orban, *supra* note 570, at p. 19-20.

883 2002/21/EC (Mar. 7, 2002) on a common regulatory framework for electronic communication networks and services (*OJ* (Apr. 24, 2002) L108/33).

884 *Eg* CA No. 128/2005 (July 13, 2005) B.1.2.

885 CA No. 132/2004 (July 14, 2004) B.5.2 ('the Court moreover remarks that the European Directives of 7 March 2002 on electronic communications and services determine that, due to convergence in the telecommunications, media and information technology sectors, all transmission networks and services must come within the scope of one single regulatory framework. When, within a member state, there are different regulatory instances, the mentioned Directives impose a duty on the member states to ensure cooperation in matters of common interest'); CA No. 128/2005 (July 13, 2005) B.6.2 (referring to No. 132/2004); CA 163/2006 (Nov. 8, 2006) B.3.1 (referring to No. 132/2004) and CC No. 112/2011 (June 23, 2011) B.3.3 (quasi-repeating the consideration).

886 John L. Austin, How to do Things with Words (2d ed., J.O. Urmson & Marina Sbisa eds. 1975) (later reframed in terms of illocutionary force, and picked up in linguistic theory by authors like Searle or Habermas).

887 *But compare* CA No. 5/98 (Jan. 21, 1998) *with* No. 79/2004 (May 12, 2004), B.8.

888 *Compare* No. 19/97 (Apr. 15, 1997) B.2.3 ('reference, in the recitals of the directive [...] is on itself without repercussion on the allocation of competences').

Worsening the intricate complexity of such a counterfactual, are some of the theoretical issues I summarily ran over in my chapter on influence. Accordingly: did Europe have an influence? It was hard to tell, but from the telecommunications judgments[889], one could reasonably infer that it was the case[890]. On the other hand, one could argue that the influence was only *indirect*[891], or *circumstantial* (given that some of the cases had direct relationships with EU law), but then again, the abovementioned theoretical questions re-emerge.

Be that as it may, the Court recently still confirmed that the Directive was important enough to mention, in a new case regarding telecommunications[892], even if here again – because it was used next to other arguments – the dogmatic question remains whether it 'separately' exacted 'influence', or whether it should be understood as part of proportionality review (in the language of the Court, it merely 'pointed out' the existence of the Directive).

140. Beyond dogmatics: a tool-like approach. Beyond these dogmatic issues, it should be understood that European law here is used as a tool which reinforces or streamlines the Court's proportionality reasoning, in particular when it has been adopted in order to impose a duty to cooperate and to coordinate certain inextricably interwoven policies[893], irrespective of 'formally' autonomous competence allocation[894]. As such, European law is instrumentalized and

[889] CA No. 132/2004 (July 14, 2004); No. 128/2005 (July 13, 2005); No. 163/2006 (Nov. 8, 2006).

[890] *Cf.* Popelier, *supra* note 16, at p. 92-94.

[891] *Eg* via the CoS Advice, *Parl. Doc.* Chamber 2001-02, No. 1937/1, at p. 56; *cf.* Werner, *supra* note 571, at p. 155.

[892] CC No. 112/2011 (June 23, 2011) B.3.3. *Cf.* Van Drooghenbroeck, *supra* note 393, at p. 258.

[893] *Compare eg* CoS Advice 51.384/VR (June 12, 2012), 2012 Tijdschrift voor Wetgeving 327-328 (need for a common approach to the implementation of Directive 2010/40/EU).

[894] New questions arise here. For instance, one could wonder what 'formal' means here, in a context where we stressed the importance of looking at competence allocation in terms of *tools*, rather than in an overly legalistic manner. I will not eludicate the question of what it expressly means here, however, since my answer would depend on complex theoretical issues I only dealt with eclectically in this book. However, the reason why I nonetheless do not refrain from adding the subordinate clause, is to show, first, that it is *überhaupt* possible for European law to *have* an influence (*compare supra*, ch. 1), and, next to that, because the structure which my sentence implies (*ie* 'proportionality' duties, as 'exceptions' to principled autonomy) is also the structure which undergirds the Court's judgments.

operationalized as a(n additional[895]) reason for limiting the autonomy of the constitutive parts of the Belgian state.

[895] I do not find it plausible to perceive it as a *necessary* (in a logical legal-dogmatic sense) condition for a duty, if only in the telecommunications cases, no explicit reference to European law was made, at least not as explicit as the CoS was (CoS Advice, *Parl. Doc.* Chamber 2006-07, No. 2761/11, at p. 6; *but see* CC No. 112/2011 (June 23, 2011) B.3.3). The Court at least nowhere stated explicitly that for a duty of cooperation to arise, European law must support this duty. Such a rule – at first sight moreover – would also lack a rationale by itself, and even if it could be read in some judgments, it seems hard to elaborate it or to infer it (as a matter of dogmatic understanding) from these judgments.
Moreover, and perhaps more importantly, Melchior & Vandernoot have pointed out, comparing Cases 6/96 (Jan. 18, 1996) *esp.* B.2.8 and 32/92 (Apr. 23, 1992) (a change in competence law on public tenders) that European law can in fact also reinforce the exclusivity (in light of the EMU) of a specific legal area in light of Directive requirements: 'the circumstance that federal legislation limiting the autonomy of federated entities is in reality the transposition of European directives has here reinforced the obligatory character of the rule of concurrence that the legislation and the directive boasted' (*supra* note 842, at p. 23). *Also see* their comments on the earlier 'general and sectorial norms', in reference to Cases 47 and 55 (*ibid.* p. 21-22) – I do not treat this issue separately here, however.

4.4 Rule of law values and the limits of instrumentalization by the Constitutional Court

141. European law as a precarious tool. Even if the Constitutional Court, in the latter case(s), invoked European law to justify limiting autonomy, it nonetheless utilized European law as a tool, since it reinforced or streamlined a conclusion that it seemed to want to reach. In this section, at least partially relying on the fact that the instrumental nature of the tools is limited, I will argue that European law can become precarious as a tool, because it comes in tension with constraints that the Court feels it must abide by. Moreover, I suggest that European law in fact exacerbates the already inherent tension between the constraints and the instrumental conceptualization of the Court's functioning and reasoning.

142. Two preliminary issues: no full systematization and no integration into existing categories of legal reasoning. Some preliminary issues should be reiterated[896] or elaborated, however, as the answer to the problems they pose indeed influence the considerations which are relevant in rendering my main line of argument.

A first issue that arises here is how to adequately construe the limits which are imposed, a question we already broached (rather theoretically) above[897]. I propose to rely here on what I coined rule of law values: the values incorporated herein are multifarious, and indeed I will not treat them all here, nor will I theorize them[898].

It should be re-emphasized that even if we can conceive of the jurisprudence as a toolbox, this does not mean that 'law' in itself offers no constraints. The rule of law itself, although there is controversy abound on this subject, indeed constrains the judge in her interpretation[899]. At the outset, we notice that even if

---

[896] *Supra* No. 101.

[897] *See supra* Nos. 119-121.

[898] Theoretically, I am inspired here by Ronald Dworkin's discussion of legality as the underlying value of the legal system (*see esp.* DWORKIN, JUSTICE IN ROBES, *supra* note 62, at p. 168 *et seq.*). However, the interpretative framework I propose can be seen to differ from Dworkin's in obvious ways, at least when it comes to emphasis.

[899] Some recent works (and many older ones too, for that matter) can be read as trying to to unite the 'instrumental' dimension with the 'legalistic' dimension into a broader concept of the Rule of Law (*eg* BEATTY, *supra* note 554 (recharacterizing the rule of law in terms of the principle of proportionality); *also see* SHAPIRO, *supra* note 37, at p. 119 ('the fundamental rules of legal system are plans. Their function is to structure legal activity so that participants can work together and thereby achieve goods and realize values that would otherwise be unattainable

the (subconscious) psychology of a judge's decision-making does not exclude an insertion of personal or political preferences into the decision-making process, it is a rule of law value that interpretation occurs (or at least is represented) as *objectively* as possible, in light of the requirements of legal texts, precedents and coherence requirements. In Belgium, where several (jurisprudential) authors have for quite a while now pleaded for a reversal of methodology, towards a more 'principled' (open-ended, argumentative, ...) approach to and in law[900], which arguably has been developing in or redeemed by dogmatics, there is an almost unanimous acknowledgment that a judge *should* still try to interpret law 'objectively', meaning now in light of underlying principles such as separation of powers and legal certainty, which is turn is also conceived as a legal principle, both processual (*eg* judicial independence and impartiality[901]) and contentious[902]. This is just to illustrate that the *rule of law* might be, and in fact in light of the overarching meaning it takes up here, should be very broadly construed. I can imagine that even factors which blatantly fall beyond the concept of the rule of law as a value underlying the system, and which cannot conceivably be brought within the concept thereof, might still exert an influence which limits

[by] settl[ing] on [some] goals' (*emphasis omitted*); *compare though* (in the context of courts) at p. 126-127, 155, and *esp.* 234 *et seq.; also compare* at p. 127 (ultimate basis in 'instrumental rationality'); *compare* Jack M. Balkin, Living Originalism (2011) (trying to show how both (in their interpretive dimensions) can be reconciled in a constitutional interpretive project)). In fact, many debates in legal theory seem to be amenable to a characterization in terms of diminishing this tension, or in terms of pleading for one side or another (*eg* Tamanaha, *supra* note 67). Even if I presuppose that a sensible distinction can be drawn between *tools* as instruments and *rule of law* values, I do not comprehensively theorize the distinction here, but rather first and foremost rely on intuition, suffused by argument, in order to establish the legitimacy and validity of the distinction in this context (*compare* Shapiro, *supra* note 716, *esp.* at p. 388-400; *compare* Shapiro, *supra* note 37, at p. 122 (on the changing relationship of means and ends)).

900 *Eg* Chaïm Perelman, *Ce qu'une réflexion sur le droit peut apporter au philosophe* in Justice et Raison 244 (Chaïm Perelman ed. 1972); Walter van Gerven, Het beleid van de rechter (1973); François Ost & Jacques Lenoble, Droit, mythe et raison: essai sur le dérive mytho-logique de la rationalité juridique (1980); Mark Van Hoecke, Intepretatievrijheid van de rechter (1979) and the different articles in L'Interprétation en droit. Approche pluridisciplinaire (Michel van de Kerchove ed. 1979).

901 *Eg* Cass. (Oct. 13, 1975), 1976 Pasinomie (I) 181 or CA 30/2005 (Feb. 9, 2005), B.4.2; *compare eg* CC 66/2011 (May 5, 2011), B.4.2 (relating the principle to article 6 ECHR). A specific *constitutional* example of this (with a focus on Germany), can be found in Alen & Peeters, *supra* note 13, at p. 1123 *et seq.*, *esp.* 1150 *et seq.* (which is nonetheless still 'partial' (depending on the base line) in some regards, *see eg* at p. 1130-31, 1133-34, 1148; *but see* 1139, 1147 on the relationship between text and non-text on the one hand, and between interpretation and application on the other hand).

902 For one recent example, which at the same time thematizes the subtle distinction between legality and legal certainty (in light of European law), *see* Jan Theunis, *Tussen wettigheid en rechtszekerheid* in 3 Leuvense Staatsrechtelijke standpunten, *supra* note 67, at p. 355.

the instrumentality of the Constitutional Court's reasoning. However, I will not address that question here.

Even if the these categories (text, precedent and coherence), to the extent that they are understood broadly, can capture quite a bit of the meaning of *rule of law*, certainly certain aspects of the values expressed by the concept of the rule of law are not readily reducible to these categories, or at least do not seem to fit them neatly. That, in turn, does not mean that these unincorporated aspects are unimportant, quite to the contrary. Often even, these aspects of rule of law values are so obvious for legal scholars that they either do not actively think about them, or at least refrain from theorizing them extensively[903]. Arguably, an example of both last categories would be the notion of exclusivity itself, as we described it (*ie* as a guarantee for avoiding antinomies). It would both be hard to catch this under any of the categories, and at the same time it would be easy to overlook that this indeed could be characterized – if theorized – as a translation of a rule of law value (*ie* consistency)[904].

What is offered here accordingly is *not* a full systematization of how or why *rule of law* values might either constrain or streamline the toolbox approach of the Constitutional Court's jurisprudence in general, or even constrain the European tools the Constitutional Court deploys. The following three elaborations on *rule of law* values could be understood as eclectic[905] means of showing how, on different levels of generalization and abstraction, the versatility of European law and the concomitant 'discretionary'[906] powers of Constitutional judges are kept within certain bounds (in a colorful variety of ways).

Second – and this is a point I have not alluded to above yet – the fact that judges are constrained by some rule of law values, does not imply a belief that rule of law values such as text, precedent and coherence can or do themselves form a coherent whole. Coherence, for instance, can be conceived of in terms of an idea of primacy of European law, in terms of a uniform interpretation of the EMU,

[903] *See eg* Rigaux, *supra* note 156, at p. 319-320. *See, even more broadly,* Kelsen, *supra* note 37, at p. 71 *et seq.*, *esp.* 74 ('[l]ogical principles are applicable, indirectly, to legal norms to the extent that they are applicable to the rules of law which describe the legal norms and which can be true or false') and *also see* p. 267 *et seq.*

[904] For a theoretization of the problem – albeit at a quasi-dogmatic level – *see* Vanpraet, *supra* note 190 (arguing for a recharacterization of the implications of the principle of exclusivity (as opposed to the dogma) in light of its purpose(s)).

[905] Electic both in terms of examples and their contextualization, as in terms of the conceptual relationship between the different values (*cf. supra* No. 119 *et seq.*).

[906] I do not intend this to explicitly mean *discretion* without *any binding* to law whatsoever, but will not engage in the debate that exists on the scope thereof (*see eg* Dworkin, *supra* note 99, at p. 30-39).

in terms of judicial restraint, or in other terms (perhaps even *overall* coherence). Indeed, theoretically, the question of what is the most foundational constraint has been much debated. I will not discuss this issue here[907]. Suffice it to say that I have opted for exactly *these* three 'categories', because they more or less, and admittedly in some cases poorly, reflect some general jurisprudential positions about how constitutional reasoning works.

We can easily associate the *textual* constraint with some brand of 'positivism'[908], whereas the 'coherence' constraint could be associated with more 'interpretive' theories of law. 'Precedent' on point could then be construed as a specific instantiation of *textual* constraints, but because I deal with the issue of *concepts* themselves under the heading of text, I have opted for a separate category here[909]. Even so, I am the first to admit that these categories are neither mutually exclusive, nor exhaustive, nor for that matter perhaps even the best elaboration of how the rule of law must be deemed to be instantiated in legal reasoning.

143. Tension 'in terms of' rule of law values and the difficulty of distinction. Be that as it may, what I do believe the following can show, is how European law can sometimes cause increased[910] tension '*in terms of*' certain rule of law values that the Constitutional Court seeks to uphold.

Let me further elaborate on how I understand 'in terms of' here. I do not argue *how* these values constrain, but rather presuppose *that* they constrain, and argue that in their constraining function, they pose limits on the instrumentality of (the Belgian deployment of) European law, thus again reinforcing the *inherent* tension between instrumentality and rule of law values. As such, the colorful reality I try to describe should not be overshadowed by the analytics which are inserted for purposes of rendition.

Accordingly, I do not elaborate several presuppositions of my argument, which are nonetheless important, in that they account for some of the complexity of the relationship between *instrumentality* and *constraint*. The point we seek to make

---

907 *But see* Raz, *supra* notes 728 and 733, and accompanying text.

908 *See eg* HART, in ESSAYS IN JURISPRUDENCE AND PHILOSOPHY, *supra* note 716, at p. 63-64. For ample other references (including to influential authors such as Fuller, Posner or Eskridge), *see* SHAPIRO, *supra* note 37, at p. 428. It should be noted that Shapiro, however, refutes this connection by restricting positivism to being a *theory* of law (and not of legal reasoning) (*ibid.* at p. 253-254)). He does recognize, that the rule of law 'is served only when those who engage in legal interpretation are faithful to the vision of the Rule of Law that the legal system presupposes and embodies' (*ibid.* at p. 398).

909 *Compare supra* No. 120-121.

910 Compare Popelier contentions about the strenghtening function of European law on internal integrating and disintegrating factors (Popelier, *supra* note 11, at p. 21).

is that the complexity of the relationship is ever-present. Take the following example: imagine case X that could have been solved by Belgian law alone, there being an apparent[911] *precedent* on point. Even so, a preliminary reference to the Court of Justice was made, and the result thereof came in tension with the result warranted by the Belgian precedent. In this case, one could argue that there is an initial conflict between two distinguishable rule of law values, namely the precedential value of either precedent. In this simple case, already, numerous complexities obviously arise: for the determination of the precedential value of any of the cases, can rely upon other rule of law values (*eg* the hierarchy of norms), or upon some instrumental reasons, or even on (a reconciliation of) both. Accordingly, it is clear that a case like this can be represented in a myriad of ways, especially *in terms* of the relationships between rule of law values and instrumentality. Furthermore, that implies that the categories of *instrumentality* and *rule of law values* should not be conceived of too abstractly, nor should their mutual relationship be presupposed to be exclusive. The very difficult theoretical issues of their *concrete* elaboration and the *interlocking* relationships of instantiations that come under the concepts are consciously *not* discussed at length here. Recognizing this limitation, I nonetheless believe that these two concepts are (the most) suitable for investigating how European law can exacerbate tensions in constitutional reasoning, not in the least because the concept of a *tool* seems to come closer to the colorful reality of competence allocation than many other conceptualizations. In that sense, it will be argued that – despite a whole array of underlying conceptual issues – the distinction between rule of law values and instrumentality, and their relationship of either harmony or *in this case* discord, allows for an explanation of the relationship between EU law and constitutional reasoning that goes beyond the classic understanding in terms of primacy, and even adds to the already more sophisticated discourse based on constitutional dialogue and pluralism.

In short: EU law in this context no longer *streamlines* constitutional reasoning[912], but rather, in conjunction with (its or other) rule of law values, it appears to fall prone to and perhaps create additional tension in constitutional reasoning[913].

---

911 We bracket possibilities of distinguishing, overruling and adequately analogizing precedents for the purposes of discussion only.

912 *Cf. supra* Ch. 4.2.1.

913 Neither will I extensively describe how the various forms of tension can be best understood with reference to the specific rule of law values. Here I refer to three rule of law values, but at the same time, I sometimes presuppose other rule of law values (*eg hierarchy of norms / judicial restraint / …*). Accordingly – I emphasize it again – my remarks here should not be comprehended as to create a *system*.

144. The Care Insurance saga as an exemplary case. In elaborating what follows the Care Insurance saga functions as an exemplary case for several reasons. First, it is probably the case in which the tension between European law and Belgian constitutional requirements regarding federalism comes to the fore most clearly[914]. Moreover, the saga has been widely commented upon, both in European and in Belgian legal circles[915]. Third, the saga knits together several cases on the same issue, which allows or at least should allow one to perceive some consistency in the (Belgian Constitutional) Court's reasoning[916]. Finally, the case is about a particularly hot issue in federalism, that is social security[917], which again underscores the importance of the judgment.

---

914 *Eg* Thomas A.J.A. Vandamme, *Case note accompanying Case C-212/06*, 46 Common Market Law Review 287, 299 (2009); Vanpraet, *supra* note 190, at p. 193 (*et seq.*). *Also see* Danny Pieters, De Europese Unie tegen een Vlaamse Sociale Zekerheid? Woonplaatsbeginsel versus werklandbeginsel in de sociale zekerheid: beslist de E.U.? 7-8, 55 *et seq. and also see* 23 *et seq.* (2010).

915 *See,* for instance, the references made by Verschueren in his contribution, especially those made in the first two footnotes, and notes 63-64 (*supra* note 842). Even if this list is not exhaustive at all, it does provide an interesting introduction. The most elaborate list of references available can be found in Storme, *supra* note 142, at p. 1508 n392 and Jürgen Vanpraet, *Naar een Vlaamse Sociale Bescherming binnen het Bestaande bevoegdheidsverdelend kader?* in De gelaagde welvaartsstaat. Naar een Vlaamse Sociale bescherming in België en Europa 155, 157 n7 (Bea Cantillon, Patricia Popelier & Ninke Mussche eds. 2010). Even this list is not exhaustive. It should be noted that due to the large number of sources, I will only be referring to authors *selectively* here, not pursuing any exhaustivity. The best short English-language introductions to facts and background are provided in the book on social federalism, mentioned *supra* note 45, or the following case-note: Peter Van Elsuwege & Stanislas Adam, *Belgium. The limits of constitutional Dialogue for the Prevention of Reverse discrimination* (Case note accompanying CC No. 11/2009 (Jan. 21, 2009)), 5 European Constitutional Law Review 327, 328-330 (2009).

916 This at least, and notwithstanding my earlier remarks (Nos. 119 *et seq.* and 142), allows reasoning in function of the *presupposed* ideal consistency, understood as a corollary of coherence.

917 This is certainly the case in Belgium, where, on the one hand, negotiators are still implementing the sixth round of State reform on the one hand, while, on the other hand, the Flemish Government, continues to develop its own 'care system' (*cf.* Vlaamse Regering (2009-2014), Een daadkrachtig Vlaanderen in beslissende tijden. Voor een vernieuwende, duurzame en warme samenleving 11 (2009)). The recently translated book on the layered welfare state (*supra* note 45) should be understood in this context. Moreover, the social issue is ever more present on the European agenda as well, especially after the ECJ's *Viking* and *Laval* judgments. In that sense, some important European scholars are pleading for a new approach to European constitutionalization in light of the Union's social agenda (*see eg* Christian Joerges, *Reconceptualising the Supremacy of European Law: A Plea for a Supranational Conflict of Laws* in Debating the Democratic Legitimacy of the European Union 311 (B Kohler-Koch & B. Rittberger eds. 2007), best read accompanied by the contributions in Conflict of Laws and Laws of Conflict in Europe and Beyond. Patterns of Supranational and Transnational juridification (Rainer Nickel ed. 2010)).

More reasons could be proffered or conjured up, but before I start, I want to stress that the point I am making here does *not* merely apply to the Care Insurance saga[918], even if I rely on it as a primary example. It is important to reiterate the point, as it is momentarily too early to tell whether the *Belgian* 2009 Care Insurance Judgment will constitute a real precedent[919]. Conversely, it will be explained that the European Care Insurance Judgment could have influence on other issues in Belgian federalism[920].

Using the Care Insurance Judgments as cases which are emblematic of the issues examined allows me to already elaborate some of the context here. In these cases, the Belgian Constitutional Court had to review whether the Flemish Care Insurance scheme could pass constitutional muster. The scheme was established for persons with a serious disability, on the basis of the Flemish Community's conferred autonomy in social assistance matters. It confers entitlements to have an insurance fund take responsibility for the payment of certain costs occasioned by a state of dependence for health reasons on certain persons (members) who come within the ambit of the scheme. Being financed by members' annual contributions and by a grant paid out of the Flemish budget for expenditure, the scheme imposes obligations and confers entitlements primarily on the basis of a residence criterion. Taking into account the adaptations the Flemish legislature adopted after several European Commission objections, the scheme applied (1) compulsorily to residents of the Dutch-speaking language area and (2) on a voluntary basis to residents of the bilingual Brussels-capital language area, excepting, under both 1 and 2, all persons to whom on the basis of the

---

918 *Also see* van Drooghenbroeck, *supra* note 393, at p. 245-246.

919 There is an important distinction to make here between the precedential value of the *Belgian* and the *European* Care Insurance cases. Whereas I *arguendo* accept the precedential value of the European case – in fact, my remarks about the sixth state reform turn on its precedential value – it should be noted that the Belgian case somewhat stands apart. Many authors have inferred specific consequences from this case. Some have succeeded in embedding the case in a broader conceptual logic – for instance, Jürgen Vanpraet in his doctoral dissertation defends the *double aspect thesis*, which implies that certain regulations can be qualified under different competence concepts or objects, implying that certain competences can be exercised in a *parallel fashion* (*supra* note 190). Even so, and notwithstanding the ruckus that emerged as a consequence of the Belgian judgment, we should be careful not to overemphasize the importance of the case. This is not in the least the case, because clearly – even if there is no hard evidence for this – what was reached in Case No. 11/2009 was a compromise. And if the compromise here was not completely incoherent, it has at least been undertheorized by the Court itself. Van Drooghenbroeck makes a similar point (*supra* note 393, at p 245 *et seq.*). *But compare supra* note 826.

920 *See infra* Nos. 179 and 183. *See, in more detail*, Pieters, *supra* note 914, at p. 71-73; Vanpraet, *supra* note 914, at p. 160 *et seq.* (explicitly discussing the possibility of a Flemish hospitalization insurance and a Flemish financial support system for children).

Social Security Regulation (No 1408/71) a social security scheme of another European Member State applies, and including, under both 1 and 2 in their respective modalities, all persons not residing in Belgium, but working either in the Dutch-speaking or the bilingual language area who, on the basis of the Social Security Regulation, are subject to Belgian social security law.

The Belgian Constitutional Court had earlier accepted that the Flemish Community had stayed within the bounds of its material and territorial constitutional authority when it adapted the Care Insurance Decree.[921] Nonetheless, in 2006, the Court still referred the case to the Luxembourg for a preliminary ruling on a number of questions, the most important ones of which pertained to whether the scope of the scheme violated the European provisions on the free movement of persons. The scheme indeed, even taking into account the modifications that had been adopted in light of the Social Security Regulation, still excluded persons working in the Flemish or Brussels Regions who were living in the Walloon Region from its scope[922].

The Court of Justice distinguished in its ruling between purely internal situations and situations falling within the scope of the European Treaties[923]. More precisely, it held that EU law would be applicable to Walloon residents who both worked in Flanders and had exercised their freedom to move within the EU. Excluded from the scope of EU law were residents in Wallonia who were working in Flanders, but who had never exercised their European free movement rights. The Court then ruled that the condition of residence, which triggered either the obligation or ability to join the Care Insurance Scheme, violated the free movement requirements of articles 45 and 49 TFEU[924], but – more or less obviously – only for persons coming within the scope of EU law[925].

A couple of months later in 2009 back in Brussels, the Constitutional Court accepted the distinguishing criterion deployed in Luxembourg, namely persons 'hav[ing] made use of their right to freedom of movement within the European

[921] In CA No. 33/2001 (Mar. 13, 2001) B.3.4, B.3.7 and B.3.9, the Court had held that the Flemish Community had stayed within the bounds of its material competence. In CA No. 51/2006 (Apr. 19, 2006) B.7-B.9.8, the Court ruled that the scheme respected the principle of exclusive territoriality, because it tried to accommodate the earlier European objections.

[922] *Cf.* CA No. 51/2006 (Apr. 19, 2006) B.12.3, B.12.4 and B.13.4.

[923] Case C-212/06 (GC; Apr. 1, 2008) *Government of the French Community and Walloon Government v Flemish Government* [hereinafter: *Flemish Care Insurance*], paras 37-39.

[924] *Ex* articles 39 and 43 TEC.

[925] Case C-212/06 (GC; Apr. 1, 2008), *Flemish Care Insurance,* para 38-39; *but see ibid.* para 40.

[Union]'[926], and in fact dichotomized its own judgment[927]. As for the European part, *ie* the part of the judgment considering persons falling within the scope of EU law, the Belgian Court faithfully copied the considerations made by Luxembourg[928]. As regards the 'purely internal [Belgian] situations', the Court was more equivocal. Surely it concluded that the residence criterion did *not* violate the Belgian EMU, but its reasoning here is uncommon at best, and probably just plainly ambiguous.[929] One reason underlying this ambiguity will be discussed further on. Now, however, we first turn to the *text* as a rule of law value that precludes the Court from instrumentalizing European law.

4.4.1 Authoritative texts

145. Between freedom and constraint. Legal texts which are deemed authoritative on a particular issue are not only amenable to function as tools, but – simultaneously, and as a result of a complex process of interaction the systematic elaboration of which falls beyond the scope of this book – as constraints. Above, I suggested that *texts* do not only have a constraining function, but also lend themselves to *instrumentalization*. I am aware of the fact that I am stretching the analysis here, in the following sense. One could ask: if the tool-like account is not radically realist, why can rule of law values not be incorporated into the account? Or perhaps the other way around: why can the 'more instrumental' considerations of functions not be entrenched within a *rule of law* account of the Court's reasoning? I readily concede the pertinence of such questions, but I am not theorizing the issue at large. For pragmatic purposes, I think working with a distinction between tools and rule of law values – or between what Duncan Kennedy' called *freedom and constraint* in adjudication[930] – remains justified, not only for the reasons elaborated above[931], but also because – notwithstanding complexities in practice – the distinction remains analytically and intuitively intelligible.

Such a "justification", however, still leaves many issues unsolved, such as the question *to which extent* a text can or should indeed constrain judicial behavior, or what methods of interpretation can or should be used in constitutional adjudication. In fact, it could be argued that many of the jurisprudential debates of the last century indeed turn upon the question to what extent a *text* can or

926 *Ibid.* para 34; *cf.* CC No. 11/2009 (Jan. 21, 2009) B.8.1.

927 *Ibid.* B.7.

928 *Ibid.* B.8.1 *et seq.*, *esp.* B.9 and B.10.1. *Also see* Feyen, *supra* note 792, at p. 173-74.

929 On the ambiguity, *see* Feyen, *supra* note 32.

930 *Supra* note 93.

931 *See supra* note 110 and accompanying text.

should constrain a judge, or at least whether from a legal point of view, it should be deemed to constrain a judge.

Even if I do not enter this debate here, I would like to argue that European law, on the one hand, is sometimes limited in its tool-like function by authoritative texts, and furthermore suggest, on the other hand, that European law exacerbates the existing tension between the instrumental modus of reasoning (admittedly possibly on the basis of texts and principles that have been developed in due course) and the constraining function that an authoritative text performs (admittedly possibly constraining for an instrumental reason).

146. Implicit constraint. Reading through the Constitutional Court's jurisprudence in general, one could argue that European law obligations[932] are often curtailed by national texts[933]. Still, it is difficult to find occasions where an explicit constitutional text[934] stands in the way – at least directly – of European

[932] Depending of course on how these obligations are construed and on the question of whether a real conflict can be thought to have emerged. This of course also has ramifications on the meaning of 'to curtail', which I refrain from further defining here.

[933] *See eg* CA No. 57/2005 (Mar. 16, 2005) B.9.2 (on legality, at least to the extent that *law* is thought to emerge as an explicit constitutional *concept*, rather than principle, in which case European law would indeed not be constrained as such by the *text* but rather by the *principle*, and arguably *precedent* and *coherence* – *compare supra* No. 119 *et seq.*, read in light of how art. 170 Cons. might be an 'exception')). *But compare* CA No. 110/2001 (Sep. 20, 2001) B.3.3 *et seq.* (on facultative exceptions foreseen in Directive 94/19/EC on deposit guarantees, which were not followed by the Belgian government) *with* CA No. 118/2003 (Sep. 17, 2003) B.3.4 ('the way in which a legislature deploys an opportunity foreseen in a Directive, must be justified in light of art. 10 and 11 Cons.'). *Also compare* CA No. 32/2000 (Mar. 21, 2000) B.3.7 (on introducing a criterion not foreseen by a Directive) (on these last three cases, *see* Van Nuffel, *supra* note 828, at p. 261-63).

[934] Constitutional, on the one hand, because we for now accept that mere (special) *laws* are subject the prevalence of European law. Moreover, it should be noted that here, the distinction between *text* and *interpretation* thereof becomes particularly problematic. Accordingly, it could be argued that the *text* of the Constitution (instead of its interpretation) itself constrains European law as a tool in the Care Insurance case (one could even characterize my own case note in this sense; *cf.* Feyen, *supra* note 792, at p. 172-73). This issue, however, on the one hand turns on solutions to difficult hermeneutical problems. If we are, for example, to follow Roland Barthes' post-modernist position, the *text* of the Constitution viewed isolatedly could be argued to have no separate meaning from its interpretation (*eg The Death of the Author* in Image, Music, Text 142 (Stephen Heath trans. 1977)). Less radical voices are ubiquitous, but the most profound works in hermeneutics, at least recognize the difficulties of separating a text and its interpretation (*eg (mutatis mutandis* applicable vis-à-vis legal interpretation) Paul Ricoeur, Interpretation Theory: Discourse and the Surplus of Meaning 9 *et seq., esp.* 12-13 (1976) (on the distinction between, or rather dialectic of event and meaning, and the doubly noetic-noematic structure of meaning)). On the other hand, it raises questions on how the Constitutional Court would deal, in light of the hierarchy of norms, with European norms conflicting with either provisions of the Constitution, or provisions of the Special Law which have a 'quasi-constitutional' status, such as the EMU (*also see infra* on coherence).

law exerting an influence on competence allocation problems. This is not eminently surprising. On the one hand, knowing that the constitutional text will be the first point of reference for the Belgian Court, which is – at least historically – steeped in a positivist tradition, it is to be expected that the Court will have difficulties explicitly putting aside a text as reference norm. On the other hand, European law's ambiguous position in the hierarchy of norms, coupled with a growing importance of judicial dialogue, will prevent the Court from explicitly putting aside European law[935]. Accordingly, if we are to look for instances where the text curtails European law as a tool, we are likely to find these *implicitly* in the Court's jurisprudence. Conversely, the implicit nature renders the tension more indirect, and hence precludes us from finding any explicit instantiations – leaving generalizations aside – of where European law's influence on competence allocation is curtailed by a text. That of course lands us in a (far-fetched) hypothetical (were the *text* might be argued to indirectly (or implicitly) constrain European law), and we declared not to discuss these earlier. Nonetheless I discuss the *text* in a separate section, primarily because generally, it seems to be the most direct point of reference, in terms of discerning meaning, or at least that seems to be the presupposition which has been institutionalized in what is often called 'positivistic' legal reasoning.

147. Article 34 of the Constitution: constraint? Even if in the field of competence allocation the Court has not yet had to deal with an explicit text allocating competences causing a stir or direct tension in terms of European legal obligations, I nonetheless want to mention article 34 of the Constitution here, which allows for the 'exercis[e] of specific powers [...] to be assigned by a treaty or by a law to institutions of public international law', since recently, the Constitutional Court seems to have been relying on this article to conceptualize the relationship between constitutional law in general and (secondary) European law[936]. Although no general theory is readily

[935] The Court, in the determination of its jurisdiction vis-à-vis European law, seems to have tried to find some sort of balance here (with reference to the *Lanaken* jurisprudence; *cf. supra* notes 747-749).

[936] *Compare* CA No. 32/2000 (Mar. 21, 2000) B.3.7 (the Court cannot review measures in light of article 34 of the Constitution) *with* CA No. 126/2005 (July 13, 2005) A.3.3 and B.10-B.12 (where one could argue that the Court implicitly accepted art. 34 as a fulfilling a bridge-function, but where at the same time, the validity of a Directive was in play; *cf.* CC No. 17/2009 (Feb. 12, 2009) B.6.1-B.6.3 read in light of A.3.1 and CC No. 128/2009 (July 24, 2009)) and *especially with* CC No. 130/2010 (Nov. 18, 2010) B.8.1 (European law as a justification for a difference in treatment). *Also see* CC No. 37/2010 (Apr. 22, 2010) B.10 (on regulations having direct applicability in Belgium *through* article 34 Cons.). *See* (all critically, albeit from different perspectives) Stéphanie De Somer, *Internationale impuls en nationale zelfbeheersingsdrang inzake bestuurlijke verzelfstandiging: het Grondwettelijk Hof en de*

available[937], we already pointed out that the answer to particular questions may or at least could turn on the question of primacy. Even if the Court seems to rely on article 34 of the Constitution to account for European law taking an ever more important place in Belgian constitutional discourse, there is little doubt that when the constitutional text itself *clearly* prohibits a situation European law requires or *vice versa*, that the Constitutional Court will not easily side with the European law arguments[938], or if it would, that some legal scholars will cry havoc over it[939].

Of course these contemplations are too general and simplistic to make a profound point, as they leave aside important – often interdependent – issues such as 'what is a conflict?', 'how relevant is the question of primacy?', and so on. However, it remains an important broad conceptual point to make that in acknowledging the growing influence of European law on Belgian constitutional – be it through more preliminary references, more reliance upon European law in general, or evinced differently – and in at the same time relying on article

casus van de energie-regulator, case note accompanying CC No. 130/2010, 2012 TBP 214, 217 *et seq*.; Koen Muylle, *Het Grondwettelijk Delegatieverbod en het Unierecht: welke democratisch verkozen beraadslagende vergadering*, in 3 LEUVENSE STAATSRECHTELIJKE STANDPUNTEN, *supra* note 67, at p. 340 *et seq*., *esp*. 351-352; and Emmanuel Slautsky, *Droit européen, Constitution et autorités administratives indépendantes*, case note accompanying CC No. 130/2010 and CoS No. 212.557, 2012 APT 99, 111-112.

937 The CoS has tried to devise such a 'theory' – it is only one paragraph actually – on the basis of article 34 of the Constitution. *See* the *Orfinger* case (CoS No. 62.922 (Nov. 5, 1996) at p. 14-17 (where the Council stresses, on the one hand, that it is not generally adjudicating the issue of primacy as such, but rather the issue of interpretation but on the other hand, that European law prevails in general in case of conflict), where the Council held that a provision of the TFEU (back then TEC), when in conflict with the non-discrimination prohibition in the Constitution, should prevail. *Also see* VELAERS, DE GRONDWET EN DE RAAD VAN STATE, *supra* note 13, at p. 236-41.

938 Accordingly, former Constitutional Judge Paul Martens urged in considerations which are (anachronistically reminiscent of the German Constitutional Court's now famous Lisbon Judgment; *cf.* SOTTIAUX, *supra* note 210, 1 *et seq*., for an in depth discussion) that whereas the issue about European influence is 'the most delicate question being considered', as long as Europe is not a nation state, 'it would be rash to want to renounce our control or to reduce its scope' (Paul Martens, *Final Conclusions*, in 2 LES RELATIONS, *supra* note 15, at p. 777, 779).

939 An analogy can here be drawn with the Maastricht treaty that did in fact impose requirements that were quite blatantly unconstitutional, *ie* pertaining to voting rights of EU citizens. Whereas the CoS argued that a constitutional revision was necessary before the Treaty could be approved (*eg Parl. Doc.* Chamber 1991-92 SS, No. 482/1, at p. 69-71, and *also see* 74-85), the Government failed to take this advice into direct account (*ibid.* at p. 90), and it took up till 1998 to adapt art. 8 Cons. to European law. The CoS said in the context of art 34 Cons. in this regard that although this article renders its possible to transfer certain powers to the Union, it 'cannot justify that European citizens are granted political rights that render it possible for them to cooperate in the organization of municipal councils' (*ibid.* at p. 71). *Also see eg* VELAERS, DE GRONDWET EN DE RAAD VAN STATE, *supra* note 13, at p. 61, with references in n13.

34 of the *Constitution* to construe the relationship between international (or perhaps more narrowly: secondary European) law and constitutional law, the Court has worked itself into an ever more broad conceptual split, which might exacerbate the tension between instrumentality and rule of law values in general by adding a surplus layer of complexity to the equation, both in terms of hierarchy (as a rule of law value) and in terms of legal foundations (as perhaps *the* rule of law value).

148. Congruent concepts and constraint? This is not even nearly the end of the story, however. Not only European law can be limited in its tool-like functions by concepts elaborated in Belgian authoritative texts. Indeed, the interpretation of the Belgian texts, and more specifically, the concepts deployed in the Belgian rules governing the allocation of competences might also be constrained by European law, which in the latter case can be represented as a 'rule of law'-like[940] restraint on the tool-like deployment of Belgian texts.

The example of 'waste' (as a competence category) has often been brought up in the past[941]. The Constitutional Court in earlier cases has explicitly adopted the European definition of waste, in order to define the concept contained in the SLIR. Other, more recent examples include 'product norms'[942] or of 'regulated'

[940] That again depends on the hierarchy of norms. It should be noted that the examples pertain to concepts elaborated in the SLIR, which has the quality of a *law* (albeit a *special* law), and is hence subject to – according to established jurisprudence of the Constitutional Court – the primacy of European law. *Also see*, very explicitly (but not a constant in case law: *compare* A.21.5 of the judgment and *see* Vanden heede & Goedertier, *supra* note 226, at p. 263-64) CC No. 84/2010 (July 8, 2010) B.22.2. ('interpreting a provision contrary to European Union law is not reasonable justifiable and the resulting difference in treatment is incompatible with art. 10- 11 Cons., read together with the Second Gas Directive') *juncto* Case C-241/09 (Dec. 9, 2010) *Fluxys*.
That, however, is only one way to look at the problem: as the European definition of waste was proffered by the Belgian special legislature in the *travaux préparatoires*, it might as well be argued that it is pursuant to a *specifically* Belgian obligation that the Constitutional Court elaborated and defined the concept as it did. Expounding upon this debate would, however, once again, drag us into several hard theoretical issues which we want to avoid confronting right now. *Cf. supra* introductory chapter.

[941] *Eg* CA No. 52 (Mar. 17, 1988) III.B.1.2. (where the Court even implied that *because* the definition was in conformity with European law, there could be no violation of competence allocation – III.B.1.4), with references to Directive 75/442/EEC on waste; *cf.* CA No. 1/89 (Jan. 31, 1989) III.B.2.1 (*but compare* III.B.2.3). *See* Lavrysen, *supra* note 333, *passim* (especially look at the discussion of cases 1/89 and 12/89); Melchior & Vandernoot, *supra* note 842, at p. 22 (providing further references to case law); Popelier, *supra* note 16, at p. 148; Van Nuffel, *supra* note 828, at p. 40-41 (both further elaborating). *Also see* Jadot, *supra* note 646, at p. 727 *et seq.* (discussing the issue from a broader environmental perspective).

[942] CC No. 149/2010 (Dec. 22, 2010) B.5.1-B.5.2, with references to Advice 2007/0266/B of the European Commission on biofuel. *Compare* Toon Moonen, *De afbakening van het begrip*

and 'unregulated traffic'[943] as concepts which have been *defined* in terms of European law.

Even if it should be noted that, in this latter case, European law again tends to *streamline* constitutional reasoning, it is no constant that concepts are congruently defined or interpreted. On the contrary, we will argue that the autonomous nature of the concepts is one of the reasons why European law might sometimes fail to streamline constitutional reasoning[944].

149. More inherent tension? We have now pointed out how European law sometimes plays a role in the determination of the *concepts* deployed in constitutional reasoning so as to establish who is competent for what. It yet remains the question whether European law here exacerbates the *inherent* tension between instrumentality and rule of law. At first sight this is not the case, for in this case the Court *streamlines* its reasoning in line with the European definition. However, additional considerations have to be taken into account, and one simple hypothetical might clarify how the tension can indeed be increased in practice.

If European law indeed *defines* the meaning of 'waste' or 'product norm', and if – as the Court has sometimes stressed[945] – the concepts working in the SLIR are mutually exclusive, then a European change in the definition of 'waste' or 'product norm' by implication might change the meaning of other competence-allocating concepts. When this meaning is changed in turn, this not only unsettles the relationships between the different principles which are at hand in *interpreting* what the law is[946], but it can also put some tension on the *text* itself,

productnorm als aanknopingspunt voor de federale restbevoegdheden inzake leefmilieu, case-note accompanying CC No. 149/2010, 2011 MER 110, 112 (the federal government sought to obtain environmental goals, like the European legislators, but if this occurs through settling product norms, the goal is of less importance).

943 CC No. 117/2010 (Oct. 21, 2010) B.3.3-B.3.4.

944 *Infra* Ch. 5.3.

945 *See eg* CA No. 11 (Feb. 25, 1986) III.3.B.2 ('[i]t stems from the fact that the special legislature [...] has introduced different conferrals of competences that these conferrals necessarily have a distinct content'). This premise of the line of reasoning deployed here has also recently been put under pressure by Jürgen Vanpraet's doctoral thesis, who argues that different regulations might come under *several* competence headings (double aspect thesis). Vanpraet, *supra* note 190; Vanpraet, *supra* note 914 (a shorter English version of the latter article has been published in Jürgen Vanpraet, *Towards a two-speed social security system in federal Belgium?* in Social Federalism, *supra* note 45, at p. 161 *et seq*.). As will be clear from what precedes, and from what follows on reification, we do not accept this doctrinal argument as dispositive in any sense (*also see the subsequent notes*).

946 I submit that the force of this logical implication *prima facie* depends on the presupposition that the meaning of the concepts deployed in the texts is settled, and that there is *prima facie*

to the extent that a *clear* Belgian competence allocation text might be at odds with a European definition of a specific concept[947]. In that case, it will be far less easy for the Constitutional Court to freely deploy European reasons in a piece of Belgian constitutional reasoning, at least if it does not explicitly opt to follow along European lines[948].

The examples elaborated here are obviously non-exhaustive, neither in the sense that there are no other conceivable examples in the *categories* of concepts that have been either accorded a *European* meaning or have been limiting of European influence in a specific authoritative text, nor in the sense that no other examples could be provided in which it becomes clear that a *text* might, in terms of European law, constrain the tool-like use of competence-allocation law.

150. Limits of constraint. Even if it is hard to deny the *text* here was represented as a vehicle of constraint on the Court's freedom to deploy different sets of reasoning in order to solve federalism problems, this does not mean that the Court looses all, or for that matter even a lot of its grip on the representation and constitution of this reasoning. Indeed, in the case of waste and products norms, the Court relied on the *travaux préparatoires* that explicitly referred to the European law definitions of waste and product norms[949]. Even if the European definition would change, the question could be raised whether the Constitutional Court would have to modify its own definitions. The same considerations in turn apply *vice versa*[950].

---

uniformity between European law and Belgian law as regards the concept at play. An easy argument could accordingly be made that *since* the meaning is not settled this implication looses much of its *exacerbating* force. That, however, would at least partially miss the point: for the core of this particular argument is the added layer of complexity that European law provides, as it might, if the interpretative principle of meaningful variation is held constant, *destabilize* the compromise or balance the (special) legislature struck in elaborating the meaning of the SLIR. On how the other presupposition (uniformity) plays out, *see infra* Ch. 5.

[947] The parties in proceedings before the Constitutional Court sometimes rely upon this line of argumentation implicitly or explicitly. *Compare* CC No. 147/2010 (Oct. 21, 2010) A.1, A.4 *and* B.3.3 (on definitions of regulated traffic and unregulated traffic, where the Flemish concept of 'traffic on one's own account' constituted a potential problem); *compare supra* note 776 (on case 75/2012).

[948] Indeed, some of the preliminary references to the Court of Justice can be understood as trying to attain just that. *See eg* CA No. 6/97 (Feb. 19, 1997), as discussed in Vuillermoz, *supra* note 42, at p. 580 *et seq., esp.* 585-88; *also see supra* No. 124.

[949] CC 149/2010 (Dec. 22, 2010) B.5.1, referring to *Parl. Doc.* Chamber 2008-09, No. 2037/001, at p. 5 and 8 and *see* references *supra* note 941 (on waste). *Adde* Vuillermoz, *supra* note 42, at p. 412-17.

[950] Would it be that much of a stretch to see for instance No. 121/2008 (Sep. 1, 2008) *esp.* B.15.3 as an instantiation of this problem, at least from a conceptual relational perspective, further giving meaning to the concepts by which the larger concept of waste is defined, in this case

Finally, and this closes the circle, because of the myriad of unarticulated and unsolved underlying issues here, the conceptualization will turn on how *interpretation* and *influence* are construed as concepts or principles themselves[951].

4.4.2 Precedent

151. Limits on instrumentality by precedent: the example of exclusive territoriality. The instrumental nature of the (European) tool is limited not only by authoritative texts, but also by the Constitutional Court's own precedents. My focus here does not lie so much on the definition of concepts, but rather on contentious points of law which have been explicitly decided upon by the Court and which come back into play afterwards[952]. The example I find most relevant in this context is that of exclusive territoriality: when the Court has held that a particular law or decree does not violate the requirements of territorial exclusivity, but the issue is brought back up later and indirectly under a different argument, the precedent decision constrains the Court's free use of the new (European) argument. I believe that is how the Care Insurance cases can be understood.

152. Care Insurance precedents. When the Care Insurance issue landed on the doorsteps of the Court of Justice in Luxemburg, the Constitutional Court had set at least[953] two precedents in the case[954]. In 2001, the Court had held that the Communities, on the basis of their social assistance competence, could assist persons which were not expressly named in the

burning as a means of disposing of waste? *Also see* Nicolas De Sadeleer, *La definition juridique de déchet est-elle évolutive?* (case note accompanying CA No. 19/97 (Apr. 15, 1997)) 1997 Aménagement-Environnement 279, at p. 283 and Vuillermoz, *supra* note 42, at p. 585 (both on the relationship between CA No. 1/89 and 19/97 in light of the definition of waste).

951 *See supra* Ch. 1.

952 Although the distinction is not sacred at all (*cf. supra* note 934 and accompanying text).

953 I disregard the first suspension case, which was deemed inadmissible for lack of standing (CA No. 9/2000 (Jan. 19, 2000)), as well as the interstitial judgment where the case was opened for redeliberation (CA No. 16/2006 (Jan. 25, 2006)) and which led up to CA No. 51/2006. I do not expressly discuss the 2003 case in which the Court held that the Care Insurance Scheme did not resort under the federal 'insurance control' competence heading (CA No. 8/2003 (Jan. 22, 2003) B.3 *et seq., esp.* B.7, where the Court held that the Scheme did not have 'as its object or objective to modify the federal legislation pertaining to insurance law nor the regulations or controls on insurance companies').

954 I do not discuss the different modifications of the Decree, sometimes in response to comments by the European Commission. For a relevant overview up till 2006, *see eg* CA No. 51/2006 (Apr. 19, 2006).

SLIR[955] through a system the modalities of which could be freely chosen, at least within the bounds of the principle of proportionality and the EMU[956] and taking the constraints into account which are imposed by specific reservations of competence[957]. In the 2006 companion case[958], it expressly[959] held that the scheme respected the principle of exclusive territoriality[960], because it tried to accommodate the European aspirations[961] but it still referred – what was framed to be – another set of issues to the Court of Justice[962]. The latter quite unsurprisingly held that the Flemish Care Insurance Scheme fell within the ambit of the Social Security Regulation[963] and it found a problem with non-Belgian nationals working in Flanders but residing in the Walloon Region, who

---

955 CA No. 33/2001 (Mar. 13, 2001) B.3.4. (here it relied on the extensive interpretation of social assistance). *See* B.3.7 and B.3.9.3 (the fact that the same persons are addressed as those envisaged by other schemes does not abridge the Community's competence). Here the concept of 'matter' clearly helps the Court to sidestep the issue (*cf.* Vansteenkiste, *supra* note 551, at p. 57; *also see* CA No. 51/2006 (Apr. 19, 2006) B.9.4; *cf. supra* No. 96).

956 CA No. 33/2001 (Mar. 13, 2001) B.3.5., B.3.9.1-B.3.9.3. The Court argued that the EMU was respected because of the 'limited amount and effect' of the measures (B.3.9.2). *Also see* CA No. 8/2003 (Jan. 22, 2003) B.5. The considerations were repeated for the new version of the decree in CA No. 51/2006 (Apr. 19, 2006) B.10.1 *et seq., esp.* B.10.3.

957 CA No. 33/2001 (Mar. 13, 2001) B.3.7 (where the Court held that the Care Insurance scheme constitutes neither a regulation of the subsistence minimum, nor a regulation of financing subsidies for disabled persons). *See* B.3.9.3, where the Court distinguished the Care Insurance Scheme from schemes falling under the federal 'social security' competence heading, by emphasizing that a conflict regulation was built in to the decree vis-à-vis specific benefits, and by stressing that the scheme set up by the decree was 'distinct' from the federal schemes. *Also see* CA No. 51/2006 (Apr. 19, 2006) B.10.4-B.10.5. *But compare* Xavier Delgrange, *La Cour d'Arbitrage momifie la compétence fédérale en matière de sécurité sociale*, 2001 RBDC 209, esp. 237; Popelier, *supra* note 45, at p. 98 *et seq.*; Vanpraet, *supra* note 945, at p. 161 *et seq.*; Velaers, *supra* note 531, at p. 146-48; Velaers & Vanpraet, *supra* note 388, at p. 214-16 (all critical of the alleged 'distinct' nature of the federal schemes, albeit on different grounds: whereas Delgrange pleads for federal exclusivity, Velaers and especially Vanpraet stand by a more parallel interpretation of social security powers on the basis of No. 11/2009 and Popelier argues, *de lege ferenda*, for more shared powers) and Storme, *supra* note 142, at p. 409 (critical of the argument relying on conflict regulation due to its lack of generalizability).

958 Notice how all the relevant considerations from the previous cases are requoted in CA No. 51/2006 (Apr. 19, 2006) B.1.5, quoting CA No. 33/2001 (Mar. 13, 2001) B.3.1-B.5.5 and CA No. 51/2006 (Apr. 19, 2006) B.2.3, quoting CA No. 8/2003 (Jan. 22, 2003) B.3-B.8 (underscoring the precedential value).

959 It already had held the same in 2001, at least pertaining to the regulation in Brussels, where people could freely choose to either adhere to the schemes or not (CA No. 33/2001 (Mar. 13, 2001) B.4.1-B.4.4). Hence, the care insurance scheme regulation did not infringe the principle of non-subnationality in Brussels.

960 CA No. 51/2006 (Apr. 19, 2006) B.7-B.9.8.

961 CA No. 51/2006 (Apr. 19, 2006) B.9.6-B.9.7.

962 CA No. 51/2006 (Apr. 19, 2006) B.11 *et seq.*

963 Case C-212/06 (GC; Apr. 1, 2008) *Flemish Care Insurance*, paras. 19-23.

were excluded from the Decree's applicability[964]. Whereas it emphasized that Union law cannot be applied to internal situations[965], it relied on the criterion of 'hav[ing] made use of their right to freedom of movement within the European [Union]'[966] to distinguish the internal situations from those to which EU law could (directly) apply. The result was that under a European obligation – and indeed one stemming directly from the treaty[967] – the connecting factor of residence could not be accepted due to lack of adequate justification[968], not only with reference to non-Belgian residents living in the Walloon Region and working in Flanders but also regarding Belgian residents who had made use of their European freedom of movement.

153. 2009 Care Insurance Case: splitting the difference. Now the Constitutional Court in the 2009 care insurance case was faced with a mind-twisting puzzle[969]. On the one hand, it was almost inconceivable for the Constitutional Court in light of this specific European dictum to simply ignore the Court of Justice[970]. On the other hand, the Court of Justice had rejected the arguments

[964] For stylistic purposes, I simplify the issue here, and exclude, for instance, comments on the Decree's applicability in Brussels, from the generalizations in the (main) text.

[965] Case C-212/06 (GC; Apr. 1, 2008) *Flemish Care Insurance,* paras. 38-39. The Court notoriously suggested that 'interpretation of provisions of [Union] law might possibly be of use to the national court, having regard too to situations classed as purely internal, in particular if the law of the Member State concerned were to require every national of that State to be allowed to enjoy the same rights as those which a national of another Member State would derive from [Union] law in a situation considered to be comparable by that court' (*ibid.* para 40).

[966] Case C-212/06 (GC; Apr. 1, 2008) *Flemish Care Insurance*, para. 34.

[967] Velaers & Vanpraet, *supra* note 388, at p. 204, relying on Herwig Verschueren, *De regionalisering van de sociale zekerheid in België in het licht van het arrest van het Europees Hof van Justitie inzake de Vlaamse zorgverzekering*, 2008 Belgisch Tijdschrift voor Sociale Zekerheid 177, 225. *See* Verschueren, *supra* note 842, at p. 203-04.

[968] Case C-212/06 (GC; Apr. 1, 2008) *Flemish Care Insurance*, paras. 42 *et seq.*, *esp.* 56 and 59. The Court refused to accept justifications based on the internal constitutional situations of the member state (*ibid.* paras 57-58). Interesting in this regard is the Opinion by A-G Mengozzi (Mar. 4, 2010) accompanying case C-46/08, *Carmen Media Group v. Land Schleswig-Holstein et al.*, §§ 58-59, where he deals with the territorial division of powers in a member state in light of Treaty obligations. The Court itself, Case C-46/08 (GC; Sep. 10, 2010), *Carmen Media Group v. Land Schleswig-Holstein et al.* did not readdress this issue.

[969] I do not mean to suggest that the Court brought this conundrum upon itself. It was indeed the French Community Government which raised the specific European issues here (CA No. 51/2006 (Apr. 19, 2006) A.3.1, A.3.3, A.4.1), and the Court had little room to outmaneuver these arguments, since the Flemish Government itself, by adapting its decree several times, acknowledged that European influence was salient here. My point is accordingly not that the Court set up a trap itself, but rather that it faced pressure from rule of law values which undermined its possibility to deploy European law in a tool-like manner. *Compare supra* Nos 128-129.

[970] I do not mean that to suggest *in this consideration* that the Constitutional Court necessarily accepted the primacy of European law in general (*compare* Feyen, *supra* note 792, at p.

stemming from the internal allocation of powers explicitly. If the latter arguments were merely relevant without preliminaries, the Court could have perhaps still found a way around them, but in this case, the Court had already explicitly adjudicated the issues of the EMU and the territorial basis of the judgment.

Hence, the Court adopted a solution trying to split the difference.

First, it accepted the governance of the issue by European law, insofar as persons would come within the ambit of European law. The Court was clearly aware of the tension between the discrimination that had been established by the Court of Justice dictum, and the requirements of Belgian constitutional law. On the one hand, the Court believed that European law required it not to ratchet down protection, accordingly allowing the 'extra persons' to enjoy the benefits of the care insurance[971]. On the other hand, it was duly aware that this would create tension in terms of the principle of territoriality. It could have chosen to ignore this issue, but it in first instance preferred to follow the Court of Justice here. In line with and referring to Luxembourg, it accepted that the 'requirements inherent in the allocation within Belgium's federal structure and especially the

---

173 *with* Velaers & Vanpraet, *supra* note 388, at p. 206). Furthermore, it is not wholly inconceivable that the Court *interprets* specific legal obligations differently from these imposed by Europe. Elke Cloots has pointed out the very relevant example of the Laundering cases, where also a preliminary reference was involved (Elke Cloots, *Rechterlijke samenwerking in een pluralistische Europese rechtsorde. De 'witwasdialoog' als casus*, 197 Nieuw Juridisch Weekblad 146, 154-57 (Feb. 25, 2009) and Cloots, *supra* note 795). Even so, in these Laundering cases, the distinction in interpretation did not pertain to the 'core' of the case, in several respects. Cloots itself points out that an 'attentative reading' of the Belgian case was necessary and that the Belgian Court's construal is 'not necessarily congruent with the European interpretation' – Elke Cloots, *Grondwettelijk Hof plaatst grondrechten boven secundair EU-recht,* Juristenkrant (Mar. 12, 2008) 15). I concede her point, and her construal of the conflict is anything but unreasonable. However, it remains an interpretative collision that would in no way be comparable to the Court, in the care insurance cases, directly ignoring the particularly clear dictum of the Court of Justice pertaining to situations coming within the ambit of European law. Surely, most scholars have argued that even in the Care Insurance case the dialogue between the Constitutional Court and the Court of Justice went somewhat astray (*eg* Buelens & Judo, *supra* note 851, at p. 185 *et seq.*), but that pertains to the *second* part of the 2009 Constitutional Court judgment (on internal situations), and not so much on the dictum of the Court of Justice itself, the prevalence of which is by and large uncontested even by those who explicitly seem to plead against drawing broad inferences on question of primacy of European law from the 2009 judgment (*eg* Velaers & Vanpraet, *supra* note 388, at p. 207-08). *Cf.* Pieters, *supra* note 914, at p. 65-66. I do not further discuss here how the Constitutional Court was thought in *Bressol* to diverge from the interpretations by the Court of Justice (CC No. 89/2011 (May 31, 2011); *see* Verrijdt, *supra* note 743, at p. 79 (noting that the Constitutional Court here did not follow the Court of Justice, and criticized it for not taking financial aspects sufficiently into account)), since *Bressol* was not an important *communautarian* case (*cf. infra* note 1104).

971 *See eg* CC No. 11/2009 (Jan. 21, 2009) B.10.2 and B.18.

fact that the Flemish Community is not competent pertaining to care insurance vis-à-vis persons residing on the territory of a different community, cannot justify the questioned difference in treatment'[972]. Conversely, going this far, the Court had to find a way to justify the European 'extension' of the scope *ratione personae* of the Flemish decree in light of the principle of exclusive territoriality. It here relied upon 'necessity flowing from European [Union] law', the fact that a relatively limited group of persons was involved and the conflict-avoiding provisions in the Flemish decree[973]. Velaers and Vanpraet have discerned a parallel with the implied powers doctrine here[974], which could be deployed in a *territorial* context on the basis of European necessity. That could be a fine dogmatic characterization of what the Court has been doing. However, in the broader context, the Court did not need these considerations to adjudicate the issue before it. The reason why it added them, is clearly to underscore that European law *cannot* in principle be thought to seriously derange the allocation of powers, even if, as it was the case here, it can put pressure on the principle of territoriality to some extent. If the Court would have explicitly taken up the implied powers discourse, it could have reopened some of the issues discussed during the Carrefour saga.

However, as regards the purely internal situations, the Court merely roughly upheld its precedents. The 'roughly' is important here. Velaers and Vanpraet are right to criticize the Court for succeeding to decide upon none of the relevant issues in this regard[975]. However, it is clear that the reason why the Court did not streamline its decision according to the suggestion the Court of Justice had provided in paragraph 40 of the Flemish Care Insurance case, was to be found in its adherence to the principle of territoriality[976]. The added difficulty seemed to be the EMU, but I will revisit that issue later[977].

154. Two "perspectives" allowing generalization: empirical and normative. How can we now adequately generalize the issues raised here in terms of the relationship between European law and constitutional rules governing allocation of powers? I believe two distinct "perspectives" could be offered.

---

[972] CC No. 11/2009 (Jan. 21, 2009) B.10.2

[973] *Compare supra* notes 956-957.

[974] Velaers & Vanpraet, *supra* note 388, at p. 206

[975] *Supra* note 388, at p. 210 et seq.

[976] *Supra* note 388, at p. 211.

[977] *See infra* Ch. 4.4.3.

The first perspective is more or less empirical.

Of course, many philosophical debates have turned upon the distinction between 'empirical' (factual) arguments and 'normative' (evaluative) arguments, often reflecting a problematic that has been described along the lines of 'Hume's law'. Even if I do not necessarily accept the is-ought dichotomy unconditionally[978] and even if the issue takes on a specific significance in methodological debates over law[979], I at least provisionally accept that different perspectives can be taken up in this regard. Taking no position here on the most adequate one, at least in this debate, little in what follows will turn on the intricacies of the (possibility and intensity of the) dichotomy.

Because of European law, a new compromise had to be reached within the Court in the 2009 Care insurance case, and throughout this reaching of a compromise, European law added an extra layer of complexity, for instance in terms of its primacy. Metaphorically, it created, or forced the Constitutional Court to create, a Learnaean Hydra[980]: a polycephalous series of judgments in which solving one issue seemed to raise at least two others. If the Court had solved the issues of territoriality and EMU in the 2001 and 2006 judgments, European law now forced it to at least partially revisit these solutions, and hence to at least distinguish[981] its precedents. A hydra, moreover, because the final solution in the 2009 Care Insurance Case can be called ugly: some considerations are uninsightful[982], others are in patent mutual tension (if not contradiction)[983], still

978 For some reasoning behind that claim, *see, eg* Putnam, *supra* note 98. Moreover, in Kelsenian logic, the adequate distinction does not track this dichotomy, as he accepts the possibility of descriptive norm(ative)(-)statements.

979 *See eg* Luhmann, *supra* note 29, at p. 54 *et seq.* (from a more (social-)theoretical perspective) or Coleman, *supra* note 95, at p. 310 *et seq.* (from the viewpoint of the Hart-Dworkin debate).

980 Yet another way, in which a new 'head' sprung from the saga, was by the annulment itself, which brought the decree in tension with the Court of Justice's case law in in *Hosse* (Case C-286/03 (Feb. 21, 2006)) on art. 19 (2) of Regulation No. 1408/71. On the issue, see explanatory memo, *Parl. Doc.* Flemish Parl. 2008-09, No. 2156/1, at p. 4-6.

981 From a a perspective of classical legal rationality, the Court indeed did its best to *distinguish*. In fact, perhaps, it is better to speak of *unsettling* or *recharacterizing* its earlier precedents, in light of the specific precedential policies (*see* Vansteenkiste, *supra* note 170, at p. 101-08, 121 *et seq.*; *compare, mutatis mutandis*, Frederick Schauer, Thinking like a lawyer: a new introduction to legal reasoning 59-60 (2009)).

982 *Esp.* CC No. 11/2009 (Jan. 21, 2009) B.16 (on not having to investigate the possible discrimination) reads like a very odd consideration, especially in light of the jurisprudence and function of the Court. It has been widely criticized, *eg* Velaers & Vanpraet, *supra* note 388, at p. 212-13. It also diverges from the point of view of the CoS (CoS Advice, *Parl. Doc.* Flemish Parl. 2003-04, No. 1970/2, at p. 12-13).

983 *Eg* Velaers & Vanpraet, *supra* note 388, at p. 212 note 92.

others seem impracticable...[984] Succinctly, the Court does not clearly answer the legal issue raised before it[985].

A second perspective is more normative.

But here, I do not intend *normative* to mean *evaluative*, in the sense of the is-ought debate. I employ the word *normative*, in the sense that the analysis *presupposes* the existence of a norm-system, *ie* law, no matter how broadly (methodologically) conceived[986]. Without wanting to take a position on the sometimes-difficult distinction between the function of *doctrinal* analysis (in the sense of dogmatic analysis) and a more reflexive legal theory or philosophy[987], I rely primarily on the reader's intuition here to understand the change in perspective. This, conversely, does not exclude an implicit or explicit reliance on evaluative considerations in elaborating one's representation of a specific judgment or theory.[988]

From a more normative perspective, accordingly, it seems important to see how European law in the Care Insurance case exacerbated the inherent tension between the principle of non-discrimination and the territorial allocation of competences[989]. We indicated before that in principle the Constitutional

---

984 *Eg* Velaers & Vanpraet, *supra* note 388, at p. 207 ('the implementation of this judgment will require showing one's paces'). This problem is not specifically a Belgian problem, however. *See eg* D. Martin, *Comments on* Gouvernment de la Communauté française and Gouvernement wallon (Case C-212/06 of 1 April 2008) and *Eind* (Case C-291/05 of 11 December 2007), 10 European Journal of Migration and Law 365, 371-72 (2008); Verschueren, *supra* note 842, at p. 213-15; *also see* Moritz Am Ende, *But not the Walloons! Internal quarrel – or a case for the Court.* Case note accompanying Case C-212/06 (GC; Apr. 1, 2008) *Flemish Care Insurance*, 2008 European Law Reporter 114, 116 ('[b]eing unable to identify nationals having made use of their freedom, Member States would *de facto* be forced to refrain from any measure which might be contrary to the four freedoms, even if this measure would concern purely internal situations'). For some examples of the problems associated with the implementation, *see* Report (Dehaene & Strackx), *Parl. Doc.* Flemish Parl. 2008-09, No. 2156/3, at p. 5-6 and Explanatory Memo, *Parl. Doc.* Flemish Parl. 2008-09, No. 2156/1, at p. 3-4 (both on the new adaptations of the decree in light of Case No. 11/2009) or Report on a Petition on the exclusion of frontier workers from the Flemish Care Insurance, *Parl. Doc.* Flemish Parl. 2009-10, No. 156/1. *Compare* Joined Cases C-363, 407 and 411/93 (1994) *Lancry*, para. 31. More generally, *see infra* Ch. 5.

985 Velaers & Vanpraet, *supra* note 388, at p. 210.

986 *Compare* Kelsen's explanations in the Pure Theory of Law, or Hart's rebuttal to Dworkin his *Postscript* to The Concept of Law.

987 *See eg* G.C.G.J. Van Roermund, Wetten en weten: 'theorie van het recht': een wijsgerige kritiek (1983).

988 For a more or less clear example (of rather singular emphasis), *see* Pieters, *supra* note 914, at p. 67-68.

989 *Cf.* Vandamme, *supra* note 914, at p. 296 ('[t]wo conflicting principles are at stake: non-discrimination and federalization'); Vandamme, *supra* note 21, at p. 144. *Compare, mutatis mu-*

Court, in its territorial exclusivity review, merely checks whether a territorial criterion deployed is co-existent with the principle exclusive territoriality, but that in practice[990], this often comes down to constitutionalizing one criterion or another[991]. The Constitutional Court indeed explicitly rejected the notion that Flanders could unequivocally rely on a *lex loci laboris*-criterion to set up its own scheme, as this would violate rules governing competences[992]. Next to that however, the Court offered little but an unappealing argumentation that primarily seemed geared towards not answering important questions[993]. Scholars have nonetheless pointed out that dangers lurk around the corner here[994]: if the Court does not accept that the principle of exclusive territoriality,

---

tandis (in the context of alien expulsion), ECtHR No. 12313/86 (Feb. 18, 1991) *Mostaquim v. Belgium*, para 49; ECtHR No. 21794/93 (Aug. 7, 1996), *C. v. Belgium,* para 38 and ECtHR No. 5335/05 (June 21, 2011) *Anatoliy Ponomaryov and Vitaliy Ponomaryov v. Bulgaria*, para 54 (justification of difference in treatment on the basis of the European Union as a 'special legal order').

990 Storme can be read to doubt the precedential value of No. 51/2006 (Storme, *supra* note 142, at p. 401). He even concludes there that 'judgment 51/2006 reveals little or nothing about the vision of the Constitutional Court on the acceptability of deployed criteria of application by the Flemish Care Insurance decree' (*ibid.* at p. 401). Even so, his criticism is primarily geared towards the fact that the Constitutional Court did not recognize the tension between allocation of competences and free movement more explicitly there (*ibid.* at p. 401-02).

991 *Supra* note 947 (*compare* note 942). With specific reference to the Care Insurance Case, *see eg* Storme, *supra* note 142, at p. 394 n1512; *Compare* Marc Joassart & Pierre Joassart, *La repartition des competences en matière de sécurité sociale: l'érosion progressive de la compétence fédérale*, 2006 RBDC 167, 183-85 (similarly criticizing the material allocation of competences in this regard).

992 CC No. 11/2009 (Jan. 21, 2009) B.12.1 *et seq., esp.* B.14 ('an extension of the scope of application of the questioned decree to Belgian citizens living in the French or German linguistic areas and which do not have to enjoy the benefits pursuant to European [Union] law, could bring the Flemish Community to exercize measures of control and inspection which are incompatible with the [...] rules governing the allocation of competences').

993 The Court conjured up a distinction between the EMU itself, the principles of which were not as such violated, as decided in precedent (*cf.* CC No. 11/2009 (Jan. 21, 2009) B.12.1, referring to CA No. 51/2006), and a discrimination in exercise of the rights of free movement in Belgium (*cf.*CC No. 11/2009 (Jan. 21, 2009) B.13.2). It explicitly refused to answer the question whether there was a discrimination in the exercise of these rights, as it proferred that if the difference in treatment could either be unsettled by a regulation of the French or German Communities (*ibid.* B.15.1), or even by a regulation by the federal government (*ibid.* B.15.2), and *accordingly* (which is somewhat strange in light of its other jurisprudence on constitutional lacunae; *also see* Velaers & Vanpraet, *supra* note 388, at p. 213), that the alleged discrimination would surely not find its 'origins in the questioned decree, but in the lack of analogous provisions' (CC No. 11/2009 (Jan. 21, 2009) B.16).

994 In fact, the issue has been anticipated. *See eg* Joint Report (Noreilde & Déom), *Parl. Doc.* Senate and Chamber 2005-06, Nos. 3-578/1 and 2438/001, at p. 7-8 (discussing the *Kohll* and *Decker* judgments as a problematic in light of the principle of territoriality in the context of the adoption of a resolution) or Velaers, de grondwet en de raad van state, *supra* note 13, at p. 757 (referring to CoS jurisprudence on the place of residence-criterion).

as it has been constitutionally enshrined, can erect boundaries against claims of discrimination of the basis of treatments which are different pursuant to autonomy, the autonomy is put under pressure, certainly if European law is so conceived as to necessitate the adoption of this or that criterion[995].

155. A pragmatic view? The practical question nonetheless remains: what was the Court to do in light of judgments 33/2001 and 56/2006? Were the options so manifold, also taking the more practical side into account (which criterion *would* work unequivocally) and having regard to the emerging problem of reverse discrimination? Of course a different compromise could have been reached *en banc*, but the compromise would probably still have been hideous, arguably then again from a different perspective. Even so, I do not believe resignation or acquiescence are in order. I offer some considerations further on to justify that belief, but first, I address how the Care Insurance saga can be seen as not only raising issues in terms of precedents, but also in terms of coherence.

4.4.3 Coherence, with the example of coherent EMU-principles

156. Coherence and the EMU. Coherence is yet another rule of law value that might constrain the tool-like use of European law by the Constitutional Court. I discuss coherence here from one particular point of view[996], although I do not *a priori* exclude similar cases from other points of view[997], or even from a more

[995] Vandamme, *supra* note 21, at p. 144; Velaers & Vanpraet, *supra* note 388, at p. 211-14 (with references to earlier positions in scholarship and jurisprudence – *ibid.* at p. 212-13 n93-94); Velaers, *supra* note 531, at p. 148-157 (proffering, next to the implied powers arguments, hierarchy of norms argument to support the Court's solution, but recognizing the 'pressure on the principle of exclusivity' (*ibid.* at p. 157)); Verschueren, *supra* note 842, at p. 206 *et seq., esp.* p. 209-10 (discussing the problematic in terms of precedence) and p. 212 *et seq.* (critical of the COJ's reliance on the treaty, the ensuing legal uncertainty and on the rather imperialistic understanding of the social security coordination). *Compare* Pieters, *supra* note 914, at p. 71-73 *and* Verschueren, *supra* note 842, at p. 225-27 (both emphasizing the distinction between a rule of conflict and a rule of personal scope of a regulation, but differing on the degree of congruence between a proposed internal Belgian coordination of social security). *But compare* Storme, *supra* note 142, at p. 406 (arguing that nothing in the Belgian Constitution *requires* the place of residence criterion, and rather that the Belgian conception of the EMU should oppose it) and p. 408 (accepting that reading No. 11/2009 seems to imply a constitutionalization of the place of residence requirement) *with* Vandamme, *supra* note 914, at p. 297-99 (arguing for a more coordinated European approach on the basis of diverse cases like *Van Schijndel* or *Azores*).

[996] Moreover excluding such issues as I mentioned before, on the justification of coherence and its meaning.

[997] In fact, the distinction between coherence in *concepts* (as discussed above), and the coherence *in principle* I discuss here, has been postulated before and has been advanced by some, for instance in light of legal force according to some (*supra* note 643 and accompanying text). However, although I recognize the *prima facie* cognizability of the distinction, I do not take a position on its foundational or representational merits.

holistic point of view of coherence. The coherence perspective I investigate here, is that of the principle of the EMU. This does not mean coherence vis-à-vis the *justification* of the principles, nor vis-à-vis their *application*. Accordingly, we do not investigate pleas such as those of Verschueren for an internal application of internal constitutional law, also with regard to EU migrants[998]. However, I concede that the distinction between justification, application and structure is not always easily made and depends on complex methodological issues[999]. I rely primarily on the work of Delgrange, Keppene[1000] and Van Ypersele[1001] for an elaboration of such a structural inquiry, but I try to be aware not to fall in the pitfall of reifying conceptual analysis[1002].

157. Diverging EMU-conceptualizations. Notwithstanding the generally recognized similarity between the European EMU and the Belgian EMU, most Belgian authors agree that Judgment No. 11/2009 has established that the EMU-principles which are deployed at the different levels are not identical[1003]. They by and large base themselves on a rather unusual set of considerations on the situation pertaining to Belgian citizens that have not made use of their right to free movement in the European Union. The Court in this regard first affirmed its precedent on EMU[1004] and then "reasoned" as follows:

> B.13.2. Consequently the question could be asked whether the Belgian citizens [...] are discriminated against in the exercise of their right to free movement of persons within Belgium, insofar it

[998] *Eg* Verschueren, *supra* note 842, at p. 224.

[999] An example of why is found in Schauer, *supra* note 56, and the entire debate of the link between law and the entrenched mode of decision-making.

[1000] *Supra* note 527.

[1001] Together with Delgrange, *Le juge du fond, la Cour d'Arbitrage et la Cour de Justice,* 1995 RBDC 413, 418 *et seq.*

[1002] Coleman, *supra* note 95, at p. 345 et seq. (trying to steer a middle ground between strict conceptualism and Leiter's naturalized jurisprudence); *see, more broadly,* Willard V.O. Quine, *Two Dogmas of Empiricism*, 60 The Philosophical Review 20 (1951).

[1003] *Eg* Eric Van Brustem, *L'affaire de la "zorgverzekering": comment concilier la libre circulation des travailleurs et l'organisation fédérale des Etats*, 2009 Sociaalrechtelijke Kronieken 193, 198-99; Vandamme, *supra* note 914, at p. 294-95; Vanpraet, *supra* note 190, at p. 192 *et seq.*; Velaers & Vanpraet, *supra* note 388, at p. 210-11. *Also see* Peter Van Elsuwege & Stanislas Adam, *Situations purement internes, discrimination à rebours et collectivités autonomes après l'arrêt sur* l'assurance soins flamande, 44 Cahiers de Droit Européen 655, 691-92 (2008) (already inferring this conclusion from No. 51/2006). *Compare* Storme, *supra* note 446, at p. 622-23 (accepting the inference that the principles are interpreted differently here, but pleading for convergence).

[1004] CC No. 11/2009 (Jan. 21, 2009) B.12.1, quoting No. 51/5006 (Apr. 19, 2006) B.10.3. ('taking into account the limited amount and the limited consequences of the criticized measures [...] no violation has occurred of the federal competence pertaining to the EMU').

is accepted for that category of persons that the certain obligation to contribute to a care fund in exchange for the future enjoyment of a care insurance, constitutes a situation that could engender a restriction to free movement within Belgium.

B.14. Nonetheless an extension of the scope of the questioned decree to Belgian citizens living in the French or the German language area, who do not have to enjoy the benefit pursuant to European [Union] law, would bring the Flemish Community to exercise measures of control and inspection which are incompatible with the [...] rules governing territorial competence.

B.15.1. The argued difference in treatment could be undone by measures taken by the French and the German Community [...] adapting an analogous scheme of care insurance.

B.15.2. From what precedes and from Judgment No. 33/2001 [one] can moreover not infer that the federal legislature, in exercising its social security competence [...] cannot take measures of social security for persons with a reduced capacity of self-care that would be valid on the territory of the entire country, without infringing upon the Community competences in the area of personal assistance.

[....]

B.16. Without the Court having to investigate whether the persons meant in B.13.2 could be discriminated against in the exercise of their right to free movement, as meant in article 6, §1, IV (3) SLIR, it must be ascertained that this possible discrimination in any case would not originate from the questioned decree, but rather in the lack of analogous provisions in decrees of the French and German Community or in the absence of federal social security measures [...] so that the measures of internal law directed against the provisions of the decree, are without merit.[1005]

[1005] CC No. 11/2009 (Jan. 21, 2009).

The authors recognizing that there is a notable difference between the European and the Belgian principles have a fair point, but often, they disregard some relevant considerations, like the question of what convergence consists in, whether there is a need for convergence, and how the principle-like properties of the EMU should be characterized[1006]. Constantly, the question about the conceptualization of the breadth (and sometimes primacy) of the legal order lurks on the background[1007].

Having said that, I do not have to take a position on these issues here[1008], as I *arguendo* accept that there is indeed a divergence between *EMU-principles* – however defined separately – and that this divergence leads to *incoherence* between different principles ("convergence = coherence"). The point I try to make seemingly applies, regardless of the hypothesis one adapts, even if perhaps, under some hypotheses, 'coherence' might not be the most adequate conceptualization of the rule of law value that is in play.

158. Coherence as a constraint. Accordingly sidestepping these issues, it remains the case that the idea of coherence still poses limits to a free applicability of European law in a tool-like manner. On the one hand, the *coherence* concept implies convergence; in fact, it has been proffered that '[w]ith the hesitation, befitting a youthful institution, the Court has sometimes silently, but nonetheless clearly, walked the European trail in fundamental matters, without however explicitly referring to the European legal system'[1009]. Accordingly, in earlier case law, notwithstanding some critical voices[1010], the Court made both EMU principles cohere as much as possible. In fact, that was the streamlining function we observed in the inheritance tax case[1011]. Now, some of the previous

[1006] *Cf.* the considerations raised *supra* on the EMU.

[1007] *Eg* CA No. 136/2000 (Dec. 21, 2003) B.49-B.50 (whereas the Court recognized that there is a connection between European competition principles and the principles enshrined in art. 10 and 11 Cons., a *general coherence* amongst these principles was deemed insufficient to trigger the Court's jurisdiction: 'the Court would exceed the competence allocated to it by the Constitution if it would decide that every violation of [Union] law would constitute a violation of art. 10 and 11 Cons.' (B.50)). *Cf.* Vandamme, *supra* note 21, at p. 133-34.

[1008] *See further*, Feyen, *supra* note 32.

[1009] Delva, *supra* note 744, at p. 639. *Also see* VELU, *supra* note 744, at p. 97 (noticing that in judgment No. 47, the Constitutional Court reviewed the conformity of the decree with European Union law).

[1010] These voices are first and foremost critical of CA No. 32/91 (Nov. 14, 1991) 5.B.1.9, where the proportionality review has been called 'hurried' (Delgrange & Keppene, *supra* note 527, at p. 85-87) and of CA No. 33/91.

[1011] Discussed *supra* No. 135. *But see* CA No. 132/2005 (July 19, 2005) B.6.1-B.6.3 (*cf. infra* note 1013).

considerations in the Care Insurance case *could* be characterized[1012] as coherence constraining the instrumentalization of European law, in the sense that the Court refused to answer the question whether there was a breach of the EMU, in light of the principle of non-discrimination, in the specific constellation of having created a difference between areas governed by European law and those governed by merely internal laws.

On the other hand, the specific constellation itself already presupposes a *divergence*. Even if this divergence is framed (merely) in terms of the distinction in scope of different legal orders – an argument the Court has relied on before[1013] – it nonetheless remains the case that *coherence* as convergence is influenced by this distinction. That is then perhaps the point the aforementioned scholars have wanted to make. By conceptually endorsing the *scope of legal order*-distinction (the internal situation rule), the Court had to conceptually distinguish between two at least potentially different EMU-principles. At the same time, the precedent on the EMU was still in play and, because of the precedential rule of law value, had to be confirmed.

159. Complex constraint, but increased tension. Accordingly, coherence, in an interaction with other rule of law values, plays a complex role in constraining the Court from deploying European law instrumentally. It is certainly the case that European law, in this constellation, also exacerbated the tension already extant between the Court's different approaches to constitutional decision-making. Of course, the Care Insurance Judgment, as I mentioned, is not the

[1012] Perhaps a variant of the more *political* characterization discussed above is even more appropriate, in the sense that the second part of the judgment (on *internal situations*), should be best characterized as an area on which there was compromise, already presupposing the (alleged) compromise made to distinguish between situations coming within the scope of European Union law and purely internal situations.

[1013] Most explicitly in CC No. 56/2009 (Mar. 19, 2009) B.4.3-B.4.4 and *also see* B.7.3 (postulating incomparability due to the distinction in legal scope, and at same time upholding the constitutionality of a regulation in which an obligation rested on principals and contractors who have recourse to non-registered contracting partners to both withhold a sum of all payments for social security and through which a joint and several liability was imposed on these formers with regard to social security debts, accordingly both formally denying direct application of Case C-433/04 (Nov. 9, 2006) *Commission v. Belgium*, and refusing to analogize the Court of Justice's argumentation, which primarily relied on the disproportionate impact of the regulatory scheme), as confirmed in CC No. 124/2009 (July 16, 2009). *See* CA No. 132/2005 (July 19, 2005) B.6.1-B.6.3 (applying the internal situation rule in the context of crematoria). *But compare eg supra* No. 135. *Also (strangely) compare* CC No. 174/2009 (Nov. 3, 2009) B.8.1 *et seq., esp.* B.11 to which A-G Sharpston referred in her conclusions in the *Ruiz Zambrano* case (C-34/09 (Sep. 30, 2010), §41 n17), where the Court – according to the A-G – solved the issue of *reverse discrimination*, by substantively extending the European arguments). *Further on the issue, see infra* note 1045, with accompanying text and reference.

most usual case. Often there will be no precedent on point, and the Court will have more leeway to integrate the EMU-concepts. Here, both in terms of rule of law values, and probably also in a more political sense of *en banc* negotiations, the Court had few really decent options.

160. More adequate apparatus for analysis. Even so, and notwithstanding the fact that my text here has perhaps raised more questions than it has answered, I would like to believe that the conceptual apparatus offered here provides for a more adequate characterization, generally for two reasons. Primarily, the general toolbox model (in interaction with rule of law values) seems to capture more of the realities of constitutional decision-making than other models of exposition. Next to that, the interaction model allows for more *considered generalization* – arguably the goal of any intellectual inquiry[1014] – in the interaction between European and municipal law.

As we noted, the relationship between European law and municipal law has been deemed ambiguous at best. Scholars have tried to approach the issue from different perspectives, and often in this area, legal doctrine has been surprisingly innovative. Even so, the contributions made in this (even innovative) context often either refer back to quasi-outdated conceptual means[1015] or lack a coherent *methodological* framework to structure the investigations. I surely do not want claim that the framework I offer is capable of explaining or capturing the full range of constitutional jurisprudence on federalism. I merely believe it to have explanatory virtues reaching beyond those incorporated in more traditional approaches to the relationship between European law and constitutional law.

[1014] *See eg* John Dewey, How we Think 134 (1910).

[1015] I would be the first one to admit that I – to the extent that it could be deemed real *contribution* – contributed to this line of work (*cf. supra* note 792).

4.5 More explanatory value? Two caveats

161. Two further caveats: substance and methodology. Two more caveats concerning what has been said, both *qua* substance in terms of legal scholarship, and *qua* methodology pertaining to the subject matter at hand, should be emphasized before I embark upon some more abstract explanations for the tension between European law and Belgian constitutional law in terms of federalism.

162. Relationship with existing legal scholarship. First, this is not a plea *against* existing arguments on the relationship between European and Belgian constitutional law. In fact, if it were, it would have hardly reached its purpose, since I rely on the arguments of authoritative scholars throughout my work. It is merely a plea for opening up and deepening the array of reasons that are traditionally deemed constitutionally relevant reasons in decision-making, for the purpose of better understanding (and perhaps for purposes of prediction).

163. Federalism[1016]**.** Second, even if I believe the approach taken up here has more explanatory power than some other more traditional approaches, this does not mean that there is no virtue in the more rule-like, entrenched representation of the judgments of the Constitutional Court[1017]. However, I believe *federalism* to be an area in which such entrenched decision-making representation fails to live up to virtue of entrenchment in other areas. Even leaving aside the general question whether scholars are or should be in the same business as judges when *interpreting* the law[1018], it cannot be the purpose of legal scholars in general to totally disregard the realities of decision-making as such, even if these should be mediated by broader rule of law values.

If only to remain an autonomous field of inquiry, surely law must be conceived of, at least to some extent, as a positivized fiction[1019], that is as a scheme of (potential) *reifications*. According to Lukács classic 'definition' (although that term might be a misnomer) in his essay on Marxist thought, reification's 'basis is that a relation between people takes on the character of a thing and thus acquires a 'phantom objectivity', an autonomy that seems so strictly rational and all-embracing as to

[1016] *Compare supra* Ch. 1.2.

[1017] SCHAUER, *supra* note 56, *eg* at p. 229 (they are 'life-simplifying').

[1018] *Compare supra* note 987 (for some further theoretical reflections).

[1019] 'Fiction' here should not only be contrasted to mere 'statement of fact' (*cf.* AUSTIN, *supra* note 886, at p. 4 n2, *also see* 19; *but see* 33), but also to non-fixated forms of inquiry (taking into account *all* considerations in play).

conceal every trace of its fundamental nature: the relation between people'[1020]. 'As applied to law, reification presents a kind of infection within legal doctrine and legal theory because it is essentially an error, a delusion, and a mystification that blinds people to alternative legal arrangements by "naturalizing" the existing legal system as inevitable'[1021]. It could of course be argued that my choice of words here is problematic, and I acknowledge that to some extent it is, at least in that 'reification' as a concept is susceptible to be 'reified' as well. I would not go so far as to name it '[o]ne of those ten cents philosophical words'[1022], but elaborating why this is the case, falls beyond the scope of this book since it would force me not only to interact with many great thinkers who have shed their light on the meaning and importance of reification[1023], such as Lukács,

[1020] Lukács, *supra* note 101, at p. 83.

[1021] Litowitz, *supra* note 56, at p. 401. *Also see* Peter Gabel, *Reification in Legal Reasoning,* 3 Res. L. & Soc'y 25 (1980) (which has been called the 'classic' and 'leading' piece on reification in legal theory by Linz Audain (*Critical Legal Studies, Feminism, Law and Economics, and the Wall of Intellectual Tolerance: A Tentative Case for Cross-jurisprudential dialogue,* 20 Hofstra L. Rev. 1017, 1035 n61 (1992); Litowitz, *supra* note 56, at p. 414), and which characterizes reification primarily as a breakdown in communication: 'everybody knows the fallacy, and yet denies that the fallacy exists' (Gabel, *supra* this note, at p. 26).

[1022] Anthony J. Fejfar, *An analysis of 'reification' as used in Peter Gabel's* reification of legal reasoning, 25 Cap. U. L. Rev. 579, 580 (1996).

[1023] In fact, one could argue that the term *reification* has been malappropriated, also by some (though not all: *see eg* Patrick J. Glen, *The Deconstruction and Reification of Law in Franz Kafka's "Before the Law" and* The Trial, 17 S. Cal. Int. L.J. 23, 50 *et seq.* (2007)) lawyers and legal philosophers who deploy the term, at least for two general reasons: first, because a (history of the) discourse of reification is hard to separate from the social diagnostics and cultural critique of (hyper-)instrumental reason(ing) (*cf.* Axel Honneth, Reification: A New Look at an Old idea 17 *et seq.* (2007)), which takes its sole form in law in terms of formalism (Lukács, *supra* note 101, at p. 95 *et seq.*; Glen, *supra* this note, at p. 54 *et seq.* (summarizing); *compare* Csaba Varga, The Place of Law in Lukács' World 40 *et seq.* (2d ed., 2012) (critical)) – a point we do not necessarily subscribe to using the term, since we deploy it to first and foremost to legal concepts, and only in a secondary sense to the legal *system* (/idea of law/legality) itself. On the other hand, criticism of conceptualism/formalism and even positivism as being covered by an '*Ideeenkleid*', to use Husserl's terminology (Edmund Husserl, The Crisis of the European Sciences and Transcendental Phenomenology: An Introduction to Phenomenological Philosophy, 51 (David Carr transl. 1970)), has been formulated by many other (legal) philosophers, and indeed social and legal theorists, without having recourse to the controversial – indeed even pugnacious – term. This has furthermore been connected to philosophical criticism of the subject-object dualism, à la Heidegger (who also argues against the idea of reification with his concept of 'care' in Being and Time, or Dewey (who argues against what he calls the 'spectator model' of knowledge (John Dewey, The Quest for Certainty (1960)). Be that as it may – and without wanting to engage in the philosophical dispute, nor wanting to analyze *per se* to which extent 'reification' from a conceptual point of view can be imposed on law-like thinking – the term single-handedly captures the meaning of what is perceived here to be one of the flaws of dogmatics, namely a sort of forgetfulness – in the words of two Frankfurter school theorists: 'All reification is forgetting' (Max Horkheimer & Theodor W. Adorno, Dialectic of Enlightenment 191 (Gunzelin Schmid Noerr ed.,

Habermas, Sartre, Nussbaum, Taylor or Honneth, but also to explore its specific impact, not only on life, but perhaps more significantly on the concept and the *practice* of (dogmatizing) law. I do want to add, however, that this *reification* problem does not undermine the (debatable) points made by Frederick Schauer in his work on rules as entrenched generalizations[1024], even more so, because the rule-like structure of constitutional law (and competence allocation as such), is itself a matter of debate. For the same reasons, I do not *necessarily* wish to interpret the words with a negative connotation.[1025]

Hence, I restrain myself to proffering some eclectic remarks on the subject, connecting it with federalism and law. If reifications are often thought to be *central* to even start comprehending some departments of law – how would start to understand contract law, without presupposing and reifying the concept of an autonomous will?[1026] –, this is not entirely clear as regards the allocation of competences we are discussing here. Of course, the very idea of law presupposes some conceptual abstractions of its constitutive elements. But how one deals with these abstractions can make an all-important difference. Indeed: some concepts in law, like property, seem to have an accepted abstract core of meaning that is at least relied upon in legal practice[1027]. However, this is not so much the case for the idea of *competence* which lies at the basis of federalism: even if there

Edmund Jephcott trans. 2002)) – of the true relations underlying the conceptual apparatus (and even normative presuppositions) of law, because one turns those relationships (accepting that law indeed regulates social relationships) into objects, apt to be analyzed into distinct parts and in their mutual relationships without necessarily tracking back to the underlying reality. On the other hand, *reification* might be thought indeed to "execute" one of the normative presupossitions of the law, *ie* its objectivity (*compare* SHAPIRO, *supra* note 37, at p. 15-16). This renders the analysis more complex. Therefore, *reification* here is first and foremost used in an etymological and rhetorical way, which nevertheless is not wholly unconnected with the history of the idea, and especially the notion of alienation it seeks to express (albeit not necessarily in ontological-*cum*-existential (*eg* Lukács), biological (*eg* Kuhlman, as referred to in HONNETH, note 11), economic (*cf.* Marx' idea of commodity fetishism) or moral (*eg* Nussbaum) terms).

[1024] SCHAUER, *supra* note 56, *esp*. ch.s 2 and 3.

[1025] *Cf.* JOHN DEWEY, *Qualitative Thought* in PHILOSOPHY AND CIVILIZATION 93 (1931); *also see* HONNETH, *supra* note 1023, at p. 17 *et seq.* (2007).

[1026] For instance, Litowitz notices that 'the actual rules of law are not reified, but the conceptions lying below the legal rules are replete with reified notions of selfhood and agency', which for him, are examples of deep-structure reifications (Litowitz, *supra* note 56, at p. 418): 'nothing per se wrong with the creation of artificial legal entities – the problem lies with the inability of people to see themselves reflected in their own creations' (*ibid.* at p. 422).

[1027] I leave open the question whether this abstract core should be conceptualized either as a *core* in the Hartian sense (as opposed to a penumbra), or as a *concept* in the Dworkinian sense (as opposed to a conception). I furthermore ignore the fact that the *concept* of *right*, which is often connected in legal discourse to concepts like property, is indeed very controversial, and in that sense, one could try to extrapolate the arguments offered here.

has been quite some debate pertaining to how to conceptualize a *competence* (either as Hohfeldian empowerment[1028], or as Kelsenian application of a rule and creation of a norm[1029], or as attribute of a Hartian secondary rule[1030]...), this debate does not seem to have any consensual reflections on the legal practice of constitutional law itself[1031]. Moreover, this debate reflects and interacts other debates about the *content* of these competences in ways too complex to elaborate here.

I do not rely on the idea here that there are no disagreements in other areas of law, nor that they are not as ferocious or problematic in these areas. My mere assertion here is that *federalism* issues are especially prone to reification in Belgium, and this in different complex ways. In general, the basic problem seems to be that most of the (necessary) abstractions in law on federalism do

1028 *Cf.* WESLEY N. HOHFELD, *Some Fundamental Legal Conceptions as Applied in Judicial Reasoning*, 23 YALE L.J. 16, 55 (1913-14) and *Fundamental Legal Conceptions as Applied in Judicial Reasoning*, 26 YALE L.J. 710 (1916-17), *both reprinted in* FUNDAMENTAL LEGAL CONCEPTIONS AS APPLIED IN JUDICIAL REASONING AND OTHER ESSAYS 23, 65 (1923) (which is to be conceptually and analytically distinguished from a right, and first and foremost be represented as a 'superadded fact or group of facts which are under the volitional control of one or more human beings'). For a modern application, *see* ALEXY, *supra* note 3, at p. 156 *et seq.*

1029 *Cf.* KELSEN, *supra* note 37, at p. 148-149 (where competences are equated to 'rights' or 'legal powers': '[t]raditional terminology blurs the essential similarity between all these functions exercising legal power' (*ibid.* at p. 149)). *Also see* ROSS, *supra* note 475, at p. 32 *et seq.* ('norm of competence is thus an indirectly expressed norm of conduct' (*ibid.* at p. 32) or 'norms of competence are reducible to norms of conduct' (*ibid.* at p. 33)) or Torben Spaak, *Norms that confer competence*, 16 RATIO IURIS 89 (2003). *But compare* Carsten Heidemann, *The Creation of Normative Facts*, 19 LAW AND PHILOSOPHY 263 (2000) (relativizing the alleged unequivocal nature of Kelsen's equation).

1030 HART, *supra* note 109, 26-49, 80-81 and 283-86 (fundamentally distinguishing primary and secondary rules, and offering a criticism of Kelsen's theory) (marking how norms of competence are reducible to (duty-imposing) norms of conduct) .

1031 *See, generally,* Eugenio Bulygin, *On norms of competence*, 11 LAW AND PHILOSOPHY 201 (1992) (discussing the theories of Kelsen, Ross, von Wright, Kanger, Searle and Lindahl and arguing that competence norms cannot be reduced to norms of conduct). For some more recent references, *see* Gerard Conway, *Conflicts of Competence Norms in EU Law and the Legal Reasoning of the ECJ*, 11 GERMAN LAW JOURNAL 966, 973-979 (2010). This does not mean that I deem the concept of competence to be useless. Within many theories of laws, there is a direct connection between the concept of competence and the concept of validity, which can be of utter importance for practical reasons. Nonetheless, the concept of competence should be explored, if even analytically, from a more relational perspective (one always has a competence in a certain respect), nonetheless keeping the aspirations of legal certainty in mind. In this sense, Neil MacCormick, apparently inspired by Perelman's *New Rhetoric*, has argued that 'clarity', as a legal aspiration concomitant to certainty, should be understood in a dialogical way (MACCORMICK, *supra* note 62, at p. 26). Even if some (mainstream) legal theorists have acknowledged this fact, it is entirely unsure whether (and how adequately) dogmatics have redeemed it.

not fulfill their goal (of clarification and systematization), but instead render the materials more confusing and obfuscating. In that case, the reified concepts and their progeny do not only loose their explanatory value, but also infuse the state actors relying on explanations with utter confusion. This is therefore not an argument against abstraction (for how could we rationalize without it), but rather against artificially trying to classify different phenomena into categories which *apparently* – witness of which the confusion – have not come to serve their explanatory goals[1032].

[1032] *Also see* Mark G. Kelman, *Interpretive Construction in the Substantive Criminal Law*, 33 STANF. L. REV. 591, 592-93 (1981) (arguing that rational legal reasoning can only start after 'a fact pattern is characterized by interpretive constructs', *ibid.* at p. 593). *Compare* JOHN FINNIS, NATURAL LAW & NATURAL RIGHTS 3-18 (2[d] ed. 2011) (*very generally* arguing that even in the selection of which concepts are relevant and important, a researcher must rely on some practical reasonableness).

5.

Three partial[1033] explanations and the road ahead

[1033] And at the same time probably too general. The reason why I add this caveat is because I refrain from taking a *general* position on the question of whether it is überhaupt possible to conceptualize competence allocation in a fully abstract (universalizable) manner. As regards the Constitutional Court – employing the toolbox conception – I argue that an overly abstract elaboration of competence allocation as a manner of representation of judicial reasoning is susceptible of distorting constitutional reality. However, this by no means implies that I take a position on the question in general. Even so, taking a position does have ramifications on the object under discussion here (*compare* in the latter regard *eg* Paul Craig, *Competence and Subsidiarity*, 2006 EU ADMINISTRATIVE LAW 40, 44 (arguing against universalizability) and Conway, *supra* note 1031, at p. 973, 983-84 (2010) (accepting universalizabity)). Be that as it may, I explicitly formulate this caveat to emphasize that I do not necessarily accept the repercussions of the abstractions that I make in this explanatory model.

164. Internal substantive logic? If anything can be noticed when reading through the foregoing passages, it is that – while they try to grasp certain phenomena into particular broader concepts or principles, they do lack some kind of internal *substantive* logic of what influence constitutes of. That is a criticism I cannot refute, because I believe it to be true, and – what is more – I even believe it to be my point. Although I do not argue that it is downright impossible to construe a fully *substantive* coherent account of the relationship between EU and Belgian constitutional law and apply it to the field of federalism (even if I do find it highly implausible), and although I am not of the opinion that coherence (perhaps, after the interpretive turn[1034], as the epitomization of all rule of law values) is not something a judge should not strive for as a regulative ideal, the main point of this book has been to construe European law as a *tool* in a (pre-existing, though evolving) *toolbox*, so as to remain as faithful as possible to what could be deemed a representation of how constitutional law in action works. And – from my point of view – in federalism matters there might be far less coherence than some authors either fallaciously elaborate or erroneously presuppose.

Primary suspect for this lack of coherence in practice seems to be the complexity of considerations which are or have to be taken into account, such as rule of law values – however broadly construed[1035] –, institutional or political considerations, and often even considerations pertaining to the specific facts of the case. I have not purported to try to fully grasp and elaborate the complexity of the issues here but nonetheless have tried to argue that the heuristic model of *tools* might indeed constitute a more adequate vocabulary to talk about the issues raised, without disavowing their complexity.

165. Partial and abstract explanations. In light of the foregoing, the following 'explanations' of complexity and interaction can only be partial. Moreover, they are probably too abstract, in the sense that they rely on considerations that have no immediate connection to specific case law. However, having run through the sources, it seems to me that the tension which European law produces *within* constitutional adjudication in Belgium is *potentially* serious primarily because

[1034] *Eg* DWORKIN, JUSTICE IN ROBES, *supra* note 62, at p. 168 *et seq.* (explaining how legalism should be understood in terms of broader coherence). *Compare* Robin West, *The meaning of equality and the interpretive turn,* 66 CHI.-KENT L. REV. 451, 465 *et seq.* (1990) (explaining how *law* can constrain in an interpretive age, based *not* primarily on coherence, but rather on the law-like nature of the Constitution, which imposes constraints that traditional interpretivism cannot capture). In this sense, our *rule of law values* concept tries to capture as much of the constraint as can be reasonably categorized under the concept.

[1035] Surely the outline of the SLIR in Belgium has not not made matters easier.

of three reasons, the first being 'Belgian', the second clearly 'European' and the third hinging upon the relationship of both.

5.1 Integration of European law in constitutional jurisprudence

166. Factor 1: thorough integration. Notwithstanding early criticism of not acting completely in accordance with European obligations[1036], it has often been acknowledged that the Belgian Constitutional Court is first in the European class of constitutional courts, at least pertaining to the amount of preliminary rulings referred to the Court of Justice. Without wanting to extensively compare constitutional courts in Europe in this regard, I believe it not unfair to say that *from a European perspective* the Belgian Constitutional Court is also amongst the top of the class when it comes to deploying European law in its constitutional jurisprudence[1037].

It seems to be a truism to state that *if* the Constitutional Court would not rely so often on European law in its constitutional jurisprudence, that the chance of conflicts and tensions *within* constitutional jurisprudence would be diminished. At the same time, it is quite doubtful that this would be a suitable solution. Assuming that European law would not lose its normative force due to a lack of reliance upon it in Constitutional Court jurisprudence, the tension would just be displaced to debates on European law in constitutional reasoning by scholars, and it is highly doubtful that the Constitutional Court in this case would remain free of criticism. More importantly, I do not offer a solution to the tension, but rather an explanation of it. Because of the fact that European law is (comparatively) *often* deployed in constitutional reasoning in Belgium, and apparently increasingly so, the chance of conflict is increased.

167. Factor 2: lack of theoretical framework. I should nonetheless emphasize one unarticulated assumption in this ascertainment of chances of tension. At least, it is unarticulated in the previous paragraph, but I have mentioned it before. It is the lack of *more definitive theorization* of the relationship between constitutional law and European law.

This is not to say that a *definitive theorization* is either possible or warranted[1038]. Nor do I imply that in other jurisdictions, a definitive theorization has in fact taken

[1036] *Eg* Van Nuffel, *supra* note 828.

[1037] *Cf. supra* note 774.

[1038] *See eg* Cass Sunstein's plea for incomplete theorization (Legal Reasoning and Political Conflict (1996)), which admittedly is situated in a completely different context, but some arguments are transposable to our cause here (*see esp. ibid.* at p. 121 et seq.); *adde supra* note 719.

ground[1039]. Nor do I want to point fingers to anyone for this lack of theorization[1040]. I am merely suggesting that an agreed upon[1041] theoretical framework, insofar as it is adequately elaborated, would decrease the possibility of tensions.

168. EMU as framework? Arguably, one could characterize the EMU, as a broad idea which is part of the foundation of the European Union and part and parcel of Belgian federalism, as indeed trying to abstractly theorize the relationship between European law and constitutional law, and then more specifically, the provisions governing the allocation of powers. However, partly in light of the problem of coherence issues discussed above, and partly due to the expansion of European law[1042], this provision might be said to have failed at adequately theorizing the relationship between European law in general and the Belgian provisions governing the allocation of powers.

This book tries to offer an alternative framework. Admittedly, it is not fully theorized, nor is it free from (internal) difficulties. However, the framework does allow to sidestep some of the most controversial (dogmatic) issues in law, and seeks to provide a basis for a broader understanding of the case of law of the Constitutional Court, or at least an understanding with increased explanatory potential.

[1039] Often for the relationship between constitutional law and European law, the German Federal Constitutional Court's jurisprudence in the *Solange* cases and their progeny are mentioned. However, this is only *indirectly* relevant here, for these cases, and recently the Lisbon treaty case (BVerfG, 2 BvE 2/08 (June 30, 2009)), primarily deal with who has the last word on what, under which conditions. Even if we have shown the question of primacy to be important in solving some issues in the relationship between European and Constitutional law, and even if, for instance, the Lisbon treaty case reads as a bulwark of theorizing about the nature of the relationship between both legal orders, these cases in general do not address how European law *functions* in general in constitutional reasoning as such, addressing such questions as, when is it relevant, should it exert influence beyond its formal scope, et cetera.

[1040] Responsibility, if there is any in this regard, must be held to be shared, not only by the Constitutional Court, but also – and perhaps all the more so – by the Constituent Assembly (perhaps a misnomer: *cf.* DICEY, *supra* note 215, at p. 37-39, 65 *et seq.*), and by scholarship in general, failing to provide a sensible and accepted theoretical framework for comprehending the relationship between both legal orders.

[1041] This term here is equivocal. I should first specify that the agreement must pertain to the *law as it is elaborated*, and not to *the law as it should be* (according to whichever perspective). For instance, I would argue that the primacy of *international* law in general over Belgian laws has been widely agreed upon, if not in scholarship, than at least in practice, since the Court of Cassation ruled on this matter in 1971 (*supra* note 748). However, since in 2004, the Court had rendered a verdict implying that international law would under certain conditions also prevail over the Constitution, a *guerre des juges* more or less broke out (especially on the matter of a coinciding protection of rights). Accordingly, what was agreed upon was now pulled in a context of doubt, at least partially.

[1042] *See infra* Ch. 5.2.

5.2 The (ever) expanding Europe

169. Expansion of regulatory scope. There has been little debate about the question whether the European Union has been expanding its regulatory scope. Europe, through different treaty reforms, has ventured into areas which could not be foreseen when the European Communities were given their first form some sixty years ago. Especially since the Maastricht treaty and the establishment of Union citizenship, the (potential) applicability of EU law has reached unknown heights[1043]. In that sense, the so-called 'internal situation which has no link with [Union] law'[1044], remains one of the few terrains in which the EU does not immediately regulate[1045].

170. The Court of Justice: a limited consideration of the federated nature of states. Even if, in accordance with the TEU[1046], the Court of Justice in some areas recognized the importance of federated entities for the application of Union law, it seems to have failed to take the specific federal nature of some states into account in other areas.

On the one hand, the Court for instance has developed a specific framework for federalism problems in state aid cases[1047]. Important cases on (regional) state aid

---

[1043] *See eg* Lenaerts, *supra* note 849, at p. 31 *et seq.* Recently, this debate has connected to the one about the scope of the EU Charter (*see* some reflections in Koen Lenaerts, *Exploring the Limits of the EU Charter of Fundamental Rights*, 8 EuCons 375, 392 *et seq.* (2012)).

[1044] *Eg* Case C-353/06 (GC; Oct. 14, 2008) *Grunkin and Paul*, para 16; Case C-148/02 (GC; Oct. 2, 2003) *Garcia Avello*, paras 25-26 (with further references); Case C-235/09 (Dec. 22, 2010) *Omalet Nv v. Rijksdienst voor Sociale Zekerheid*. Further comments and references are found in Van Elsuwege & Adam, *supra* note 1003, at p. 659 *et seq.*, *esp.* 666-69, 672-73 or in Verbist, *supra* note 849.

[1045] At least not directly: indirectly it could regulate here too, through spontaneous harmonization, or even through courts reading the constitutional equality provisions in a specific way (*see* Valérie Verbist, *Omgekeerde discriminatie en de Belgische rechtsorde: op zoek naar een standpunt* in 3 Leuvense Staatsrechtelijke Standpunten 3, *supra* note 67, at p. 406-410 (offering examples of spontaneous harmonization in Belgium) and p. 411-427 (deploring the fact that the Belgian Constitutional Court has taken no principled stance on the issue of reverse discrimination). It should be noted that it is very likely that the Constitutional Court will formulate a principled point of view in 2013, since several cases regarding family unification have been referred to it, which do not easily allow sidestepping the issue).

[1046] Art. 4 (2) TEU ('[t]he Union shall respect [...] the national identities [of Member States], inherent in their fundamental structures, political and constitutional, inclusive of regional and local self-government').

[1047] *See eg* Opinion A-G Kokott (July 2, 2009) accompanying Case C-169/08, *Presidente del Consiglio dei Ministri v. Regione autonoma della Sardegna* (where Kokott assessed a regional tax on stopovers for tourist purposes by recreational craft only on persons whose tax domicile is outside the region in light of state aid provisions, and considered that it 'cannot be presumed that advantages conferred by a regional authority upon certain undertakings within the area

in this regard are *Altmark*[1048] and the *Azores*[1049] cases, which render it possible to make the federated entity the relevant entity for purposes of EU law, accordingly nuancing the EU's federal blindness[1050].

I do not discuss this case law in detail because it does not seem to directly influence the contours of Belgian federalism. Moreover, it should be noted that the *Azores* case law does not *prima facie* seem to directly apply to Belgium at this point in time, since that line of case law only applies to federal or regional states in which the sub-national entity can be coined *asymmetric* as regards the allocation of competences[1051] which – it has been said – is not the case in

in which it exercises its powers are not selective and therefore cannot be categorised as aid' (§ 132)). The Court in its judgment concurred, noting that 'in order to determine whether a measure is selective, where it is adopted by an infra-State body which enjoys autonomy vis-à-vis the central government of the kind enjoyed by the Region of Sardinia, it is necessary to determine whether, with regard to the objective pursued by that measure, it constitutes an advantage for certain undertakings as compared with others which, within the legal framework in which that body exercises its competences, are in a comparable legal and factual situation' (Case C-169/08 (GC; Nov. 19, 2009) *Presidente del Consiglio dei Ministri v. Regione Sardegna*, para 61 (*also see* para 36-37)).

[1048] Case C-280/00 (July 24, 2003) *Altmark*, paras 87-94 (disqualifying state compensations for certain public services under certain conditions (paras 89-93) from the qualification as state aid).

[1049] Case C-88/03 (GC; Sep. 6, 2006) *Portugal v. Commission*, para 58 *et seq*. (where tax reductions adopted by the Azores region for their own fiscal residents were assessed in light of state aid requirement, and where the ECJ judged that the appropriate framework of reference in the assessment of selectivity could be the Region, insofar as it was procedurally, institutionally, economically and financially autonomous, *quod non in casu* (para 67 read together with Joined Cases C-428/06 to C-434/06 (Sep. 11, 2008), *Unión General de Trabajadores de la Rioja et al. (UGT-Rioja)*, para 51)). *Also see* Lenaerts & Cambien, *supra* note 755, at p. 629-633 (discussing the empowered regions in Europe after the Lisbon reforms, and referring back to state aid cases further specifying the *Azores case* framework, such as the 2008 *Rioja* judgment, concerning Basque tax measures). *Compare* Opinion by A-G Jääskinen (Apr. 7, 2011), accompanying Joined Cases C-106/09 P and C-107/09 P, *European Commission and Kingdom of Spain v. Government of Gibraltar and United Kingdom* (in which the applicability of the jurisprudence vis-à-vis Gibraltar's is examined; *see esp.* §§ 77-89 (on Gibraltar specific, alleged, status as a 'colony') and §§ 92 *et seq.* (on the application of the *Azores* case law, especially §§ 103 *et seq*., where the A-G rebuts Spain's argument that there is a fourth condition in the *Azores* case law, aiming at the protection of the common market), and the ensuing GC Judgment on Nov. 15, 2011 (*esp.* paras 97 *et seq.*).

[1050] *Compare supra* note 754.

[1051] Case C-88/03 (GC; Sep. 6, 2006) *Portugal v. Commission*, para 64; Decision Commission 11 December 2002 concerning the part of the regulation pertaining to the modification of the national tax system to the specific characteristics of the Azores autonomous region, which concerns the reduction of the income tax rate, 150/52 OJ (L) (June 28, 2003) §§ 17; Opinion A-G Geelhoed (Oct. 20, 2005) accompanying Case C-88/03, *Portugal v. Commission*, §§ 50-54; Opinion A-G Kokott (May 8, 2008), accompanying Case C-428-434/06, *UGT Rioja*, §§ 45-47; Opinion A-G Jääskinen (*Gibraltar appeal*), *supra* note 1050, § 58; Axel Haelterman, *Corporate income tax regionalisation. Feasibility, compliance issues and EU requirements. The*

Belgium[1052]. Two evolutions are quite unclear, however, and in light of these, *Azores* and its progeny might become directly related to issues of Belgian federalism. First, it is possible that Belgium – during its later state reforms – could become more asymmetric from a fiscal perspective, which would render the abovementioned case law very relevant. Furthermore, even if the Court in the *Azores* case[1053] seemingly acknowledged that the *Azores* three-fold test does not apply to states in which tax competences are allocated symmetrically, this does not preclude re-evaluation of this acknowledgment in light of the rationale of the *Azores* test or in light of the broader rationale of article 107, §1 TFEU. Indeed, as Peeters rightfully asked: 'why does the economic-financial autonomy requirement not count in case of a symmetrical repartition of fiscal competences?'[1054]. It remains to be seen how the Court of Justice shall cope with this line of criticism[1055]. What is more, in that case, some difficulties may arise, as 'it is the applicable laws as interpreted by the national courts which determine the limits of the areas of competence of an infra-State body and which must be taken into account for the purpose of verifying whether that body has sufficient autonomy'[1056]. The Constitutional legal provisions as such become facts to be ascertained in a procedure before the European Courts[1057], but this becomes problematic if these *facts* may be offset in light of Union law, such as in the

Belgian Case. Working Paper A2A (Oct. 5, 2007), at p. 9-10, available at www.steunpuntfb.be and Bruno Peeters, *European Legal Limitations to the Repartition of Fiscal competences in a federal state structure* in SOCIAL FEDERALISM, *supra* note 45, at p. 237-39, 245-49. *Compare* Opinion A-G Geelhoed (*Azores*), *supra* this note, §§ 48-49 (where he argues that a tax increase does not fall within the scope of state aid, on the assumption that this territory represents a minor part of the total geographical territory of the member state and thus has to be characterized as a 'specific burden').

1052 *Also see* Evi Mattioli, Manuela Vervoort & Tim Bruynickx, *Fiscale voordelen vanwege regionale en lokale overheden: onder staatssteunbedreiging?*, 361 TIJDSCHRIFT VOOR FISCAAL RECHT 387, 397-99 (2009) (discussing modulations thereof).

1053 Para 64.

1054 Peeters, *supra* note 1051, at p. 247; *also see* p. 248-49 (arguing to replace the appropriate frame of reference to 'the normal situation of competition in the internal market'.

1055 *Compare* Frans Vanistendael, *Wanneer wordt fiscale autonomie fiscale soevereiniteit, voor toepassing van fiscale staatssteun?* in 1 MAATSCHAPPELIJK HEFFEN. OPSTELLEN OP 8 DECEMBER AANGEBODEN AAN PROF. L.G.M. STEVENS 591, 611 (Dirk A. Albregtse & Peter Kavelaars eds. 2006) ('the current situation leads paradoxically to Member States being allowed to bedevil each other fiscally, but sub-member state entities being held firmly on a leash'); *but see* Mattioli, Vervoort & Bruyninckx, *supra* note 1052, at p. 402 (applauding the less rigid approach of symmetric regions in light of their fiscal autonomy); *see more generally (from a European perspective)* Suzaenne Kingston, *The European Court of Justice and the Devolution of Taxation Powers* in FEDERALISM, *supra* note 32, at p. 249.

1056 *Rioja* judgment, *supra* note 1049, para 82.

1057 Opinion A-G Jääskinen, *supra* note 1050, §§ 47-48.

case on the Flemish decree on land and buildings policy (evacuating issues to Europe).[1058]

On the other hand, pertaining to free movement of goods, the Court has sometimes judged that the Member State is not necessarily the relevant entity to take into account when assessing whether there has been a cross-border movement[1059].

Even so, in the Care Insurance Judgment, for instance, it did refuse to take some important arguments relying on the constitutional structure of Belgium into account[1060].

171. Reverse discrimination as a second factor. But even if the Court of Justice would strictly apply its (old) 'purely internal situation'-rule, the issue of reverse discrimination (as a consequence thereof) lingers and indeed gives rise to a whole array of new problems. In a fairly recent parliamentary debate in Belgium implementing the family reunification directive[1061], for instance, the issue of reverse discrimination was subject of some fierce debate[1062]. That debate illustrates that, even if Europe keeps its hands off the issue (formally

[1058] The same problem seems to have laid at the basis of the *Rioja* judgment, *cf.* Javier Muguruza, *De fiscale autonomie van het Baskenland in het raam van de Europese Unie*, in EEN VLAAMSE, *supra* note 615, at p. 93, 98, 109-113. *See, generally,* Koen Lenaerts, *The Law of the European Union and the exercise by regions of their tax powers* in FISCAL FEDERALISM IN THE EUROPEAN UNION. EU PRESIDENCY SEMINAR 10 (Flemish Department of Finance and Budget ed. 2012) (*cf.* http://fin.vlaanderen.be/nlapps/docs/default.asp?fid=144).

[1059] Foundational cases in this regard were Case C-163/90 (July 16, 1992) *Legros*, paras 16-17; Joined Cases C-363, 407 and 411/93 (1994) *Lancry*, paras 27-29; Joined Cases C-485-486/93 (Sep. 14, 1995) *Simitzi*, para 17. This theory has been consequently applied: *see eg* Case C-72/03 (Sep. 9, 2004) *Carbonati Apuani*, para 22; Case C-293/02 (GC; Nov. 8, 2005) *Jersey Produce Marketing Organisation*, paras 26-28 or Case C-161/09 (Mar. 3, 2011) *Kavaketsos-Frakopolous AG*, paras 28-29. *Also see* Tryfonidou, *supra* note 859.

[1060] Case C-212/06 (GC; Apr. 1, 2008) *Flemish Care Insurance*, paras 57-58.

[1061] Council Directive 2003/86/EC (Sep. 22, 2003) on the right to family reunification, OJ (L) (Mar. 10, 2003) 251/12, as found valid by the Court of Justice (Case C-540/03 (GC; June 27, 2006) *Parliament v. Council*).

[1062] Bill 443 was adopted in the Chamber after fierce debate (*Summarized Report* Plenum Meeting Chamber 2010-11 (May 26, 2011) at p. 112; *also see* p. 36, 43, 45, 48 and 79-80 (on national sovereignty, the relationship between *Ruiz Zambrano* and *McCarthy*, and reverse discrimination); *see*, more elaborately, *Full Report* Plenum Meeting Chamber 2010-11 (May 26, 2011) *passim*. *Also see* Report (Dierick & Fonck) *Parl. Doc.* Chamber 2010-11, No. 443/018, at p. 59-63, 184-89, 206-09, read together with Amendments Nos. 19, 20, 147, 162 and 169 (Nos. 443/004 and 443/014) and with the CoS Advice (No. 443/015, at p. 3-7 (on Amendment 147, but not taking *McCarthy* into account, which was decided one month later). The Bill was promulgated on July 8, 2011. For some further reflections hereupon, *see* Verbist, *supra* note 1045.

allowing reverse discrimination[1063]), the issue remains a problem. It could even be said that recent European developments have exacerbated the issue, as the Union citizenship provisions seem to push the boundaries of European law ever further, without always taking into account the specific constitutional structure of Member States[1064]. Despite important efforts to clarify the issues[1065], they are far from *solved*.

European law will indeed 'obligate the federated entities to adopt regulations which are both well-thought through and take into account the need for nuances and/or expansions of the measures or policy choices which are merely directed at a local context'[1066], but the question remains: will the federated entities take such obligations seriously, and moreover, can they? This question does not only pose itself from a policy perspective. Storme noted that in fact 'up till now, the Belgian Economic Union has not yet played a prominent role in the jurisprudence of the Constitutional Court, whereas the development of European law nonetheless has demonstrated that the impact of the economic union on the policy and regulatory freedoms of the Member States can be very deep'[1067]. More importantly, the question must be addressed from an epistemological and a constitutional angle. Can federated entities indeed know what exactly European law requires? And even if they can and if they are willing to accept the far-reaching implications in terms of policy[1068],

1063 *Eg* Opinion A-G Sharpston (June 28, 2007), accompanying Case C-212/06, *Flemish Care Insurance*, §§ 116 *et seq.*; *also see* Opinion A-G Mengozzi (Sep. 29, 2011) accompanying Case C-256/11, *Dereci*, §§ 44-45 (looking at some 'paradoxical' implications). For further general references, *see eg* Craig & De Búrca, *supra* note 627, at p. 829-33 (in light of citizenship) and 732, 754, 776-79 (more generally).

1064 This is not to say that the Court has not taken the constitutional structure into account (*see eg* Case C-428/07 (GC; July 16, 2009) *Horvath*, paras 55-58; *cf.* Lenaerts & Cambien, *supra* note 755, at p. 633-635), but rather that it has not done so in all cases where it was possible. Accordingly, in the Care Insurance Case, and notwithstanding the fact that A-G Sharpston had argued against this possibility (Opinion A-G Sharpston (June 28, 2007) accompanying Case C-212/06, *Flemish Care Insurance*, §§ 84-97), the Court refused to apply *lex loci laboris* to denote the competent part of the State, a solution which could – according to some authors, like Herwig Verschueren (*supra* note 842) – have relieved some of the tension between European law and Belgian constitutional law.

1065 For instance, if Lenaerts conceptualization of the new case law after *Ruiz Zambrano* is correct (*see supra* note 849, at p. 31 *et seq.*) it is not sure that the *national* courts will automatically accept the expansion of power accompanied with this conceptualization.

1066 Storme, *supra* note 142, at p. 207; *also see* Velaers & Vanpraet, *supra* note 388, at p. 217.

1067 Storme, *supra* note 446, at p. 622.

1068 For an arguable instance hereof, *see eg* Explanatory Memorandum, *Parl. Doc.* Fl. Parl. 2012-2013, No. 1867/1, at p. 53 *et seq.* (regarding the Flemish (civic) integration policy, where it is contended that the exclusion of European citizens from the scope is defended on the basis of discrete arguments; at the same time, the Care Insurance hypothesis is taken into account (*ibid.*

the question remains whether this all can be squared with constitutional requirements.

172. Territorializing effect. As regards the latter, it has been noted that European Union law has had a primarily *territorializing* influence on Member State regulations altogether, arguably, as some other international institutions have had.[1069] Ninke Mussche[1070] provides some examples in the social security sphere, where Court of Justice jurisprudence extended Guaranteed Income for the Elderly[1071] and Guaranteed Income for Handicapped persons[1072] to non-Belgian nationals under certain conditions.

Even if 'nationality' as a criterion of distinction often fails to pass European muster, a primarily territorial criterion of distinction does not always suffice to pass European review either[1073]. Accordingly, relinquishing any criterion of nationality and determining the scope *ratione personae* of a national regulation as linked with territory (who has been working *here*, who has been living *here*, ...) does not foreclose the possibility of contravening European law, certainly in light of the broadly conceptualized freedoms of movement, which often relies on the open concept of *restriction*, which provides the Court of Justice with quite some leeway of bringing situations under Union law[1074].

at p. 58-59)).

[1069] Ninke Mussche mentions the ILO recommendation to extend eligibility of the Guaranteed Income for the Elderly read in conjunction with the ILO Convention on Migrating Workers (*cf.* Law (July 10, 1953) approving the international Convention (No. 97) on Migrant workers and the annexes, revised in Geneva on July 1, 1949, by the International Labor Organization during its thirty-second session (ratified by Belgium on July 10, 1953), *BSG* Aug. 20, 1953), which influenced Belgian law (*cf. Parl. Doc.* Chamber, 1979-80, No. 323/1, at p. 27), as regards the application of the principle of territoriality (*see* art. 122 Law (Aug. 8, 1980) on budgetary propositions 1979-80, *BSG* Aug. 15, 1980). Ninke Mussche, *Social citizenship vs. the territoriality principle: Lessons for Flanders' Solidarity Circle* in SOCIAL FEDERALISM: *supra* note 45, at p. 194.

[1070] Mussche, *supra* note 1069, at p. 194.

[1071] Case 1/72 (June 22, 1972) *Rita Frilli* (the lack of reciprocity could not be argued in order to withhold guaranteed income for the elderly, which came within the scope of Regulation No. 3); Case 261/83 (July 12, 1984) *Carmela Castelli* (extending the protection to depending relatives in the ascending line).

[1072] Case 187/73 (May 28, 1974) *Odette Callemeyn* (the Court decided that the Belgian State could not withhold these benefits, which needed to be classified as social security benefits, to a person of French nationality married to a Belgian and residing in Belgium).

[1073] It should be noted that *nationality* as such does not necessarily determine whether a law is applicable or not. Of course there is a need for a determination of the scope of a law *ratione loci* and *ratione materiae*, which also matter. However, what has often changed, is that nationality *in the determination of the scope ratione personae* has faded away in favor of other determinants, linked more directly to territory.

[1074] *See* Tryfonidou, *supra* note 656.

5.3 Diversity in unity: autonomous concepts

173. Converging concepts as a solution to decrease tension. It seems that the integration of European law within Belgian law and the expansion of the scope of European law would be rendered less problematic if there were to be more internal coherence between the (competence) concepts deployed. Of course, I am not asserting that when concepts are *not* autonomous, but defined coherently amongst different legal orders, that all problems of interaction would automatically fade away. They surely would not, as the issue of reverse discrimination itself can show.

However, it has been pointed out, for instance by Koen Lenaerts in a Parliamentary Report[1075], that if the concepts deployed in European law and in municipal law are brought more into conformity with each other, the conflict potential would certainly be reduced. As he explains, under the *Dzodzi* jurisprudence[1076], the Court of Justice may indeed authoritatively interpret provisions of national law if they refer to Union Law, and accordingly, uniformity would be increased[1077].

174. The engine of convergence? Lenaerts' point is of course clear: if the concepts deployed in both legal systems – and concept here should be understood widely[1078] – are authoritatively interpreted by one and the same Court, risks of divergence would presumably decrease. However, the most salient issue of course would be to whom this power would be relegated. As the recent *Melki* controversy on the coinciding of human rights shows[1079], this question is often central in the relationship between European and municipal law. So, notwithstanding the fact that there is a certain interest in the existence of some sort of minimal framework of references, including concepts and basic rules, to be defined at the European level, and even granting that this does not per se

[1075] Koen Lenaerts' hearing in Report (Caluwé *et al.*), *Parl. Doc.* Senate 1998-89, No. 1-1333/1, at p. 818 et seq.

[1076] *See* references *supra* note 860.

[1077] Koen Lenaerts' hearing in Report (Caluwé *et al.*), *Parl. Doc.* Senate 1998-89, No. 1-1333/1, at p. 820-21. *Compare* Opinion A-G Jacobs (Sep. 17, 1996) accompanying Joined Cases C-28/95, *Leur-Bloem* and C-130/95 *Bernd Giloy*, § 47 (doubting its use for the uniformity of EU law as such).

[1078] Although Lenaerts focuses on the example of specific concepts, like waste (*Parl. Doc.* Senate 1998-99, No. 1-1333/1, at p. 822 *et seq.*).

[1079] *See* next to the references provided *supra* note 27. *See* more generally Claes, *supra* note 774; Patricia Popelier, *Belgium. The supremacy dilemma: the Belgian Constitutional Court caught between the European Court of Human Rights and the European Court of Justice* in Human Rights Protection in the European Legal Order: the interaction between the European and national courts 149 (Patricia Popelier, Cathérine van de Heyning & Piet Van Nuffel eds. 2011); Van de Heyning, *supra* note 725, *passim.*

infringe upon the possibility of decentralization or federalization[1080], Lenaerts' solution certainly does not focus enough[1081] upon the power of the definition or explanation of alone-standing concepts themselves and their influence upon the *content* of the law, which is arguably even more important in cases regarding the allocation of competences.

175. Far reaching results of convergence. For sure, when we think of the grand allocation of competences between Europe and the Member States, we often think in the rhetoric of proportionality to assess the results to a particular inquiry. For instance, when a judge in the Court of Cassation argues that the Belgian Court takes less of an economic perspective and grants more room for social considerations, then this almost 'naturally' seems to imply that in proportionality review, the Belgian Court will provide more room for 'competing' considerations[1082]. However, concepts themselves, by defining the scope of their application and by sheer definition, already weigh in the larger balance of considerations[1083]. To give but one example, again using the Flemish Care Insurance saga: if the concept of *social security* was defined according to European terms, the first question which was referred to the Court of Justice – does the Care Insurance scheme fall within the scope of *social security* in the sense of the Regulation at hand? – would have ended the dispute and rendered the Care Insurance Scheme unconstitutional on grounds of the lack of a Regional social security competence[1084]. As we pointed out above, however, such a way of approaching the issue is not in line with the (earlier) thoughts of the Belgian

[1080] *Cf.* Lenaerts, *Parl. Doc.* Senate 1998-99, No. 1-1333/1, at p. 822.

[1081] Although he does mention – summarily – that indeed the Belgian Courts would loose some of their competence, but frames it in a way that this seems 'natural' (*ibid.* at p. 823). More pertinent in this regard, seems to be the remark by Mr. Coenraets, who infers from Lenaerts' suggestions that 'Belgian constitutional law would have to adapt to European law' (*ibid.* at p. 825).

[1082] Accordingly, a former First Chamber President of the Court of Cassation argues that the Belgian Court would be more lenient in the interpretation of a 'public interest' than the Court of Justice is (Ivan Verougstraete, *Een nieuw soort rechters?* in LIBER AMICORUM WALTER VAN GERVEN 77, 88 (2000)).

[1083] A similar (or at least *mutatis mutandis* applicable) point was made forcefully by Robert Hale in the private law context almost a century ago (*see* Robert L. Hale, *Coercion and Distribution in a Supposedly Non-Coercive State*, 38 POLITICAL SCIENCE QUARTERLY 470 (1923); *also see supra* note 680).

[1084] An additional complication lies in the fact that the Court of Justice recognizes that the concept of 'social security' is prone to reification, and is therefore hard to distinguish from 'social assistance' (Case 1/72 (June 22, 1972) *Rita Frilli*, para 13 or Case 187/73 (May 28, 1974) *Odette Callemeyn*, para 6). Finally, one should mention that the concept of social security, according to Velaers, is a polysemic legal concept under Belgian law as well (Velaers, *supra* note 531, at p. 143).

Constitutional Court (which in that case would lose quite a bit of its decision-making power).

176. What to do with the tensions? Accordingly, those are three possible reasons why conflicts have emerged and why they might be exacerbating. In light of this, the question becomes what Belgium can do, especially in light of the ongoing sixth reform of state, and in light of the implementation of the *Butterfly Agreement*.

5.4 The road ahead

177. Institutional Agreement: basic scope. Central in the new political-institutional agreement[1085] are (1) the federalization of certain competences, including[1086] full employment policy federalization[1087], a couple of social assistance/security mechanisms[1088], as well as child support[1089], some further economic leverage mechanisms[1090], (2) a federal financial reform, increasing fiscal autonomy for the Regions[1091] and, (3) more generally, an attempt to rebalance the power structures amongst the different sociological groups[1092].

178. Problem of connecting factors: economic versus non-economic policies. Here, we focus on the problem of the connecting factor deployed by the Communities or the Regions when imposing their different policies. In the most simplistic terms, it could be argued that many of the Regional competences are generally *economy*-related, and therefore by themselves already

---

[1085] I will also refer back to the different negotitation documents here (meaning the Di Rupo, the Vande Lanotte and the De Wever negotiation documents), to emphasize the generality of the problem I am addressing.

[1086] *See* Butterfly Agreement, *supra* note 10, at p. 45 (student migration), 37 (on youth sanctioning, here integrated in a broader *justice* policy federalization; *also see* p. 20), and 38-40 and 42-44 (on energy and mobility). *Also see,* amongst other new competences, Di Rupo, *supra* note 129, at p. 59 (on migration), 62-63 and 82-83 (on youth protection and regional jurisdictional competence) and 67-69, 83-84 and 86-87 (on energy and mobility); De Wever, *supra* note 129, at p. 10 and 32 (migration), 26-28 (on youth protection and regional jurisdictional competence), and 30-31 (on energy and mobility); Vande Lanotte, *supra* note 129, at p. 15 and 34 (on migration), 26-29 (on youth protection and regional jurisdictional competence) and 24-25 (on energy and mobility).

[1087] Butterfly Agreement, *supra* note 10, at p. 29-32; Di Rupo, *supra* note 129, at p. 33-35, 74-77; *see* De Wever, *supra* note 129, at p. 7-10; Vande Lanotte, *supra* note 129, at p. 11-15 and 56-57.

[1088] Butterfly Agreement, *supra* note 10, at p. 32-36; Di Rupo, *supra* note 129, at p. 52-56, 77-81; *see* De Wever, *supra* note 129, at p. 12-16; Vande Lanotte, *supra* note 129, at p. 16-21 and 58-59.

[1089] Butterfly Agreement, *supra* note 10, at p. 36-37; Di Rupo, *supra* note 129, at p. 58-59, 81-82; *see* De Wever, *supra* note 129, at p. 24-25; Vande Lanotte, *supra* note 129, at p. 22-23 and 60.

[1090] Butterfly Agreement, *supra* note 10, at p. 40-42; Di Rupo, *supra* note 129, at p. 42-43, 84-86; *see* De Wever, *supra* note 129, at p. 29-30; Vande Lanotte, *supra* note 129, at p. 31-32.

[1091] Butterfly Agreement, *supra* note 10, at p. 51-65 and 67-69; Di Rupo, *supra* note 129, at p. 30-33, 93-105; *see* De Wever, *supra* note 129, at p. 11, 17-23, 39-48; *see* Vande Lanotte, *supra* note 129, at p. 36-38, 46-54 and 62.

[1092] Remarkable here is the increasing politicization of the Constitutional Court's docket (*compare eg* Di Rupo, *supra* note 129, at p. 25 to Butterfly Agreement, *supra* note 10, at p. 20 (notice the procedural resemblance, with a vote for the alternating president in case of a tie of votes); *also see* ibid. at p. 11 and 62-63 (granting review in terms of federal loyalty)).

prone to European influence, whereas Community competences are generally more *non-economy*-related, and therefore by themselves less prone to European influence[1093].

Of course this is a simplification, in need of several basic nuances. Some of the Community competences are clearly economically inspired (*eg* tourism[1094]), whereas some Regional competences are not (*eg* environment). Moreover, as the Care Insurance Case shows, specifically in the *social* field economic and non-economic competences intertwine, also – moreover – because Europe does no longer pursue a merely economic integration, or at least conceives of what *is* economic in more broad terms. Finally, it could be argued that exactly the *federal* legislature remains competent for economic matters, insofar as divergence in this regard may influence the unity of the market (EMU).

An additional twist lies in *fiscal* competences, especially those of the Regions, which allow them to pursue policy goals which do not exactly lie within the normal scope of their competences, at least if they take the same EMU into account.

179. Problems in construing social and fiscal policies? In light of the jurisprudence discussed before, we may expect problems to especially rise in the *social* field, insofar as certain policies are tied – based on a circle of solidarity – to the *territory*, and do not take into account the general principle of *lex loci laboris* as elaborated in European law[1095]. Moreover, as some of the precedents we will

---

[1093] *Compare* Velaers, *supra* note 531, at p. 149-151 (establishing a link between the place-of-residence criterion and so-called 'person-related matters' falling within the scope of Community powers, as 'the choice for the place-of-residence criterion in person-related matters is conductive to a system of solidarity between residents of the same region', *ibid.* p. 150). Paul Van Orshoven and Bea Cantillon, dissenting in an expertise done on Flemish Care Insurance, argue on the basis of EMU that free movement is applicable in internal situations, depending on whether Care Insurance is to be situated in the Flemish *economic* policy or not (*cf.* Stijn Rottiers, *De weerbaarheid van de Vlaamse zorgverzekering: Waalse klachten en Europese Bedenkingen,* Bercihten Centrum voor Sociaal Beleid Herman Deleeck 23-24 (2005), available at www.centrumvoorsociaalbeleid.be/sites/default/files/20060208101253BPUA.pdf, referring to Expertencommissie, *Verslag van de Expertencommissie Europese regelgeving aan de Vlaamse Regering* (2003)).

[1094] *Also see* Butterfly Agreement, *supra* note 10, at p. 27-28 and 42, *esp.* n17 (tourism will become a Regional matter, under auspices of some cooperation agreements, without prejudice to the Community's competences in promoting Brussels at the national and international level, and maintaining the possibility for the Communities to grant touristic subsidies in Brussels) and p. 27 (on the link between employment and vocational activities); *compare* CC 45/2012 (Mar. 15, 2012), *esp.* B.13.

[1095] *Also see* CoS Advice, *Parl. Doc.* Flemish Parl. 2003/04, No. 1970/2, at p. 13 (judging that there is no tension between European law and Belgian law in this regard); *compare (from a European perspective)* Verschueren, *supra* note 51, at p. 267 *et seq.*

discuss show, also the *fiscal* field may pose specific problems, at least insofar as fiscal benefits are awarded on the basis of a residence criterion.

180. Some precedents. Some precedents show how these problems may occur. We of course already pointed out the Care Insurance Scheme issues. These are specific in that they pertain especially to residents of different Belgian federated entities who have exercised their rights to freedom of movement.

The problem does not stop there, however. The inheritance tax case was one example where the issue of a residence requirement (*as investment* requirement) played[1096]. The Commission has threatened several Flemish programs with an action for non-compliance with European law, and the problems were often situated in the fiscal area.

For example, the Commission took issue with a flat-rate reduction of personal income tax as established by the Flemish Region for all having fiscal domicile in Flanders[1097]. The underlying issue of course was that the Flemish Region could not fiscally regulate those not having residence in Flanders. This issue resurfaced

[1096] *Supra* No. 110. *See* Opinion A-G Kokott (Feb. 15, 2007) accompanying Case C-464/05, *Geurts & Vogten v. Belgium,* § 40 (explaining how she was not interested in the internal division of competences in Belgium). *Also see* Case C-256/06 (Jan. 17, 2008) *Jäger*, para 51 (where the German government could not show the necessity of excluding agricultural properties outside Germany from a tax rebate under the inheritance tax in light of free movement of capital requirements); also regarding the Flemish Inheritance Tax, *see* Case C-11/07 (Sep. 11, 2008) *Eckelkamp et al.*, paras 61-63 (on a woman whose property in Germany was taxed (to be paid by the heirs), but could not bring debts to bear on that tax, unlike Flemish residents can); Peeters, *supra* note 1051, at p. 249-52.

[1097] Decree Fl. Parl. (June 30, 2006) containing a flat-rate reduction of personal income tax, *BSG* Sept. 26, 2006, as amended by four subsequent decrees (resp. May 23, 2008; Dec. 19, 2008; Dec. 18, 2009 and Dec. 23, 2010). Art. 2, §1, 2° however, still stipulates as a condition for application of the reduction that the person during the fiscal year must be taxable within a Flemish municipality. Even if it now has been abolished (starting in 2011: art. 86-87 Decree (Dec. 23, 2010) regarding measures guiding the 2011 budget, *BSG* Dec. 31, 2010), still, important questions arise as to the applicability of the reduction to non-residents (for the period that it was valid), *see eg* Question (Eric Van Rompuy & Martine Fournier) in the Commission for General Policy, Finances and Budget (Nov. 9, 2010), No. 417 and 445 (2010-11) (where Flemish Minister Muyters answered that the Flemish Government did not yet know what to do with the European threat of instituting proceedings). *Contra Integral Report* Flemish Parl. No. 15 (2010-11) (Dec. 21, 2010) (where the decrease of the amount of reduction is seen as an answer to European objections). *Compare* Question E-0876/10 (Feb. 22, 2010) by Ria Oomen-Ruijten to the Commission regarding the Flemish job rebate, which was answered by Mr. Semeta (Apr. 6, 2010) on behalf of the Commission (available at the European Parliament Website) (pointing out the relevance of the care insurance case).

in other cases as well[1098]. In one recent case, the Flemish Government argued that even if the Special Finance Law in principle only allows for a general reduction for regional *residents,* the Flemish decree on land and buildings policy has to take the supranational nature of article 63 TFEU regarding free movement of capital into account. 'Judging differently', so it was said, 'would mean that the fiscal competences of the regional legislator are *de facto* diluted, because the regional legislator could only adopt fiscal measures violating European law'[1099]. If the problems are somewhat more "public" in Flanders than in Wallonia, that does not mean they do not occur there too[1100].

181. Territoriality versus free movement. Accordingly, in the areas of fiscal policies and social policies at least, there are potential problems, which – perhaps

[1098] For instance, in the case of the "win-win-loan" (Decree Fl. Parl. (May 19, 2006) on the win-win-loan, *BSG* June 30, 2006) or "ARKImedes" (on the activiation of risk capital: Decree Fl. Parl. (Dec. 19, 2003) on the activation of risk capital in Flanders (*BSG* Feb. 2, 2004).
See Report by the Commission for Economy, Work and Social Economy, brought by Ms. Annick de Ridder and Anissa Temsamani, *Parl. Doc.* Flemish Parl. 2005-06, No. 754/2, at p. 6 (not even seeing a European problem when adapting the win-win-decree). Some adaptations to European requirements were made over time (Decree (Dec. 10, 2010) modifying diverse provisions of the May 19, 2006 Decree on the win-win-loan and the Dec. 19, 2003 Decree on the activation of risk capital in Flanders, *BSG* Dec. 23, 2010; *also see Parl. Doc.* Fl. Parl. 09-10, No. 640/2, at p. 6 (diluting a requirement to invest risk capital in Flanders), but still only residents would get a tax cut (*ibid.* p. 9).
An adaptation to the other European requirements was hard, because art. 6, §2 and 7, §1 SLFCR only permit tax cuts for residents (*see Parl. Doc.* Flemish Parl. , No. 640/2 (2009-10) at p. 10; Question (Eric Van Rompuy) in the Commission for General Policy, Finances and Budget (Jan. 11, 2011) No. C90 – FIN 6 (2010-11) p. 3-5 (dicussing the European problems with the 'win-win-loan', where a resident of Flanders 'wins' when he acts as a lender to a Flemish company, and where Minister Muyters again had no straighforward answer and pointing out that the Flemish government cannot reduce the tax for non-residents and that the appropriate nexus for personal taxes is fiscal domicile); *also* see Dirk de Wilde & Katrien Verstraete, *EU remt Vlaamse ambities af,* De Tijd Nov. 26, 2010, at p. 11); *but see* (a new answer by Muyters) Question by Mr. Bothuyne, *Integral Report* Flemish Parl. (2010-11) Economics Commission Meeting: C213-ECO25 (Apr. 28, 2011), at p. 20-22.
Compare eg Axel Haelterman, *Regionalisering Personenbelasting. Huidige bevoegdheden werkbaarder maken.* Working Paper A2 (Apr. 19, 2008), available at www.steunpuntfb.be.

[1099] Explanatory Memo, *Parl. Doc.* Flemish Parl. 2008-09, No. 2012/1, at p. 108 (on the so-called *parent-loan*).

[1100] *See eg* the Commission Decision regarding Belgium (where a reasoned opinion was sent by the Commission (Apr. 6, 2011): BE 2006/2431/TAXU) regarding a higher duty on gifts and inheritances coming from different member states. Or, in Brussels for that matter, *see eg* the Commission Decision regarding Belgium (a case which was nonetheless closed (Nov. 24, 2010): BE 2008/4784/TAXU), regarding lower inheritance duties for real estate left by a resident than for real estate left by a non-resident in Brussels.

somewhat different in nature[1101] - share some interesting characteristic because they translate a tension between European law and constitutional law.

In both areas the problem lies in the connecting factors deployed to establish the scope of a particular regulation. More generally, it could be argued that the tension here reigns explicitly between the requirements under constitutional law pursuant to the principle of territoriality, and the requirements under European law pursuant to the freedoms of movement, largely conceived. Both have also been set in the framework of a tension between the principle of residence and the *lex loci laboris* principle[1102].

182. Specific issue of European tension in federated policies. Of course there might be problems in terms of European law when the *federal* legislator deploys a wrong connecting factor. If, for instance, the federal government were to reserve some benefits on the basis of territorial requirement that could be construed as either indirectly discriminating or at least unjustifiably restricting trade in terms of free movement of persons, that would obviously contravene European law[1103]. However, the problem becomes exacerbated in terms of

[1101] I disregard, next to disregarding other policy fields, the specific question whether the Azores case law (discussed above) can find application in Belgium (due to Brussels or German-speaking Community asymmetry). *Compare* Peeters, *supra* note 1051, at p. 245-49; TRAVERSA, *supra* note 51, at p. 513 (arguing that now Belgium is still symmetrical, but that future state reforms should take the risk of asymmetry into account) or Mattioli, Vervoort & Bruyninckx, *supra* note 1052, at p. 387 *et seq.* (and other references *supra* note 479).

[1102] *Eg* PIETERS, supra note 914, 7-8, 55 *et seq. and also see* 23 *et seq.*; Axel Haelterman Working Paper A23 (Jan. 2, 2008), available at www.steunpuntfb.be; Velaers, *supra* note 531, at p. 152 *et seq.*; Velaers & Vanpraet, *supra* note 388, at p. 216-17. *Also see* Van Elsuwege & Adam, *supra* note 1003, at p. 701 *et seq., esp.* 707-09 (assessing the issue from the point of the internal market).

Velaers and Vanpraet argue that it is not the 'consequence of the principle of territorial exclusivity, but of the specific conceptualization thereof in this case by designating the principle of residence as the most meaningful criterion' (Velaers & Vanpraet, *supra* note 388, at p. 217). However, although in principle the federated entities remain free to adopt their own criteria, we also pointed out that important practical issues of internal coordination arise which have sometimes brought the Constitutional Court to conceive of a criterion as a constitutional requirement, rather than as a constitutional permission.

[1103] Examples of this point are legion, although the scope of the prohibition of discrimination is not always clear: *compare eg* Case C-175/88 (May 8, 1990) *Biehl*, para 14 (criticizing the place of residence criterion as a precondition for tax refunds) *with* Case C-279/93 (Feb. 14, 1995) *Schumacker*, paras 30-35 (allowing for a heavier tax on non-residents, due to a objective differences, except when these non-residents do not pay taxes in the state of residence). *Also see* some of the examples in MASSIMO CONDINANZI, ALESSANDRA LANG & BRUNO NASCIMBENE, CITIZENSHIP OF THE UNION AND FREEDOM OF MOVEMENT OF PERONS (2008). *But compare* A. PIETER VAN DER MEI, FREE MOVEMENT OF PERSONS WITHIN THE EUROPEAN COMMUNITY. CROSS-BORDER ACCESS TO PUBLIC BENEFITS 5-7 (2003).

federalism when federated entities adopt these measures, not in the least because the criterion 'having exercised the right to free movement' becomes paramount, and is susceptible of causing differentiations (discriminations?) between a group of people who, under a federal logic, normally are regulated by similar policies. In this sense, the special balance acquired or at least sought within federalism, is put under pressure by European law that differentiates differently. Of course, such reverse discrimination already looks arbitrary from the point of view of specific nationals (having either used their right to free movement or not), but the arbitrariness is sometimes[1104] worsened in the federal case because here the non-discrimination-logic (because of autonomous policies) is put under extra pressure by European law.

183. A real problem in social and fiscal areas, as of yet by and large unsolved by the Institutional Agreement. In many social areas, the residence principle is the first deployed connecting factor[1105]. Given the fact that these areas are the ones in which Flemish political parties are hoping to elaborate their competences, the abovementioned mechanism might produce extra tensions.

Perhaps even worse[1106], some connecting factors have been inserted into (special) laws, as part of the general balance in Belgium. Accordingly, the residence criterion is presupposed for many provisions of the SLFCR[1107], and this criterion

[1104] Not always though, as for instance the *Bressol* case shows (*supra* notes 590 and 970), because of the sheer fact that the interest of Flemish people in French Community education is not so high, the conflict potential of this case was rather low. That is one of the other reasons why I opted for the social and the fiscal policy areas, as examples, because in these areas, the conflict potential (as shown in the negotiation agenda) is large.

[1105] *See* the examples provided for in Velaers & Vanpraet, *supra* note 388, at p. 199-200 (especially mentioning art. 13 Decree Fl. Comm. (May 7, 2004) establishing an internally autonomous agency for disabled persons, art. 16 Decree Fr. Comm. (Apr. 6, 1995) regarding the integration of disabled persons or art. 18 Decree Germ. Comm. (June 19, 1990) establishing a service of the German-speaking Community for disabled persons). *Also see* Verschueren, *supra* note 842, at p. 219.

[1106] From a specifically legal perspective, however, it is conceivable (but improbable) that the Constitutional Court would find these (special) legal requirements to be unconstitutional in light of the EMU (which could be, on the basis of No. 47), be conceived of as a *constitutional* (rather than a special law) requirement. Perhaps more probable would be a *partial* invalidation of the articles in play, as soon as they are relevant in terms of European law obligations (*cf.* No. 11/2009 (Jan. 21, 2009)). *Compare* CA No. 35/2003 (Mar. 25, 2003) B.5.1.

[1107] *See eg* art. 6, §2, 3° and 4° ('all persons owing the personal tax') or art. 7, §1, 1° *juncto* art. 5, 4° SLFCR (on where inheritance rights should be levied). *Compare* art. 1*ter* SLFCR (double tax clause), in light of the example provided in Explanatory Memo, *Parl. Doc.* Chamber 2000-01, No. 1183/001, at p. 13 and 70 (on the question whether a judge would be able to annul one of two inheritance taxes, levied by two different Regions, where one region determines *residence* in terms of registration, but where the other region disputes that it is the *real* residence) and *also see* p. 72.

itself might be problematic in terms of EU law[1108].

However, it should be noted that in the implementation of the *Butterfly agreement*, a special provision will be inserted into the SLFCR, according to which 'the exercise of fiscal competences of the regions occurs observing federal loyalty and notably the following principles: [...] the principle of free movement of persons, goods, services and capital *and* of the Economic and monetary Union'[1109]. The '*and*' might point to the fact that the 'first' *freedom movement*-requirements are in fact requirement of European law. It seems but logical that they are, as otherwise, this provision would be quasi-tautology. Moreover, whereas the SLIR explicitly refers to international obligations in the context of the EMU, here, no reference to European law is made. On the other hand, the text of the agreement further specifies that, although the federal government remains exclusively competent for taxing non-residents, it will 'take into account' the regional tax schemes, 'thereby guaranteeing the observance of the EU Treaty provision regarding the four fundamental freedoms'[1110].

A first reading of these 'provisions' may point to a continuance of the Constitutional Court's practice of dichotomizing on the basis of the scope of the legal order[1111]. Currently, however – and this is not so remarkable since we are relying on the text of a *political* agreement[1112] – the text is unclear about the matter[1113]. Therefore, we will have to wait for further determination of the issue, not only in the *Travaux Préparatoires* for the new SLFCR, but, perhaps even more importantly, for (constitutional) case law on the issue.

184. Need to take European law seriously. If the Belgian government wants to conform European law as it stands, it is imperative that the (special) legislature take the aforementioned considerations into account more seriously[1114].

1108 *See eg* Axel Haelterman, *Regionalisering Personenbelasting. Huidige bevoegdheden werkbaarder maken.* Working Paper A2 (Apr. 19, 2008), available at www.steunpuntfb.be (focusing on the fiscal autonomy provisions, and their scope of applicability) or Flemish Minister-President Peeters in *Parl. Doc.* Fl. Parl. 2009-10, No. 640/2, at p. 6 and 10. *Also see* Lenaerts, *supra* note 1058, at p. 10 (explaining the limits of the Regions taxing powers under European law, both from the perspective of free movement, as from the perspective of state aid).

1109 Butterfly Agreement, *supra* note 10, at p. 63 (*emphasis added*).

1110 *Ibid.* at p. 63.

1111 *Cf.* Feyen, *supra* note 32.

1112 *Cf.* Butterfly Agreement, *supra* note 10, at p. 65 (anticipating disagreement).

1113 This is *a fortiori* the case now that the same agreement emphasized that the 'federal government is exclusively competent for taxing non-residents' (Butterfly Agreement, *supra* note 10, at p. 63).

1114 Johan Vande Lanotte, De Belgische Unie Bestaat uit Vier Deelstaten 5-7 (2011). *Compare* Butterfly Agreement, *supra* note 10, at p. 32.

Negotiators were aware of them right now, as the *Butterfly Agreement* seems to suggest, but no solid solution has been given yet. Yet offering such a solution will be hard, for at least two reasons. On the one hand, the European law requirements are not by themselves eminently clear. Not only as regards scope of applicability, but also as regards the question when certain *internal constitutional* reasons might justify some deviation from the general free market rules, there has been quite some debate. On the other hand, even if it has been pointed out by Prime Minister Elio Di Rupo that he wants to proceed in accordance with European law[1115], he will have difficult *conceptual* choices to make.

One example suffices to make the point. If the principle of economic and monetary union *within* the Belgian borders (the Belgian EMU) is conceptualized in conformity with the European EMU, Velaers rightly concludes that 'the territorial distribution of competences would [...] be entirely eroded'[1116]. If the principle of economic and monetary union, however, is conceptualized differently in the European and in the Belgian context – as arguably was the case in the No. 11/2009 on the Care Insurance – the problem of reverse discrimination will arise ever more vehemently, as it did there[1117]. A catch 22 situation does seems to be occurring, and some fundamental choices will have to be made.

[1115] *See esp.* Di Rupo, *supra* note 129, at p. 77 and *also see* p. 29, *but compare* p. 67.

[1116] Velaers, *supra* note 531, at p. 156, to be read in conjunction with the remarks made in Vanpraet, *supra* note 914, at p. 164 *et seq.* (on *internal* issues of federalizing social security competences).

[1117] If the Court of Justice would have followed A-G Sharpston's suggestion in *Ruiz Zambrano* to also adjudicate 'purely internal situations', which it did not (*compare supra* notes 1063-1064), this would not have solved the issue (*compare* moreover Pérez, *supra* note 708, at p. 117-118), as in that case, in order to follow the COJ judgment, the Constitutional Court would at least have to strongly reduce the strength of the principle of territorial exclusivity. Other 'European' solutions have been contemplated however (*see eg* Christian Joerges, *Reconceptualising the Supremacy of European Law: A Plea for a Supranational Conflict of Laws* in Debating the Democratic Legitimacy of the European Union 311 (B Kohler-Koch & B. Rittberger eds. 2007); *also see* Conflict of Laws and Laws of Conflict in Europe and Beyond. Patterns of Supranational and Transnational juridification (Rainer Nickel ed. 2010); *compare* Storme, *supra* note 142 (proposing a Belgian conflict of laws approach to the problem)), but discussing these in detail falls beyond the scope of this inquiry, and it is uncertain whether they would really help to solve the issue.

Conclusion

185. The Constitutional Court: looking for the right balance, with many weights in the scales. The Belgian Constitutional Court holds an ambiguous position towards European law. Whereas, generally, it has recognized its power to review the conformity of a legislative act approving a treaty with the Constitution, it also deploys these treaties, and more broadly European law as enshrined in treaties and other instruments, to decide upon the constitutionality of other laws. Especially in reviews that rely upon the constitutional principle of non-discrimination, European law can play an important role, providing content to that principle.

At the same time, the Constitutional Court has had to fulfill the difficult task of finding an adequate balance between different political forces in Belgium. Especially communautarian political forces have had to be held in check, so as to give *content* to the so-called federal principle, establishing a balance between different (sociological) communities.

186. A pragmatic stance as the best representation of the Court's action. I have argued throughout this book that the Court has tried to accomplish its task rather pragmatically, both employing pre-existing texts and context and developing new principles. Accordingly, the different 'principles' underlying Belgian federalism have been described as tools, which the Court deploys in order to restore or ensure the necessary balance between Communities and Regions amongst themselves, and between these federated entities and the federal government. Even if this characterization of Constitutional Court jurisprudence is not entirely novel, it does stress – (much) more than more 'classic' rendition of constitutional law in Belgium – the leeway the Court has in deciding different cases on federalism issues. At the same time however, I stress that the Court is bound by some rule of law values.

187. European law as a precarious tool: adding complexity, but also opportunity. Furthermore, I have tried to show how European law fits in this picture. European law for the Court seems to create a new tool for solving practical conflicts. Indeed, the Court has not only availed itself of European law *politically*, in the sense that it sometimes allows for an evacuation of conflicts, but also more *legally*, in the sense of supports arguments imposing cooperation or supporting the Belgian EMU principle.

Even so, European law has shown itself to be a precarious tool. I have argued that also when European law is brought into play before the Court, rule of law values sometimes get in the way of it being employed merely as a (politico-legal) instrument. I have moreover suggested that in fact, European law can sometimes exacerbate the existent tension which exists in the constitutional toolbox, a tension primarily caused by an already utterly complex interplay of rule of law related and more instrumental forms of reasoning by the Constitutional Court.

188. A problem for the future. In the final chapter, I have first tried to point out some explanations for the tension. Although these explanations are somewhat too abstract, I have pointed out that the conflict potential comes (ever more) to the fore because of an increasing integration of EU law into constitutional jurisprudence, an ever expanding reach of European law, and a lack of coordination between concepts constituted within different legal orders.

Finally, I have warned for some possible increased tensions due to the imminent sixth stage of state reform. Focusing on one aspect of the relationship between European law and constitutional law[1118], I have tried to establish that the Belgian legislature should be careful to avoid a catch 22 situation: for relying on the premise that federalization of social and fiscal competences is warranted, a severe tension is observed between the (European) EMU and the principle of territorial exclusivity.

[1118] To bring the issue back to the Constitutional Court: if the Court 'widens' its own perimeters and brings issues of 'discrimination' (EMU) to bear on federalism matters, rationalization in terms of a classic sectorial classifying system such as exclusivity becomes utterly problematic, and it seems that European law plays a (precarious) role primarily in this dimension. To recharacterize it (and simplify it) in the language of the book: European law presents itself here, not so much as a tool, but as (constraining) rule of law values (hierarchy (primacy)/coherence (EMU)), here in conflict with other rule of law values, which were deployed as tools, earlier, especially the principle of territorial exclusivity, as enshrined in the constitutional text and in precedent (at least insofar as the residence criterion is concerned – *cf. eg* Storme, *supra* note 446, at p. 622-23).